Taste of Nepal

The Hippocrene Cookbook Library

Taste of Nepal

Jyoti Pathak

HIPPOCRENE BOOKS, INC.
New York

Illustrations by Tekbir Mukhiya at Sajha Prakashan.
Book design by Michael Yee.

For more information, address:
HIPPOCRENE BOOKS, INC.
171 Madison Avenue
New York, NY 10016

ISBN-13: 978-0-7818-1121-7
ISBN-10: 0-7818-1121-X
Cataloging-in-Publication Data available from the Library of Congress.

Printed in the United States of America.

This book is dedicated to my parents in Nepal,
Shree Badaguruju Kesari Raj Pandey and Kiran Kumari Pandey.

Contents

Dhanyabaad

ACKNOWLEDGMENTS

It is a great pleasure to thank the many people who have helped me put this cookbook together. I would first like to thank my husband, Kamal, for planting the seed for this project many years ago. This book would not have been possible without his continuous encouragement and help, as well as his eagerness to sample the recipes.

I also owe a great debt to my three children for their constant advice and moral support. Special appreciation and thanks go to my oldest daughter, Rachana, for her countless hours of editing and research. I am forever grateful to her and would not have been able to finish this book without her help. My thanks also go to my younger daughter, Sapana, and son-in-law, Prabhat Adhikari, for steady encouragement, advice, as well as patient recipe testing. Special thanks to my son, Parag, who provided me with his time and wisdom in every way, and most importantly pushed me to finish what I started so many years ago by constantly reminding me, "when I turn 45, the Nepali cookbook will be ready." (This was said when he was a college freshman six years ago!)

My appreciation to my older brother, Prakash A. Raj, who provided steady encouragement, moral support, and advice while I worked on this book. I would like to thank my mother, Kiran K. Pandey, who generously offered her expertise and guidance over the years and shared many family recipes. Many thanks to my late mother-in-law, Aama Hazoor, who lived with us for seventeen years, and taught me that cooking is about more than food. She always said, "*masala le jeeteko khaana mitho hudaina*" or that the essential nature of food should not be overpowered or masked with heavy spices, and I have tried to incorporate her advice into this cookbook.

My thanks to Gregg and Anne Heist and Dr. James Hamilton for encouraging me and sharing their culinary wisdom and continued support for this project. My thanks to Dr. Ramesh Pokharel for assisting me with research on Nepali vegetables and spices. I also owe a great debt to my friends Amar and Meena Giri, Madhu Sen Gupta, Pratima Thapa, Ruma Rajbhandari, Shanti Jonchhe, Dinesh Sthapit, Raja Singh, Indira Sharma, Bhadrika Sharma, Shakun Tuladhar, Amrit Tuladhar, Renu Shukla, Reeta Stecklein, and Hema Zala for giving me encouragement and advice, which has left me richer both in knowledge and friendship.

Finally, this book would not have been possible without Rebecca Cole, my editor at Hippocrene Books. My thanks for the extensive amount of time and effort she spent editing the manuscript. I would also like to thank Barbara Keane-Pigeon, managing editor, for the final editing and great attention to details, and the publisher, George Blagowidow, for giving me the opportunity to bring this book to light!

Bhumika

PREFACE

I have been interested in food and cooking since my childhood. My earliest memories are of my grandparent's house in Kathmandu, Nepal. I remember watching Thuli Bajai, our family's cook, sitting on a wooden platform (*pirka*) in front of a wood-fire stove. Although she never allowed me to help or interfere, by watching I learned a few basic techniques, which served as a foundation for my lifelong interest in cooking.

In college, I majored in Home Economics and taught at NVTC, a vocational college in Sano Thimi, Nepal. My real interest in cooking, however, began when I arrived in the United States in the spring of 1970. I came as a young bride, to join my husband, Kamal Pathak, beginning a new life in a new world. Because he longed for the Nepali foods he had eaten all his life, I searched for a Nepali cookbook in local libraries, bookstores, at Nepali travel agents, even at the Royal Nepali Embassy in Washington, D.C. To my disappointment, I discovered that there was no such resource available here. To further my culinary education, I began asking my family and friends who lived all over the United States for their recipes. I also called my mother in Nepal for tips on some dishes from my childhood.

Each time I visited Nepal, I continued my research. Whenever I met friends and relatives for a meal, I inquired about their cooking methods. These Nepali cooks frequently described a dish by saying, "Add a little bit of this and a little bit of that, mix everything and cook together." Even when I asked for more exact measurements, they would explain with hand gestures to indicate how much to be used for particular ingredients. I quickly learned that *alikiti* (very little), could be anything from 1 teaspoon to 1 cup and *yeti* (some) could be anything from 1 to 2 cups. *Sabai masala haalera pakaaune basaalne* means mix all the spices and start cooking, but it was not clear which spices or how much of each to use. As I talked to these cooks, I wrote down every word, even with these fuzzy measurements. I watched and observed their techniques and then experimented in my own kitchen. In trying these recipes, I found that Nepali cooking is very rewarding; with a little effort, you can produce a wonderfully delicious meal. These experiences prompted me to write a complete book of Nepali home cooking and so my journey began.

This cookbook includes hundreds of recipes. The majority use ingredients that are familiar to Western cooks, so that authentic Nepali flavors can be recreated even outside of Nepal. I have incorporated dishes both traditional and modern, dishes from both Kathmandu and rural areas, for special occasions and everyday fare.

This cookbook is for anyone curious about Nepali cuisine, whether the interest stems simply from a desire to cook or to learn about a different culture. I also hope that this book will assist first-generation Nepalese living abroad, who wish to learn to cook Nepali food. Finally, this book may also serve as a resource for people who have visited Nepal: returned Peace Corps volunteers and tourists who want recipes for the food they enjoyed in Nepal. If I am able to preserve Nepali culture and traditions even on a small scale, this will be a great accomplishment!

Jyoti Pathak
Painted Post, New York
November 2006

Nepal ko Baaremaa

ABOUT NEPAL

The kingdom of Nepal is a landlocked country bordered by Tibet on the north and India to the east, west, and south. It is well-known as the birthplace of Buddha and for the Himalayas. Although it is a small country, it contains the greatest variation in altitude on earth, from the lowlands of the Tarai in the south, to the world's tallest mountain, Mt. Everest (29,028 feet). The length of the country is 550 miles from east to west and it averages 125 miles from north to south. Nepal can be roughly divided into three geographic areas: the high Himalayan region, the mountain region, and the Tarai region, each with its own distinct customs, history, economy, and environment. These different land-scapes have shaped the culinary traditions of Nepal's more than twenty-five million people.

For centuries, Nepal had relatively little contact with the rest of the world. Because of this isolation, Nepali foods and traditions were not influenced by foreign ingredients, resulting in a unique culinary culture. After 1950, when Nepal opened its borders to the outside world, this cuisine, especially in the capital of Kathmandu, was increasingly influenced by the culinary traditions of neighboring areas. It evolved to incorporate many ideas from Indian, Chinese, and Tibetan fare. Modern Nepali cooking, foods, and eating habits have also been shaped by exposure to many Western influences, a process that has been facilitated by Nepal's popularity as a tourist destination. However, in rural villages, cooking has stayed close to its traditional foundations, and in some areas, villagers still cook the same food their ancestors made centuries ago.

Given Nepal's vast geographic and cultural diversity, it is difficult to generalize about what constitutes Nepali cuisine. It is, however, characterized by its simplicity, lightness, and healthfulness. A typical meal uses only the freshest local ingredients, minimal fat, and an artful combination of herbs and spices. This balanced cuisine is just waiting for discovery!

Nepali cuisine varies by region, from the tropical Tarai region to the arctic Himalayas, but most meals consist of some form of rice or other grain accompanied by dried beans, lentils, or peas, and fresh vegetables. A common meal in many areas is *daal-bhaat-tarkaari*, boiled rice accompanied by lentil soup and vegetables. Meat, poultry, and fish are served only occasionally, mostly during celebrations. Nepali meals are almost always enhanced by freshly made or preserved pickles.

Another common dish, *momo*, bite-size dumplings, has roots in the north. The Tibetan influence brings ingredients such as bamboo shoots *(taama)*, salted and pickled radish *(sinki)*, and sun-dried fish *(sukeko maacha)*. In southern Nepal, many dishes are influenced by North Indian cuisine, although these tend to be milder in Nepal. Other Nepali dishes are inspired by the indigenous Newari culture that exists largely in the Kathmandu Valley. Typical Newari dishes include grilled and spiced meat *(chowela)*, sprouted bean soup *(kwanti)*, rice flour bread *(chataamari)*, ceremonial sweet bread *(lakha-mari)*, stuffed steamed rice bread *(yoh-mari)*, and sweetened yogurt *(juju dhau)*. In the mountainous regions, the local staple is roasted flour *(sattu* or *tsaampa)* and boiled potatoes with salted yak butter tea. In the rural and hilly regions where there is a scarcity of rice, Nepalese typically consume a simple meal of cornmeal or millet porridge *(dhindo)*, usually accompanied by some kind of pickle and fermented dried leafy vegetables *(gundruk)*.

The joint family system, where the father, mother, married sons and their spouses and children all live together, is still widespread in Nepal. During meals, family members gather on the kitchen floor, sitting cross-legged, on a low wooden stall or mat *(pirka* or *chakati)*. Dining together is a joyful occasion. Customs are deeply ingrained and food taboos are taken seriously. To begin the meal, family members offer a small amount of food to their gods and ancestors and bow their heads to express gratitude for the food provided. Usually, the food is first served to the eldest or most respected family members or friends. The men and children often dine first, followed by the women. Food is served on flat, compartmentalized plates *(khande-thaal)* or on metal plates *(thaal)* with accompanying bowls. Rice and bread are placed directly on the plate or in the largest compartment, while vegetables, lentils, and meats are placed in the individual bowls or in the smaller compartments. This way one can taste each dish individually, or mix them according to preference. According to Nepalese customs, all the dishes are served at the same time. If a second helping is desired, dishes are not passed around; instead, the cook or homemaker spoons the prepared food onto the plate.

It is common to make noisy slurping sounds while eating. Traditionally, Nepalese eat with their hands, but Western influences have introduced silverware. Some Nepalese, however, are convinced that food tastes better if eaten with the hands. Eating with one's hand has its own etiquette: only the right hand and just the tips of the fingers are used to mix the rice with vegetables, leaving the palm perfectly clean. Leftover food is called *baasi-khaana* and is traditionally given to animals as a gesture of kindness to all living things. Before and after eating, water is provided to wash hands, rinse the mouth, and gargle. Some people with orthodox views never eat food cooked by castes other than their own. Some also believe that fish and meat (*maacha-maasu*) may not be mixed and eaten together.

Although Nepal is one of the poorest countries in the world, it is known for its hospitality. Guests are always looked upon as gods and Nepalese consider it an honor to welcome visitors, including strangers and passersby, and treat them with kindness and courtesy.

In Nepal, food is a constant topic of conversation and no meal is complete without an extended discussion about the food, such as how it is cooked, how it is served, and recent meals. It is also common to talk about one's health, weight loss or gain, and which foods treat various ailments. Dining in restaurants is not a common custom. Most people eat at home, and a lot of time is spent preparing family meals. Entertaining is always done at home and the most authentic food is always found in individual homes.

In Nepal, culinary traditions and recipes are passed down by word-of-mouth from mother to daughter or daughter-in-law, or from grandmothers and aunts over time, with each generation adding their own special touches. Young girls learn to cook by watching and helping in the kitchen. Nepali cooks are not accustomed to measuring devices and cooking is mostly guided by basic principles and common sense, like most culinary traditions.

Most Westerners who go to Nepal for trekking and vacation do not explore the culinary heritage of traditional Nepali home cooking. Tourists primarily eat cooked *daal-bhaat-tarkaari* (a rice-lentil-vegetable combination), a meal that has developed a bad name particularly among trekkers, who often refer to it as "tasteless." This book, however, reveals that Nepali food is not boring or bland. It may indeed be simple, but when well prepared can be extremely delicious. Unfortunately, the most scrumptious home-cooked meals are found in Nepali homes, which are not usually accessible to tourists— although these days a large number of home-style restaurants have opened in Kathmandu and other popular tourist areas.

This book is an attempt to showcase the art of Nepali cooking and make Nepali cuisine available to a wider audience. It reflects the recipes and traditions of my home and cultural upbringing. Thank you for inviting me into your kitchen. My hope is that you will broaden your culinary horizons with these Nepali dishes and turn to these recipes again and again.

Khaajaa ra Chamena

SNACKS and APPETIZERS

Nepalese eat two full meals a day, one around mid-morning and another after sunset. It seems that they are always snacking in between, perhaps because the gap between the two meals is so long. When friends and family visit each other, serving and eating snacks is a common activity. Guests are automatically offered a beverage accompanied by some kind of snack as a welcoming gesture.

A typical Nepali snack does not have to be salty but can be sweet as well. There are so many varieties of snack food enjoyed by Nepalese, it is hard to name each one here. The most common and popular snacks are pressed rice flakes (*cheura*) served with any combination of fried or curried vegetables, meat, egg, or yogurt. Other favorite savory snacks include fritters made from seasonal vegetables and potato (*pakauda*), stuffed samosas, vegetable patties (*tarkaari ko chop*), savory snack mixes (*furindaana*), and a variety of sweet dishes. Look for meat appetizer dishes in the meat section of this book. Snacks are most often served in the mid-afternoon with hot or cold beverages. Although the traditional Nepali meal does not usually start with an appetizer, many of the dishes in this chapter make interesting appetizers.

Nimki
AJOWAN CRACKERS

Nimkis are deep-fried crackers flavored with ajowan seeds, which provide a distinct flavor and can be used whole or crushed. They are a popular light snack food, usually served with hot tea or cold beverages. They can be made ahead of time, but should be stored in an airtight container.

2½ cups all-purpose flour plus extra for rolling
1 teaspoon ajowan seeds, crushed in a mortar and pestle
1 teaspoon salt
A small pinch baking soda

3 tablespoons clarified butter (*gheu*) or unsalted butter, melted
2 tablespoons plain yogurt, mixed with 2 tablespoons water
2 to 3 cups vegetable oil

In a medium-size bowl, mix the flour, ajowan seeds, salt, and baking soda. Add the butter and rub it into the flour mixture with your fingers, until the mixture resembles a coarse meal. Stir in the yogurt mixture and then gradually add ¼ to ½ cup of water, to form a dough that comes together. Knead until the dough is semi-firm. If it is too sticky, add 1 to 2 tablespoons more flour. If it feels too firm, add a little water and knead some more. Cover the dough with a damp kitchen towel and set aside at room temperature for 10 minutes.

When the dough is well rested, place it on a lightly floured flat surface and knead for 1 minute. Divide the dough into four balls. Dust one of the balls generously with flour, and roll it out ⅛ inch thick. Cut the rolled dough into 1-inch diamond shapes. Repeat the process with the remaining dough. Set aside.

Heat the oil in a heavy deep skillet over medium-high heat until it reaches 350° to 375°F. Test the readiness of the oil by placing a small piece of dough into the hot oil. If it bubbles and rises to the surface slowly, it is ready. Add several pieces of dough at a time and fry, stirring as needed, until they are golden brown and crisp, 3 to 4 minutes. With a slotted spoon, remove them, draining as much oil as possible, and transfer to a paper towel-lined platter. Fry the remaining pieces the same way. When they have cooled, store them in an airtight container. These crackers keep well for 1 month.

Makes 4 to 6 servings.

Tarkaari-Maasu ko Samosa

SAMOSAS

These fried turnovers filled with vegetables, meat, or a combination, are one of Nepal's most popular snacks. Traditionally served with chutney or dipping sauce, I like to serve them as a light lunch with yogurt or with a cucumber, onion, and tomato salad (page 287).

DOUGH
2½ cups all-purpose flour plus extra for rolling
¼ cup fine-grain semolina
½ teaspoon ajowan seeds, crushed
½ teaspoon salt
¼ cup vegetable oil

VEGETABLE FILLING
2 pounds boiling potatoes
2 to 3 cups vegetable oil
1 teaspoon cumin seeds
1 medium onion, finely chopped (about 1 cup)
2 fresh mild green chilies, chopped
1 tablespoon minced fresh ginger
3 medium cloves garlic, minced
2 teaspoons ground coriander
1 teaspoon ground cumin
1 teaspoon cayenne pepper
1 teaspoon salt
½ teaspoon ground turmeric
2 cups frozen peas, thawed and thoroughly drained
1 cup finely chopped cilantro

4 to 5 green onions (white and green parts), finely chopped
2 tablespoons fresh lemon or lime juice

MEAT FILLING
2 tablespoons vegetable oil
2 medium onions, finely chopped (about 2 cups)
1 large shallot, minced
1 tablespoon minced fresh ginger
2 large cloves garlic, minced
1 teaspoon Nepali Garam Masala (page 398)
½ teaspoon ground turmeric
½ teaspoon cayenne pepper
1½ pounds ground lamb, chicken, or turkey
2 cups frozen peas, thawed and thoroughly drained
2 fresh mild or hot green chilies, chopped
½ teaspoon salt
1 cup finely chopped cilantro
4 to 5 green onions (white and green parts), finely chopped

To make the dough, combine the flour, semolina, ajowan, and salt in a bowl. Rub in the oil until the mixture resembles a coarse meal. Gradually add ¾ to 1 cup of water until the dough holds together. Knead until semi-firm, adding a little flour if it feels too sticky or a little water if it is too firm. Cover with a damp towel and set aside for 1 hour.

Prepare either the vegetable or the meat filling. For the vegetable filling, in a large saucepan, combine the potatoes and water to cover, and bring to a boil. Reduce the heat to low, cover, and cook until the potatoes are tender, 20 to 25 minutes. Drain, and when cool enough to handle, peel and cut the potatoes into ¼-inch cubes and set aside. Heat 3 tablespoons of the oil in a medium-size saucepan over medium-high heat until hot, but not smoking. Add the cumin seeds and fry until lightly browned and fragrant, about 5 seconds. Add the onion, green chilies, ginger, and garlic. Stir frequently, until the onions are soft but not brown, about 5 minutes. Stir in the coriander, cumin, cayenne pepper, salt, and turmeric. Add the peas and potatoes and cook, stirring for 5 minutes. Remove from the heat and stir in the cilantro, green onions, and lemon juice. Transfer to a bowl and cool to room temperature.

For the meat filling, heat the oil in a large skillet over medium-high heat until hot. Add the onions, shallot, ginger, and garlic and cook, stirring constantly, until the onions are soft, about 5 minutes. Stir in the turmeric, cayenne pepper, and garam masala. Lower the heat to medium, add the meat, and cook, stirring to break up the lumps, until the meat is lightly browned, about 10 minutes. Add the peas, green chilies, and salt and cook until all the moisture has evaporated. Remove from the heat, stir in the cilantro and green onions, and set aside to cool.

Place the dough on a lightly floured work surface. Knead it again until it is soft and pliable. Divide into fifteen balls and coat them with flour. Flatten a ball with a rolling pin and roll into a 7-inch circle. Cut the circle in half. Moisten the straight edge with water and fold the semicircle in half again squeezing along the moistened edge to seal it. Now you have a triangular-shaped cone. Pick it up with your thumb and forefinger. With your other hand, fill the cone with 3 to 3½ tablespoons of filling. Moisten the top edges and press together. Do not overstuff or the samosa may open while frying. Repeat with the remaining dough and filling. While working, make sure to keep the dough covered so it does not dry out. Place the filled samosas in a single layer on a tray, cover, and set aside until you are ready to cook.

Heat oil in a deep, wide skillet over medium-high heat until it reaches 350° to 375° F. Gently drop the samosas in the oil, cooking 4 to 5 at a time. Fry turning frequently, until they are crisp and golden brown. Remove with a slotted spoon and drain on paper-towel-lined platter. Serve immediately.

Makes 25 to 30 samosas.

Alu ko Chop
POTATO PATTIES

Alu ko chop are small oval-shaped spiced mashed potato patties. They are generally eaten warm, accompanied by a spicy chutney or assorted condiments. Traditionally, they are served as a mid-afternoon snack but they can also be served as an appetizer or side dish. Each cook uses their own blend of spices to prepare them and some prefer to dip the patties in chickpea-flour batter before frying. This is my version, a family favorite. I usually serve it with any variety of tomato chutney.

2 pounds boiling potatoes
1 cup finely chopped cilantro
4 to 5 green onions (white and pale green parts), finely chopped
3 to 4 mild fresh green chilies, chopped
1 small red onion, finely chopped (about ½ cup)
2 tablespoon fresh lemon or lime juice
½ teaspoon salt
2 cups plus 2 tablespoons vegetable oil
½ teaspoon cumin seeds
½ teaspoon ajowan seeds
1 medium yellow onion, finely chopped (about 1 cup)
1 tablespoon minced fresh ginger
3 medium cloves garlic, minced
1½ teaspoons ground coriander
1 teaspoon cayenne pepper
1 teaspoon ground cumin
½ teaspoon ground turmeric
2 to 3 eggs, lightly beaten
1 cup dry bread crumbs plus more if needed

In a large saucepan, combine the potatoes and water to cover, and bring to a boil over high heat. Reduce the heat to low, cover the pan, and cook until the potatoes are tender, 20 to 25 minutes. Drain, and when cool enough to handle, peel and mash the potatoes in a medium-size bowl. Mix in the cilantro, green onions, green chilies, red onion, lemon juice, and salt.

Heat 2 tablespoons of the oil in a small skillet over medium-high heat. When the oil is hot, but not smoking, add the cumin seeds and ajowan seeds and fry until lightly browned and fragrant, about 5 seconds. Add the yellow onion, ginger, and garlic and fry until the onion is soft, but not brown, about 5 minutes. Stir in the coriander, cayenne pepper, cumin, and turmeric. Mix the onion mixture with the potatoes and then set aside.

Scoop out about 3 tablespoons of the potato mixture and with lightly oiled hands, roll them into a ball, then flatten slightly into a 3-inch long oval-shaped patty. Repeat with the remaining mixture and place the patties on a tray. Dip each patty into the beaten eggs and let the excess drip off. Roll the patty in the bread crumbs and shake off the excess. Repeat this procedure until all the patties are coated. Set them aside.

Heat the remaining 2 cups of oil in a large nonstick or cast-iron skillet over medium-high heat until it reaches 350° to 375°F. Test the readiness of the oil by sprinkling a pinch of bread crumbs in the hot oil. If they bubble and rise to the surface immediately, it is ready. Place four to five patties in the skillet and cook, turning carefully once or twice, until they are reddish brown and crispy on both sides, 4 to 6 minutes. With a slotted spoon, remove them, draining as much oil as possible, and transfer them to a paper towel-lined platter to drain. Repeat the process with the remaining patties. Skim the surface of the oil occasionally to remove any burnt bread crumbs before adding the next batch. Transfer the patties to a platter and serve hot or at room temperature.

Meat-Filled Potato Patties: Prepare the potato mixture as directed above. Heat 2 tablespoons of vegetable oil in a skillet and sauté 1 chopped medium onion until lightly browned. Stir in 2 minced cloves of garlic, 1 teaspoon minced fresh ginger, 1 teaspoon ground cumin, 1 teaspoon ground coriander, $\frac{1}{2}$ teaspoon ground turmeric, and $\frac{1}{8}$ teaspoon black pepper and cook for 1 minute. Add 1 pound ground lamb or chicken and cook, stirring to break up lumps until the meat is lightly browned and nearly cooked through, about 10 minutes. Add 1 cup drained frozen peas and salt to taste. Cook until all the moisture has evaporated, about 5 minutes. Allow the mixture to cool. Scoop up 2 tablespoons of the potato mixture and with lightly oiled hands, form balls. Flatten each ball slightly and place $1\frac{1}{2}$ tablespoons of the meat filling in the center. Fold the potato mixture to enclose the meat filling and create a smooth oval-shaped patty. Cook as directed above.

Makes 4 to 6 servings.

Tarkaari ko Chop
MIXED VEGETABLE PATTIES

Mixed vegetable patties can be prepared from any combination of chopped vegetables, but the potatoes are essential. These patties are pan-fried and generally served hot with chutney as a snack or appetizer.

1 ½ pounds boiling potatoes	1 teaspoon salt
1 cup vegetable oil	½ teaspoon ground turmeric
½ teaspoon cumin seeds	½ teaspoon cayenne pepper
1 medium onion, finely chopped (about 1 cup)	⅛ teaspoon freshly ground black pepper
1 tablespoon minced fresh ginger	1 cup finely chopped cilantro
3 medium cloves garlic, minced	4 to 5 green onions (white and pale green parts), finely chopped
5 cups finely chopped mixed vegetables (carrots, cauliflower, green peas, bell peppers)	3 to 4 mild fresh green chilies, chopped
2 teaspoons ground coriander	2 tablespoons fresh lemon or lime juice
1 teaspoon ground cumin	

Combine the potatoes and water to cover in a large saucepan, and bring to a boil over high heat. Reduce the heat to low, cover the pan, and cook until the potatoes are tender, 20 to 25 minutes. Drain, and when cool enough to handle, peel the potatoes, roughly mash, and set aside.

Heat 2 tablespoons of the oil in a saucepan over medium-high heat. When the oil is hot, but not smoking, add the cumin seeds and fry until lightly browned and fragrant, about 5 seconds. Add the onion, ginger, and garlic and fry, stirring frequently, until the onion is soft, about 5 minutes. Stir in the chopped vegetables, coriander, cumin, salt, turmeric, cayenne pepper, and black pepper. Mix well. Reduce the heat to medium-low, cover the pan, and continue cooking, stirring from time to time, until the vegetables are soft, about 10 minutes. Add the potatoes, mix well, and continue cooking until any liquid evaporates. Remove the pan from the heat, add cilantro, green onions, green chilies, and lemon juice and mix well. Transfer the mixture to a bowl and cool it to room temperature before proceeding.

Scoop out about 3 tablespoons of the mixture and with lightly oiled hands, roll them into a ball, flatten slightly, and shape into a 2½-inch patty. Place it on a tray and repeat the procedure until all the patties are made.

Heat 2 tablespoons of the oil in a wide non-stick or cast-iron skillet over medium heat. Place 4 to 5 patties in the skillet and cook, carefully turning once or twice, until browned and crispy on both sides, 4 to 5 minutes. Repeat the process with the remaining batch, adding more oil as needed while cooking. Transfer the vegetable patties to a serving dish and serve hot or at room temperature.

Makes 4 to 6 servings.

Pakaudas
BATTER-FRIED VEGETABLES

Pakaudas, *battered-based savory fritters, are very popular in Nepal. This recipe is versatile, so feel free to choose your favorite ingredients and spices. The key to making the perfect* pakauda *lies in the quality of the ingredients and heating the oil to the proper temperature. If the oil is not hot enough, they absorb too much oil. Also, a thick batter will overwhelm the vegetables and make doughy fritters, but if the vegetables are too wet, the batter will be runny. Serve with chutney or any dipping sauce.*

2 cups chickpea flour (*besan*)
½ cup finely chopped cilantro
2 fresh mild green chilies, minced
1½ teaspoons salt
1 teaspoon ajowan seeds
1 teaspoon minced fresh ginger
1 teaspoon ground cumin
1 teaspoon ground coriander
½ teaspoon ground turmeric
½ teaspoon cayenne pepper
¼ teaspoon freshly ground black pepper

A small pinch ground asafetida
2 cups vegetable oil
1 medium potato, peeled and sliced ⅛ inch thick
1 medium onion, sliced ¼ inch thick and separated into rings
1 small eggplant, sliced ⅛ inch thick
¼ head cauliflower, cut into 1-inch florets (about 2 cups)

In a medium-size bowl, combine the chickpea flour, cilantro, green chilies, salt, ajowan seeds, ginger, cumin, coriander, turmeric, cayenne pepper, black pepper, and asafetida. Gradually add 1 to 1½ cups of water to make a smooth batter with the consistency of thick cream. Cover and set aside for 20 minutes. When the batter is well rested, it will thicken slightly. If the batter seems too thick, add some water; if it feels too thin, add more chickpea flour.

Heat the oil in a heavy deep skillet over medium-high heat until it reaches 350° to 375°F. Test the readiness of the oil by placing a drop of batter into the hot oil. If it bubbles and rises to the surface immediately, it is ready. Dip a vegetable slice into the batter, making sure it is completely coated. Shake off any excess and gently place it in the hot oil. Fry, turning a few times, until golden brown and crispy, 2 to 3 minutes. Fry a few pieces at a time, but do not crowd the pan. With a slotted spoon, remove the *pakauda*, draining as much oil as possible, and transfer it to a paper towel-lined platter. Repeat with the remaining vegetables. Transfer the *pakaudas* to a platter and serve immediately while still crispy.

Makes 4 to 6 servings.

Pakauda Variations: 1/8-inch-thick slices of Asian eggplant; 1/8-inch-thick slices of zucchini; stemmed spinach; stemmed, seeded, and thinly sliced bell peppers; shredded cabbage; whole green chilies, with a small slit cut in the middle; thin slices of crustless bread, cut into triangles; peeled and deveined shrimp, patted dry; bite-size pieces of fish fillets or boneless chicken; 1/2-inch-thick slices of paneer cheese; and sliced hard-boiled eggs.

Mismaas Tarkaari ko Pakauda
VEGETABLE FRITTERS

Unlike the preceding recipe mixed vegetable pakaudas are made from chopped vegetables mixed with batter.

2 cups finely chopped fresh
    spinach
I cup frozen peas, thawed and
    drained
I small onion, thinly sliced
I medium potato, peeled and
    grated
¼ head cauliflower, finely
    chopped (½ cup)
I small zucchini, chopped
    (½ cup)
½ cup shredded green cabbage
2 fresh mild green chilies, minced

I½ teaspoons salt
I teaspoon ajowan seeds
I teaspoon minced fresh ginger
I teaspoon ground cumin
I teaspoon ground coriander
½ teaspoon cayenne pepper
½ teaspoon ground turmeric
¼ teaspoon freshly ground
    black pepper
A small pinch ground asafetida
I½ cups chickpea flour (*besan*)
    or as needed
2 cups vegetable oil

In a large bowl, combine the spinach, peas, onion, potato, cauliflower, zucchini, and cabbage. Stir in the green chilies, salt, ajowan, ginger, cumin, coriander, cayenne pepper, turmeric, black pepper, and asafetida. Add the chickpea flour a little at a time, mixing well after each addition. Make sure all the vegetables are well coated. Cover and let the mixture stand at room temperature for 15 to 20 minutes. When the mixture is well rested, the vegetables should have released enough moisture to form a sticky batter. If the batter is too thick, sprinkle in some water; if it is too runny, add some chickpea flour. The mixture should be just thick enough to form into fritters.

Heat the oil in a deep heavy skillet over medium-high heat until it reaches 350° to 375°F. Test the readiness of the oil by adding a drop of the batter. If it bubbles and immediately rises to the surface, it is ready. Scoop up about 2 tablespoons of the mixture and gently drop it into the oil. Fry, turning a few times, until golden brown and crispy, 2 to 3 minutes. With a slotted spoon, remove the *pakauda*, draining as much oil as possible, and transfer it to a paper towel-lined platter. Fry four to five pieces at a time, but do not crowd the pan. Repeat with the remaining batter. Transfer the *pakaudas* to a platter and serve immediately, while still crisp.

Makes 4 to 6 servings.

Makai Poleko
NEPALI-STYLE CORN ON THE COB

Fresh sweet corn is so good all by itself that it does not need much spicing up, but this recipe adds a new dimension. Each row of kernels is scored and marinated with spices. The corn is roasted on a grill, bringing out the intense flavor of the spices.

6 to 8 ears corn	1 medium clove garlic, minced
¼ cup butter, softened	½ teaspoon cayenne pepper
2 fresh mild green chilies, minced	⅛ teaspoon Szechwan pepper (*timmur*), freshly ground with a mortar and pestle
1 tablespoon fresh lemon or lime juice	⅛ teaspoon freshly ground black pepper
1 teaspoon salt	1 lemon, cut into wedges
1 teaspoon minced fresh ginger	

Preheat a charcoal or gas grill to medium-high heat for 10 minutes. Remove and discard the husks and silk from the corn. Hold each ear firmly, and score each row of kernels with a sharp knife. When the kernels are pierced, a milky liquid may be released.

In a small bowl, combine the butter, green chilies, lemon juice, salt, ginger, garlic, cayenne pepper, Szechwan pepper, and black pepper and mix well. Spread the spice mixture evenly over each ear of corn and rub the entire surface, making sure each kernel is covered. Set them aside about 10 minutes to allow the flavors to be absorbed. Place the ears of corn directly on the grill and roast, turning occasionally, until they are dotted with black and brown marks. Transfer the corn to a platter, garnish them with the fresh lemon wedges, and serve warm.

Makes 6 to 8 servings.

Farsi ko Phool Taareko
FRIED SQUASH BLOSSOMS

Squash blossoms (farsi ko phool) are the edible flowers of squash plants. In Nepal, they are dipped into a spiced batter and deep-fried. They are delicious and have a pleasant, moist, and silky texture. Fried squash blossoms are among the most appreciated snack in Nepal, and can be served alone or with a spicy chutney. These snacks are popular during the summer months when squash is abundant. They are harvested early in the morning before they open to the sun. Like any flower, they are extremely perishable and fragile and should be used the day they are picked. To keep them fresh until preparation time, store them in a bowl of cold water in the refrigerator. The surest way to come by squash blossoms is to grow them yourself. They may also be available in farmer's markets or in health food stores.

10 to 12 squash blossoms
1½ cups chickpea flour (*besan*)
2 fresh mild green chilies, minced
1 teaspoon minced fresh ginger
½ teaspoon ground turmeric
¼ teaspoon ground cumin
¼ teaspoon ground coriander
¼ teaspoon salt

¼ teaspoon ground cayenne (optional)
⅛ teaspoon freshly ground black pepper
1 cup vegetable oil

Check the inside of each blossom for bugs. Rinse gently, shake to remove excess water, and then pat it dry on a paper towel. If there is a tiny squash attached to the stem, remove it.

In a medium-size bowl, combine the chickpea flour, green chilies, ginger, turmeric, cumin, coriander, salt, cayenne pepper, and black pepper and mix well. Gradually add ¾ to 1 cup of water, stirring well, to make a smooth batter with the consistency of heavy cream. Cover and set aside to rest for 20 minutes. When the batter is well rested, it will thicken slightly. If the batter is too thick, add a little water; if it feels too thin, add more chickpea flour.

Heat the oil in a large heavy skillet over medium-high heat until it reaches 350° to 375°F. Test the readiness of the oil by placing a drop of batter into the hot oil. If it bubbles and rises to the surface immediately, it is ready. Dip each blossom into the batter, making sure to coat the entire blossom. Shake off the excess batter and gently lower it into the hot oil. Fry, turning a few times, until crisp and golden brown on all sides, about 2 minutes. Remove the blossoms with a slotted spoon, draining as much oil as possible, and transfer to a paper towel-lined platter to drain. Repeat the process with the remaining blossoms. Transfer to a platter and serve immediately while still crispy.

Makes 4 to 6 servings.

Maas ko Baara
URAD BEAN FRITTERS

Maas ko Baara are light and spongy urad daal fritters that resemble small doughnuts. Traditionally, the batter is ground on a stone slab and roller (silouto), giving it a smooth and fluffy consistency, but this recipe uses a food processor or blender to produce an equally good result. They are best served fresh but can be stored overnight.

Baara *are associated with religious and ceremonial occasions. During the ten days of the Vijaya Dashami festival, they are prepared each morning, and are offered to the deities as sacred offerings* (naivedya). They are also distributed among friends and families and consumed as a blessed food (prashaad).

2 cups split black urad beans,
    with skins (*kaalo maas*
    ko daal)
1 teaspoon salt
1 teaspoon minced fresh ginger
A small pinch ground asafetida
2 cups vegetable oil

Sort and wash the beans as described on pages 69-70. In a large bowl, soak them in the refrigerator for at least 6 hours or overnight, until doubled in volume. Rub the beans between your hands vigorously to loosen the outer black skins. The coating will come off easily and float in the water. Drain, add fresh water, and rub again until most of the coatings are removed. Drain the beans in a colander.

Place the drained beans in a food processor or blender and process, adding just enough water to make a semi-thick smooth puree with no grainy bits of beans remaining. You may have to do this in two batches. Place the batter in a bowl and add the salt, ginger, and asafetida and whisk until it is light and spongy. Cover the bowl and allow the mixture to rest at room temperature for at least 10 minutes.

Heat the oil in a large heavy skillet over medium-high heat until it reaches 350° to 375°F. Test the readiness of the oil by dropping a little batter into the hot oil. If it bubbles and rises to the surface immediately, it is ready. With moistened fingertips, scoop up 2 tablespoons of the batter and shape it into a round flat patty. Make a hole in the center of the patty. Immediately gently slide the patty into the hot oil. The *baara* will sink to the bottom first, but will rise up and double in size. Flip it over a few times, until both sides are light brown and it is cooked through, 2 to 3 minutes. Remove with a slotted spoon, draining the excess oil, and place the fritter on a paper towel-lined plate. Repeat with the remaining batter. Serve the *baara* hot.

Makes 6 to 8 servings.

Croquette Variation *(Maas ko Phulaura)*: Prepare the beans as described above through the pureeing step. Transfer the batter to a bowl and stir in 2 minced mild green chilies, I teaspoon salt, I teaspoon minced fresh ginger, $\frac{1}{8}$ teaspoon ground Szechwan pepper, and a small pinch asafetida. Set aside to rest for I0 minutes. Heat the oil as above. Form the batter into balls using 2 tablespoons of the mixture. Drop the balls into the hot oil and fry until brown, about 3 to 4 minutes. Drain on paper towels and serve warm or at room temperature.

Moong ko Daal Taareko
FRIED YELLOW MUNG BEANS

This crunchy treat is a perfect mid-afternoon snack to be nibbled alone like peanuts or combined with Savory Snack Mix (page 34). Although fried mung beans are available in Indian grocery stores and most families purchase them ready-made, they are easy to make.

2 cups split yellow mung beans without skins (*pahelo moong ko daal*) or whole green mung beans (*singo moong ko daal*)	A pinch baking soda 2 cups vegetable oil Salt to taste

Sort and wash the mung beans as described on page 69-70. In a large bowl, combine the beans with the baking soda and water to cover, and soak them in the refrigerator for 6 to 8 hours or overnight. Drain the beans and place them on paper towels until the excess moisture is removed.

Heat the oil in a large heavy cast-iron skillet over medium-high heat until it reaches 350° to 375°F. Test the readiness of the oil by adding a few beans. If they bubble and rise to the surface immediately, it is ready. Put half of the mung beans into the oil and gently fry, stirring frequently, until crispy, about 7 minutes. With a slotted spoon, remove the beans, draining as much oil as possible, and transfer to a paper towel-lined platter. Repeat with the remaining beans. Be careful not to overfry the beans or they will become too hard. Toss the fried beans with salt and any other seasoning of your choice and cool to room temperature before storing. The snack will stay fresh for 2 months if kept in an airtight container.

Fried Split Chickpeas: Substitute dried chickpeas for the mung beans, increasing the baking soda to 1 teaspoon because they tend to be harder. After frying, toss the chickpeas with ½ teaspoon cayenne pepper, ⅛ teaspoon ground cumin, 1 teaspoon mango powder (*amchoor*), and salt to taste.

Makes 4 to 6 servings.

Taareko Piro Kaaju-Badaam
SPICED NUTS

This nut mixture makes a crunchy, salty, spicy snack. The nuts are fried until crisp and then coated with spices for flavor. This recipe is versatile, so adjust the spices to your liking and use any variety of nuts. It can be prepared a few weeks ahead and kept in an airtight container at room temperature.

¼ teaspoon ground cumin
¼ teaspoon granulated garlic
¼ teaspoon cayenne pepper
¼ teaspoon mango powder
   (*amchoor*)

Salt to taste
¼ cup vegetable oil
1½ cups raw cashews
1½ cups raw almonds

In a plastic bag or a sealable container combine the cumin, garlic, cayenne pepper, mango powder, and salt. Set aside.

Heat the oil in a skillet over medium heat. When the oil is hot, add the cashews and almonds and sauté until they are lightly browned and crisp, 2 to 3 minutes. Make sure the nuts do not get too dark; otherwise, they will have a bitter and burned taste. With a slotted spoon, transfer the nuts to a bowl. Cool slightly, add the fried nuts to the plastic bag with the spices, and shake to coat. The nuts keep in an airtight container for up to 2 weeks.

Makes 4 to 6 servings.

Furindaana
SAVORY SNACK MIX

Most Nepali homes are well stocked with furindaana, a popular mixture of nuts, seeds, lentils, beans, peas, rice flakes, dry fruits, and potato sticks. Furindaana is a flexible dish, and there are no rigid measurements or spice proportions. In fact, each family uses their own formula. Although the ingredient list is long, this snack is easy to put together if you substitute ready-made ingredients, which are often just as good and more convenient. Ready-made packages of sev noodles, fried split chickpeas, and fried mung beans can be purchased at Indian grocery stores. If you wish, you can make a large batch and store it in an airtight container at room temperature for up to six months.

1½ cups vegetable oil
1½ cups pressed rice flakes
   (*cheura*)
¼ cup sugar
1 teaspoon salt
½ teaspoon ground turmeric
½ teaspoon cayenne pepper
¼ teaspoon mango powder
   (*amchoor*)
2 cups canned fried potato
   sticks
2 cups chickpea flour noodles
   (*sev*), thin or thick
1 cup Fried Split Chickpeas
   (page 32 or store-bought)
1 cup Fried Yellow Mung Beans
   (page 32 or store-bought)
1 cup Assorted Spiced Nuts
   (page 33 or store-bought)

1 cup roasted peanuts
¼ cup roasted sunflower seeds
1 tablespoon coconut chips
8 dried red chilies
1 cup finely chopped cilantro
6 to 8 fresh mild green chilies,
   finely diced
½ cup peeled and finely
   julienned fresh ginger
4 to 6 large cloves garlic, thinly
   sliced
½ cup golden raisins
½ teaspoon cumin seeds
½ teaspoon ajowan seeds
¼ teaspoon brown mustard
   seeds
2 tablespoons sesame seeds

Using 1 cup of the oil, fry the cheura as described on page 36. Place the fried rice flakes in a large bowl and combine with the sugar, salt, turmeric, cayenne pepper, and mango powder. Stir in the potato sticks, noodles, chickpeas, mung beans, spiced nuts, peanuts, sunflower seeds, and coconut. Set aside.

Heat the remaining ½ cup of vegetable oil in a skillet over medium-high heat. When hot, but not smoking, add the dried chilies and fry until they become reddish-brown and fully fragrant, about 5 seconds. Remove with a slotted spoon and add to the rice flake mixture. In the same oil, fry the cilantro, green chilies, ginger, and garlic until lightly crisp, 2 to 3 minutes. Remove them from the skillet, draining as much oil as possible, and add them to the rice flake mixture. Fry the raisins until they puff up, remove them, and add them to the rice flake mixture. In the remaining oil, fry the cumin, ajowan, and mustard seeds until the mustard seeds pop and the other spices turn dark brown and become fully fragrant, about 5 seconds. Reduce the heat to low, immediately add the sesame seeds, and fry until they crackle. The spices will smoke, but do not let them burn. Remove the spices with a slotted spoon, draining the excess oil, combine them with the *furindaana* mixture, and mix thoroughly until the spices are well coated. Serve immediately or cool and store in an airtight container.

Makes 10 to 12 cups.

Taareko Cheura
FRIED PRESSED RICE FLAKES

This is a delicious and quick method of converting pressed rice flakes into a crunchy snack. When fried, rice flakes double in size and become snow white in color. Fried cheura is versatile and can be served sprinkled with sugar or salt as a mid-afternoon snack with beverages or with meat, vegetables, or pickles. The fried flakes can also be combined with nuts, fried potato shreds, fried lentils, and spices to make a crunchy snack mix.

2 cups pressed rice flakes (*cheura*), thick variety	**2 to 3 tablespoons sugar, or to taste**
2 to 3 cups vegetable oil	

Spread the *cheura* on a large platter and pick out any foreign matter such as unhusked rice, stems, or powdery flakes and discard.

Heat the oil in a deep skillet over medium-high heat until it reaches 350° to 375°F. If the oil is too hot, the rice flakes will brown too quickly, but if the temperature is not hot enough, they will absorb too much oil and be soggy. Test the readiness of the oil by placing a few rice flakes into the hot oil. If the flakes expand and rise to the surface immediately, the oil is ready. If you have a fine-mesh metal strainer, place ½ cup of rice flakes at a time in the strainer and lower them into the hot oil. After the flakes have fried, lift the strainer and drain the oil. Otherwise, you can use a slotted spoon. The flakes will sink first, then bubble and foam, and within a minute, they will expand to fluffy white flakes. Stir constantly and fry until the flakes float to the surface, which occurs very quickly. Immediately remove the flakes from the oil and drain on paper towels. Repeat with the remaining rice flakes. Mix the fried *cheura* with the sugar and serve. Cool to room temperature and store in an airtight container for 2 to 3 weeks.

Makes 6 to 8 servings.

Dahi-Cheura
YOGURT WITH PRESSED RICE FLAKES

Dahi-Cheura *is a mixture of yogurt and pressed rice flakes and is one of the most popular foods in Nepal. This soothing comfort food is eaten at any time of the day, as a mid-afternoon snack or as a light lunch, but I usually serve it for breakfast. In Nepal, one very common demeaning slogan is to call someone "dahi-cheure," which translates to "a person who is untrusting, shady, tricky, undependable, and untrustworthy."*

1 cup pressed rice flakes (*cheura*), thick variety	1 to 2 tablespoons sugar, or to taste
2 cups plain yogurt (preferably whole-milk)	Chopped nuts and/or fruit (optional)

Spread the *cheura* on a large platter and pick out any foreign matter such as unhusked rice, stems, or powdery flakes and discard. In a small bowl, combine the rice flakes, yogurt, and sugar. Let the mixture stand, covered at room temperature, until the yogurt is absorbed and the flakes soften, about 10 minutes. Add the chopped nuts and/or fruits, if using.

Makes 2 servings.

Matar-Cheura
PRESSED RICE FLAKES WITH GREEN PEAS

Matar-cheura is my father's favorite mid-afternoon snack. I like to make this dish at the height of the season from spring to early summer when fresh peas are tender and can be easily bought at the local farmer's market. Although shelling fresh peas is tedious, it is worth the delicate taste it adds to this snack.

3 cups pressed rice flakes (*cheura*), thick variety
2 tablespoons clarified butter (*gheu*)
1 dried red chili, halved and seeded
½ teaspoon cumin seeds
2 small bay leaves
1 medium onion, finely chopped (about 1 cup)
4 small cloves garlic, chopped
1½ teaspoons minced fresh ginger

A small pinch ground asafetida
2 cups shelled fresh peas
2 fresh mild green chilies, split lengthwise
1 teaspoon salt
½ teaspoon ground turmeric
½ teaspoon ground cumin
½ teaspoon ground coriander
½ cup finely chopped cilantro
4 to 5 green onions (white and pale green parts), finely chopped

Spread the *cheura* on a large platter, pick out any foreign matter such as unhusked rice, stems, or powdery dusty flakes and discard. Wash, rinse, and drain the *cheura* until the water runs clear. Put the rice flakes in a medium-size bowl, cover with plenty of cold water, and soak for 1 minute. The softened rice flakes should be firm, not mushy. Drain.

Heat the clarified butter in a heavy saucepan over medium-high heat. When it is hot, add the dried chili, cumin seeds, and bay leaves, and fry until lightly browned and fragrant, for about 5 seconds. Add the onion, garlic, ginger, and asafetida and cook until soft. Mix in the peas, green chilies, salt, turmeric, cumin, and coriander and cook, covered, stirring occasionally, until the peas are cooked, 8 to 10 minutes. Gently stir in rice flakes. Reduce the heat to medium-low, cover, and cook until the spices have soaked into the rice flakes, for about 5 minutes. The finished dish should be moist, tender, and fluffy. If the mixture is too dry, stir in ¼ cup of warm water and cook for 5 minutes more. Mix in the cilantro and green onions, and serve the mixture hot or at room temperature.

Makes 4 to 6 servings.

Hariyo Bhatmaas Saandheko
SOYBEAN SALAD

Fresh green soybeans (bhatmaas) are an important crop in Nepal. They are harvested before maturity while they are still tender and sweet. They are similar to green peas in size, but have a silkier texture. Bhatmaas are very flavorful and high in fiber and protein. I use these beans in salads, stir-fries, or serve them simply steamed. For this recipe, I use shelled frozen soybeans, which are readily available at many Asian markets.

I pound frozen shelled soybeans, thawed and thoroughly drained
Salt to taste
I small red onion, finely chopped (about ½ cup)
4 to 5 green onions (white and pale green parts), finely chopped
½ cup finely chopped cilantro

3 fresh hot green chilies, finely chopped
I tablespoon fresh lemon or lime juice
2 medium cloves garlic, minced
½ tablespoon vegetable oil
I teaspoon minced fresh ginger
⅛ teaspoon Szechwan pepper (*timmur*), finely ground with a mortar and pestle

Bring a medium-size pot of salted water to a rolling boil over medium-high heat. Add the soybeans and boil until tender, 3 to 4 minutes. Immediately drain in a colander and run the beans under cold water. Transfer them to a medium-size bowl and combine with the remaining ingredients. Mix well. Cover, and set aside for 30 minutes to allow the flavors to set in. Transfer the mixture to a platter and serve at room temperature.

Makes 4 servings.

Bhogate Saandheko
POMELO SALAD

Pomelos (bhogates) are large, thick-skinned citrus fruits native to tropical and subtropical regions throughout the world. The fruit is covered by a thick, tough, loose-fitting skin which peels off easily. Bhogates are abundant in the winter months in Nepal. *The preparation of this refreshing salad is a leisurely family affair. Typically, family members, relatives, and friends gather in the sunniest part of the house, usually the open-air top floor (kausi) on a warm sunny day. A large amount of pomelos are brought in and everyone helps to peel the fruit, separate it into segments, and mix it with spices.*

¼ cup sesame seeds
4 medium white or red pomelos, peeled and sectioned
4 medium navel oranges, peeled and sectioned
2 cups plain yogurt, stirred well
¾ cup sugar
2 tablespoons fresh lemon or lime juice
I teaspoon cayenne pepper

½ teaspoon freshly ground black pepper
⅛ teaspoon Szechwan pepper (*timmur*), finely ground with a mortar and pestle
Salt to taste
2 tablespoons mustard oil
½ teaspoon fenugreek seeds
½ teaspoon ground turmeric
A small pinch ground asafetida

Heat a small cast-iron skillet over medium heat and toast the sesame seeds for about 2 minutes, stirring constantly to prevent the seeds from flying out, until they give off a pleasant aroma and darken. Transfer the seeds to a dry container. Cool, place them in a spice grinder or a mortar and pestle, and grind to a fine powder.

Combine the ground sesame seeds, pomelos, oranges, yogurt, sugar, lemon juice, cayenne pepper, black pepper, *timmur*, and salt and mix gently.

Heat the mustard oil in a small skillet over medium-high heat. When the oil is hot, but not smoking, add the fenugreek seeds and fry until dark brown and fragrant, for about 5 seconds. Remove the skillet from the heat and sprinkle in the turmeric and asafetida. Immediately pour these spices into the citrus mixture and stir well. The finished dish should be spicy, sweet, tangy, and tart.

Adjust the seasonings accordingly. Cover and set aside for 15 minutes to allow the seasonings and flavor to develop. Transfer the pomelo salad to a bowl and serve.

Note: Pomelos are available at Asian food stores and occasionally in regular grocery stores. Be careful to select ripe pomelos. Immature pomelos can be very bitter, dry, and overpowering, and may not be suitable for this salad. When ripe, the fruit is slightly dry, the flesh is firm, and it has a slightly sweet-tangy taste. You may substitute grapefruit if pomelos are not available.

Makes 4 to 6 servings.

Saandheko Bhatmaas-Badaam-Kukhura
SPICED PEANUTS, SOYBEANS, AND SHREDDED CHICKEN

Even when guests arrive unexpectedly, snacks and beverages must be served in Nepalese homes and the following recipe can be put together quickly. It combines soybeans, peanuts, fresh herbs, and spices with cooked shredded chicken. This simple dish is delicious and flavorful.

2 cups shredded cooked chicken
1 cup roasted or fried soybeans, split or whole
1 cup roasted peanuts
6 to 7 green onions (white and pale green parts), finely chopped
½ cup finely chopped cilantro
2 to 3 fresh hot green chilies, chopped
1 tablespoon mustard oil

2 medium cloves garlic, minced
2 teaspoons fresh lemon or lime juice
1 teaspoon minced fresh ginger
½ teaspoon salt
½ teaspoon cayenne pepper
½ teaspoon ground cumin
⅛ teaspoon Szechwan pepper (*timmur*), finely ground with a mortar and pestle

In a large bowl, combine all the ingredients. Taste and adjust the seasonings. Cover and set the mixture aside to allow the seasonings to blend well for 15 minutes. Transfer the mixture to a platter and serve it at room temperature.

Makes 4 to 6 servings.

Maacha ko Chop
FISH STICKS

Maacha ko chop *is a delicious fried snack or appetizer that can be made from any variety of fish. In this recipe, fish is cooked with fresh herbs and spices, shaped into sticks (resembling store-bought fish sticks), and deep-fried. These are generally served warm with chutney and dipping sauce or just a squeeze of lemon juice.*

1 pound red-skinned potatoes
2 cups vegetable oil
1 medium onion, finely chopped (about 1 cup)
3 to 4 mild fresh green chilies, finely chopped
2 teaspoons minced fresh ginger
2 medium cloves garlic, minced
1 teaspoon cayenne pepper or to taste
1 teaspoon ground cumin
1 teaspoon ground coriander
½ teaspoon ground turmeric
2 to 2½ pounds firm white fish fillets, picked over for bones and cut into 2-inch pieces

½ teaspoon salt
1 cup finely chopped cilantro
4 to 5 green onions (white and pale green parts), finely chopped
2 tablespoons fresh lemon or lime juice
2 eggs, lightly beaten
1 cup dry bread crumbs, plus more if needed
1 lemon, cut into wedges

In a small saucepan, combine the potatoes and water to cover, and bring to a boil over high heat. Reduce the heat to low, cover, and cook until the potatoes are tender, 20 to 25 minutes. Drain, and when cool enough to handle, peel, mash roughly, and set aside.

Heat 2 tablespoons of the oil in a medium-size skillet over medium-high heat. When the oil is hot, add the onion and fry until lightly browned, about 5 minutes. Stir in the green chilies, ginger, garlic, cayenne pepper, cumin, coriander, and turmeric. Reduce the heat to medium, add the fish and salt, and cook, stirring frequently, until the fish is cooked through and all the moisture has evaporated, about 8 minutes. Add the mashed potatoes, cilantro, green onions, and lemon juice and continue cooking until the mixture is dry. Transfer it to a bowl and cool to room temperature before using.

With lightly oiled hands, scoop out 2½ tablespoons of the mixture and roll into a 2-inch-long cylinder. Place on a platter and repeat with the remaining mixture. Dip each stick in the beaten eggs, let the excess drip off, then roll it in the bread crumbs, and shake off the excess crumbs. Repeat until all the sticks are coated with bread crumbs.

Heat the remaining oil in a large nonstick or cast-iron skillet over medium-high heat until it reaches 350° to 375°F. Test the readiness of the oil by sprinkling a pinch of bread crumbs into the hot oil. If it bubbles and rises to the surface immediately, it is ready. Place six or seven fish sticks in the oil and fry, turning carefully once or twice, until browned and crispy, 2 to 3 minutes. With a slotted spoon, remove them, draining as much oil as possible, and transfer to a paper towel-lined platter to drain. Repeat with the remaining fish sticks. Skim the surface of the oil occasionally and remove any burnt bread crumbs before adding the next batch. Transfer the fish sticks to a platter and serve with the lemon wedges.

Makes 4 to 6 servings.

Bhaat-Bhuja

RICE DISHES

Rice is cultivated in many regions of Nepal, and is one of its most important crops. The rice seedling transplanting and harvesting seasons are times of great anticipation and happiness in the community. Nepali farmers celebrate the occasion with a feast accompanied by music and dance. In the hilly part of the country, however, land conditions and lack of rain make rice difficult to grow and thus an expensive luxury. In these higher elevations, locals eat corn, millet, wheat, barley, and buckwheat.

Rice is a versatile food, and can be simply boiled, steamed with butter, or cooked with a variety of ingredients such as spices, herbs, nuts, vegetables, meat, lentils, and beans. Plain boiled rice acts as a neutral food to eat with highly spiced curries, chutneys, pickles, and gravies. Nepalese like their rice tender, light, and fluffy with each grain separated and not mushy.

Uncooked rice is called *chaamal,* and cooked rice is referred to as *bhaat* or *bhuja.* Rice is grown under a wide range of conditions and a number of varieties are produced, varying in size, shape, color, flavor, and fragrance. In Nepal, the most expensive variety is long-grain white rice (*masino chaamal* or *basmati chaamal*), which is prized for its delicate, distinct flavor and texture. Medium- to short-grain white rice (*saano-thulo marsi chaamal*) is usually flatter and oval in shape. Parboiled rice (*usineko chaamal*) is slightly yellowish in color, less flavorful, less expensive, and takes longer to cook. Pressed or flattened rice flakes known as *cheura* are one of the most common rice products consumed in Nepal. Rice is also ground to make flour and made into fried or steamed snacks, breads, and sweet dishes.

Preparing Rice

Rice is very easy to cook and does not require any special skills. If you follow a few basic guidelines, you will not have any trouble making perfectly cooked rice. Most of the recipes in this chapter use long-grain white rice or basmati rice, both of which are readily available in most supermarkets or Indian grocery stores. I usually cook rice after preparing the accompanying dishes, which can be easily reheated, so that it is steaming hot when served.

Cleaning

Most commercially bagged rice, such as the supermarket variety (in plastic, cloth, or burlap bags) has been cleaned and sorted, so there is rarely any need to pick through it. Be sure however, to pick over imported rice or rice from open bulk containers for unhulled grains, stems, pebbles, or broken rice. To clean it, spread the rice on a large platter or a wide round wicker tray (or a *naan-glo*, if available). Pick through a small portion at a time, and discard any foreign particles.

I always rinse rice thoroughly under cold running water before cooking to remove any floating husks or impurities that may have collected during milling and processing. To wash the rice, place it in a large bowl and cover with cold water. Gently rub the grains between your hands and remove anything that floats. Slowly pour the milky water out, holding back the grains with one hand. Repeat this process several times until the water runs clear.

Soaking and Draining

I recommend soaking rice (especially basmati) before cooking it as it shortens the cooking time and keeps each grain separate and fluffy. Soaking also makes the rice grains less likely to stick together. I recommend soaking for at least 20 minutes, but recipes vary, and some dishes only need washing and rinsing. To soak the rice, place it in a large bowl and cover with cold water, set aside, and drain thoroughly. For cooking everyday rice (long-grain rice) by the absorption method (see below), soak the rice for 20 to 25 minutes before cooking, but if you are in a hurry, omit the soaking. You will still get good results. I also prefer to cook the rice in the same water in which it has been soaking.

Cooking

Rice can be cooked in any pot that has good heat distribution and a tight-fitting lid. In Nepal, rice was traditionally cooked in a heavy, round-bottomed, brass pot called a *kasaudi*. The pot has a narrow neck to retain moisture, and the heavy bottom distributes the heat evenly so that the rice cooks in an energy-saving fashion and can be kept warm for a long time. Today there are several methods of cooking rice and each cook has their own preferred technique. Some prefer to boil rice in plenty of water on the stovetop. When the rice is almost cooked, the starchy water is poured off, and the rice is cooked over low heat until each grain is light and fluffy. In the absorption method, an exact amount of water is added to the rice and boiled, then covered and simmered on the stovetop until the water has been absorbed and the rice becomes tender and fluffy. Rice can also be cooked by first sautéing it in oil, adding a measured amount of water, and then simmering it, covered, until the water has been absorbed.

Finally, if you own an electric rice cooker, and follow the directions correctly, you should be able to make perfect, fluffy rice that stays warm for hours without losing quality every time. If you enjoy rice and cook it often, it may be worth purchasing a rice cooker.

Whichever method of cooking you use, be sure to leave the rice undisturbed for five to ten minutes, covered in the pot so that the trapped steam finishes off the cooking process (*tharak marne*). Sometimes while cooking rice, the grains stick together on the bottom of the pan and form a thin, golden brown crust (*mamuri*), considered the most delicious part of cooked rice.

Most Nepali cooks do not measure water for rice, but make an educated guess based on a finger measurement. Typically, rice is washed, drained, and placed in a pot. The water is poured into the pot, and the cook inserts a finger into the water. The level of water above the rice should be just above the first joint of the middle finger. The rice is then cooked by the absorption method. When cooking a large quantity of rice I add about $1\frac{1}{4}$ inches of water above the rice.

However, the measurement and cooking time depend on many factors, such as the age of the grain, type of rice, type of pot, whether the rice has been presoaked or not, and the heat source. With each type of rice, it is necessary to cook it once in order to find out the best way to cook it. A little experimentation will help to achieve the best results. I have found that I need to adjust the amount of water and cooking time with each variety of rice, but the basic guideline is for a cup of long-grain white rice, use $1\frac{1}{2}$ to 2 cups of water, and for 2 cups of rice, use $3\frac{1}{2}$ to 4 cups of water. Rice expands to two or three times its original size after cooking so that generally, 1 cup of uncooked rice yields $2\frac{1}{2}$ to 3 cups of cooked rice.

THE ROLE OF RICE IN NEPALI CULTURE

My husband and I were raised in households where rice was served two or three times a day. Although he has lived outside Nepal longer than in the country itself, he takes rice seriously. If he does not eat rice with dinner, it is as if no meal was eaten at all. Growing up in Kathmandu, breakfast often started with creamy rice porridge (*jaulo*) early in the morning, which was considered very soothing and nutritious. Lunch eaten before heading to school or work consisted of rice, lentils, and vegetables. Snacks eaten throughout the day contained pressed rice flakes or rice flour. Supper was freshly cooked rice accompanied by lentils, gravy-based or fried vegetables, and perhaps a small quantity of meat or fish with pickle and chutney.

In addition to its many culinary uses, rice is also integral to Nepali traditions, ceremonies, rituals, and religious observances. Morning is considered the holiest time of the day, and some devotees start the day with a visit to neighborhood temples and shrines at dawn. A small copper or silver tray is filled with uncooked rice, vermilion powder, flowers, and incense known as *pooja ko saamaan* and taken to temples as offerings to the gods.

Many Nepalese consider rice grains to be sacred. Annapurna, the goddess of prosperity and abundance, whose name literally translates as grain (*anna*) and prosperity (*purna*), is worshiped during and after harvest time to bring a bountiful harvest. Throwing away or wasting food is considered disrespectful to the goddess of grain. As children, we were often reminded of the common Nepali saying that if you waste food in your present life, the goddess will curse you and in your next life you will suffer from starvation: "*anna le saraap-chha.*"

On religious occasions, raw rice, vermilion powder, and yogurt are mixed into a paste (*achheta ko tika*). This paste is applied to the forehead for family blessings and given to travelers for good luck. On the tenth day of *Vijaya Dashami*, an important religious festival, also called *Tika* day, Nepalese receive *tika* from elders as a blessing of good health, happiness, and prosperity. Rice also plays an important part in Nepali Hindu marriage ceremonies. During the wedding ritual, the groom's party is welcomed with a sprinkling of unhusked puffed rice (*lava*). A sacred flame is lit to start the wedding and an offering of puffed rice, raw rice, and rice mixed with butter is added to the fire. In the bride's welcoming ceremony, rice grains are placed across the doorway of her husband's home, symbolizing that she brings prosperity and happiness to her new family. Following the bride welcoming ceremony, the bride and her mother-in-law play a ceremonial game with rice grains called *pathi bharne*. In some families, the bride is given the job of serving rice when she moves into the groom's house.

Rice flour is also used on religious occasions. It is mixed with water to form a thin paste that is used to draw intricate religious symbols called *aipan* on the ground. During the *Laxmi Pooja* festival, small footprints are drawn with rice paste at the entrance of many households, on the stairs, and all over the house to welcome the goddess of wealth and prosperity and ask her to bless the family with good luck.

Rice and rice flour are also used to prepare sacred offerings (*naivedya*) for deities and consumed as blessed food (*prashaad*). Under Nepali Hindu traditions, a religious ceremony known as the rice-feeding ceremony (*anna-prasana*) is performed when a child reaches six months of age. It is observed by feeding the infant rice grains, which represent knowledge, wisdom, and purity as his or her first solid food along with Vedic rites. Rice continues to be a part of daily religious activity throughout adulthood and in death. During the mourning period, only certain foods are considered pure. Plain boiled rice is one of the few foods that can be consumed by the next of kin as a mourning food for the first thirteen days.

Finally, even some customary Nepali greetings have to do with rice. For instance, a common greeting spoken when relatives, friends, or family members meet each other is, *"bhanchha garnu bhayo?"* (in Nepali) or *"jane dhuna la?"* (in Newari), "have you had your rice?" or "have you finished your meal?" This is the first question asked regardless of the time of the day and establishes care and concern for the other's well being. An invitation to dinner would be, *"aaja bhaat khaana aunus,"* which means, "come over for a rice dinner."

Bhaat-Bhuja
PLAIN STEAMED RICE

This is my basic everyday recipe for cooking rice using the absorption method. It works for any variety of long- or medium-grain white rice. I prefer to make moist and tender rice with each grain separated, so that it is not sticky or dry. Plain rice is a versatile dish that can be served with mild or highly seasoned curries, vegetables, or lentils.

2 cups long-grain white rice

Clean the rice according to the instructions on page 46. Put the rice in a medium-size bowl, pour 3¾ cups water over it and soak for 20 minutes.

Transfer the soaked rice and water to a heavy saucepan over medium-high heat. Bring to a rapid boil, uncovered, stirring gently from time to time. Once it comes to a full boil, reduce the heat as much as possible, cover, and simmer until the liquid has been absorbed by the rice and each grain is separate and tender, 15 to 20 minutes. Do not stir or uncover while the rice is simmering. Remove the pot from the heat and let the rice rest, undisturbed, for 5 to 10 minutes before serving. Uncover, fluff the rice gently, and serve. If you are not planning to serve it immediately, leave the rice covered in the pan to prevent it from drying out.

Makes 4 to 6 servings.

Umaaleko Bhaat-Bhuja
PLAIN BOILED RICE

This is another basic method of cooking rice, using a larger quantity of water than the absorption method (see page 47). When the rice is almost cooked, the starchy water is drained off, and the rice is cooked until it is fluffy. Although with this method much of the nutrients are drained away from the rice, the milky water (bhaat ko maad) is always reserved and used as a thickening agent for soups and curries or as animal feed.

2 cups long-grain white rice

Prepare the rice according to the instructions on page 46. Put the rice in a large heavy saucepan with 8 cups of cold water and bring it to a boil over medium-high heat, uncovered. Cook for 8 to 10 minutes. Pinch a grain of rice between your thumb and finger. If it is cooked but still a little hard in the center, the rice is three-quarters cooked, indicating that it is ready to be drained. Drain the milky water through a fine-mesh strainer or sieve. Adjust the heat to the lowest possible setting and cook, covered, until the rice is tender, with each grain separated, 10 to 15 minutes more. Remove from the heat and let the rice rest undisturbed for 5 to 10 minutes before serving. Uncover, fluff the rice gently, and serve.

Makes 4 to 6 servings.

Gheu Haaleko Bhuja
BASMATI RICE WITH BUTTER

Basmati rice is a high-status grain cultivated in the foothills of the Himalayas. When cooked with clarified butter, it increases to twice its length and has a distinct delicate flavor and fluffy texture. This variety of rice is expensive and is reserved for special occasions. Basmati rice can be found in large supermarkets or Indian markets, where it is less expensive. Imported basmati rice needs to be picked over, rinsed in several changes of water, and soaked before cooking. Each type of basmati rice absorbs water differently, so you may need to adjust the water depending on the dryness and age of the grain.

2 cups basmati rice	½ teaspoon salt
2 tablespoons clarified butter	2 bay leaves
(*gheu*) or regular butter,	4 whole cloves
at room temperature	

Prepare the rice according to the instructions on page 46. Drain and place in a heavy saucepan with the butter, salt, bay leaves, cloves, and 3¾ cups of cold water over medium-high heat. Bring it to a rapid boil, uncovered, stirring gently from time to time. Once it comes to a full boil, adjust the heat to the lowest possible setting, cover, and simmer until the liquid has been absorbed and the rice is tender with each grain separated, 15 to 20 minutes. Do not stir or lift the lid during simmering. Remove the pan from the heat and let the rice rest, covered and undisturbed, for 5 to 10 minutes before serving. Uncover, fluff the rice gently, and serve. If you are not planning to serve it immediately, leave the rice covered in the pan to prevent it from drying out.

Makes 4 to 6 servings.

Note: This recipe can be prepared with any variety of good-quality long-grain white rice and can also be cooked in an electric rice cooker.

Jhanne ko Saada Bhaat
TEMPERED STEAMED RICE

This is a family recipe, our favorite way of adding flavor to cooked rice by pouring spice-infused butter (jhanne) over the rice just before serving it. Traditionally, homemade butter (nauni) is melted and added to the rice directly on the individual plates before serving. The spices listed below are the most commonly used. However, each family has their own spice blend. Sometimes a fried egg is served on top of the rice.

2 cups long-grain white rice	2 dried red chilies, halved and
3 tablespoons clarified butter	seeded
(*gheu*)	2 cloves garlic, thinly sliced
½ teaspoon ajowan seeds	¼ teaspoon salt

Prepare the rice according to the instructions on p. 51. In a small skillet, heat the clarified butter over medium heat. Add the ajowan seeds and chilies and sauté until lightly browned and fragrant, 5 to 7 seconds. Immediately add the garlic and salt and sauté until the garlic is crisp. Pour the entire contents directly over the prepared rice. Cover and let the rice rest for 5 minutes so the flavor develops. When you are ready to serve, uncover and fluff the rice.

Makes 4 to 6 servings.

Kesari Bhuja
SAFFRON RICE

In Nepal, serving dishes with saffron is regarded as a mark of honor to the guests, as saffron is the world's most expensive spice. This delicious, festive rice dish is cooked for special occasions. Saffron gives the rice an intense yellow color, exquisite flavor, and delicate aroma. Because saffron is a costly spice, some people substitute ground turmeric. However, while turmeric may give a similar yellow color to the rice, it cannot replace saffron's distinctive flavor.

2 cups long-grain white or basmati rice
¼ teaspoon saffron threads
2 tablespoons clarified butter (*gheu*)
3 bay leaves
4 green cardamom pods, crushed
2 black cardamom pods, crushed
4 whole cloves
1 (1-inch) stick cinnamon, halved
½ teaspoon salt

Prepare the rice according to the instructions on page 46. Drain.

Rub the saffron threads between your fingers to crush them and place them in a mortar and pestle or small bowl with 2 tablespoons of warm water. Mix with a pestle or spoon until the saffron is thoroughly dissolved and set aside.

Heat the clarified butter in a heavy saucepan over medium-high heat. Add the bay leaves, green and black cardamom pods, cloves, and cinnamon stick and sauté until fragrant, slightly puffed, and beginning to brown. Be careful not to let the spices burn. Add the rice and continue sautéing, stirring constantly until it is slightly translucent, about 2 minutes. Add 3¾ cups of cold water and the salt and bring it to a rapid boil, uncovered, stirring gently from time to time. Once it comes to a full boil, reduce the heat to the lowest possible setting, cover, and simmer until the liquid has been absorbed and the rice is tender, with each grain separated, 15 to 20 minutes. Uncover, pour the saffron-infused water over the rice, and replace the lid. There is no need to stir the rice. Remove it from the heat and let the rice rest, covered, for 5 to 10 minutes. The rice will be partly white and partly bright yellow. Uncover, fluff gently, and serve. If you are not serving the rice immediately, leave it covered in the pan to prevent it from drying out.

Makes 4 to 6 servings.

Jeera Bhaat
CUMIN-FLAVORED RICE

This is an easy to prepare rice dish with black cumin seeds, also called king of cumin (shahi jeera or kaalo jeera). This variety of cumin is darker than regular cumin, resembles caraway seeds, and when heated in oil, imparts a special nutty and warm flavor.

2 cups long-grain white rice
(any variety)
3 tablespoons clarified butter
(*gheu*)
2 teaspoons black cumin seeds
2 small bay leaves
½ teaspoon salt or to taste

¼ cup vegetable oil
2 tablespoons raw cashew halves
¼ cup blanched sliced or
slivered raw almonds
¼ cup golden raisins
I medium onion, halved
lengthwise and thinly sliced

Prepare the rice according to the instructions on page 46. Drain.

Heat the clarified butter in a heavy saucepan over medium-high heat. When hot, add the cumin seeds and bay leaves and sauté until they release a pleasant aroma, 5 to 7 seconds. Add the rice and continue sautéing, stirring constantly until slightly translucent, about 2 minutes. Add 3¾ cups of cold water and the salt and bring to a rapid boil, uncovered, stirring gently from time to time. Once it comes to a full boil, adjust the heat to the lowest setting, cover, and simmer until the liquid has been absorbed, and the rice is tender, with each grain separated, 15 to 20 minutes.

Meanwhile, heat the oil in a small skillet over medium heat. When the oil is hot, but not smoking, add the cashews and almonds and sauté until golden brown and crisp. Remove with a slotted spoon and drain on a paper towel. Add the raisins to the same oil and fry until they puff up. Remove them from the pan and drain on paper towels. Raise the heat to medium-high, add the onion and sauté until light brown and slightly crisp. Remove from the heat and set aside.

Remove the rice from the heat and let it rest covered, undisturbed, for 5 to 10 minutes. Uncover, fluff the rice gently, and transfer it to a platter. Garnish with the nuts, raisins, and onion and serve.

Makes 4 to 6 servings.

Jwaano Bhuteko Bhaat
AJOWAN RICE

This recipe is one of the quickest and most flavorful ways of using leftover rice (baasi bhaat) to create a delicious dish. In addition, ajowan seeds are known to aid and stimulate digestion. Rice usually hardens as it cools, so add a little water while cooking. This dish can be served as a light lunch with vegetables, pickles, and yogurt.

¼ cup clarified butter (*gheu*)
1 teaspoon ajowan seeds
2 dried red chilies, halved and seeded
1 medium onion, halved lengthwise and thinly sliced

3 medium cloves garlic, finely chopped
4 to 6 cups cold cooked rice
½ teaspoon salt
4 to 5 green onions (white and green parts), thinly sliced

Heat the clarified butter in a heavy skillet over medium-high heat. When hot, add the ajowan seeds and chilies and fry until lightly browned and aromatic, 5 to 7 seconds. Add the onion and garlic and cook, stirring until soft. Adjust the heat to medium-low and mix in the rice, a little at a time, separating any clumps. Add the salt and continue stirring until the rice is heated through and begins to brown slightly. If the rice becomes dry and sticks to the skillet, add 1 to 2 tablespoons of water at a time and keep stirring. Let the rice absorb the water before adding more. The finished rice should be soft. Mix in the green onions, transfer to a serving dish, and serve hot.

Makes 4 to 6 servings.

Kerau ko Pulau
RICE WITH GREEN PEAS

This is an easy recipe and makes a perfect light lunch with any gravy-based meat dish or with plain yogurt. To make it more festive, use basmati rice, which will give it a special touch. If fresh peas are not available, frozen peas are a good substitute.

2 cups long-grain white rice (any variety)
2 tablespoons clarified butter (*gheu*)
1 teaspoon cumin seeds
3 small bay leaves
4 green cardamom pods, crushed
2 black cardamom pods, crushed
4 whole cloves
1 (1-inch) stick cinnamon, halved

1 medium onion, finely chopped (about 1 cup)
1 teaspoon minced fresh ginger
2 small cloves garlic, finely chopped
2 cups shelled fresh or frozen peas, thawed and drained
1 teaspoon Nepali Garam Masala (page 398)
½ teaspoon salt
½ teaspoon ground turmeric

Prepare the rice according to the instructions on page 46. Drain.

Heat the clarified butter in a heavy saucepan over medium-high heat. When hot, add the cumin seeds, bay leaves, green and black cardamom pods, cloves, and cinnamon and fry until they begin to puff up, darken, and give off a pleasant aroma, 5 to 7 seconds. Add the onion, ginger, and garlic and cook until they are soft, about 5 minutes. Add the rice and continue frying, stirring constantly, until the onion is translucent, about 2 minutes.

If fresh peas are used, add them with 3¾ cups of cold water, the garam masala, salt, and turmeric and bring the mixture to a rapid boil, uncovered, stirring gently occasionally. Once it comes to a full boil, adjust the heat to the lowest setting, cover it with a tight-fitting lid, and simmer until the liquid has been absorbed and the rice is tender, with each grain separated, 15 to 20 minutes. If frozen peas are used, add them now, and cover. There is no need to stir. Remove the pan from the heat and let the rice rest covered, undisturbed, for 5 to 10 minutes so that the trapped steam cooks the peas. Uncover, fluff the rice, gently mix in the peas, and transfer the rice to a platter. If you are not planning to serve it immediately, leave the rice covered in the pan to prevent it from drying out.

Makes 4 to 6 servings.

Masala Bhaat
FRAGRANT RICE WITH RAISINS AND NUTS

In this recipe, rice is cooked with whole spices that provide a subtle flavor. Fried nuts give a crunchy texture and a pleasant toasty flavor. Any combination of dried fruits and nuts can be used. This dish may be served with almost any meat curry, gravy-based vegetable dish, plain yogurt, lentils, or chutney.

2 cups long-grain white rice (any variety)
3 tablespoons clarified butter (*gheu*)
½ cup raw cashew halves
¼ cup blanched slivered raw almonds
¼ cup dried coconut chips
¼ cup dark or golden raisins
2 small bay leaves

6 green cardamom pods, crushed
3 black cardamom pods, crushed
6 whole cloves
1 (1-inch) stick cinnamon, halved
1 small onion, finely chopped (about ½ cup)
½ teaspoon salt
3 hard-boiled eggs, quartered lengthwise (for garnish)

Clean, wash, and soak the rice according to the instructions on page 46. Drain.

Heat the clarified butter in a heavy saucepan over medium-low heat. When hot, add the cashews, almonds, and coconut chips and lightly toast, stirring constantly, until golden. Remove with a slotted spoon and drain on paper towels. In the same pan, sauté the raisins until they puff up. Remove them to drain on paper towels and set aside.

Raise the heat to medium-high and add the bay leaves, green and black cardamom pods, cloves, and cinnamon. Fry the spices until they begin to puff up, darken, and give off a pleasant aroma, 5 to 7 seconds. Add the onion and cook, stirring constantly until it softens. Add the rice and stir constantly, until it is slightly translucent, about 2 minutes. Add 3¾ cups of cold water and the salt and bring it to a rapid boil, uncovered, stirring gently from time to time. Once it comes to a full boil, adjust the heat to the lowest setting, cover and simmer until the liquid has been absorbed and the rice is tender, with each grain separated, 15 to 20 minutes. Add the reserved nuts, coconut, and raisins and cover. Remove the pan from the heat and let the rice rest covered, for 5 to 10 minutes before serving. Uncover, fluff the rice gently, and transfer it to a platter. Garnish with the hard-boiled eggs and serve.

Makes 4 to 6 servings.

Baasi-Bhaat Bhutuwa
FRIED RICE

This recipe is so versatile that any combination of vegetables, meats, eggs, nuts, and spices can be used. If you do not have leftover rice, you can cook fresh rice, but make sure to cool it completely before frying, or else it will be mushy. Rice usually hardens when cooled, but cooking over low heat and occasionally sprinkling in a little water will soften it. Fried rice is considered a complete one-dish meal and can be served by itself or with salad, yogurt, and pickles.

1 tablespoon vegetable oil	2 medium carrots, peeled and
2 eggs, lightly beaten	cut into ½-inch slices
¼ cup clarified butter (*gheu*)	(about 1 cup)
½ teaspoon cumin seeds	1 cup frozen peas, thawed and
1 medium onion, halved length-	drained
wise and thinly sliced	1 cup finely diced cooked meat
3 to 4 cloves garlic, finely	(chicken, turkey, pork, or lamb)
chopped	4 to 6 cups cold cooked rice
8 ounces fresh mushrooms,	1 teaspoon salt
sliced (about 2 cups)	½ teaspoon freshly ground black
1 small red or green bell pepper,	pepper
cored and chopped	4 to 5 green onions (white and pale
(about 1 cup)	green parts), finely chopped

Heat the oil in a small skillet over medium-high heat. Add the eggs and cook, without stirring, until set. Transfer the eggs to a platter. When cool enough to handle, julienne and set aside.

Heat the butter in a heavy skillet over medium-high heat. When hot, add the cumin seeds and fry until lightly browned and aromatic, 5 to 7 seconds. Add the onion and garlic and cook until they are soft. Stir in the mushrooms, bell pepper, carrots, peas, and meat and sauté until the vegetables are half cooked, 5 to 7 minutes. Stir in the rice, salt, and pepper, breaking up any clumps of rice and stirring until the rice is heated through and lightly browned. If the rice becomes dry and starts to stick to the skillet, add 1 to 2 tablespoons of water at a time, keep stirring and let the rice absorb the water before adding more. Stir in the green onions and julienned egg. Transfer the rice to a serving dish and serve hot.

Makes 4 to 6 servings.

Maas ko Khichari
RICE WITH DRIED BEANS

Khichari *is a delicious and nutritious Nepali comfort food of rice and daal cooked into a creamy porridge. Warm spiced gheu is added just before serving for extra flavor. It is accompanied by vegetables, pickles, or yogurt. The rice and daal are usually soaked to shorten the cooking time, but you can omit this step if you wish.* Khichari *made with split black urad beans is traditionally served during the celebration of Maghe Sankranti. During this festive occasion, people take holy baths in the rivers and visit temples. Other sacred foods, such as lentil balls* (maas ko phulaura), *sweet potato* (sakhar khanda), *yam* (tarul), *spinach* (paalungo), *and sesame seed candy* (til ko laddu) *are also prepared. Family members visit each other and share these foods, which is believed to ensure health.*

1½ cups long- or short-grain white rice	½ teaspoon ground turmeric
	A small pinch ground asafetida
1½ cups split black urad beans, with skin *(kaalo maas ko daal)*	3 tablespoons clarified butter *(gheu)*
1 tablespoon minced fresh ginger	1 teaspoon cumin seeds
1 teaspoon salt	

Prepare the rice and urad beans according to the instructions on pages 46 and 69-70.

Combine the rice, urad beans, ginger, salt, turmeric, asafetida, 1 tablespoon of the clarified butter, and 7 to 8 cups of cold water in a heavy saucepan and bring to a boil over medium-high heat. Reduce the heat to low, cover, and simmer, stirring frequently, until the rice and daal disintegrate, 25 to 30 minutes. If the *khichari* is too thick, add a few tablespoons of boiling water a little at a time. Remove from the heat and keep it covered until ready to serve.

Before serving, heat the remaining 2 tablespoons clarified butter in a small skillet over medium-high heat. When hot, add the cumin and fry until lightly browned and aromatic, 5 to 7 seconds. Pour the entire contents over the *khichari*, mix well, transfer to a serving dish, and serve hot.

Makes 4 to 6 servings.

Tarkaari ko Jaulo
SPICY VEGETABLE JAULO

Jaulo is a one-dish meal of rice and daal, considered a soothing comfort food in Nepal. This version is spicier than most and is enhanced with herbs and a variety of vegetables to round out the flavor. A mild version, given to infants and people suffering from stomach pain or other digestive disorders and served for breakfast in my home growing up, is also listed.

I cup long- or short-grain white rice
½ cup split yellow mung beans, without skins (*pahelo moong ko daal*)
¼ cup clarified butter (*gheu*)
¼ teaspoon fenugreek seeds
2 small bay leaves
½ teaspoon ground turmeric
A generous pinch ground asafetida
I medium onion, finely chopped (about I cup)
I tablespoon minced fresh ginger

4 small cloves garlic, finely chopped
2 medium potatoes, peeled and cubed (about 2 cups)
¼ head cauliflower, separated into 1-inch florets (about 2 cups)
I teaspoon ground cumin
I teaspoon ground coriander
I teaspoon salt
I cup frozen peas, thawed and drained

Prepare the rice and mung beans according to the directions on pages 46 and 69-70.

Heat the clarified butter in a heavy pot over medium-high heat. When hot, add the fenugreek seeds and fry until they darken and become fragrant, 5 to 7 seconds. Add the bay leaves, turmeric, and asafetida, then immediately add the onion, ginger, and garlic. Fry, stirring constantly until they are lightly browned, 5 to 7 minutes. Stir in the potatoes, cauliflower, rice, mung beans, cumin, and coriander. Add 7 cups cold water and the salt and bring the mixture to a boil, then reduce the heat to low and simmer, partially covered, until the beans are soft, stirring frequently, 25 to 30 minutes. The mixture should disintegrate into a creamy porridge. Stir in the peas and cook for 5 minutes more. If the porridge seems too thick, add a few tablespoons of boiling water. Transfer to a serving dish and serve.

Mild Jaulo: Replace the chopped ginger and garlic with 2 (¼-inch) pieces ginger and 6 peeled cloves garlic, and reduce the butter to 3 tablespoons. Combine the rice, mung beans, garlic, ginger, 1 tablespoon of the clarified butter, salt, turmeric, bay leaves, and 7 cups water and bring to a boil. Reduce the heat and simmer, stirring frequently, until the mixture forms a porridge, 25 to 30 minutes. Heat 2 tablespoons clarified butter over medium-high heat and fry the fenugreek seeds, 5 to 7 seconds. Remove from the heat and add the asafetida. Pour the mixture over the rice and cover for 5 minutes. Uncover, mix well, and remove the bay leaves and ginger.

Makes 4 to 6 servings.

Tarkaari ko Pulau
MIXED VEGETABLE PULAU

Pulau is a rice dish made with chicken, meat, lentils, nuts, dried fruits, or vegetables. A typical festive Nepali meal always includes pulau, *most commonly this vegetarian version of the popular dish.*

2 cups long-grain white or
 basmati rice
¼ cup clarified butter (*gheu*)
4 green cardamom pods, crushed
2 black cardamom pods, crushed
1 teaspoon cumin seeds
2 small bay leaves
4 whole cloves
1 (1-inch) stick cinnamon, halved
1 medium onion, finely chopped
 (about 1 cup)
3 medium cloves garlic, finely
 chopped
1 tablespoon minced fresh ginger
¼ head cauliflower, cut into
 1-inch florets (1 cup)
1 cup shelled fresh or frozen
 peas, thawed and drained

1 small carrot, peeled and
 cut into ½-inch slices
1 cup green beans, cut into
 ½-inch pieces
1½ teaspoons Nepali Garam
 Masala (page 398)
½ teaspoon ground turmeric
½ teaspoon salt

GARNISH
¼ cup vegetable oil
¼ cup raw cashew halves
¼ cup blanched slivered raw
 almonds
¼ cup dark or golden raisins
1 large onion, halved lengthwise
 and thinly sliced

Prepare the rice according to the instructions on page 46. Drain.

Heat the clarified butter in a heavy saucepan over medium-high heat. Add the green and black cardamom pods, cumin, bay leaves, cloves, and cinnamon, and fry until they begin to puff up, darken, and give off a pleasant aroma, about 5 seconds. Add the onion, garlic, and ginger and cook, stirring until lightly browned. Add the cauliflower, fresh peas, carrots, green beans, garam masala, and turmeric and sauté for 1 minute. Add the rice and cook, stirring, about 3 minutes. Add the salt and 3¾ cups of cold water, and bring the mixture to a boil, uncovered, stirring gently from time to time. Once it comes to a full boil, adjust the heat to low, cover it with a tight-fitting lid, and simmer until the liquid is absorbed and the rice is tender, with each grain separated, 15 to 20 minutes.

For the garnish, heat the oil in a small skillet over medium heat until hot, but not smoking. Add the cashews and almonds, and sauté until golden brown and crisp. Remove them with a slotted spoon to drain on paper towels. Sauté the raisins in the same oil until they puff up, remove them and drain on paper towels. Raise the heat to medium-high and sauté the onion until light brown and slightly crisp. Remove from the heat and set aside.

If using frozen peas, add them on top of the rice, and cover with the lid. There is no need to stir. Cover and let the rice rest, undisturbed, for 5 to 10 minutes. Uncover, fluff the rice, transfer it to a platter, and garnish with the nuts, raisins, and onion.

Makes 4 to 6 servings.

Kukhura ko Pulau
CHICKEN PULAU

I make this family recipe for special occasions or dinner parties. It may seem time-consuming, but the savory reward will truly be appreciated. Serve hot with gravy-based vegetables, poori, lentils, yogurt, pickles, and any variety of chutney.

CHICKEN
1 (2½- to 3-pound) chicken
3 medium onions, 2 quartered
   and 1 halved lengthwise
   and thinly sliced
9 cloves garlic, 6 peeled and
   3 minced
1 (½-inch) piece fresh ginger,
   peeled and halved, and 1
   tablespoon, peeled and minced
1 (2-inch) stick cinnamon
2 green cardamom pods, crushed
1 black cardamom pod, crushed
1 teaspoon cumin seeds
10 whole black peppercorns
½ teaspoon fennel seeds
½ teaspoon salt
3 small bay leaves
2 tablespoons vegetable oil
½ teaspoon ground turmeric
½ teaspoon ground cumin
½ teaspoon ground coriander

RICE
2 cups basmati rice
¼ teaspoon saffron threads
2 tablespoons clarified butter
   (*gheu*)
2 green cardamom pods, crushed
6 whole cloves
2 small bay leaves
1 (1-inch) stick cinnamon
¼ teaspoon salt

GARNISH
¼ cup vegetable oil
2 tablespoons halved raw
   cashews
3 tablespoons blanched, slivered,
   raw almonds
2 tablespoons shelled raw
   pistachios
¼ cup dark or golden raisins
1 medium onion, halved lengthwise and sliced paper-thin

For the chicken: Combine the chicken, onion quarters, 6 whole garlic cloves, piece of ginger, cinnamon, green and black cardamom, cumin seeds, peppercorns, fennel seeds, ¼ teaspoon of the salt, bay leaves, and 8 cups of water in a deep saucepot. Bring it to a boil over high heat, reduce the heat to medium-low, cover tightly, and simmer until the chicken is very tender, 35 to 40 minutes. Remove from the heat and cool. Remove the chicken from the stock, separate the meat from the bones, shred, and set it aside. Strain the stock and discard the spices and bones. There should be about 4 cups of stock. Add milk, if necessary, to make a total of 4 cups.

Heat the oil in a heavy skillet over medium-high heat until hot, but not smoking. Add the sliced onion, minced ginger, and minced garlic and fry until golden. Add the chicken, turmeric, cumin, coriander, and remaining ¼ teaspoon of salt and fry until lightly browned. Remove from the heat and set aside.

For the rice: Prepare the rice according to the instructions on page 46. Drain and set aside. Rub the saffron threads between your fingers to crush them and place them in a mortar and pestle or small bowl with 2 tablespoons of warm water. Mix until the saffron is thoroughly dissolved and set aside.

Heat the butter in a heavy saucepan over medium-high heat. Add the cardamom pods, cloves, bay leaves, and cinnamon and fry, stirring, until they puff up, darken, and give off a pleasant aroma, about 5 seconds. Add the rice and salt and stir until the rice becomes transparent, 2 to 3 minutes. Pour in the reserved stock and bring it to boil, then reduce the heat to low and simmer, covered. When the rice is almost cooked, or most of the liquid has been absorbed and steam holes appear in the rice, remove the lid and gently stir in the chicken and saffron-infused water. Cover and cook for 5 to 7 minutes, until the rice is tender, with each grain separated.

For the garnish: Heat the oil in a small skillet over medium-low heat. Add the cashews, almonds, and pistachios and sauté, stirring, until they are golden brown and crisp. With a slotted spoon remove them to drain on paper towels. Sauté the raisins in the same oil, until they puff up, then drain on paper towels. Raise the heat to medium-high and fry the onion, until it is light brown and slightly crisp. Remove it with a slotted spoon, drain on paper towels, and set aside.

Remove the rice from the heat and leave it to rest for 5 to 10 minutes, undisturbed. Uncover and fluff the rice. Transfer it to a platter, sprinkle it with the garnish, and serve hot.

Makes 4 to 6 servings.

Lamb Pulau: Heat 2 tablespoons of oil until hot, but not smoking. Add 1½ cups chopped onion, 4 minced cloves of garlic, and 1 tablespoon peeled and minced ginger and fry until soft, 5 minutes. Add 2 to 2½ pounds cubed boneless lamb, 1½ teaspoons Nepali garam masala, 1 teaspoon turmeric, 1 teaspoon cayenne pepper, and ½ teaspoon salt and stir frequently, until the meat is lightly browned, about 5 minutes. Add 1 cup plain yogurt, 1 tablespoon at a time, stirring constantly. Lower the heat and simmer, stirring from time to time, until the lamb is tender, 20 to 25 minutes. If the meat has not cooked through in that time, add ¼ to ½ cup of water and cook until tender. Remove from the heat and set aside. Continue as directed above, adding the lamb in place of the chicken.

Daal

DRIED BEANS, LENTILS, AND PEAS

No Nepali meal is complete without daal—made from any dried legume, such as lentils, beans, and peas. Most varieties of daal are available in Indian grocery stores and some larger supermarkets. Daal is either cooked by itself, with vegetables, and/or rice. When cooked daal is paired with rice, the meal is called *daal-bhaat*. It is eaten throughout Nepal. Daal is prized for its high protein content and is perhaps the primary protein source in Nepal. Nepalese generally prefer soupy daal rather than thicker porridge-like forms of it, making it suitable to eat over boiled rice.

Daal is very easy to cook and does not require any special skills. There are just two simple steps: First, the legumes are simmered with spices until they disintegrate into a puree. Then, spices are tempered or fried in oil, and added for extra flavor. The main spices used are asafetida, cumin, Himalayan herb *(jimbu)*, mustard seeds, cloves, cinnamon, bay leaves, and dried red chilies. In some recipes, onions, garlic, ginger, and tomatoes are also added toward the end of the cooking process. Daal can be prepared one or two days in advance and stored covered in the refrigerator. It can be reheated by simmering gently with additional water. It is a versatile food; you can make it highly spicy or mild according to your taste. Daal doubles in volume after cooking, and when cooled it thickens, but you can add water to make it thinner. These days, many Nepalese cook daal in a pressure cooker to speed up the cooking process. Dried legumes are also made into fried snacks and breads, sprouted, mixed with vegetables, and used in sweet dishes.

There are a few basic things to be aware of before cooking daal. All imported daals must be picked over for tiny stones, dirt, or any foreign matter.

To clean the daal, spread it on a large platter, pick through it carefully, and discard any foreign matter. Wash the daal, by placing it in a large bowl and cover it with cold water. Remove anything that floats. Gently rub it between your hands, and slowly pour off the water, holding the daal back with one hand. Rinse and drain the cloudy water several times until the water runs clear. I, personally, discard the soaking water and rinse the daal with fresh cold water before using it in a recipe. Some kinds of daal may need to be soaked before cooking to soften them.

Pahelo Moong ko Daal
YELLOW MUNG BEANS

This is a delicious daal made from skinless split yellow mung beans, which cook quickly without soaking. Be careful not to overcook the beans or they will become pasty and gooey. This dish is considered a comfort food in Nepal and soothes an ailing stomach when served with plain boiled rice.

I cup split yellow mung beans, without skins (*pahelo moong ko daal*)
1½ teaspoons minced fresh ginger plus I tablespoon finely julienned
I bay leaf
½ teaspoon salt
½ teaspoon ground turmeric
3 tablespoons clarified butter (*gheu*)
I teaspoon cumin seeds
A small pinch ground asafetida
2 large cloves garlic, thinly sliced
I tablespoon fresh lemon or lime juice
¼ cup finely chopped cilantro
I small tomato, chopped (about ½ cup)

Sort and wash the mung beans as described on pages 69-70. Combine the mung beans, minced ginger, bay leaf, salt, turmeric, I tablespoon of the clarified butter, and 3½ cups of water in a large, heavy saucepan. Bring the mixture to a quick boil over medium-high heat, uncovered, stirring occasionally to make sure the beans do not boil over or stick together. There is no need to skim off the foam that rises to the surface, as it contains flavor. When it comes to a full boil, reduce the heat to low, cover, and simmer gently until the beans are tender and have doubled in volume, 20 to 25 minutes. Add more water if necessary, to attain a soupy consistency. Simmer for 5 minutes. Remove from the heat and set aside, covered.

In a separate small skillet, heat the remaining 2 tablespoons of clarified butter over medium-high heat. Add the cumin and fry until lightly browned and fragrant, about 5 seconds. Add the asafetida and then immediately add the julienned ginger and garlic and fry until crisp. Remove the skillet from the heat, immediately pour the entire mixture into the daal, and stir well. Cover and allow the seasonings to develop for 5 minutes. Mix in the lemon juice. Transfer to a serving dish, sprinkle the cilantro and tomato on top, and serve.

Makes 4 to 6 servings.

Musuro ko Daal
PINK LENTIL DAAL

Brightly colored split lentils are known as musuro ko daal *in Nepal and are nutritious, quick to cook, light, and easily digestible. These shiny round lentils are coral colored, but turn golden yellow after cooking.*

I cup *masoor daal* (split pink or red lentils), without skins (*musuro ko daal*)
2 large cloves garlic, finely chopped
1½ teaspoons minced fresh ginger
½ teaspoon salt
½ teaspoon ground turmeric
¼ teaspoon ground cumin
¼ teaspoon ground coriander
3 tablespoons clarified butter (*gheu*)

I to 2 dried red chilies, stemmed
½ teaspoon cumin seeds
⅛ teaspoon Himalayan herb (*jimbu*)
A small pinch ground asafetida
I tablespoon fresh lemon or lime juice
¼ cup finely chopped cilantro
2 to 3 green onions (white and pale green parts), finely chopped
I small tomato, chopped (about ½ cup)

Sort and wash the lentils as described on pages 69-70. Combine the lentils, garlic, ginger, salt, turmeric, ground cumin, coriander, I tablespoon of the clarified butter, and 3½ cups of water in a large, deep, heavy pot. Bring the mixture to a quick boil over medium-high heat, uncovered, stirring occasionally to make sure the lentils do not boil over or stick together. Do not skim away the foam that rises to the surface, as it contains flavor. Reduce the heat to low, cover, and simmer gently until the lentils are tender and fully cooked, 20 to 25 minutes. If necessary, add more water to attain a soupy consistency. Simmer for 5 more minutes. Remove the pot from the heat and set aside.

In a separate small skillet, heat the remaining 2 tablespoons of clarified butter over medium-high heat. Add the chilies, cumin seeds, and *jimbu* and fry until they darken and become fragrant, about 5 seconds. Sprinkle in the asafetida and immediately pour the entire mixture into the cooked daal, stir well. Cover and allow the seasonings to develop for 5 minutes. Mix in the lemon juice, transfer the daal to a serving dish, sprinkle with the cilantro, green onions, and tomato, and serve.

Makes 4 to 6 servings.

Chhata ko Daal
SPLIT WHITE URAD BEANS

The pale ivory-colored split urad beans are called chhata ko daal *in Nepalese. These beans do not require soaking and can be cooked in a pressure cooker to speed up the cooking process. As the beans swell and thicken, they become slippery and are called slippery daal (*chiplo daal*).*

I cup split white urad beans, without skins (*maas ko chhata ko daal*)
¼ cup clarified butter (*gheu*)
2 dried red chilies, stemmed
I teaspoon cumin seeds
½ teaspoon Himalayan herb (*jimbu*)
I teaspoon ground turmeric
2 small bay leaves

A generous pinch ground asafetida
I medium onion, halved and thinly sliced
4 to 5 medium cloves garlic, finely chopped
I½ tablespoons minced fresh ginger
I medium tomato, chopped (about I cup)
½ teaspoon salt

Sort and wash the daal as described on pages 69-70.

Heat the clarified butter in a large, heavy pot over medium-high heat. When hot, add the chilies, cumin, and *jimbu* and fry until fragrant and dark, about 5 seconds. Add the turmeric, bay leaves, and asafetida, then immediately add the onion, garlic, and ginger. Cook until the onion is soft, about 5 minutes, stirring frequently, then add the tomato and cook until slightly soft. Add the daal, salt, and 4 cups of water and bring the mixture to a boil, stirring occasionally to make sure it does not boil over or stick together. After it comes to a full boil, reduce the heat to low, cover, and simmer gently, stirring from time to time, until the daal are tender and fully cooked, 30 to 40 minutes. If needed, add ¼ cup water or more to attain a soupy consistency and simmer an additional 5 minutes. Transfer the daal to a serving dish and serve hot.

Makes 4 to 6 servings.

Jhaaneko Kaalo Maas ko Daal
BLACK URAD DAAL

Maas ko daal *or black gram beans are among the most popular daals in Nepal. They are flavorful, satisfying, and extremely nutritious.* Maas ko daal *differ from other daals in that they are traditionally cooked in an iron pot* (falaam ko tapke), *which imparts a deep black color and rich flavor. The cooked daal is tempered with Himalayan herb* (jimbu) *for an authentic Nepali taste.*

I cup split black urad beans, with skins (*kaalo maas ko daal*)
I tablespoon finely julienned fresh ginger plus 1½ teaspoons minced
½ teaspoon salt
½ teaspoon ground turmeric
⅛ teaspoon Szechwan pepper (*timmur*)

3 tablespoons clarified butter (*gheu*)
2 to 3 dried red chilies, halved and seeded
½ teaspoon Himalayan herb (*jimbu*)
A generous pinch ground asafetida
2 large cloves garlic, thinly sliced

Sort and wash the beans as described on pages 69-70. Combine the beans, minced ginger, salt, turmeric, Szechwan pepper, I tablespoon of the clarified butter, and 3½ cups of water in a deep, heavy pot (or *falaam ko taapke*). Bring the mixture to a quick boil over medium-high heat, uncovered, stirring occasionally to make sure the beans do not boil over or stick together. Cook for about 20 minutes. Reduce the heat to low, cover, and simmer gently until the beans are tender and have doubled in volume, about 55 minutes. If necessary, add more water to attain a soupy consistency, and simmer 5 more minutes. Remove the pot from the heat and set aside.

In a small skillet, heat the remaining 2 tablespoons of clarified butter over medium-high heat. Add the chilies and *jimbu*, and fry until light brown and fragrant, about 5 seconds. Add the asafetida, then immediately add the julienned ginger and garlic and fry until crisp, about 10 seconds. Immediately pour the entire mixture into the daal and stir well. Cover and allow the seasoning to develop for 5 minutes. Transfer the daal to a serving dish and serve hot. The daal will thicken if not served at once, so reheat it with 3 to 4 tablespoons of water if it needs to be warmed again.

Makes 4 to 6 servings.

Rahar ko Daal
SPLIT PIGEON PEA DAAL

Here is a mild daal made with yellow split pigeon peas, which are available dry or lightly coated with oil. The oil preserves freshness and protects the daal from insects. If you are using this type, make sure to wash them several times in hot running water to remove the oil completely.

1 cup split yellow pigeon peas, without skins (*rahar ko daal*)	½ teaspoon ground turmeric
	2 small bay leaves
	1 teaspoon cumin seeds
2 tablespoons clarified butter (*gheu*)	2 whole cloves
	A small pinch ground asafetida
1 (1-inch) stick cinnamon	1 tablespoon fresh lemon or lime juice
1½ teaspoons minced fresh ginger	
½ teaspoon salt	¼ cup finely chopped cilantro

Sort and wash the split peas as described on pages 69-70. Combine the daal, 1 tablespoon of the clarified butter, cinnamon, ginger, salt, turmeric, bay leaves, and 3½ cups of water in a deep, heavy pot. Bring the mixture to a boil over medium-high heat, uncovered, stirring occasionally to make sure the mixture does not boil over or stick together. When it comes to a full boil, reduce the heat to low, cover, and simmer, stirring from time to time, until the daal is tender and has doubled in volume, 25 to 30 minutes. If necessary, add more water to attain a soupy consistency. Simmer for 5 minutes. Remove the pot from the heat and set aside.

In a separate small skillet, heat the remaining 2 tablespoons of clarified butter over medium-high heat. When hot, add the cumin and fry until lightly browned and fragrant, about 5 seconds. Add the cloves and asafetida, remove the skillet from the heat, immediately pour the entire mixture into the daal, and stir well. Cover, and allow the seasoning to develop for 5 minutes. Mix in the lemon juice. Transfer the daal to a serving dish, sprinkle the cilantro on top, and serve.

Makes 4 to 6 servings.

Daal Makhani
BUTTERED DAAL

Here is a delicious, rich, and filling daal prepared from whole urad and mung beans. This dish tastes even better the next day, as the aromatic spices gently infuse the daal, adding more flavor.

1½ cups whole black urad beans (*singo maas ko daal*)
½ cup whole green mung beans (*singo moong ko daal*)
4 small cloves garlic, minced
1½ teaspoons minced fresh ginger
1 teaspoon ground coriander
½ teaspoon salt
½ teaspoon ground turmeric
½ teaspoon ground cumin
½ teaspoon cayenne pepper
2 bay leaves

¼ cup clarified butter (*gheu*)
2 dried red chilies, stemmed
A small pinch ground asafetida
1 medium onion, halved lengthwise and thinly sliced
1 medium tomato, chopped (about 1 cup)
1 tablespoon fresh lemon or lime juice
¼ cup finely chopped cilantro
2 to 3 green onions (white and pale green parts), thinly sliced

Sort and wash the mung beans as described on pages 69-70. Combine the beans, garlic, ginger, coriander, salt, turmeric, cumin, cayenne pepper, bay leaves, and 6 cups of water in a deep, heavy pot. Bring the mixture to a boil over medium-high heat, uncovered, stirring occasionally to make sure the beans do not boil over. When they come to a full boil, lower the heat, cover, and simmer gently until the mixture is soft and the beans are tender, about 1 hour. Add more water if the liquid evaporates. The beans are cooked when they break easily and flatten when pressed between your fingers. Remove the pot from the heat and set aside, covered.

In a separate small skillet, heat the clarified butter over medium-high heat. When hot, add the chilies and fry until lightly browned and fragrant, about 5 seconds. Add the asafetida, then immediately add the onion and cook until light brown, about 7 minutes. Add the tomato and stir until soft, about 2 minutes. Remove the skillet from the heat, immediately pour the entire mixture into the cooked beans, and stir well. Bring the pot back to a simmer, covered, for 10 minutes to bring out the flavors. Add more water if the mixture has thickened, to attain a moderately thick consistency. Mix in the lemon juice. Transfer the daal to a serving dish, sprinkle the cilantro and green onions on top, and serve.

Makes 4 to 6 servings.

Maharani Daal

MAHARANI DAAL

Maharani *means "fit to serve a queen" and indeed this dish is. This is my family's favorite daal. A succulent and delicious slow-cooked dish, it is easy to prepare and extremely nutritious. This recipe combines three varieties of lentils, each with a distinct flavor and texture. This is the traditional combination of daals, but any varieties can be used.*

½ cup split yellow mung beans, without skins (*pahelo moong ko daal*)
½ cup masoor daal, (split pink or red lentils), without skins (*musuro ko daal*)
½ cup split yellow pigeon peas, without skins (*rahar ko daal*)
1 tablespoon minced fresh ginger plus 1 tablespoon finely julienned
4 medium cloves garlic, 2 finely chopped and 2 thinly sliced
½ teaspoon salt
½ teaspoon ground turmeric
2 bay leaves

5 tablespoons clarified butter (*gheu*)
2 dried red chilies, halved and seeded
1 teaspoon cumin seeds
⅛ teaspoon Himalayan herb (*jimbu*)
A small pinch ground asafetida
1 medium onion, finely chopped (about 1 cup)
2 medium tomatoes, finely chopped (about 2 cups)
½ cup finely chopped cilantro
3 to 4 green onions (white and green parts), finely chopped

Sort and wash the daal as described on pages 69-70. Combine all 3 daal with the minced ginger, chopped garlic, salt, turmeric, bay leaves, 1 tablespoon of the clarified butter, and 4 cups of water in a large, deep, heavy pot. Bring the mixture to a boil over medium-high heat, uncovered, stirring occasionally to make sure the beans do not boil over. When it comes to a full boil, reduce the heat to low, cover, and simmer gently until the mixture is soft and fully cooked, 20 to 25 minutes. If needed, add more water to attain a soupy consistency. Simmer for 5 minutes. Remove the pot from the heat and set aside, covered.

In a separate small skillet, heat the remaining 4 tablespoons of clarified butter over medium-high heat. When hot, add the chilies, cumin, and *jimbu*, and fry until lightly browned and fragrant, about 5 seconds. Add the asafetida first, then immediately add the onion, julienned ginger, and sliced garlic and cook until soft. Add the tomatoes, cilantro, and green onions and cook, stirring constantly, about 2 minutes. Remove from the heat, immediately pour the entire mixture into the cooked daal, and stir well. Lower the heat to medium-low, bring the pot back to a simmer, and cook for 10 minutes to develop the flavors. Transfer the daal to a serving dish and serve hot.

Makes 4 to 6 servings.

Mismaas Daal
MIXED DAAL

This recipe combines five different varieties of daal in equal amounts. Each has a distinct taste and texture, giving this dish a lot of flavor and making it a delicious accompaniment to any rice dish, roti bread, stir-fried vegetables, and pickles.

¼ cup split yellow mung beans, without skins (*pahelo moong ko daal*)

¼ cup masoor daal (split pink or red lentils), without skins (*musuro ko daal*)

¼ cup split white urad beans, without skins (*maas ko chhata ko daal*)

¼ cup split yellow pigeon peas, without skins (*rahar ko daal*)

¼ cup split yellow chickpeas, without skins (*chana ko daal*)

3 tablespoons clarified butter (*gheu*)

1 teaspoon cumin seeds

1 (1-inch) stick cinnamon

2 small bay leaves

½ teaspoon ground turmeric

A large pinch ground asafetida

1 large onion, finely chopped (about 1½ cups)

3 to 4 medium cloves garlic, chopped

1 tablespoon minced fresh ginger

2 medium tomatoes, chopped (about 2 cups)

1 teaspoon salt

½ cup finely chopped cilantro

Sort and wash the daal as described on pages 69-70.

Heat the clarified butter in a large heavy-bottomed pot over medium-high heat. Add the cumin seeds and fry until lightly browned and fragrant, about 5 seconds. Add the cinnamon, bay leaves, turmeric, and asafetida, then immediately add the onion, garlic, and ginger. Cook until the onion is soft, about 5 minutes, stirring frequently, then add the tomatoes and cook until slightly soft. Add the daal, salt, and 4½ cups of water and bring the mixture to a quick boil, stirring from time to time to make sure it does not boil over. Reduce the heat to medium-low, cover, and cook until the daal are tender, 40 to 45 minutes. If necessary, add ½ cup of water or more, to maintain a moderately thick consistency. Transfer the daal to a serving dish, sprinkle the cilantro on top, and serve hot.

Makes 4 to 6 servings.

Daal ra Paalungo ko Saag
SPINACH DAAL

In this dish, mung beans are cooked with spinach, making a delicious and healthy meal. You may substitute any variety of daal for this recipe, but I prefer mung or masoor daal *(split pink or red lentils) because they cook the fastest. Serve over freshly steamed rice or flat breads, any meat curry, and a fiery chutney.*

I cup split yellow mung beans, without skins (*pahelo moong ko daal*)
3 tablespoons clarified butter (*gheu*)
½ teaspoon cumin seeds
A small pinch ground asafetida
I small onion, finely chopped (about ½ cup)

3 to 4 small cloves garlic, chopped
1½ teaspoons minced fresh ginger
½ teaspoon ground turmeric
I medium tomato, chopped (about I cup)
I teaspoon salt
I large bunch spinach, stemmed and finely chopped (about 3 cups)

Sort and wash the mung beans as described on pages 69-70.

Heat the clarified butter in a large heavy-bottomed pan over medium-high heat. Add the cumin seeds and fry until lightly browned and fragrant, about 5 seconds. Add the asafetida, then immediately add the onion, garlic, ginger, and turmeric. Cook until the onions are soft, then add the tomatoes and cook until the liquid evaporates, about 5 minutes. Add the mung beans, salt, and 3½ cups of water and stir well. Bring the mixture to a quick boil, stirring occasionally to make sure the beans do not boil over or stick together. Reduce the heat to medium-low, cover, and simmer until almost cooked, about 20 minutes. Add the spinach, and continue to simmer, stirring from time to time, until the mixture softens into a thick puree, about 10 minutes. If needed, add ½ cup water or more, to maintain the consistency. Transfer the daal to a bowl and serve hot.

Makes 4 to 6 servings.

Chana ko Daal ra Lauka
YELLOW SPLIT CHICKPEAS WITH SQUASH

Yellow split chickpeas have a sweet nutty flavor and hold their shape well. Mild bottle gourds enhance the flavor and texture of the daal. To reduce the cooking time, soak the daal for at least five hours in cold water before cooking. Bottle gourds are available at Indian food stores, where they are called lauki or ghiya. They may also be found in the specialty produce sections of some larger supermarkets. Substitute any summer squash of your choice if fresh bottle gourds are not available.

1½ cups split yellow chickpeas, without skins (*chana ko daal*)
2 tablespoons vegetable oil
1 teaspoon brown mustard seeds
½ teaspoon ground turmeric
A large pinch ground asafetida
2 cups peeled and cubed bottle gourd
4 small cloves garlic, finely chopped
1 tablespoon minced fresh ginger
1 teaspoon salt
½ teaspoon ground cumin
½ teaspoon ground coriander
½ teaspoon cayenne pepper
¼ teaspoon Nepali Garam Masala (page 398)

Sort and wash the chickpeas as described on pages 69-70.

Heat the oil in a large heavy saucepan over medium-high heat. When it is hot, but not smoking, add the mustard seeds and fry until they pop and become fragrant, about 5 seconds. Add the turmeric and asafetida, then immediately add the daal and fry for 2 minutes, stirring frequently. Add the squash, garlic, ginger, salt, cumin, coriander, cayenne pepper, and garam masala and cook, stirring, for about 5 minutes. Add 4 cups of water and bring the mixture to a boil, stirring occasionally. Reduce the heat to medium-low, cover, and cook until the daal is tender and the squash has become soft, 30 to 40 minutes. If necessary, add ½ cup of water or more, to maintain a moderately thick consistency. Transfer the daal to a serving dish and serve hot.

Makes 4 to 6 servings.

Chana ko Tarkaari
EASY CHICKPEA CURRY

This quick and easy curry comes from my daughter, Rachana, who uses canned chickpeas for convenience. Rinse the chickpeas well before cooking. Serve with warm poori bread (page 110).

2 tablespoons plus
  1½ teaspoons vegetable oil
2 large onions, finely chopped
  (about 2½ cups)
4 to 6 small cloves garlic, finely
  chopped
1 tablespoon minced fresh ginger
2 large tomatoes, chopped
  (about 3 cups)
3 (15½-ounce) cans chickpeas,
  drained and rinsed
1½ teaspoons Nepali Garam
  Masala (page 398)

½ teaspoon ground cumin
½ teaspoon ground coriander
½ teaspoon cayenne pepper
½ teaspoon salt
1 tablespoon plus
  1½ teaspoons fresh lemon
  or lime juice
1 medium red onion, cut into
  ¼-inch slices and separated
  into rings
½ cup finely chopped cilantro

Heat the oil in a heavy saucepan over medium-high heat. When the oil is hot, but not smoking, add the onion, garlic, and ginger and cook, stirring occasionally, until light brown, about 7 minutes. Stir in the tomatoes and cook until soft and the juices evaporate, about 5 minutes. Add the chickpeas, garam masala, cumin, coriander, cayenne pepper, and salt and cook, stirring constantly for about 2 minutes. Add 1½ cups of water and bring the mixture to a boil. Reduce the heat to medium-low and cover the pot. Cook, stirring from time to time, until the mixture thickens, about 20 minutes. Add the lemon juice and mix well. Transfer the curry to a serving dish, place the red onion and cilantro on top, and serve.

Makes 4 to 6 servings.

Kaalo Chana ko Tarkaari
BROWN CHICKPEAS WITH ONIONS

Dry-cooked chickpeas have a delicious, nutty flavor and will not become musby after cooking like some other beans. I usually serve this as a snack with pressed rice flakes (cheura). Make sure to soak the chickpeas before cooking them; this gives them a better texture and reduces the cooking time.

2 cups dried whole brown chickpeas (*kaalo chana*)
4 medium cloves garlic, peeled
1 (1-inch) stick cinnamon
½-inch piece fresh ginger, peeled quartered and 1 tablespoon peeled and minced
2 tablespoons plus 1 teaspoon vegetable oil
1 teaspoon salt
1 small bay leaf
A large pinch ground asafetida

1 teaspoon ajowan seeds
1 dried red chili, halved and seeded
1 large onion, finely chopped (about 1½ cups)
1 teaspoon ground cumin
1 small red onion, finely chopped (about ½ cup)
½ cup finely chopped cilantro
2 to 3 fresh mild green chilies, split lengthwise
1 tablespoon fresh lemon or lime juice

Sort and wash the chickpeas as described on pages 69-70. Place them in a large bowl, cover with cold water, and soak for at least 8 hours.

Drain the chickpeas and place them in a large, heavy pot with the garlic, cinnamon stick, sliced ginger, 1 teaspoon of the oil, ½ teaspoon of the salt, bay leaf, asafetida, and 7 cups of water. Bring the mixture to a full boil over medium-high heat. Reduce the heat to medium-low, cover, and simmer gently, stirring occasionally, until the chickpeas are tender, about 1 hour. If there is any liquid left, adjust the heat to medium-high and cook until it evaporates. Remove the pot from the heat and discard the bay leaf, cinnamon, and ginger slices.

Heat the remaining 2 tablespoons of oil in a deep skillet over medium-high heat. When hot, but not smoking, add the ajowan and red chili and fry until lightly browned and fragrant, about 5 seconds. Add the onion and minced ginger and cook until soft, about 5 minutes. Stir in the chickpeas, cumin, and remaining ½ teaspoon salt and cook, stirring as needed, until the liquid evaporates, about 10 minutes. Mix in the red onion, cilantro, green chilies, and lemon juice, transfer to a serving dish, and serve.

Makes 4 to 6 servings.

Raajma ko Tarkaari
KIDNEY BEAN CURRY

Traditionally, this dish is made from dried kidney beans, but I use the canned variety, which is less authentic, but still delicious. If you prefer to cook with the dried variety, soak the beans in water for at least eight hours, boil or pressure-cook them until very soft, and follow the recipe below.

2 tablespoons vegetable oil
½ teaspoon cumin seeds
1 medium onion, finely chopped
    (about 1 cup)
2 medium cloves garlic, minced
1½ teaspoons minced fresh ginger
½ teaspoon ground turmeric
2 medium tomatoes, chopped
    (about 2 cups)

1 small red or green bell pepper,
    cored and cut into 1-inch
    cubes
1 teaspoon Nepali Garam Masala
    (page 398)
½ teaspoon cayenne pepper
½ teaspoon salt
3 (15½-ounce) cans red kidney
    beans, rinsed and drained
½ cup finely chopped cilantro

Heat the oil in a large skillet or a heavy saucepan over medium-high heat. When the oil is hot, but not smoking, add the cumin seeds and fry until lightly browned and fragrant, about 5 seconds. Stir in the onion, garlic, ginger, and turmeric and cook, stirring occasionally, until the onion is soft, about 5 minutes. Add the tomatoes, bell pepper, garam masala, cayenne pepper, and salt and cook until the tomatoes and peppers are soft, about 5 minutes. Add the kidney beans and 1 cup of water and bring the mixture to a boil. Reduce the heat to medium-low, cover the pot, and cook, stirring from time to time, until the mixture thickens and a sauce forms, about 10 minutes. Add more water if you prefer a thinner sauce. Transfer the beans to a serving dish, sprinkle with the cilantro, and serve hot.

Makes 4 to 6 servings.

Bodi ko Tarkaari
BLACK-EYED PEA CURRY

Nepalese use dried black-eyed peas in various ways: cooked with bamboo shoots to make a curry, mixed with other dried legumes to make sprouted beans (page 97), or mixed with vegetables in a stew-like dish. Soak the dried black-eyed peas for at least six hours for a better texture and so that it cooks faster. The outer coverings of the soaked beans are somewhat thick and tough, so the beans should be boiled or pressure-cooked until soft.

1½ cups dried black-eyed peas (*bodi*)	1 teaspoon freshly ground cumin
2 tablespoons vegetable oil	1 teaspoon freshly ground coriander
1 teaspoon fenugreek seeds	1 teaspoon salt
1 large onion, finely chopped (about 1½ cups)	½ teaspoon cayenne pepper
1½ tablespoons minced fresh ginger	2 large tomatoes, chopped (about 3 cups)
2 to 3 medium cloves garlic, minced	3 to 4 green onions (white and pale green parts), finely chopped
½ teaspoon ground turmeric	2 to 3 fresh mild green chilies, halved lengthwise
A large pinch ground asafetida	½ cup finely chopped cilantro
2 medium potatoes, peeled and cut into 1-inch cubes (about 2 cups)	

Sort and wash the black-eyed peas as described on pages 69-70. Place the peas in a large bowl, cover with cold water, and soak for 6 hours or more at room temperature.

Drain the peas and place them in a large saucepan with 5½ cups of water. Bring to a boil over medium-high heat. Reduce the heat to medium-low, cover, and simmer gently, stirring occasionally, until the peas are tender, 45 minutes to 1 hour. If there is any liquid left, adjust the heat to medium-high and continue to cook until it evaporates. Remove from heat.

Heat the oil in a heavy saucepan over medium-high heat. When the oil is hot, but not smoking, add the fenugreek seeds and fry until browned and fragrant, about 5 seconds. Add the onion, ginger, garlic, turmeric, and asafetida and cook, stirring until the onion softens, about 5 minutes. Mix in the peas, pota-toes, cumin, coriander, salt, and cayenne pepper and continue cooking, stirring as needed, for 5 minutes. Stir in 1½ cups of water and bring the mixture to a boil. Cook uncovered for 5 minutes, then reduce the heat to medium-low, cover, and cook until the potatoes are tender, about 10 minutes. Add the toma-toes, green onions, and chilies, and cook, stirring for 5 minutes. Transfer to a serving dish, top with the cilantro, and serve.

Makes 4 to 6 servings.

Thulo Kerau ko Tarkaari
CURRIED DRIED PEAS

Thulo kerau is the Nepali name for whole dried peas. This recipe calls for whole green peas, but feel free to substitute yellow peas, as both varieties have a wonderful earthy flavor. Like with any daal, slowly simmer the mixture to let the peas absorb the flavors of the herbs and spices.

1½ cups dried whole green peas (*sukeko hariyo thulo kerau*)
1 bay leaf
½ teaspoon salt
A small pinch baking soda
3 to 4 medium cloves garlic, chopped
1 tablespoon minced fresh ginger
½ teaspoon ground turmeric
½ teaspoon ground cumin
½ teaspoon ground coriander

2 tablespoons vegetable oil
1 teaspoon fenugreek seeds
1 dried red chili, halved and seeded
1 medium onion, finely chopped (about 1 cup)
A large pinch ground asafetida
1 tablespoon fresh lemon or lime juice
1 teaspoon Nepali Garam Masala (page 398)

Sort and wash the peas as described on pages 69-70. Put them in a large bowl, cover with cold water, soak for at least 8 hours, and drain.

Bring 6 cups of water to a boil in a heavy saucepan over high heat. Add the peas, bay leaf, salt, and baking soda. Boil uncovered for 10 minutes and then reduce the heat to medium-low. Cover and simmer gently, stirring occasionally, until the peas are tender, about 25 minutes. Stir in the garlic, ginger, turmeric, cumin, and coriander and continue cooking, covered, until the peas are tender, about 15 minutes. Remove the pan from the heat and keep covered.

In a medium skillet, heat the oil over medium-high heat. When the oil is hot, but not smoking, add the fenugreek seeds and chili and fry until dark brown and fragrant, about 5 seconds. Add the onion and asafetida and cook, stirring frequently, until the onion is soft, about 5 minutes. Remove the skillet from the heat, immediately pour the entire mixture into the cooked peas, and stir well. Adjust the heat to medium-low, return the pot to the heat, cover, and simmer until the peas have softened, about 5 minutes. Mix in the lemon juice and garam masala, transfer to a serving dish, and serve.

Makes 4 to 6 servings.

Maseura ko Ras
URAD BEAN NUGGET SOUP

In this recipe, maseura nuggets are sautéed and then simmered in a delicious sauce. The nuggets may become soft, but will maintain their shape and texture. I usually serve this dish with plain boiled rice, fried vegetables, and any meat dish.

3 tablespoons vegetable oil
8 to 10 homemade Maseura
   Nuggets (page 91)
1 small onion, finely chopped
   (about ½ cup)
1 tablespoon minced fresh ginger
2 large cloves garlic, minced
1 teaspoon ground cumin
1 teaspoon ground coriander
½ teaspoon ground turmeric
½ teaspoon cayenne pepper
⅛ teaspoon freshly ground
   black pepper

2 medium potatoes, peeled and
   cut into 1-inch cubes
   (about 2½ cups)
1 teaspoon salt
2 medium tomatoes, finely
   chopped (about 2 cups)
3 to 4 green onions (white and
   green parts), cut into
   ½-inch pieces
2 fresh mild green chilies,
   halved lengthwise
½ cup finely chopped cilantro

Heat the oil in a heavy saucepan over medium-low heat. Add the nuggets and fry until brown on all sides, stirring constantly, about 2 minutes. Watch carefully and do not let them burn. With a slotted spoon remove the nuggets to drain on paper towels, and set aside. In the oil remaining in the pan, sauté the onion, ginger, garlic, cumin, coriander, turmeric, cayenne pepper, and black pepper, stirring constantly, until the onion is soft, about 5 minutes. Increase the heat to medium, add the potatoes, and continue cooking until lightly browned, about 3 minutes. Mix in 3 cups of water and the salt and bring to a boil. Add the browned nuggets, reduce the heat to medium-low, cover, and simmer gently, stirring from time to time, about 20 minutes. Add the tomatoes, green onions, green chilies, and half the cilantro and continue cooking until the potatoes and nuggets are tender and the sauce has slightly thickened, about 5 minutes. Transfer the soup to a serving dish, garnish with the remaining cilantro, and serve hot.

Note: If you use the store-bought Indian variety of lentil nuggets known as *dal badi* or *badian*, break them into small pieces before browning. The Nepali home-made variety are usually smaller and do not require breaking.

Makes 4 to 6 servings.

Dahi Kadi
YOGURT KADI

Yogurt kadi *is a smooth and creamy dish of spiced yogurt and chickpea flour.* Kadi *is typically served with plain boiled rice. This dish is light, soothing, easily digested, and prescribed to those suffering from a delicate stomach. I prefer to make* kadi *with homemade yogurt, which usually becomes tart after a few days. If you like a smooth and mellow kadi, use freshly made yogurt.*

¼ cup chickpea flour (*besan*)
2½ cups plain yogurt, stirred
1 tablespoon minced fresh ginger
1 teaspoon salt
½ teaspoon ground turmeric
2 tablespoons clarified butter (*gheu*)
½ teaspoon brown mustard seeds

½ teaspoon fenugreek seeds
1 dried red chili, halved and seeded
A large pinch ground asafetida
½ cup finely chopped cilantro
1 to 2 fresh mild green chilies, chopped

In a large, heavy saucepan, whisk the chickpea flour and yogurt together to make a smooth batter. Add the ginger, salt, turmeric, and 4 cups of water and mix thoroughly. Bring the mixture to a boil over medium-high heat, stirring constantly. Reduce the heat to medium-low and continue cooking, uncovered, stirring from time to time, until the mixture thickens to the consistency of heavy cream, 10 to 12 minutes. If you prefer a thinner sauce, add ½ cup water and simmer for 3 to 5 minutes more. Remove the pan from the heat, cover, and keep warm.

In a separate small skillet, heat the clarified butter over medium-high heat. When hot, add the mustard, fenugreek, and chili and fry until the mustard seeds pop, the fenugreek seeds darken, and the chili becomes reddish-brown and fragrant, about 5 seconds. Remove the skillet from the heat, sprinkle in the asafetida, immediately pour the entire mixture into the *kadi*, and mix well. Return the saucepan to medium-low heat, cover, and simmer for 5 minutes to develop flavor. Transfer the *kadi* to a serving dish and stir in the cilantro and green chilies. Serve piping hot. The sauce will thicken once cooled, so add 2 to 3 tablespoons of water and reheat it before serving.

Yogurt Kadi with Dumplings: Prepare the kadi as directed on page 89. Combine 1 cup chickpea flour, ¼ teaspoon turmeric, ¼ teaspoon salt, ⅛ teaspoon cayenne pepper, ⅛ teaspoon baking soda, and a small pinch asafetida. Gradually beat in ½ cup cold water to make a smooth batter, the consistency of heavy cream. Cover and set aside at room temperature for 10 to 15 minutes, until thickened slightly. Heat 1½ to 2 cups vegetable oil in a deep skillet over medium-high heat to 350° to 375°F. Drop tablespoons of the batter into the oil, frying a few at a time. The dumplings will sink, but will swell and slowly rise to the surface. Fry, stirring constantly, until crisp and golden on all sides. Remove the dumplings with a slotted spoon and transfer to paper towels to drain. Repeat the process with the remaining batter, frying a few at a time without overcrowding. Gently add the dumplings to the *kadi* and simmer, covered, for about 5 minutes. Transfer to a bowl and serve hot.

Makes 4 to 6 servings.

Maseura
URAD BEAN NUGGETS

Maseura *are common throughout Nepal and usually made at home. Traditionally, these nuggets are prepared from split black urad beans and taro leaves and stalks, but any finely chopped vegetable, such as radishes, cauliflower, green cabbage, spinach, or mustard leaves can be combined with lentils to prepare the maseura. The nuggets have a light and spongy texture when dried.*

The following recipe comes from my mother-in-law, Aama Hazoor, who prepared maseura each summer. She preferred sun drying which takes five to six days in the direct hot sun. To speed up the drying process, use a food dehydrator, which is faster and more convenient.

3 cups split black urad beans, with skins (*kaalo maas ko daal*)
I large bunch (6 to 8) fresh taro leaves, stalks, and young shoots, finely chopped (about 2½ cups)

2 tablespoons minced fresh ginger
I teaspoon salt
A generous pinch ground asafetida
I to 2 tablespoons chickpea flour (*besan*)
Vegetable oil, as needed

Sort and wash the beans as described on pages 69-70. In a large bowl, soak the beans in water to cover for at least 8 hours, until doubled in size. Rub the beans vigorously between your hands to loosen their outer black coverings. They should come off easily and float in the water. Discard the coverings, drain the beans, add fresh water, and repeat the process until the coverings are all completely removed. Drain the beans in a colander and set aside.

Separate the taro leaves from the stalks with a knife. Place the leaves on a work surface, tightly roll up, and thinly slice. Peel off the outer covering of each stalk by pulling off the fiber to get smooth and silky stems. Discard the covering and chop the stems into ⅛-inch pieces. Wash the taro thoroughly and spread it on a large tray lined with a cloth or paper towel. Dry the taro in the sun for 2 to 3 hours or in a food dehydrator until the moisture is completely removed and slightly wilted.

Place the beans in a food processor or blender and process, adding 1 to 2 tablespoons of water at a time as needed, to make a thick smooth batter that can be shaped. You may have to do this in two batches. Use just enough water to facilitate blending. Transfer the batter to a bowl and mix with your fingers or a fork until it is light and spongy, about 2 minutes. Add the chopped taro, ginger, salt, and asafetida and mix well. If the batter is too thin, add a small amount of chickpea flour to thicken it.

Grease a baking sheet with oil. With your fingers or a spoon, form ½-inch nuggets and drop them onto the baking sheet. Cover the nuggets with cheesecloth, place the baking sheet in the sun, and let the nuggets dry slowly. Always bring them indoors after the sun has set. Once they are slightly firm on top, gently turn them over to expose the bottom sides to dry evenly. The *maseura* should be completely dry before storing or using, which may take 3 to 4 days, depending upon the amount of sunlight. Make sure there is no moisture in the nuggets or they will spoil. You can also use a food dehydrator to dry the nuggets. Follow the manufacturer's instructions and make sure that they are not over-dried. You may store them in an airtight container for up to 6 months at room temperature.

Note: An Indian version of lentil nuggets is available in Indian food stores by the name *dal-badi* or *badian*. You may substitute them in the recipes calling for *maseura* but the store-bought commercial *badi* are much spicier, and may not include vegetables.

Makes 40 to 45 (½-inch) nuggets.

Gundruk ra Maseura ko Ras
GUNDRUK AND URAD BEAN NUGGET SOUP

This spicy soup contains two sun-dried ingredients: lentil nuggets (maseura) and fermented and dried greens (gundruk). The nuggets are first browned, and then added to a spicy broth made from gundruk, with fresh herbs and spices. It is served hot as a side dish with freshly boiled rice.

3 tablespoons vegetable oil
8 to 10 homemade Maseura Nuggets (page 91)
2 dried red chilies, halved and seeded
2 medium tomatoes, finely chopped (about 2 cups)
4 cloves garlic, finely chopped
1½ teaspoons minced fresh ginger
1 teaspoon salt
½ teaspoon ground turmeric
½ teaspoon ground cumin
¾ cup Gundruk (see pages 310-311), soaked in water for 10 minutes, drained, and chopped

Heat the oil in a medium-size saucepan over medium-low heat. Add the nuggets and sauté until brown on all sides, stirring constantly, about 2 minutes. With a slotted spoon, transfer the nuggets to paper towels to drain and set aside.

Add the dried chilies to the same pan and fry, stirring constantly, until they darken and become fragrant, about 5 seconds. Add the tomatoes, garlic, ginger, salt, turmeric, and cumin and continue to cook until the tomatoes are soft and the liquid has evaporated, about 5 minutes. Stir in the *gundruk* and continue sautéing, about 1 minute. Adjust the heat to medium-high, add 3½ cups of water, and bring the mixture to a boil. Add the browned *maseura*, reduce the heat to medium-low, cover, and continue cooking, stirring from time to time, until the *gundruk* swells and the *maseura* soften, about 12 minutes. Transfer the soup to a serving dish and serve hot.

Makes 4 to 6 servings.

Moong ko Titaura
MUNG BEAN NUGGETS

This is another variation of sun-dried nuggets, made from split yellow mung beans. They are easy to prepare, and dry quickly because they are small in size. The nuggets can be stored in an airtight container for up to six months.

4 cups split yellow mung beans, without skins (*pahelo moong ko daal*)
A generous pinch ground asafetida
½ teaspoon salt
I to 2 tablespoons chickpea flour, or as needed (*besan*)
Vegetable oil, as needed

Sort and wash the mung beans as described on pages 69-70. In a large bowl, soak the beans with enough water to cover for at least 6 hours, then drain.

Place the drained beans in a food processor or blender and process, adding a little water at a time as needed, to make a thick, smooth batter that can be shaped. You may have to do this in two batches. Use just enough water to facilitate blending. Transfer the batter to a bowl and mix with your fingers or a fork until the batter is light and spongy, about 2 minutes. If the batter is too watery, add a small amount of chickpea flour to thicken it.

Before shaping the nuggets, oil I or 2 trays or baking sheets. With a lightly oiled hand, form grape-size nuggets, and drop them on the tray. Place the nuggets close together, but not so they are touching. Cover the tray with cheesecloth and place in the full sun. Always bring the tray indoors after the sun has set. Once they are set and slightly firm on top, gently turn them over to expose the bottom sides. The *titaura* should be completely dried in I to 2 days, depending on the amount of sun. You may also use a food dehydrator to dry the nuggets, which should not take more than a couple of hours. Make sure there is no moisture present before storing them. Store them in an airtight container at room temperature for up to 6 months.

Note: Commercially prepared ready-made mung bean nuggets are available at Indian grocery stores by the name *mung dal badi* or *badian*. These nuggets may be substituted, but homemade *titaura* are more flavorful and fresher, and have an authentic Nepali taste.

Makes 75 to 80 nuggets.

Moong Titaura ko Ras
MUNG BEAN NUGGET STEW

This delicately flavored dish is a traditional favorite of many Nepalese and is cooked regularly in my home. This delicious soup, actually a cross between soup and stew, is prepared with mung bean nuggets. It is served with plain boiled rice and considered a soothing dish.

3½ tablespoons clarified butter (*gheu*) or unsalted butter, melted
1½ cups Mung Bean Nuggets (page 94)
2 medium potatoes, peeled and cubed the same size as the nuggets (about 2 cups)
1 tablespoon minced fresh ginger
2 small cloves garlic, chopped

1 teaspoon ground cumin
1 teaspoon ground coriander
½ teaspoon ground turmeric
1 medium tomato, chopped (about 1 cup)
2 fresh mild green chilies, split lengthwise
½ cup finely chopped cilantro
½ teaspoon salt

Heat 2 tablespoons of the butter in a heavy saucepan over medium-low heat. When hot, add the nuggets and fry them until golden brown on all sides, stirring constantly. Watch carefully and do not burn them, as this process only takes a few minutes. With a slotted spoon, remove the nuggets, drain them on paper towels, and set aside.

Increase the heat to medium, and add the remaining 1½ tablespoons butter and the potatoes to the same pan. Fry until the potatoes are lightly browned, about 5 minutes. Add the ginger, garlic, cumin, coriander, and turmeric and mix well. Stir in the tomato, green chilies, and half of the cilantro and continue cooking until the tomato is soft and all the juices have evaporated, about 5 minutes. Add 3 cups of cold water and the salt and bring to a boil. Add the browned nuggets, lower the heat to medium-low, and cook, covered, stirring from time to time, until the potatoes are tender, the nuggets soften, and the sauce thickens, about 15 minutes. Transfer the stew to a serving dish, garnish it with the remaining cilantro, and serve.

Makes 4 to 6 servings.

Taareko Kwanti
STIR-FRIED MIXED SPROUTED BEANS

This is a simple dry-cooked bean dish, served as a side with rice or a mid-afternoon snack. Typically, it is prepared from the leftover Kwanti Soup (page 99). After the broth is eaten, the remaining cooked beans are separated and stir-fried with spices.

2 cups mixed Sprouted Beans (page 97)
2 tablespoons minced fresh ginger
1 teaspoon salt
½ teaspoon ground turmeric
2 medium bay leaves
A generous pinch ground asafetida
3 tablespoons vegetable oil
¼ teaspoon cumin seeds
¼ teaspoon ajowan seeds
1 medium onion, chopped (about 1 cup)
4 to 6 large cloves garlic, finely chopped

4 fresh mild green chilies, 2 split lengthwise and 2 diced
1 teaspoon ground cumin
1 teaspoon ground coriander
1 teaspoon Nepali Garam Masala (page 398)
½ teaspoon cayenne pepper
⅛ teaspoon freshly ground black pepper
¼ cup finely chopped cilantro
3 green onions (white and pale green parts), finely chopped

Rinse the sprouts under running water. Drain and place in a large, heavy saucepan. Add 4 cups of water, 1½ tablespoons of the ginger, the salt, turmeric, bay leaves, and asafetida. Bring the mixture to a boil over high heat. Reduce the heat to medium-low, cover, and simmer until the beans become soft, and most of the water has evaporated, about 1 hour. Uncover, increase the heat, and cook until all the liquid has evaporated. Remove the pan from the heat and set aside.

In a separate large skillet, heat the oil over medium-high heat until it is hot, but not smoking. Add the cumin and ajowan seeds, and fry until lightly browned and fragrant, about 5 seconds. Add the onion and cook, stirring constantly, until lightly browned, about 7 minutes. Add garlic, chilies, and remaining ½ tablespoon ginger and cook about 1 minute more. Mix in the boiled beans, cumin, coriander, garam masala, cayenne pepper, and black pepper and cook, stirring constantly, until the moisture has evaporated, 7 to 8 minutes. Mix in the cilantro, green onions, and diced chilies, transfer to a dish, and serve.

Makes 4 to 6 servings.

Kwanti or Biraula
SPROUTED BEANS

Mixed sprouted beans are known as kwanti, quaanti, *or* biraula *in Nepal and are cooked a number of ways: in soups, vegetable stir-fries, salads, or with meats. Sprouted beans have been used since ancient times and are an excellent source of protein, vitamins, minerals, and fiber. Making your own sprouts is not as complicated as it might seem; in fact, it is quite easy and straightforward. In choosing the dried beans to sprout, I usually pick organically grown beans, which are available at Indian markets, health food stores, and some specialty shops, but you can use any good quality beans. Keep away from insect-damaged ones, which are marked by holes.*

Listed below is the traditional combination of beans, but any other combination may be substituted. Just use a total of $2\frac{1}{2}$ cups of any variety of legumes. I usually prefer smaller beans, as they yield a better flavor.

½ cup whole green mung beans, with skins (*singo moong ko daal*)
½ cup whole black urad beans, with skins (*singo maas ko daal*)
¼ cup dried black-eyed peas (*bodi*)
¼ cup dried whole green or yellow peas (*sukeko thulo kerau – hariyo, pahelo*)
¼ cup dried soybeans, brown or white (*bhatmaas*)

¼ cup dried whole brown chickpeas (*kaalo chana*)
2 tablespoons dried whole yellow chickpeas (*thulo chana*)
2 tablespoons dried kidney beans (*raato bodi*)
2 tablespoons dried fava beans (*bakulla*)
2 tablespoons dried small field peas (*sukeko hariyo saano kerau*)

Cleaning: Inspect the beans carefully before soaking and remove any foreign materials such as small stones, weeds, seeds, soil, or leaves. Once sprouted, it is very difficult to pick out and remove these foreign materials. Certain beans, such as whole black urad beans, or Nepali field peas need to be cleaned particularly thoroughly, as they often contain tiny black stones. Wash, rinse, and drain the daal several times until the water runs clear. Discard anything that floats, as well.

Soaking: As a rule, for each cup of beans, use 4 cups of room temperature water. I do not recommend hot water, because it may cause the beans to sour or the outer skins to break. Very cold water will slow the rehydration process. Once the beans are soaked, they will swell and double in size. The soaking water should always be discarded.

In a large bowl, mix all the beans together, add enough room temperature water to cover, and leave them to soak for 10 to 12 hours at room temperature. Drain and rinse the beans thoroughly.

Wrap the drained beans in a cheesecloth or muslin cloth and secure it. Place them in a colander or any porous container, as growing sprouts need ventilation. Place the colander in a cupboard, pantry, or any dark, warm, humid place, to encourage sprouting. Check them occasionally, and sprinkle with a few drops of water if needed to keep the beans moist, but not wet. By the second day, the beans will start to sprout, given proper moisture. Remove the beans from the cloth and rinse under running water. Drain the beans, tie them back in the cheesecloth, and return to the warm place. Repeat the process twice a day (morning and evening) until they begin to sprout, which may take 2 to 3 days. The size of the sprouts will vary according to the combination of beans. They are ready when the sprouts are about ¼-inch long. Do not allow the sprouts to grow too long, as they will become tasteless. To stop further sprouting, drain completely and store in a plastic bag in the refrigerator.

How to use: When preparing the sprouts for cooking, it is not necessary to remove the outer covering of the beans or pluck off the sprouts. Some sprouted beans cook faster than other beans (mung beans cook faster than other large legumes, for instance). When you are cooking the mixed beans, the soft textured beans may become mushy by the time the cooking process is finished, which is normal.

Makes 6 to 7 cups.

Kwanti ko Ras
KWANTI SOUP

According to a time-honored tradition, a delicious soup is prepared from a colorful array of mixed sprouted beans and served in July and August, during the Nepali festival of janai purnima *or* kwanti purnima. *Traditionally, the sprouts are prepared from a combination of nine different kinds of colorful beans. This wholesome soup is highly nutritious and aids digestion. Today,* kwanti *soup is cooked regularly in many Nepali households, and one does not have to wait for festival time to enjoy it. Although this dish can be prepared quickly in a pressure cooker, some cooks believe that the sprouts do not absorb the seasoning in the shorter cooking time. While cooking* kwanti, *there is no need to mash the beans to thicken the soup. Some sprouts, like mung beans, cook faster than others and by the time the whole dish is cooked, they will become mushy, making the dish just the right texture.*

2 cups mixed Sprouted Beans (page 97)
2 tablespoons clarified butter (*gheu*)
4 to 6 large cloves garlic, sliced
2 fresh mild green chilies, split lengthwise
½ teaspoon ground turmeric
A generous pinch ground asafetida
1 medium onion, halved lengthwise and thinly sliced
1½ teaspoons ajowan seeds
1 teaspoon salt
2 medium tomatoes, chopped (about 2 cups)

4 teaspoons minced fresh ginger
1½ teaspoons ground coriander
1 teaspoon Nepali Garam Masala (page 398)
1 teaspoon ground cumin
½ teaspoon cayenne pepper
2 bay leaves
1 tablespoon mustard oil
2 dried red chilies, halved and seeded
⅛ teaspoon Himalayan herb (*jimbu*)
¼ cup finely chopped cilantro

Rinse the sprouts in several changes of running water. Discard any seed coatings that come loose and float to the top of the water. Drain the sprouts and set aside.

Heat the clarified butter in a heavy saucepan over medium-high heat. Add the garlic, green chilies, turmeric, and asafetida and fry for 10 seconds. Add the onion and cook, stirring constantly, until lightly browned, about 7 minutes. Mix in the sprouted beans, 1 teaspoon of the ajowan, and the salt and cook, stirring from time to time, until lightly fried and the moisture from the sprouts has evaporated, about 5 minutes. Add the tomatoes, ginger, coriander, garam masala, cumin, cayenne pepper, and bay leaves and cook until the tomatoes have softened, about 3 minutes. Stir in 4 cups of water and bring the mixture to a boil. Reduce the heat to medium-low, cover the pan, and simmer. Check occasionally to see if the water has evaporated or the beans are soft. If not, add more water and continue cooking, covered. The beans are ready when they are soft when pressed between your fingers, 45 minutes to 1 hour. Remove the beans from the heat and keep covered.

In a small skillet, heat the mustard oil over medium-high heat until it faintly smokes. Add the dried chilies, jimbu, and remaining ½ teaspoon of ajowan and fry until dark brown and highly fragrant, about 5 seconds. Remove the skillet from the heat, immediately pour the entire mixture onto the cooked bean dish, and stir well. Cover and let stand 10 minutes before serving. Transfer the beans to a serving dish, sprinkle the cilantro on top, and serve.

Makes 4 to 6 servings.

Gundruk ko Jhol
SOYBEAN AND GUNDRUK SOUP

Gundruk ko Jhol *is a traditional thin soup prepared from fermented dried greens and dried soybeans. It is served with plain boiled rice, millet, or corn-meal porridge (dhindo). The following recipe is particularly flexible, and any ingredients (meat, fish, lentil nuggets, or potatoes) can be added.*

1 cup *Gundruk* (page 310)	1 medium tomato, chopped
2 tablespoons vegetable oil	(about 1 cup)
½ cup dried soybeans, yellow or	3 medium cloves garlic, finely
brown (*bhatmaas*)	chopped
2 dried red chilies, halved and	1½ teaspoons minced fresh ginger
seeded	½ teaspoon ground turmeric
1 teaspoon ajowan seeds	½ teaspoon salt

In a medium-size bowl, soak the *gundruk* in water to cover, for about 10 minutes. Drain thoroughly, chop, and set aside.

Heat the oil in a medium-size saucepan over medium-low heat. When the oil is hot, but not smoking, add the soybeans and cook, stirring constantly, until light brown, about 2 minutes. Remove them with a slotted spoon and set aside. In the remaining hot oil, add the dried chilies and ajowan seeds to the same pan and fry until lightly browned and fragrant, about 5 seconds. Mix in the drained *gundruk* and cook, stirring constantly, for 1 minute. Then add the tomatoes, garlic, ginger, turmeric, and salt and cook until the tomato is soft, about 2 minutes. Mix in 3 cups of water and bring the mixture to a boil. Add the soybeans, reduce the heat to medium-low, cover, and simmer until the soybeans are soft and the liquid has slightly reduced, about 10 minutes. Transfer the soup to a bowl and serve hot.

Makes 4 to 6 servings.

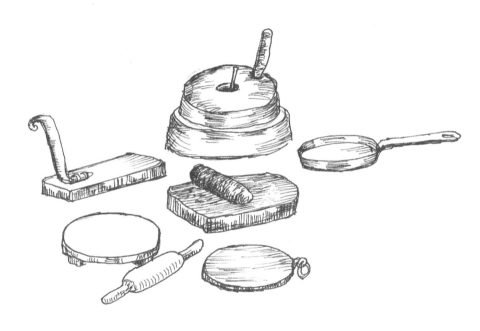

Roti

BREAD

Roti is the generic term for bread in Nepal. Bread is prepared from a variety of ground grains, including wheat, rice, corn, millet, soybean, legumes, and buckwheat. Traditionally, the flour is ground in a *jaato*, a circular milling or grinding stone on a pivot. Stone grinding is still common in many parts of Nepal, although it has largely been replaced by machine grinding. Nepali bread is as diverse as the country itself and many ethnic groups have their own specialties, including buckwheat bread (*phaapar ko roti*), rice flour bread (*chataamari*), millet flatbread (*kodo ko pitho ko roti*), rice-molasses bread (*arsa-roti*), ceremonial sweet bread (*laakha-mari*), sweet ground rice bread (*anarsa-roti*), and steamed rice bread (*yoh-mari*).

There are many ways to prepare *roti*, but it is most commonly griddle-cooked, pan-fried, or deep-fried. Nepali breads range from crispy deep-fried rice-flour bread to flat corn breads, puffed poori bread, and thin wheat-flour flatbreads. Its texture varies, ranging from very thin, to thick, chewy, and stuffed. Homemade Nepali breads are easy to make and are usually prepared fresh for each meal. They are served with various gravy-based dishes, such as meat and vegetable curries, lentil dishes, chutney and pickles, sweet dishes, and yogurt. They can be eaten with almost anything. There is no hard and fast rule as to which bread accompanies which main dish. Much depends upon one's taste, the amount of rice served, and how elaborate the meal is.

Most of the flat, unleavened breads are cooked in a heavy cast-iron skillet known as *taaba* or *taawa*, which when heated on a stovetop absorbs heat quickly and distributes it evenly, so the bread will cook thoroughly. Its concave shape holds the oil at the bottom of the pan where it is needed, so the griddle-cooked bread can be cooked with a small amount of oil. If you do not have a *taaba* you may use a cast-iron griddle or skillet.

Rolling *roti* into a perfect circle is a challenge at first. However, your skill will improve with practice. The dough is usually rolled out on a round wood, stone, or marble platform, known as a *chauka*. The *belna*, a rolling pin, is usually made of wood. Nepalese rolling pins usually have tapered ends, and are suited for rolling out thin and round breads. They provide a good grip and are the perfect weight, but a regular rolling pin will work fine.

For my everyday simple bread recipes, I prefer to use atta or chapatti flour (durum wheat), which is a finely ground whole wheat flour made from a low-gluten wheat. This flour makes dough that is easy to knead and roll, and bread with a light texture. It is found in Indian grocery stores and some supermarkets. If it is not available, you can substitute a mixture of all-purpose white flour and whole wheat flour as indicated in the recipes.

Swaari
FRIED BREAD

Swaari *is delicious, soft, fried bread prepared from all-purpose white flour. It is served at room temperature, folded in half or into a triangle. This bread is usually made for celebrations and festivals and bought from sweet shops.* Swaari *is often eaten with* jilphi *(pretzel-shaped syrup-filled loops). When served with* mana-bhog *(flour haluwa), it becomes a delicious breakfast or snack food.*

2½ cups all-purpose white flour   **2 to 3¼ cups vegetable oil**

In a medium-size bowl, combine the flour and 3 tablespoons of the oil and mix by hand until thoroughly combined. Gradually add ¾ to 1 cup of water, until the dough holds together. Knead well in the bowl until the dough is smooth and elastic, about 5 minutes. The dough should be soft but not sticky. If it is too sticky, add a tablespoon of flour; if it feels too firm, add a little water and knead some more. Cover with plastic wrap or a damp kitchen towel and set aside at room temperature for 1 hour or more.

When the dough is well rested, knead it on a flat surface with the heel of your hand until you have a pliable and smooth dough, about 5 minutes. Roll the dough into a rope about 2 inches in diameter and divide it into 12 to 14 equal portions. Roll it into a ball. Lightly oil your hands and stretch the dough between your palms to create 5-inch uneven circles, about ⅛-inch thick. Alternatively, place the dough on a greased work surface and use a rolling pin. Keep the dough covered with damp towels while working. As you work, place the stretched dough in a single layer on a tray.

Heat the remaining 2 to 3 cups of oil in a deep skillet over medium-high heat until it reaches 350° to 375°F. Test for readiness by placing a small piece of dough into the hot oil. If it bubbles and rises to the surface immediately, it is ready. Gently place the circles of dough into the oil, one at a time. The dough will sink at first, and when it rises, turn it quickly and fry for 30 to 40 seconds more. Remove from the oil with a slotted spoon while still white and soft, and drain on paper towels. Fold it in half and keep covered until ready to serve. Repeat with the remaining dough.

Makes 12 to 14 breads.

Phulka-Roti
WHOLE WHEAT FLATBREAD

Phulka-roti, *also called* sukkha-roti, *or just* roti, *is a thin unleavened flatbread prepared from durum whole-wheat flour. It is the most basic Nepali bread, very light textured, easy to prepare, and usually cooked just before serving. Typically, the dough is rolled into thin circles and cooked on a dry Nepali cast-iron griddle (taaba), but any regular griddle that has even heat distribution can be used. Expert cooks can roll and cook the bread at the same time, but the dough can also be rolled and kept covered before cooking. The bread usually puffs up during cooking and should be immediately basted with butter to maintain moistness. It is served with almost any combination of vegetables, gravy-based meat curries, lentils, and pickles.*

2½ cups chapatti (*atta*) flour or I cup whole wheat flour mixed with I½ cups all-purpose white flour, plus ½ cup for rolling	½ teaspoon salt I tablespoon vegetable oil 3 to 4 tablespoons clarified butter (*gheu*)

In a medium-size bowl, combine the flour and salt. Add the oil and mix by hand until all ingredients are well-combined. Gradually add ¾ to I cup of water, a little at a time, to form a dough that holds together. Knead well in the bowl until the dough is smooth and elastic, about 5 minutes. The dough should be soft but not sticky. If it is too sticky, sprinkle some flour over the dough and knead some more. Cover with plastic wrap or a damp towel and set aside at room temperature for 25 to 30 minutes.

Remove the dough from the bowl, and knead on a flat surface until soft and pliable, about 5 minutes. Divide the dough into fifteen portions, shape each into a ball, and coat each with a little flour. With a rolling pin flatten out one of the balls and roll it into a 6-inch circle about ¼ inch thick, using only enough flour to keep the dough from sticking. Adding too much flour will toughen the bread. Repeat with the remaining dough. Cover the unused balls and rolled circles with damp kitchen towels while working.

Heat a cast-iron griddle (*taaba*) over medium-high heat. Test for readiness by sprinkling a few drops of water on the griddle. If the drops bounce and sputter, it is ready, but if the water evaporates immediately, it is too hot, so adjust the heat accordingly. Place the circles of dough on the griddle, one at a time and cook until the top is slightly dry, and small bubbles begin to form, moving frequently. When the underside is dotted with light brown dots, turn it over. At this stage, the bread will slowly start to puff up. Take a kitchen towel and gently press down on the surface of the bread until the whole bread puffs up. Turn it over again and cook the other side until light brown spots starts to appear. The entire process should take less than 3 minutes. Spread with clarified butter on the roti, transfer to a covered dish, and keep warm while you cook the rest of the rotis.

Makes 12 breads.

Patre-roti
FLAKY ROTI BREAD

Patre-roti, *also called* tinkune-roti *or* parautha-roti, *is a triangular flatbread. Clarified butter is added at three points resulting in a slightly crispy crust and very soft flaky inside. This variety of bread is richer, slightly thicker, and more filling than most flatbreads.*

3 cups chapatti (*atta*) flour or 1½ cups whole wheat flour mixed with 1½ cups all-purpose white flour, plus an extra ½ cup for rolling

1 teaspoon salt
5 tablespoons clarified butter (*gheu*), at room temperature

In a medium-size bowl, combine the flour and salt. Add 1 tablespoon of the clarified butter and mix well by hand until all ingredients are well combined. Gradually add 1 to 1¼ cups of water to form a dough that holds together. Knead well in the bowl until the dough is smooth and elastic, about 5 minutes. The dough should be soft but not sticky. If it is too sticky, sprinkle some flour over it, and knead some more. Cover with plastic wrap or a damp kitchen towel and set aside at room temperature for 25 to 30 minutes.

Remove from the bowl and knead on a flat surface until you have a soft and pliable dough, about 5 minutes. Roll the dough into a rope about 2 inches in diameter and divide it into ten equal portions. Roll each portion into a ball and coat it with a little flour. Flatten the ball and, with a rolling pin, roll it into a 6- to 7-inch circle. Lightly brush the top with melted butter. Fold the dough into a half-circle and apply more butter. Fold in half again to form a small triangle. Do not use too much butter, as it will make the dough too slippery and the butter will leak out when the bread is re-rolled. Roll the triangle 6 to 7 inches long, taking care to maintain its shape. Place each rolled piece of dough in a single layer on a tray covered with damp kitchen towels. Repeat until all the dough is used up.

Heat an ungreased cast-iron griddle (*taaba*) over medium-high heat. Test for readiness by sprinkling a few drops of water on the griddle. If the drops bounce and sputter, it is ready, but if the water evaporates immediately, it is too hot, so adjust the heat accordingly. Place a piece of rolled-out dough on the griddle and cook until the top is dry and the bottom is dotted with brown spots, about 1 minute. Turn over, brush 1 teaspoon of butter around the edges and on the surface, and rotate frequently. Flip again and add another teaspoon of butter. At this stage, the flaky layers will separate, puff up slightly, and the outer layers will become crispy. Rotate and flip the bread frequently until it is light golden brown on both sides. The entire process should take less than 3 minutes. When cooked, transfer the bread to a covered dish and keep warm while you cook the remaining rotis.

Makes 10 breads.

Poori

POORI BREAD

Poori, *pronounced "poo-ree," is a deep-fried puffed bread, generally prepared from wheat flour. The dough can be prepared in advance, but the rolling and frying should be done just before serving.* Poori *are fried in bubbling hot oil and puff up into steam-filled balloons.* Poori *tastes best if eaten piping hot, puffed up with a crispy outside and a moist inside. Though it starts to lose its puffiness and becomes somewhat chewy and tough when cold, poori is still quite tasty when eaten that way. It is one of the most popular breads and a classic accompaniment to any Nepali meal, and it is also eaten during family celebrations and religious festivals. It is prepared for* naivedya, *sacred food that is ritualistically offered to deities during worship. At the same time, it is often packed for picnics and long journeys as a good traveling bread.*

2½ cups atta flour (*chapatti*) or ½ cup whole wheat flour mixed with 1½ cups all-purpose white flour, plus an extra ½ cup for rolling

½ teaspoon salt
2 to 3 cups vegetable oil

In a medium-size bowl, combine the flour and salt. Add 1 tablespoon of oil and mix by hand until all ingredients are well combined. Gradually add ¾ to 1 cup of water, to form a dough that holds together. Knead in the bowl until the dough is smooth and elastic, about 5 minutes. The dough should be moderately stiff. If the dough is too sticky, add 1 or 2 tablespoons of flour; if it feels too firm, add a little water and knead some more. Cover with a plastic wrap or damp kitchen towel and set aside at room temperature for 25 to 30 minutes.

When the dough is well rested, place it on a flat surface and knead it until pliable, about 5 minutes. Roll the dough into a rope about 2 inches in diameter and divide it into twelve to fourteen equal portions. Roll each portion into a ball and coat it with a little flour. Flatten the balls with a rolling pin and roll into 4 to

5-inch circles, about ¼ inch thick. Keep the dough covered with damp towels while working. Place the circles on a tray so they are not touching each other.

Heat the oil in a deep skillet over medium-high heat until it reaches 350° to 375°F (see Note below). Test for readiness by placing a small piece of dough into the hot oil. If it bubbles and rises to the surface immediately, it is ready. Place the circles into the oil, one piece at a time. The dough will sink to the bottom, but will immediately rise up. Use light pressure with the back of a slotted spoon to submerge the dough until it puffs. Then, turn it over to brown the second side. The second side of poori is slightly heavier, so fry it longer until golden. Remove the poori with a slotted spoon and drain on paper towels. Repeat the procedure with the remaining dough. Serve immediately, if possible, or keep warm, covered, until ready to serve.

Makes 12 to 14 (5-inch) breads..

Note: While frying, be careful to keep the oil at 350° to 375°F for even cooking. If the oil is too hot, the poori will brown too fast and may remain doughy and uncooked inside. If the oil is not hot enough, it will not puff up and the dough will absorb a lot of fat.

Spinach Poori: Add ½ teaspoon cayenne pepper, ¼ teaspoon turmeric, ¼ teaspoon ground coriander, and ¼ teaspoon ground cumin to the flour and salt. When you add the tablespoon of oil, stir in 1½ cups chopped fresh spinach, 2 chopped mild green chilies, and 1 tablespoon minced fresh ginger. Proceed as directed above.

Alu-Roti
POTATO-STUFFED BREAD

Alu-roti is delicious stuffed bread cooked on a griddle. The filling consists of spiced mashed potato, but any combination of vegetables, such as cauliflower, peas, spinach, radish, and homemade paneer cheese can also be used. The bread is not difficult to make, but it does take time. Experts can roll the dough, stuff, and cook simultaneously and this can be mastered with a little practice. However, the task can be simplified if you have someone to cook while you roll and assemble the bread. The bread can be prepared ahead of time and reheated just before serving. It is served as part of a meal or as a part of a light lunch with a variety of chutneys, pickles, and yogurt.

DOUGH
3 cups atta flour (*chapatti*) or
   1½ cups whole wheat flour
   mixed with 1½ cups all-
   purpose white flour, plus
   an extra ½ cup for rolling
½ teaspoon ajowan seeds
½ teaspoon salt
1 tablespoon vegetable oil
½ cup melted clarified butter
   (*gheu*)

POTATO STUFFING
3 to 4 medium potatoes
1 tablespoon vegetable oil
1 medium onion, finely chopped
   (about 1 cup)
2 fresh mild green chilies, finely
   chopped
1 tablespoon minced fresh ginger
2 large cloves garlic, minced
1 teaspoon ground cumin
1 teaspoon salt
½ teaspoon Nepali Garam
   Masala (page 398)
¼ teaspoon turmeric powder
½ cup finely chopped cilantro
3 to 4 green onions (white and
   pale green parts), finely
   chopped
2 tablespoons fresh lemon or
   lime juice

To make the dough, in a medium-size bowl, combine the flour, ajowan seeds, and salt. Add the oil and mix by hand until thoroughly combined. Gradually add 1 to 1¼ cups of water, a little at a time, to form a dough that holds together. Knead well in the bowl until the dough is smooth and elastic, about

5 minutes. The dough should be moderately stiff. If the dough is too sticky, add 1 or 2 tablespoons of flour; if it feels too firm, add a little water and knead it some more. Cover with plastic wrap or a damp kitchen towel and set aside at room temperature for 25 to 30 minutes or until ready to use.

To make the stuffing, place the potatoes in a medium-size saucepan, with water to cover, and bring to boil over high heat. Reduce the heat to low, cover the pan, and cook until the potatoes are tender, about 20 minutes. Drain, and when cool enough to handle, peel and mash the potatoes completely. Set aside.

Heat the oil in a saucepan over medium-high heat. When the oil is hot, but not smoking, add the onion and cook until soft, about 5 minutes. Add the green chilies, ginger, garlic, cumin, salt, garam masala, and turmeric and cook for 1 more minute. Stir in the mashed potatoes, and cook until the moisture has evaporated. Remove the pan from the heat and stir in the cilantro, green onions, and lemon juice. Transfer the mixture to a bowl and let it cool to room temperature before using.

When the dough is well rested, knead it on a flat surface until pliable. Divide the dough into twenty-four equal portions. Roll each piece into a ball, coat it with a little flour, and flatten it out on the work surface. Using a rolling pin, roll the dough into 4-inch circles, making sure the middle is thicker than the edges. Set aside on a tray.

Place 2 to 2½ tablespoons of the potato mixture in the center of one circle of dough and gently spread it over the dough leaving a ½-inch margin. Place another circle on top and press the edges together, pinching to seal, making sure the filling is secure inside. Gently reroll the stuffed dough into a 7-inch circle of even thickness. Make sure the stuffing does not come out while rolling. If it pokes out, seal it with a piece of dough. Repeat the process with the remaining dough and stuffing. As you assemble the breads, keep them on a tray covered with a kitchen towel.

Heat an ungreased cast-iron griddle (*taaba*) over medium-high heat. Test for readiness by placing a few drops of water on the griddle. If they bounce and sputter, it is ready, but if the water evaporates immediately, it is too hot, so adjust the heat accordingly. Carefully place one of the stuffed breads on the griddle and cook for about 1 minute. Turn it over, brush 1 teaspoon of butter on the edges and top. Flip and cook the underside until it is dotted with light brown spots. Brush 1 teaspoon of butter over the surface. Rotate and turn the bread frequently until it is lightly browned on both sides. The entire process should take less than 3 minutes. Transfer the bread to a covered dish and keep it warm while you cook the remaining breads. Serve warm or at room temperature.

Makes 12 breads.

Phaapar ko Roti
BUCKWHEAT BREAD

Phaapar ko Roti *is a delicious light gray-colored bread prepared from buckwheat flour. The bread is made from a smooth batter that is spiced and cooked on a griddle similarly to the way pancakes are cooked. It is delicious by itself, or can be served as a light lunch accompanied with a combination of vegetables, yogurt, and buttermilk.*

2 cups buckwheat flour	½ teaspoon salt
2 to 3 fresh mild green chilies, minced	⅛ teaspoon Szechwan pepper, finely ground with a mortar and pestle
1½ teaspoons minced fresh ginger	¼ cup clarified butter (*gheu*)
1 small clove garlic, minced	

In a medium-size bowl, combine the flour, chilies, ginger, garlic, salt, and Szechwan pepper. Gradually add ¾ to 1 cup of water, beating well to make a smooth batter without lumps. Beat with a fork until fluffy. Cover and set aside at room temperature for 10 to 15 minutes. If the batter thickens, add more water. The batter should have a semi-thick consistency, and should spread evenly when poured on the griddle.

Heat a heavy griddle or nonstick skillet over medium-high heat. Test the griddle for readiness by splashing on a few drops of water. If the drops bounce and sputter, it is ready. If the water evaporates immediately, it is too hot. Adjust the heat accordingly. Pour about ½ cup of the batter onto the hot griddle. Tilt the pan to distribute the batter, forming a circle. Cook until the edges start to brown and the top is covered with air bubbles. Pour 1 teaspoon of the butter around the edges and over the top. Gently flip and cook the other side. Add 1 more teaspoon of butter and continue cooking until golden brown. Remove from the heat and serve immediately. Repeat with the remaining batter.

Makes 8 to 10 breads.

Moong ko Roti
MUNG ROTI

This crisp, griddle-cooked bread prepared from split yellow mung beans is both filling and nutritious. It is easy to prepare, but it requires some practice to make them in perfect round shapes. Nepali cooks usually use their fingers to spread the batter on the griddle.

2½ cups split yellow mung beans, without skins (*pahelo moong ko daal*)
2 fresh mild green chilies, minced to a fine paste

1 tablespoon minced fresh ginger
¼ teaspoon ground turmeric
¼ teaspoon salt
A small pinch ground asafetida
3 to 4 tablespoons clarified butter (*gheu*)

Prepare the mung beans as directed on pages 69-70. In a large bowl, soak the beans for at least 4 hours or overnight. Place the drained beans in a food processor or blender and process, adding up to 1 cup of fresh water to make a semi-thick puree with no grainy bits. You may have to do this in two batches. Transfer the puree to a bowl and mix it with the chilies, ginger, turmeric, salt, and asafetida. If the batter is too thick, add 1 to 2 tablespoons water and beat with a fork or your hand until fluffy. The batter should be easily spreadable. Cover the bowl and allow to rest at room temperature for at least 10 minutes.

Heat a cast-iron griddle (*taaba*) over medium-high heat. Test the griddle for readiness by splashing on a few drops of water. If the drops bounce and sputter, it is ready. If the water evaporates immediately, it is too hot. Adjust the heat accordingly. Melt ½ teaspoon of butter on the griddle. Pour ½ to ¾ cup of batter onto the center of the griddle. Moving the back of a spoon or your fingers in a circular motion, spread the batter evenly into a 5-inch circle. The batter should cover the griddle in a thin layer. Cook until the edges start to crisp and the underside starts to brown, about 2 minutes. Turn the roti over and drizzle 2 teaspoons of butter around the edges and top. Rotate and turn the roti frequently, adding more butter, until it is browned on both sides and slightly crispy. Transfer to a serving dish and keep warm. Repeat with the remaining batter. Serve warm or at room temperature. If the batter starts to dry up while you are cooking, add teaspoons of water until smooth.

Makes 10 to 12 breads.

Makai ko Roti
CORN BREAD

Makai ko roti *is a cornmeal flatbread gently cooked on a griddle. Since cornmeal lacks gluten, the dough dries out quickly and shaping these is a little tricky. The dough can be patted between your palms to stretch and shape it or rolled gently with a rolling pin. It is served hot with almost any combination of vegetables, meats, or lentils.*

2 cups cornmeal	½ teaspoon salt
½ cup atta flour (*chapatti*)	1 to 1¼ cups hot water
2 fresh hot green chilies, minced	3 to 4 tablespoons clarified
1½ teaspoons minced fresh ginger	butter (*gheu*) or vegetable oil

In a medium-size bowl, combine the cornmeal, flour, green chilies, ginger, and salt. Gradually add the hot water to form a smooth dough. Knead in the bowl until a semi-soft dough forms. Cover with plastic wrap or a damp kitchen towel and set aside at room temperature for 10 minutes.

With lightly oiled hands, divide the dough into ten equal portions and roll each piece into a ball. Keep the dough covered with damp towels to keep it from drying. Flatten out one of the balls on an oiled work surface. With a rolling pin, roll the dough into a 5-inch circle. Use gentle pressure and turn the dough frequently when rolling. If any cracks form, pinch the dough together with your fingers. Alternately, the dough can be patted between oiled palms. Repeat with the remaining dough and place the rounds in a single layer on a tray.

Heat a cast-iron griddle (*taaba*) over medium-low heat, about 3 minutes. Brush lightly with ½ teaspoon of the butter, and place a circle of dough on it. As soon as the dough is on the griddle, it will stick, so move it carefully without tearing. Cook until the top is slightly dry and the bottom is covered with golden dots. Turn over and cook the other side until light brown spots appear. Brush about 1 teaspoon of butter around the edges and the top. Rotate frequently and cook until both sides are golden brown and crisp. Transfer to a platter and repeat with the remaining dough. Serve hot with additional butter if you like.

Makes 10 to 12 breads.

Kodo ko Pitho ko Roti
MILLET FLOUR BREAD

These thick and highly nutritious flatbreads are prepared from millet flour. They are served with almost any combination of vegetables, meat dishes, yogurt, buttermilk, or pickles and chutney. Millet flour (kodo ko pitho) *is available in health food stores, Indian grocery stores* (under the name bajri *flour), and some supermarkets* (generally in bulk containers).

2 cups millet flour	2 to 3 tablespoons melted
½ cup whole wheat flour	clarified butter (*gheu*)
1 to 1¼ cups hot water	1 tablespoon vegetable oil
½ teaspoon salt	

In a medium-size bowl, combine both flours and the salt. Gradually add the hot water until a smooth dough forms. Knead until you have a semi-soft dough. Cover with plastic wrap or a damp kitchen towel and set aside at room temperature for 10 minutes.

With lightly oiled hands, divide the dough into eight to ten equal portions and roll each piece into a ball. Flatten out one of the balls on an oiled work surface. Using a rolling pin, roll the dough into a 5-inch circle, using gentle pressure and turning frequently. If the dough tears, pinch it back together with your fingers. Keep the dough covered with damp towels so it does not dry out. Alternately, the dough can be patted into circles between oiled palms. Place the dough in a single layer on a tray. Repeat with the remaining dough.

Heat a cast-iron griddle (*taaba*) over medium-low heat, about 3 minutes. Place a circle of dough on the griddle, moving it around and cook until the top is slightly dry with small bubbles and the bottom is covered with golden dots, 3 to 4 minutes. Turn over and cook the other side until the brown spots start to appear. Rotate frequently, cooking until both sides are lightly browned. Remove the dough from the heat, spread 1 teaspoon of butter evenly over the surface, and serve immediately or transfer it to a covered dish and keep warm while you make the rest of the bread.

Makes 8 to 10 breads.

Chataamari
RICE FLOUR BREAD WITH VEGETABLE TOPPING

Chataamari *is a traditional Newari rice flour bread topped with meat, eggs, vegetables, or sugar. The bread is delicious plain or can be served with vegetables, pickles, and chutney. Here is my version with a vegetable topping.*

2 cups rice flour (*chaamal ko pitho*)
¾ cup urad bean flour (*maas ko pitho*)
½ teaspoon salt
2 medium tomatoes, chopped (about 2 cups)
1 medium red onion, finely chopped (about 1 cup)

1 small red or green bell pepper, cored and finely chopped (about 1 cup)
4 to 5 green onions (white and pale green parts), finely chopped
½ cup finely chopped cilantro
2 to 3 fresh hot green chilies, chopped
½ cup clarified butter (*gheu*)

In a medium-size bowl, combine both flours and the salt. Gradually add ¼ to ½ cup of water, beating well to make a smooth batter. Beat with a fork to make it fluffy. Cover with plastic wrap or a damp towel and set it aside at room temperature for 15 to 20 minutes. If the rested batter has thickened, stir in 1 or 2 tablespoons of water. It should be thin and spread evenly when poured on the griddle. In a separate bowl, combine the tomatoes, onion, bell pepper, green onions, cilantro, and green chilies and set aside.

Heat a cast-iron griddle (*taaba*) over medium-high heat. Test the griddle for readiness by splashing on a few drops of water. If the drops bounce and sputter, then it is ready. If the water evaporates immediately, it is too hot. Adjust the heat accordingly. Brush the griddle lightly with butter. For each *chataamari*, pour about ½ cup of the batter into the center of the griddle. Swirl the pan and spread the batter into a 5-inch circle. Sprinkle ½ cup of the mixed vegetables evenly over the batter and press lightly with a spoon. Cover the pan with a lid, adjust the heat to medium-low, and cook until the edges start to crisp and the underside starts to brown, about 3 minutes. Drizzle 2 teaspoons of butter around the edges. Rotate the bread frequently and cook, covered, until lightly browned and slightly crispy, about 2 minutes. *Chataamari* are only cooked on one side, so remove it from the heat, fold in half, and serve immediately or transfer it to a covered dish to keep warm while you cook the remaining batter.

Makes 10 to 12 breads.

Arsa Roti
MOLASSES RICE FLOUR BREAD

This chewy, sweet flatbread from Nepal's hilly region is known as arsa roti. *The dough is traditionally hand stretched in banana leaves before deep-frying. Arsa roti keeps for up to 2 months at room temperature and is usually served with yogurt or buttermilk.*

3 cups medium-grain white rice	2 to 3 cups plus 1 tablespoon
1 cup molasses	vegetable oil
¼ cup rice flour, or as needed	

Prepare the rice as directed on page 46. In a large bowl, soak the rice in water to cover for at least 4 hours or overnight. Drain and place in a blender or food processor and process, adding ¼ cup of water at a time, until finely ground. Set aside.

In a large, heavy saucepan, heat the molasses over medium-low heat. Slowly stir in the ground rice. Cook, stirring continuously, until all the moisture has evaporated. Remove the pan from the heat and cool. With oiled hands knead the mixture into a moderately stiff dough, for 3 to 4 minutes. If it is too sticky, gradually add 1 or 2 tablespoons of rice flour and knead some more. Break off walnut-size pieces of dough and form balls. With oiled hands, stretch the balls into 5-inch circles. If the dough tears, pinch it back together. Alternately, the dough can be placed on a greased work surface and stretched. Put the stretched dough onto a tray and cover.

Heat the oil in a skillet over medium-high heat until it reaches 350° to 375°F. Test the temperature by placing a small piece of dough into the hot oil. If it bubbles and rises to the surface immediately, it is ready. Gently place a circle of dough into the oil. It will sink to the bottom first, when it starts to rise, push it into the oil with a slotted spoon, and cook for 20 to 25 seconds. Flip it and fry the second side until golden. Do not let the bread become crisp or overfried. Transfer it to paper towels to drain and cool. Repeat with the remaining dough. Serve at room temperature.

Makes 10 to 12 breads.

Anarsa-roti

POPPY SEED RICE BREAD

This is an adaptation of an old recipe from Sani Bajai, a family friend from Dhading. Anarsa-roti are old-fashioned sweet rice patties (resembling large cookies). Rice flour gives this bread a crisp texture, and poppy seeds provide a pleasant nutty flavor. The dough is hand stretched into circles and deep-fried. It is served as a snack or sweet dish. Anarsa is also eaten during festivals, family celebrations, and other special occasions.

3 cups white rice or rice flour
1¼ cups sugar
¼ cup clarified butter (*gheu*) or unsalted butter

1 to 2 tablespoons plain yogurt, or as needed
3 tablespoons white poppy seeds
2 to 3 cups plus 1 tablespoon vegetable oil

Prepare the rice as directed on page 46. In a large bowl, soak the rice for at least 4 hours or overnight. Drain and grind in a food processor until very finely ground, stopping the machine frequently and scraping down the sides, if necessary.

In a bowl, combine the ground rice, sugar, and butter. Gradually add the yogurt and then knead until a soft dough forms. If the dough is too sticky, knead in a little rice flour. Cover with plastic wrap or a damp towel and set aside for 2 to 3 hours. The mixture will be sticky after resting.

With lightly oiled hands, form the dough into walnut-size balls. Flatten the balls and gently stretch them into 3-inch patties. Sprinkle poppy seeds on top, and press gently so they stick. Place the patties in a single layer on a tray.

Heat the oil in a skillet over medium-high heat until it reaches 350° to 375°F. Test for readiness by placing a small piece of dough into the hot oil. If it bubbles and rises to the surface immediately, it is ready. Carefully drop the rice patties, seeded side up, into the hot oil. Fry until crispy and just lightly browned on the bottom. Spoon oil over the rounds, but do not turn as the seeded side should remain white. Remove the *anarsa* with a slotted spoon and drain on paper towels. Repeat with the remaining patties. Once they have cooled, store them in an airtight container.

Makes 12 pieces.

Ainthe Mari
AINTHE MARI BREAD

This is a simplified adaptation of the old, classic Newari ceremonial bread
laakha-mari (page 123) from our close family friend Tata Maiya Didi.

2 cups medium-grain white rice
½ cup split white urad beans,
  without skins (*maas ko*
  chhata ko daal)

I cup all-purpose flour
¾ cup clarified butter (*gheu*)
3 to 4 cups vegetable oil
I ½ cups sugar

Prepare the rice and beans, as directed on pages 46 and 69-70. In a large bowl, combine the rice and beans and soak them with water to cover, for at least 4 hours or overnight. Drain and transfer to a blender or food processor and process until very finely ground. Add 2 to 3 tablespoons of water to facilitate grinding. In a bowl, combine the ground rice and bean mixture, flour, and butter. Gradually stir in ¼ to ½ cup of water, until the dough holds its shape. Knead well to produce a soft dough. Cover with plastic wrap or a damp towel and set aside to rest for I hour or more at room temperature.

While the dough is resting, put the sugar and ¾ cup of water in a pan, and bring to a boil over medium-high heat, stirring occasionally, until it thickens, about 5 minutes. Keep warm.

Knead the rested dough again, for I minute and roll it into a rope about 2 inches in diameter. Divide the rope into eight to ten equal pieces. Shape each piece into a 3-inch long stick. You can then shape the pieces of dough into braids, straight ropes, or twisted sticks.

Heat the oil in a skillet over medium-high heat until it reaches 350° to 375°F. Test for readiness by placing a small piece of dough in the skillet. If it sizzles, and immediately rises to the surface, it is ready. Gently drop two or three pieces of dough into the oil and fry until light golden brown on both sides. Remove the dough with a slotted spoon and dip them in the sugar glaze. Transfer the *ainthe mari* to a tray and cool. Once it cools, the glaze will set, leaving a translucent satiny finish. Repeat with the remaining pieces of dough.

Makes 8 to 10 breads.

Sel-Roti
BANANA RICE BREAD

Sel-roti, *is a sweet bread that is fried into thin, crisp rounds with a reddish-brown color. Sel is prepared by grinding soaked rice into a thick batter. Traditional Nepali cooks grind the soaked rice in a heavy rectangular stone mortar and pestle (silauto-baccha), which produces a perfectly textured batter. I grind the rice in a blender for convenience. Sel-roti is always prepared during the Nepali religious festivals of Dashai and Tihaar and for other special occasions such as weddings. It is also prepared as a sacred food for the gods (naivedya) and offered ritualistically to deities. Sel is distributed among friends and family as a blessed food (prashaad).*

Sel is delicious by itself, but can also be served with plain yogurt, fried vegetables, and pickles. It tastes best fresh, and becomes tough and chewy once it gets cold, although it still tastes good. It can be kept at room temperature for a week.

3 cups white rice	¾ cup unsalted butter, melted
I medium very ripe banana	¼ cup rice flour, or as needed
I cup sugar, or to taste	4 to 5 cups vegetable oil

Prepare the rice as directed on page 46. In a large bowl, soak the rice in water to cover for at least 4 hours or overnight. Drain and place in a blender or food processor with the banana, sugar, and butter and process, adding up to 1¼ cups of water to make a semi-thick puree with no grainy bits. You may have to do this in two batches. Transfer the batter to a mixing bowl, and beat with a fork until fluffy, 2 to 3 minutes. Cover with plastic wrap or a damp towel and set aside to rest for 20 to 25 minutes.

When the batter is well-rested, mix it again. The consistency should be similar to heavy cream. If it seems too thick, gradually add I to 2 tablespoons of water; if it feels too thin, add I to 2 tablespoons of rice flour and mix well.

Heat the oil in a skillet over medium-high heat until it reaches 350° to 375°F (see Note). Test for readiness by placing a small drop of the batter into the hot oil. If it bubbles and rises to the surface immediately, it is ready. Pour about

¼ cup of batter into the oil slowly, making a large circle (Pour the batter from a cup or a pastry bag with a medium-size opening). Stretch and move the batter using a wooden spoon or chopstick to create a round shape. As the *sel* puffs and rises, push it into the oil with the back of a spoon until it is light golden brown. Flip and fry the second side until golden brown. Remove with a slotted spoon and drain it on paper towels. Repeat with the rest of the batter.

Note: While frying *sel*, be careful to keep the oil at 350° to 375°F for even cooking. If the oil is too hot, the batter will brown too quickly and the insides may remain undercooked and doughy. If the oil is not hot enough, the batter will absorb a lot of oil. Occasionally check the batter as it may thicken while you are cooking. Add a small amount of water to adjust the consistency.

Makes 10 to 12 pieces.

Laakha-Mari
CEREMONIAL NEWARI SWEET BREAD

Sel-Roti is similar to *laakha-mari*, but easier to make, resembling twisted donuts, with a flaky and crunchy texture.

The preparation of *laakha-mari*, crunchy, coiled sweet breads, is an ancient culinary art from the Newar community. Before the formal marriage ceremony (*gwe*), the groom's family displays approval of the marriage by sending *laakha-mari* and other sweets, fruits, and flowers to the bride's family. They are also given to relatives and friends to announce the wedding. The size and the shape varies. Larger ones are sent to closer relatives to honor them and smaller ones are sent to others who are invited.

Laakha-mari are deep-fried and glazed with a light icing to create a translucent satiny finish. The sweet bread is delicious by itself or served with other ceremonial foods. The bread keeps for at least a month at room temperature.

Making this bread is time-consuming and requires significant effort, equipment, and skill, but is a glorious undertaking. These days, the bread is not often prepared at home, but can be found at specialty sweet shops (*haluwai ko pasal*).

Yoh-Mari
SESAME AND COCONUT-FILLED RICE BREAD

Yoh-mari *is a delicious stuffed and steamed bread. The filling varies according to family preference, varying from milk fudge (khuwaa), spicy ground meat and bean paste, to sesame seeds or coconut. The stuffed bread is molded into different shapes that often resemble animals, fruits, ceremonial lamp stands, and figurines of gods and goddesses. The preparation of yoh-mari is a family affair and even small children help to mold the dough. It is eaten warm or at room temperature, by itself or with beverages.*

Yoh-mari is traditionally prepared during the harvest celebration of Yomari Punhi or Dhanya Purnima, observed during the full moon from December to January. During this festival, the people of Kathmandu feast and worship the goddess of grains (Annapurna) for good harvest. Yoh-mari are prepared and offered ritualistically to the gods. Although the festival has its roots in the Newar farming community, today it is observed in almost every Newari home in Kathmandu. It is also prepared to celebrate children's birthdays, when a yoh-mari garland is used to honor the child.

3 cups rice flour
1 to 1½ cups boiling water,
   or as needed
¾ cup sesame seeds
3 tablespoons unsweetened
   shredded coconut
¾ cup dark brown sugar
Vegetable oil

In a large bowl, combine the rice flour and 1 cup of boiling water. When cool enough to handle, knead the dough until smooth and pliable. If the dough is too firm, knead in 1 teaspoon of water. Cover with plastic wrap or a damp towel and set aside to rest at room temperature for 20 to 25 minutes.

While the dough is resting, prepare the filling. Heat a small skillet over medium-low heat. Toast the sesame seeds, stirring and shaking the skillet, until lightly browned and aromatic. Remove from the heat and cool. Use a spice grinder to grind the sesame seeds into a fine powder. Add the coconut to the grinder and grind into a fine powder.

In a small bowl, mix the ground sesame seeds, brown sugar, and coconut with 1 cup of water. Place the mixture in a small saucepan over medium-low heat and simmer, stirring frequently, until the mixture thickens, about 5 minutes. Remove from the heat and set aside.

When you are ready to proceed, place the rested dough on a flat surface and knead for 1 to 2 minutes. With lightly oiled hands, divide the dough into ten to twelve equal portions. Shape each piece into ovals with a small pocket. Place about 2 teaspoons of the filling inside each and pinch the dough to seal tightly. Once sealed, you can create any shape. If there are any cracks in the surface, be sure to seal them. Cover with plastic wrap or a damp kitchen towel while forming the remaining breads.

Fill the bottom of a vegetable steamer with water and bring it to a boil over high heat. Grease the steamer tray with oil. Arrange the *yoh-mari* on the steamer tray(s), making sure that there is ½ inch of space between each, allowing the steam to circulate. You may have to do this in batches. Place the steamer trays on the steamer, cover, and steam for 8 to 10 minutes or until cooked and they appear glazed. Carefully transfer the *yoh-mari* to a serving dish and serve hot.

Makes 10 to 12 breads.

Makai ko Pitho ko Dhindo
CORNMEAL PORRIDGE

Dhindo *is a thick porridge or mush, made by cooking stone-ground cornmeal or millet flour. It has been the staple food of most rural and middle mountain area people in Nepal, especially in dry areas where rice or wheat crops are difficult to grow. This hearty and nutritious food is eaten with homemade butter (*nauni*), curried vegetables (*jhol tarkaari*), pickles, buttermilk, or yogurt.* Gundruk-Dhindo, *the most common combination, combines* dhindo *with fermented greens. Traditionally,* dhindo *is cooked in a cast-iron pan with a long handle and rounded bottom, called a* taapke, *which has excellent heat distribution qualities. It is typically stirred with a large iron spoon with a long handle (*panyu*).* Dhindo *should be eaten right away since it hardens once it cools.*

½ teaspoon salt	2 tablespoons clarified butter
I cup coarse or medium-ground cornmeal	(*gheu*)

In a heavy saucepan, bring 4 cups of water and the salt to a boil over high heat. Once it comes to a full boil, pour in the cornmeal in a slow, steady stream with the left hand, while mixing vigorously and constantly with the right hand. Mix until it is well-combined, making sure there are no lumps. Reduce the heat to medium-low and continue stirring until the mixture thickens, about 20 minutes. It is ready when the porridge begins to pull away from the sides of the pan. Remove it from the heat and stir in the butter until melted. Pour it directly onto plates and eat piping hot.

Makes 4 to 6 servings.

Kodo ko Pitho ko Dhindo
MILLET FLOUR PORRIDGE

Millet is an important source of food in the rural and hilly regions of Nepal because it is drought-tolerant and can be grown on slopes, in poor soil conditions, and even in high-elevation areas. It is a high fiber grain, nourishing and wholesome, and especially suitable for people used to hard physical labor. Millet is also used to make breads and a popular alcoholic drink called chhang. *This dish is eaten with vegetables and is often accompanied by buttermilk or yogurt.*

½ teaspoon salt   2 tablespoons clarified butter
1 cup millet flour

In a heavy saucepan, bring 3½ cups of water and the salt to a boil over high heat. Once it comes to a full boil, pour in the millet flour in a slow, steady stream, while mixing vigorously and constantly. Mix until it is well-combined, making sure there are no lumps. Reduce the heat to medium-low and continue stirring until the mixture thickens, about 20 minutes. It is ready when the porridge starts to pull away from the sides of the pan. Remove it from the heat, and stir in the butter until it melts. Pour the steaming *dhindo* directly onto plates and eat piping hot.

Note: If you prefer a creamer *dhindo*, add more water and clarified butter.

Makes 4 to 6 servings.

Tarkaari

VEGETABLES

Vegetables (*tarkaari*) are one of the most important food groups in the Nepali diet. During the peak growing season, you may see a local farmer heading to the market balancing a bamboo pole across his shoulders, holding two wicker woven baskets of freshly picked vegetables. In Nepali vegetable markets (*tarkaari bazaar*), one can witness the proud harvest of vendors filling every tiny space with elaborate displays of vegetables and fruits. Greens such as spinach and mustard are neatly tied in small bundles and arranged in piles. Potatoes, onions, and shallots are skillfully arranged in wicker trays, baskets, or burlap sacks. Most Nepali households do not store vegetables, so they are bought fresh every day. On many street corners, vendors set up small stands of freshly picked fruits and vegetables such as green gooseberry, *lapsi*, guava, or tangerines. The vegetables are weighed in a hand-held scale, known as a *taraaju*.

While the Kathmandu valley is renowned for the seasonal vegetables grown in its fertile soil, the scarcity of arable land in many rural and hilly areas, limits the consumption of vegetables to root vegetables and preserved vegetables. The most common vegetables include green beans, cauliflowers, cabbage, eggplants, greens, okra, peas, potatoes, radish, squash, and tomatoes. Green leafy vegetables such as spinach and mustard greens are eaten daily in large quantities. Vegetables are made into pickles, salads, snacks, and even desserts.

Kurelo ra Alu Taareko
SAUTÉED ASPARAGUS

Asparagus is considered the king of vegetables in Nepal. The most popular way of cooking it is sautéing it in a little oil. This brings out a depth of flavor that boiling and steaming do not.

3 tablespoons vegetable oil
⅛ teaspoon fenugreek seeds
2 medium red potatoes, peeled and cut into ¼-inch pieces
¼ teaspoon ground turmeric
A small pinch ground asafetida
2 fresh mild or hot green chilies, cut into long slivers
3 medium cloves garlic, minced
1 teaspoon minced fresh ginger

1½ teaspoons ground coriander
1 teaspoon ground cumin
1 teaspoon cayenne pepper
½ teaspoon salt
½ teaspoon freshly ground black pepper
2 pounds asparagus, trimmed and sliced diagonally into 1-inch pieces (about 6 cups)

Heat the oil in a skillet over medium-high heat. When the oil is hot, but not smoking, add the fenugreek seeds and fry until dark brown and fully fragrant, about 5 seconds. Add the potatoes, turmeric, and asafetida and cook, stirring frequently, until the potatoes brown, 6 to 7 minutes. Add the green chilies, garlic, ginger, coriander, cumin, cayenne pepper, salt, and black pepper and mix well. Add the asparagus and cook for 1 minute. Reduce the heat to medium, cover and cook, stirring occasionally, until the vegetables are tender and the liquid has evaporated, 6 to 8 minutes. Do not overcook! When you think they are done, sample a piece. It should be firm with a bit of crunch. Transfer the vegetables to a serving dish and serve warm.

Makes 4 to 6 servings.

Saandheko Kurelo
ASPARAGUS SALAD

This recipe is best when prepared with the freshest, youngest asparagus of the season. I serve this salad as a side dish, with rice, lentils, and pickles.

2½ pounds asparagus, trimmed and sliced diagonally into 1½-inch pieces
¼ cup finely chopped cilantro
1 green onion (white and light green parts), thinly sliced
1 fresh mild or hot green chili pepper, chopped
1 tablespoon vegetable oil

1 small clove garlic, finely chopped
1½ teaspoons minced fresh ginger
3 whole Szechwan pepper (*timmur*), finely ground with a mortar and pestle
½ teaspoon salt
1 tablespoon fresh lemon or lime juice

Bring a medium-size pot of salted water to a rolling boil over medium-high heat. Add the asparagus and cook until crisp-tender, about 5 minutes. Do not overcook, as they will become waterlogged and tasteless. Immediately drain the asparagus in a colander, and run cold water over it to halt the cooking. Place the asparagus in a medium-size bowl and set aside.

In a small bowl, combine the cilantro, green onion, green chili, oil, garlic, ginger, and *timmur* and mix well. Add the spice mixture to the asparagus and toss gently to mix well. Taste and add the salt and lemon juice, if necessary. Cover the bowl and allow the flavors to set for at least 10 minutes at room temperature. Transfer the asparagus to a bowl. If you are not serving it right away, cover and refrigerate until serving time.

Makes 4 to 6 servings.

Barela ko Tarkaari
SAUTÉED BALSAM APPLE

Balsam apple (barela) is a late summer vegetable measuring one to two inches in length, slightly curved at one end with a soft and delicate texture. The pale green, juicy fruit looks somewhat like a pointed gourd (parwar or parvar). Unfortunately, unless you grow barela in your home garden, it is difficult to find. The vegetable is usually picked and cooked when it is young and tender. The mature, overripe ones have rough black seeds which should be removed before cooking. Since this vegetable is very delicate, it cooks quickly.

2 tablespoons vegetable oil	25 to 30 fresh *barela*, trimmed,
I dried red chili, halved and	halved lengthwise, and
seeded	mature seeds removed
¼ teaspoon fenugreek seeds	I ½ teaspoons minced fresh ginger
¼ teaspoon ground turmeric	½ teaspoon ground cumin
	¼ teaspoon salt

Heat the oil in a wide skillet over medium-high heat. When the oil is hot, but not smoking, add the dried chili and fenugreek and fry until dark brown and highly fragrant, about 5 seconds. Sprinkle in the turmeric, and then add the *barela*, ginger, cumin, and salt. Cook, stirring frequently, until the *barela* are crisp-tender, about 10 minutes. While cooking, the *barela* will release some water. Adjust the heat to high, and cook until the liquid evaporates, about 4 minutes. Transfer the *barela* to a serving dish and serve hot.

Makes 4 to 6 servings.

Taama-Alu-Bodi ko Tarkaari
BAMBOO SHOOTS, POTATOES,
AND BLACK-EYED PEAS

Bamboo shoots (taama) are the undeveloped, young, edible shoots of the bamboo plant. They have a mild flavor and are very versatile. In fact, the young, tender shoots can be pickled, fermented, dried, or cooked with any combination of vegetables. To make fermented bamboo, fresh bamboo shoots are thinly sliced, mixed with salt, mustard seeds, turmeric, and mustard oil, and fermented in the sun until they become slightly sour. For this recipe, you may substitute packaged bamboo shoots, readily available in many forms (fresh, canned, bottled, packed in brine, or vacuum-packed in plastic) at Asian markets.

½ cup dried black-eyed peas (*bodi*)	I teaspoon salt
2 tablespoons vegetable oil	I teaspoon cayenne pepper
¼ teaspoon fenugreek seeds	3 medium tomatoes, chopped (about 3 cups)
I medium onion, finely chopped (about I cup)	I small red or green bell pepper, cored and diced (about I cup)
½ teaspoon ground turmeric	
2 medium red potatoes, peeled and sliced ½ inch thick	2 cups (bottled or canned) bamboo shoots, well rinsed, drained, and cut into bite-size pieces
2 fresh hot green chilies, halved lengthwise	
I tablespoon brown mustard seeds, finely ground	½ cup finely chopped cilantro
I tablespoon minced fresh ginger	2 tablespoons fresh lemon or lime juice

Sort and soak the peas as directed on pages 69-70.

Heat the oil in a large saucepan over medium-high heat. When the oil is hot, but not smoking, add the fenugreek seeds, and fry until dark brown and highly fragrant, about 5 seconds. Reduce the heat to medium, add the onion and turmeric, and cook, stirring frequently, until the onion softens, about 5 minutes.

Add the drained black-eyed peas and cook for 10 minutes. Mix in the potatoes, green chilies, mustard, ginger, salt, and cayenne pepper and stir for 1 minute. Stir in the tomatoes and bell pepper and continue cooking until the tomatoes soften, about 5 minutes. Increase the heat to high, add 3 cups of water, and bring the mixture to a boil for 7 minutes. Reduce the heat to medium-low, cover, and cook, stirring from time to time, until the black-eyed peas and potatoes are tender and the sauce has thickened, about 20 minutes. Add the bamboo shoots and cook for another 5 minutes to allow the flavors to blend. If you prefer a thinner sauce, add some water and boil further. Transfer the mixture to a bowl and stir in the cilantro and lemon juice. Serve hot.

Makes 6 to 8 servings.

Kera ko Bungo Tarkaari
BANANA BLOSSOM CURRY

Banana blossoms or buds are the tender heart of unopened banana flowers called kera ko bungo *in Nepali. The rust and purple colored blossom has several sheaths and is roughly shaped like a heart. It is eaten as a side dish or made into pickles and is found fresh in Indian and Asian markets or specialty food stores. The canned variety is readily available as well.*

1 small fresh banana blossom (about 2 cups chopped), or 1 (10-ounce) can banana blossoms	1 teaspoon ground cumin
	1 teaspoon ground coriander
	½ teaspoon cayenne pepper
3 tablespoons vegetable oil	½ teaspoon salt
¼ teaspoon fenugreek seeds	4 to 5 green onions (white and pale green parts), finely chopped
2 medium potatoes, peeled and cut into 1-inch cubes	
½ teaspoon ground turmeric	¼ cup finely chopped cilantro
1 tablespoon minced fresh ginger	2 fresh mild green chilies, halved lengthwise

Before handling the fresh banana blossom, rub your hands and knife with cooking oil to prevent it from sticking. Remove and discard the tough outer leaves. Quarter and core the blossom and shred into ¼-inch pieces. Soak them in salted water for 10 minutes, turning occasionally, to prevent discoloration. Drain, rinse under running water, and set aside. If using canned banana blossoms, drain and wash in several changes of cold water. Shred into ¼-inch pieces and set aside.

Heat the oil in a saucepan over medium-high heat until hot, but not smoking. Add the fenugreek seeds and fry until dark brown and fully fragrant, about 5 seconds. Add the potatoes and turmeric, and cook, stirring frequently, until light brown and half cooked. With a slotted spoon, remove the potatoes, draining as much oil as possible, and transfer them to a bowl.

Add the banana blossom to the same pan and sauté for 4 minutes. Add the ginger, cumin, coriander, cayenne pepper, salt, and reserved potatoes and stir for 1 minute. Add ½ cup of water and bring it to a boil. Reduce the heat to medium-low, cover, and cook until the vegetables are tender, 10 to 12 minutes. Stir in the green onions, cilantro, and green chilies. Transfer the mixture to a serving dish and serve warm.

Makes 4 to 6 servings.

Lauka ko Tarkaari
SPICED BOTTLE GOURD

Bottle gourd (lauka) is also known as long melon or opo squash. The musky scented gourd has a smooth skin and is pale to deep green in color. It resembles a large zucchini, has a mild flavor, and releases a lot of liquid when cooked. It is edible only when young and tender, because as it matures, it becomes bitter. Its mild taste makes it easy to blend with many other vegetables and dried legumes. It is available during the summer and early fall in Asian or Indian grocery stores and some specialty produce markets.

3 tablespoons vegetable oil
4 fresh hot green chilies, halved
  lengthwise
4 medium cloves garlic, thinly
  sliced
1 tablespoon peeled and finely
  julienned fresh ginger plus
  1 teaspoon minced
½ teaspoon ground turmeric
A generous pinch ground asafetida

1 small bottle gourd
  (2½ to 3 pounds), peeled,
  halved lengthwise, seeded,
  and cut into ½-inch pieces
1 teaspoon salt
1 teaspoon ground brown
  mustard seeds
1 teaspoon ground cumin
½ teaspoon cayenne pepper
⅛ teaspoon freshly ground
  black pepper

Heat the oil in a heavy saucepan over medium-high heat. When the oil is hot, but not smoking, add the green chilies, garlic, and julienned ginger and fry until crisp, about 30 seconds. Stir in the turmeric and asafetida, followed by the gourd and salt, and cook, stirring occasionally, for 7 minutes. Add the minced ginger, mustard seeds, cumin, cayenne pepper, and black pepper and mix well. Reduce the heat to medium-low, cover the pan, and cook, stirring and mashing the gourd with the back of the spoon from time to time, until the gourd is very soft and most of the juice has evaporated, 30 to 35 minutes. Transfer the mixture to a serving dish and serve.

Makes 4 to 6 servings.

Bakulla Simi Tarkaari
SPICED FAVA BEANS

Here is a hearty and satisfying vegetable dish from my mother-in-law, Aama Hazoor. She combined young, velvety fava pods and tender shelled beans in this dish, making sure to remove the mature beans. Likewise, you should look for young and delicate fava bean pods, without strings at Indian, Asian, or Middle Eastern markets. She always cooked this dish in a traditional Nepali cast-iron pan (falaam ko taapke) for better flavor, and the finished dish had a faint black coating from the pan. For this recipe, you may use a regular skillet.

2 pounds tender young fava beans, in the pod	**½ teaspoon ground turmeric**
3 tablespoons clarified butter (*gheu*)	**2 small cloves garlic, minced**
	1½ teaspoon minced fresh ginger
½ teaspoon fenugreek seeds	**½ teaspoon salt**
A small pinch ground asafetida	**½ teaspoon cayenne pepper**

Rinse the fava beans in cold water, drain, and trim the ends. Pull off the strings if needed, and cut or snap the pods into 1½-inch pieces. If the beans are tough, discard the outer coating with the pods, and use only the tender beans.

Heat the clarified butter in a large heavy saucepan (*taapke*) over medium-high heat. Add the fenugreek seeds and fry until dark brown and highly fragrant, about 5 seconds. Sprinkle in the asafetida and turmeric, then immediately add the fava beans and cook for 5 minutes. Add the garlic, ginger, salt, and cayenne pepper and cook, stirring, for about 1 minute. Reduce the heat to medium-low, cover the pan, and cook, stirring as needed, until the beans are tender, about 20 minutes. Transfer them to a serving dish and serve.

Makes 4 to 6 servings.

Tane Bodi ko Tarkaari
SPICY LONG BEANS

These long beans (tane bodi) are also called yard beans, asparagus beans, or Chinese long beans. Long beans should be cooked just before serving to preserve their crispy texture. For better flavor, use only tender, slim, and evenly colored beans, as over-mature beans tend to taste bitter. They are available and neatly packaged at Asian, Indian, specialty food stores, and some well-stocked supermarkets.

3 tablespoons vegetable oil	½ teaspoon ground turmeric
I dried red chili, halved and seeded	½ teaspoon salt
⅛ teaspoon fenugreek seeds	I teaspoon Nepali Garam Masala (page 398)
I½ pounds long beans, trimmed and cut into I-inch pieces	I tablespoon minced fresh ginger
2 medium cloves fresh garlic, finely chopped	½ teaspoon cayenne pepper

Heat the oil in a heavy-bottomed wide saucepan over medium-high heat. When the oil is hot, but not smoking, add the dried chili and fenugreek and fry until dark brown and fully fragrant, about 5 seconds. Add the beans, garlic, turmeric, and salt and cook, stirring frequently, for 5 minutes. Add the garam masala, ginger, and cayenne pepper and mix well. Adjust the heat to medium-low, cover the pan, and cook, stirring from time to time, until the beans wrinkle and shrink slightly, but are still crisp, 15 to 20 minutes. Transfer the beans to a serving dish and serve.

Makes 4 to 6 servings.

Simi ra Alu ko Tarkaari
GREEN BEANS AND POTATOES

Look for crisp young beans that snap when you break them. This versatile side dish can be served with any Nepali meal.

3 tablespoons vegetable oil
½ teaspoon fenugreek seeds
1 medium red onion, thinly
    sliced
3 medium cloves garlic, finely
    chopped
½ teaspoon ground turmeric
A small pinch ground asafetida
2 pounds green beans, trimmed
    and cut into 1-inch pieces
    (about 8 cups)

2 medium red potatoes, peeled
    or unpeeled and cut into
    ½-inch pieces
1½ teaspoons minced fresh ginger
1 teaspoon ground cumin
½ teaspoon salt
½ teaspoon cayenne pepper
¼ teaspoon freshly ground black
    pepper

Heat the oil in a large heavy saucepan over medium-high heat. When the oil is hot, but not smoking, add the fenugreek seeds and fry until dark brown and highly fragrant, about 5 seconds. Add the onion, garlic, turmeric, and asafetida and cook, stirring frequently, until the onions soften, about 5 minutes. Add the beans, potatoes, ginger, cumin, salt, cayenne pepper, and black pepper and mix thoroughly. Adjust the heat to medium, cover, and cook, stirring as needed, making sure the liquid has not evaporated completely and the beans do not stick to the bottom of the pan. Add 1 to 2 tablespoons of water if the vegetables begin to stick. Cook until the beans and potato are tender, and all the moisture has evaporated, 18 to 20 minutes. Transfer the mixture to a serving dish and serve.

Makes 4 to 6 servings.

Tito Karela Taareko
BITTER MELON CHIPS

Bitter melon is one of the most popular vegetables in Nepal and many other Asian countries. The Nepali variety of tito karela *is somewhat skinny and dark green in color, pointed at the blossom end, with very bumpy skin. It is much more bitter than the Chinese variety, which is larger, plumper, and pale green. It is believed to have medicinal value and acts to cure stomach ailments, as an appetite stimulant, and to purify the blood and improve circulation. Serve these chips alongside any Nepali main dish or as an appetizer.*

6 to 8 medium bitter melons (enough to make 8 cups sliced) Salt, to taste	$\frac{1}{4}$ cup vegetable oil Fresh lemon or lime juice, to taste

Wash the bitter melons thoroughly, but do not peel. Slice off 1 inch from the top and bottom ends. Rub the cut pieces against the cut surfaces in a circular motion to release a white, foamy substance. This will reduce the bitterness. Discard the ends and wash the bitter melons. This process will extract some of the bitterness. With a spoon, remove any mature seeds and spongy pulp (like coring an apple) and discard. Slice the melons into $\frac{1}{8}$-inch rounds.

In a colander, combine the melon slices with 1 teaspoon of salt, and set aside for 30 minutes in the sink. Squeeze the bitter juice from the melons, rinse, drain, and pat dry. This will further remove the bitter flavor.

Heat the oil in a nonstick skillet over medium-high heat. When the oil is hot, but not smoking, add half of the bitter melon and fry, stirring constantly, until golden brown and crunchy, about 5 minutes. With a slotted spoon, transfer them to a paper towel-lined platter, draining as much oil as possible. Repeat the process with the remaining melons. Sprinkle them with salt and lemon juice to taste and serve at room temperature.

Makes 4 to 6 servings.

Banda Govi Taareko
STIR-FRIED CABBAGE

Cabbage (banda govi) is one of the most widely used cold-weather vegetables. It is inexpensive, keeps for a long time, and is readily available almost year-round. Briefly stir-frying the cabbage in a spice-infused oil retains the freshness of the vegetable and preserves the nutrients. Overcooking the cabbage will make it mushy with a dull color.

1 small head green cabbage, shredded ¼ inch thick (10 cups)	1 medium clove garlic, minced
	½ teaspoon ground turmeric
3 tablespoons vegetable oil	¼ teaspoon ground cumin
1 dried red chili, halved and seeded	¼ teaspoon ground coriander
	¼ teaspoon ground black pepper
½ teaspoon cumin seeds	A small pinch ground asafetida
¼ teaspoon fenugreek seeds	½ teaspoon salt
1½ teaspoons peeled minced fresh ginger	

Rinse and drain the cabbage, and set aside.

Heat the oil in a large skillet over medium-high heat. When the oil is hot, but not smoking, add the dried chili, cumin, and fenugreek and fry until dark brown and fragrant, about 5 seconds. Add the ginger, garlic, turmeric, cumin, coriander, black pepper, and asafetida and stir for about 30 seconds. Add the cabbage and salt, and cook uncovered, stirring frequently, until the liquid evaporates and the cabbage is tender but still crunchy, about 15 minutes. Transfer the cabbage to a serving dish and serve.

Makes 4 to 6 servings.

Ramechhap ko Banda-Govi Tarkaari
RAMECHHAP-STYLE CABBAGE

My daughter, Sapana, who spent a summer volunteering at the Taamakoshi Healthcare project in the Manthali District of Ramechhap, contributed this simple and flavorful dish. She learned to prepare cabbage, a favorite vegetable in this hilly part of Nepal, by cooking it in spice-infused oil with potatoes and tomatoes. The cabbage is cooked in its own juice until it starts to lose its crispness. It is served with freshly boiled plain rice. Sapana enjoyed this dish while she was there, and it is now her favorite way of cooking green cabbage.

1 small head green cabbage, shredded ¼ inch thick (10 cups)	2 tablespoons vegetable oil
	½ teaspoon fenugreek seeds
1 teaspoon cumin seeds	2 medium red potatoes, peeled and thinly sliced
1 teaspoon coriander seeds	½ teaspoon ground turmeric
1 tablespoon minced fresh ginger	4 whole Szechwan peppercorns (*timmur*)
2 medium cloves garlic	
2 dried red chilies, 1 crumbled and soaked in 2 tablespoons warm water, and 1 halved and seeded	A small pinch ground asafetida
	1 medium tomato, finely chopped (about 1 cup)
	1 teaspoon salt

Rinse and drain the cabbage, and set aside.

Place the cumin and coriander seeds in a mortar and pound with a pestle until finely ground. Add the ginger, garlic, and the crumbled chili with the soaking water and pound to a smooth paste, adding 1 additional teaspoon of water, if necessary. Set aside.

Heat the oil in a heavy saucepan over medium-high heat. When the oil is hot, but not smoking, add the fenugreek and halved dried chili, and fry until dark brown and fragrant, about 5 seconds. Add the potatoes, turmeric, *timmur*, and asafetida and fry until the potatoes turn golden brown and are nearly cooked, about 10 minutes. Mix in the spice paste and stir for 1 minute. Add the cabbage, tomatoes, and salt and cook, stirring frequently, until the cabbage just begins to soften, about 10 minutes. Transfer the mixture to a serving dish and serve.

Makes 4 to 6 servings.

Phool-Govi, Alu, Kerau Tarkaari
CAULIFLOWER WITH POTATO AND PEAS

Cauliflower is one of the most beloved vegetables in Nepal. The golden rule is not to overcook it or it will become mushy.

1 medium-size head cauliflower
½ cup mustard oil
2 dried red chilies, stemmed
¼ teaspoon fenugreek seeds
¼ teaspoon cumin seeds
¼ teaspoon Himalayan herb (*jimbu*)
2 small red potatoes, peeled and cut into 1-inch cubes
2 green cardamom pods, crushed
1 (1-inch) stick cinnamon, halved
½ teaspoon ground turmeric
1 bay leaf
2 whole cloves
1 tablespoon minced fresh ginger

1½ teaspoons ground coriander
1 teaspoon ground cumin
1 teaspoon salt
½ teaspoon cayenne pepper
1 cup shelled fresh peas
1 small red or green bell pepper, cored and cut into 1-inch pieces (about 1 cup)
½ cup finely chopped cilantro
3 to 4 green onions (white and pale green parts), finely chopped
1 teaspoon Nepali Garam Masala (page 398)

Break the cauliflower into 1½-inch florets. Discard any yellow leaves, but reserve the tender green leaves attached to the stem. Peel the stem and cut into ½-inch pieces. Heat the mustard oil in a wide, heavy saucepan over medium-high heat until faintly smoking. Add the dried chili, fenugreek, cumin, and *jimbu* and fry until several shades darker and fully fragrant, about 5 seconds. Immediately add the potatoes, cardamom pods, cinnamon, turmeric, bay leaf, and cloves. Cook, stirring frequently, until the potatoes are light brown, 5 to 7 minutes. With a slotted spoon, transfer the potatoes to a bowl, draining as much oil as possible. Add the cauliflower, leaves, and stem to the pan and cook, stirring frequently, for 5 minutes. Stir in the ginger, coriander, cumin, salt, and cayenne pepper. Reduce the heat to medium, cover the pan, and cook, stirring gently, until the cauliflower is lightly browned and half cooked, about 15 minutes. Mix in the reserved potatoes, peas, and bell pepper and cook, covered, until the vegetables are tender, 10 to 12 minutes. Stir gently to avoid breaking the florets. Stir in the cilantro, green onions, and garam masala. Transfer to a serving dish and serve.

Makes 4 to 6 servings.

Piro Makai ko Tarkaari
SPICY FRESH CORN

This simple corn dish is extremely flavorful and delicious, and can be served as a snack or as a side dish. For this recipe, be sure to use fresh corn. To inspect the corn for freshness, peel back the husk, and then puncture the exposed kernels. If the juice is milky and the kernels are plump, it is fresh. Over-matured corn will not be juicy and will be hard to puncture.

3 tablespoons clarified butter (*gheu*)
½ teaspoon cumin seeds
2 fresh hot green chilies, chopped
2 medium cloves garlic, chopped
I teaspoon peeled and finely chopped fresh ginger
6 cups fresh corn kernels (from 6 to 8 ears)
½ teaspoon salt
I teaspoon Nepali Garam Masala (page 398)
½ teaspoon cayenne pepper
¼ cup finely chopped cilantro

Heat the clarified butter in a skillet or heavy saucepan over medium-high heat. When hot, but not smoking, add the cumin seeds and fry until lightly browned and fragrant, about 5 seconds. Add the green chilies, garlic, and ginger and fry until crisp, about I minute. Stir in the corn and salt. Reduce the heat to medium-low, cover, and cook, stirring occasionally, until the kernels are tender and all the liquid has evaporated, 8 to 10 minutes. Stir in the garam masala and cayenne pepper and cook for I minute more. Add the cilantro and mix well. Transfer to a serving dish and serve.

Makes 4 to 6 servings.

Ikush ko Tarkaari
SPICED CHAYOTE SQUASH

Chayote (ikush) is a type of squash that grows on a climbing vine. The plant produces a light green fruit, resembling a pear, with crispy white flesh and a single large, soft seed. Be sure to select young unblemished chayotes for the freshest flavor. While cutting this vegetable, place it under running water to prevent skin irritation from the sticky substance that it releases. Chayote squash is available at Asian markets and some large supermarkets.

2 tablespoons vegetable oil	2 medium cloves garlic, minced
¼ teaspoon fenugreek seeds	I tablespoon minced fresh ginger
½ teaspoon brown mustard seeds	I teaspoon ground cumin
4 medium fresh chayote squash, peeled, seeded, and thinly sliced	½ teaspoon salt
	½ teaspoon cayenne pepper
	¼ teaspoon ground turmeric
	A small pinch ground asafetida

Heat the oil in a medium-size saucepan over medium-high heat. When the oil is hot, but not smoking, add the fenugreek and mustard seeds and fry until the fenugreek darkens, the mustard seeds pop, and they are fully fragrant, about 5 seconds. You may want to cover the pan, as mustard seeds splatter when heated. Add the chayote, garlic, ginger, cumin, salt, cayenne pepper, turmeric, and asafetida and cook, stirring constantly, for 5 minutes. Reduce the heat to medium-low, cover the pan, and cook, stirring as needed, until the vegetables are tender but not mushy, about 20 minutes. Transfer the chayote to a serving dish and serve.

Makes 4 to 6 servings.

Hariyo Chana ko Tarkaari
FRESH GREEN CHICKPEAS

Hariyo chana *is the Nepali name for young, tender, unripe chickpeas. They are slightly larger than ordinary chickpeas, irregularly shaped, and somewhat wrinkled. The shelled green chickpeas are crispy with a delicate nut-like flavor. A favorite snack in Nepal, green chickpeas are shelled and eaten raw or cooked as a side dish. Shelling is a tedious job because each pod must be peeled individually, and a single pod encloses only one bean. To ensure a delicate flavor, use only the freshest chickpeas and avoid dried, yellowing pods. Green chickpeas may sometimes be found in farmer's markets, but if they are not available, substitute frozen green chickpeas or green soybeans (edamame).*

6 cups unshelled green chickpeas (4 cups shelled)	2 medium cloves garlic, minced
2 tablespoons clarified butter (*gheu*)	2 teaspoons minced fresh ginger
	½ teaspoon salt
2 fresh mild or hot green chilies, stemmed and chopped	½ teaspoon ground cumin
	⅛ teaspoon freshly ground black pepper
2 large shallots, minced	⅛ teaspoon ground turmeric

To shell the chickpeas, pull the string on each pod and they will pop open. Remove the chickpeas, rinse, drain, and set aside.

Heat the clarified butter in a heavy skillet over medium heat. Add the green chilies, shallots, garlic, and ginger and cook, stirring constantly, until soft, about 5 minutes. Add the green chickpeas, salt, cumin, black pepper, and turmeric and mix well. Adjust the heat to medium-low, cover the skillet, and cook, stirring frequently, until the chickpeas are tender, 10 to 12 minutes. Transfer the chickpeas to a serving dish and serve.

Makes 4 to 6 servings.

Nepali Bhanta Tarkaari
SAUTÉED ASIAN EGGPLANT

Called bhanta *in Nepalese, the Asian variety of eggplant (also known as Japanese or Chinese eggplant) is very popular in Nepal. They are usually smaller, slimmer, and slightly sweeter than large oval or round ones. They are nearly seedless, very tender, and cook quickly. This dish will deliciously complement any Nepali meal.*

2 tablespoons vegetable oil	1½ teaspoons ground coriander
½ teaspoon cumin seeds	1 teaspoon ground cumin
2 medium onions, thinly sliced	½ teaspoon cayenne pepper
1 tablespoon minced fresh ginger	½ teaspoon salt
2 medium cloves garlic, chopped	⅛ teaspoon freshly ground
½ teaspoon ground turmeric	black pepper
5 to 6 medium Asian eggplants	2 medium tomatoes, chopped
(about 2 pounds), sliced	(about 2 cups)
diagonally into ½-inch-thick	
pieces or lengthwise into	
¼-inch slices	

Heat the oil in a heavy saucepan over medium-high heat. When the oil is hot, but not smoking, add the cumin seeds and fry until lightly browned and fragrant, about 5 seconds. Add the onions, ginger, garlic, and turmeric and cook, stirring frequently, until the onions soften, about 5 minutes. Stir in the eggplant, coriander, cumin, cayenne pepper, salt, and black pepper. Reduce the heat to medium-low, cover the pan, and cook, stirring from time to time, until the eggplant is halfway cooked, 5 to 7 minutes. Stir in the tomatoes and cook until the liquid evaporates and the eggplant is tender, 8 to 10 minutes. Transfer the eggplant to a serving dish and serve.

Makes 4 to 6 servings.

Bhanta Saandheko
ROASTED EGGPLANT WITH SESAME SEEDS

For this dish, choose a variety of eggplant with a lot of pulp, rather than the slim Asian variety, making sure that they are plump, firm, and glossy.

¼ cup sesame seeds
1 large or 2 medium eggplants (about 2½ pounds total)
½ cup finely chopped cilantro
1½ tablespoons fresh lemon or lime juice
1 teaspoon cayenne pepper or to taste
1 teaspoon salt
2 tablespoons vegetable oil

⅛ teaspoon fenugreek seeds
½ teaspoon Himalayan herb (*jimbu*)
2 fresh hot or mild green chilies, julienned
4 medium cloves garlic, thinly sliced
1 tablespoon peeled and finely julienned fresh ginger
½ teaspoon ground turmeric

Heat a small cast-iron skillet over medium heat and toast the sesame seeds, stirring constantly to prevent the seeds from flying all over, until they give off a pleasant aroma and darken, 2 to 3 minutes. Pour the sesame seeds into a dry container to halt the toasting and let them cool. Transfer the seeds to a spice grinder, grind to a fine powder, and set aside.

Preheat a charcoal or gas grill to medium-high heat or preheat the broiler. Prick the eggplants all over with a fork or the tip of a knife to speed the cooking and to allow the steam to escape. Roast the eggplants over the grill, turning frequently, to cook on all sides. The eggplant is done when the skin wrinkles, the juice seeps out, and it releases a pleasant smoky aroma, 30 to 40 minutes, depending on the size of the eggplant. Set the cooked eggplant aside until cool enough to handle. Peel off the charred skin and remove and discard as many seeds as possible. The skins should come off easily. Mash the pulp by hand or with a fork and mix it with the ground sesame, cilantro, lemon juice, cayenne pepper, and salt and set aside.

Heat the oil in a small skillet over medium-high heat until hot, but not smoking. Add the fenugreek seeds and *jimbu*, and fry until dark brown and fully fragrant, about 5 seconds. Add the green chilies, garlic, ginger, and turmeric and fry until crisp, but not brown, about 7 seconds. Immediately pour the entire contents into the eggplant mixture. Stir well, cover the bowl, and allow the seasoning to develop for 20 minutes or more. Transfer the eggplant to a serving dish and serve.

Makes 4 to 6 servings.

Neuro ko Tarkaari
SAUTÉED FIDDLEHEAD FERNS

Fiddlehead ferns (neuro) are the young shoots of edible ferns. They resemble the spiral end of a fiddle, for which they are named, and taste similar to asparagus and okra. They are extremely perishable and need to be cooked shortly after picking. Fiddlehead ferns are available neatly bundled in specialty food stores or occasionally at well-stocked larger supermarkets.

1 to 2 bunches young fiddlehead ferns (6 cups chopped)	2 medium cloves garlic, chopped
2 tablespoons clarified butter (*gheu*)	1½ teaspoons peeled and julienned fresh ginger
¼ teaspoon fenugreek seeds	¼ teaspoon ground turmeric
2 fresh mild green chilies, halved lengthwise	½ teaspoon salt
	½ teaspoon ground cumin
	½ teaspoon ground coriander

Remove the fuzzy coatings of the fiddleheads by rubbing them between your hands. Trim and discard the tough ends and cut the fiddleheads into 1-inch pieces. Rinse under cold water, drain, and set aside.

Heat the clarified butter in a heavy-bottomed wide skillet over medium-high heat. When hot, but not smoking, add the fenugreek seeds and fry until dark brown and highly fragrant, about 5 seconds. Add the green chilies, garlic, ginger, and turmeric and stir well. Add the fiddleheads and salt, and cook, uncovered stirring frequently, for 5 minutes. Add the cumin and coriander and cook, covered, until the fiddleheads are tender, 5 to 7 minutes. Transfer the fiddleheads to a serving dish and serve.

Makes 4 to 6 servings.

Saandheko Neuro
FIDDLEHEAD FERN SALAD

Here is a simple, delicious way of preparing the edible shoots of the fern plant. The shoots remain coiled for a few days, before they uncurl into lacy leaves, which cannot be cooked as they become stringy and bitter.

3 small red-skin potatoes	½ teaspoon cayenne pepper
1 or 2 bunches young fiddlehead ferns (6 cups chopped)	⅛ teaspoon Szechwan pepper (*timmur*), finely ground with a mortar and pestle
2 tablespoons sesame seeds	1 tablespoon mustard oil
1 tablespoon fresh lemon or lime juice	¼ teaspoon fenugreek seeds
½ teaspoon salt	½ teaspoon ground turmeric

In a medium-size saucepan, combine the potatoes and water to cover, and bring to a boil over high heat. Reduce the heat to low, cover, and cook until tender, about 15 minutes. Drain until cool enough to handle, peel, and cut into ½-inch cubes. Set aside.

Bring a small pot of salted water to a rolling boil over medium-high heat. Remove the fuzzy paper-like covering of the fiddleheads by rubbing them between your hands. Trim and discard the tough ends, cut the fiddleheads into 1-inch pieces, rinse under cold water, and drain. Add a few drops of lemon juice and the fiddleheads to the boiling water and boil until they are crisp-tender, 3 to 4 minutes. Drain and run under cold water to halt the cooking. Transfer to a bowl and set aside.

Heat a small cast-iron skillet over medium heat and toast the sesame seeds, stirring constantly to prevent them from flying all over, until they give off a pleasant aroma and darken, 2 to 3 minutes. Remove from the skillet and pour into a dry container to halt the toasting. When cool transfer to a spice grinder and grind to a fine powder. In a bowl, combine the fiddleheads, potatoes, ground sesame seeds, lemon juice, salt, cayenne pepper, and *timmur.*

Heat the mustard oil in a small skillet over medium-high heat until the oil is faintly smoking. Add the fenugreek seeds and fry until dark brown and fully fragrant, about 5 seconds. Sprinkle in the turmeric and immediately pour the spiced oil into the fiddlehead mixture. Stir well, cover the bowl, and allow the seasonings to develop for at least 20 minutes. Transfer the mixture to a serving dish and serve.

Makes 4 to 6 servings.

Rukh-Katahar ko Tarkaari
GREEN JACKFRUIT CURRY

Jackfruit (rukh-katahar) is a large, oblong tree-borne fruit with bumpy, hard green skin. It is eaten as a vegetable when green and a dessert when it is ripe. In this recipe, the young green fruit is cut into chunks and simmered with yogurt and spices. Fresh jackfruit is available at Asian food stores, but it is available canned at Indian, Asian, and specialty food markets. This recipe can be prepared from the canned variety, but make sure they are rinsed in several changes of water before using.

In Nepal, green jackfruit is considered a festive vegetable. In the Hindu marriage ceremonies of some Brahmin families, the bride's family does not serve meat. Instead, unripened jackfruit is substituted during the wedding feast. It is believed that the texture and flavor of cooked jackfruit is similar to meat.

2 dried red chilies, halved
¼ cup hot water
1 small fresh green jackfruit
  (about 8 cups after trimming)
1 medium onion, roughly
  chopped (about 1 cup)
1½ tablespoons peeled and
  roughly chopped fresh ginger
4 medium cloves garlic, peeled
1 tablespoon ground coriander
1½ teaspoons ground cumin
½ teaspoon ground turmeric

¼ teaspoon freshly ground black
  pepper
¾ cup vegetable oil
1 (2-inch) stick cinnamon, halved
4 green cardamom pods, crushed
4 whole cloves
2 bay leaves
3 medium tomatoes, chopped
  (about 3 cups)
1 teaspoon salt
1 cup plain yogurt, stirred
1 teaspoon Nepali Garam Masala
  (page 398)
½ cup finely chopped cilantro

Soak the chilies in the hot water until soft.

Before handling the jackfruit, rub your hands and knife with oil. When the fruit is cut, a copious gummy latex accumulates that may irritate bare skin. Peel the exterior covering off the fruit and cut the fruit into 1½-inch pieces and set aside.

Place the onion, ginger, garlic, chilies and soaking water, coriander, cumin, turmeric, and black pepper in a food processor or blender and process, adding 1 to 2 tablespoons of water if needed, to make a smooth paste. Transfer the paste to a small bowl and set aside.

Heat the oil in a heavy saucepan over medium-high heat. When the oil is hot, but not smoking, add the cinnamon, cardamom pods, cloves, and bay leaves and fry until they begin to puff up, darken, and give off a pleasant aroma, about 5 seconds. Reduce the heat to medium, add the spice paste, and fry, stirring constantly, until it is light brown, 3 to 4 minutes. Add the tomatoes and cook until they soften and all the juices evaporate, about 5 minutes. Add the jackfruit and cook, stirring for 5 minutes. Add ½ cup of water and the salt and bring the mixture to a boil. Reduce the heat to medium-low, cover the pan, and continue cooking, stirring occasionally, until the jackfruit is soft and most of the water has evaporated, about 15 minutes. Mix in the yogurt 1 tablespoon at a time, stirring vigorously and constantly until well combined. Add the garam masala and continue cooking until the liquid has evaporated and the sauce has thickened and coats the jackfruit, about 5 minutes. Transfer the jackfruit to a serving dish and sprinkle with the cilantro. Serve hot.

Makes 4 to 6 servings.

Gyanth-Govi ko Tarkaari
SPICED KOHLRABI

Kohlrabi (gyanth govi) is a round, green bulb somewhat resembling a turnip. For this recipe, select small, young, tender bulbs, for they will produce a milder flavor and crisper texture. The richly colored greens are also edible and are often cooked with the bulb.

6 to 8 small kohlrabi (about 2 pounds)	I medium clove garlic, finely chopped
2 tablespoons vegetable oil	½ teaspoon salt
½ teaspoon fenugreek seeds	½ teaspoon ground cumin
I teaspoon minced fresh ginger	¼ teaspoon cayenne pepper
	¼ teaspoon ground turmeric

Remove the leaves from the kohlrabi and save them for future use. Slice off the top end of the bulbs and pull off the skins, which will come off easily. If the bulbs are very tender, do not peel them. Cut the kohlrabi into I-inch pieces.

Heat the oil in a heavy saucepan over medium-high heat. When the oil is hot, but not smoking, add the fenugreek seeds and fry until dark brown and fully fragrant, about 5 seconds. Add the kohlrabi and cook, stirring, for 4 to 5 minutes. Add the ginger, garlic, salt, cumin, cayenne pepper, and turmeric and mix well. Reduce the heat to medium-low, cover the pan, and cook, stirring from time to time, until the kohlrabi is just tender, about 20 minutes. Transfer the kohlrabi to a serving dish and serve.

Makes 4 to 6 servings.

Chyau ko Tarkaari
MUSHROOM CURRY

Many Nepalese consider mushrooms (chyau) a delicacy. This recipe works best with oyster mushrooms, which offer a delicate, mild, and velvety texture, but can be cooked with any variety of mushrooms.

1 pound fresh oyster mushrooms	1½ teaspoons minced fresh ginger
2 tablespoons mustard oil	½ teaspoon ground turmeric
¼ teaspoon fenugreek seeds	A small pinch ground asafetida
⅛ teaspoon Himalayan herb (*jimbu*)	1 teaspoon ground coriander
	½ teaspoon ground cumin
1 medium onion, finely chopped (about 1 cup)	½ teaspoon salt
	½ teaspoon cayenne pepper
2 fresh mild or hot green chilies, halved lengthwise	⅛ teaspoon Szechwan pepper (*timmur*), finely ground with a mortar and pestle
2 medium cloves garlic, minced	

Rinse the mushrooms under running cold water and drain. Do not leave them in the water for a long time, as they become water logged. Cut off about 1 inch from the bottom of the stems and discard. Break the mushrooms into bite-size pieces and set aside.

Heat the mustard oil in a wide skillet over medium-high heat until faintly smoking. Add the fenugreek seeds and *jimbu*, and fry until dark brown and highly fragrant, about 5 seconds. Add the onion, green chilies, garlic, ginger, turmeric, and asafetida and fry until the onion softens, about 5 minutes. Add the mushrooms, coriander, cumin, salt, cayenne pepper, and *timmur* and cook, uncovered, stirring frequently until most of the liquid has evaporated, about 10 minutes. Transfer the mushrooms to a serving dish and serve.

Makes 4 to 6 servings.

Sit le Khaeko Raayo ko Saag
SPICED MUSTARD GREENS

Young tender mustard greens (raayo ko saag) are one of the most common and popular vegetables in Nepal and are grown in abundance. In the winter months, when the pungent leaves are exposed to frost, they become very tender and delicate. Sit le khaeko saag *literally translates as "mustard greens tenderized by frost," and are among the most tender and delicious greens. You may use the mustard shoots (raayo ko duku), which form as the mustard plant matures.*

2 to 3 bunches fresh mustard greens (about 2 pounds)	2 dried red chilies, halved and seeded
3 tablespoons mustard oil	2 medium cloves garlic, minced
¼ teaspoon ajowan seeds	1½ teaspoon minced fresh ginger
	¼ teaspoon salt

Tear the mustard greens into bite-size pieces. Rinse the torn mustard greens in cold water. Drain and reserve.

Heat the mustard oil in a heavy saucepan over medium-high heat, until faintly smoking. Add the ajowan seeds and dried chilies and fry until lightly browned and fragrant, about 5 seconds. Add the mustard greens, garlic, ginger, and salt. Cover the pan and cook, stirring occasionally, until the greens become tender and most of the liquid evaporates, 10 to 12 minutes. Transfer the greens to a serving dish and serve immediately.

Makes 4 to 6 servings.

Sishnu ko Tarkaari
SPICED NETTLES

Sishnu is the Nepali name for edible stinging nettles which are popular in areas where there is a scarcity of vegetables. Bhagavati Bajai, an elderly Nepali woman, showed me how to pick and cook nettles. I was afraid to prepare this wild vegetable at first, because the sting of this plant is not a pleasant one. Cooking the young, tender shoots eliminates, however, their stinging effect. It is also very important that bare hands do not touch the raw vegetable so handle them with tongs (chimta). This is a unique dish and is worth trying if you can get a hold of nettles!

1 to 2 bunches (8 cups) nettle shoots	1 dried red chili, halved and seeded
1 tablespoon plus 1½ teaspoons mustard oil	¼ teaspoon salt

Wash the nettles thoroughly in several changes of water, using tongs or rubber gloves.

Heat the mustard oil in a skillet over medium-high heat. When hot, add the dried chili and fry until it becomes reddish-brown and fully fragrant, about 5 seconds. Add the nettles and salt, cover the pan, reduce the heat to medium-low, and cook, stirring occasionally, until tender. Serve immediately with rice.

Makes 4 to 6 servings.

Taareko Raam-Toriya
SAUTÉED OKRA

Okra (raam toriya), also called lady's finger, is a summer vegetable that is beloved in Nepal. It is picked while still young and tender, because once it matures it becomes fibrous and tough. The following recipe is delicious, flavorful, and easy to prepare, but be sure to wash the whole okra pods before cutting. If you wash chopped okra, it becomes sticky and slippery. Also, stir the okra as gently as possible, as over-stirring may break the okra into small pieces, which will become sticky and cling to the pan.

¼ cup vegetable oil
½ teaspoon cumin seeds
½ teaspoon ajowan seeds
½ teaspoon ground turmeric
2 pounds okra, trimmed and
    cut into ¼-inch pieces

I tablespoon peeled and finely
    chopped fresh ginger
2 medium cloves garlic, finely
    chopped
½ teaspoon salt
½ teaspoon cayenne pepper

Heat the oil in a cast-iron or nonstick skillet over medium-high heat. When the oil is hot, but not smoking, add the cumin and ajowan seeds, and fry until they are lightly browned and fragrant, about 5 seconds. Add the turmeric and okra and stir for I minute. Reduce the heat to medium, add the ginger, garlic, salt, and cayenne pepper and mix well. Cook, stirring gently, until the okra is tender and light brown, 12 to 15 minutes. Transfer the okra to a serving dish and serve.

Okra with Potatoes: Sauté 2 peeled and diced medium red potatoes until golden before adding the okra.

Makes 4 to 6 servings.

Raam Toriya ko Ras Tarkaari
OKRA, TOMATO, AND ONION MEDLEY

The following vegetable dish is flavorful and easy to prepare. When preparing okra, always use fresh small to medium pods that are plump and free of blemishes. The pods should snap easily when broken in half.

2 pounds okra, trimmed and halved lengthwise
2 tablespoons fresh lemon or lime juice
1 teaspoon salt
¼ cup vegetable oil
2 medium onions, halved lengthwise and thinly sliced
1 tablespoon minced fresh ginger
2 medium cloves garlic, minced

1½ teaspoons ground coriander
1 teaspoon ground cumin
½ teaspoon ground turmeric
¼ teaspoon cayenne pepper
⅛ teaspoon freshly ground black pepper
2 medium tomatoes, chopped (about 2 cups)
¼ cup finely chopped cilantro

In a bowl, combine the okra with the lemon juice and ½ teaspoon of the salt. Mix well and set aside for 10 to 15 minutes. This helps to reduce the sticky juice released during cooking. Drain and set aside.

Heat the oil in a heavy saucepan over medium-high heat. When the oil is hot, add the onions, ginger and garlic and cook, stirring frequently, until light brown, 5 to 7 minutes. Add the coriander, cumin, turmeric, cayenne pepper, and black pepper and mix well. Toss in the tomatoes and remaining ½ teaspoon of salt and cook until the tomatoes soften, 4 to 5 minutes.

Add the okra, mix well, and cook for 1 minute. Reduce the heat to medium-low, cover the pan, and simmer until the okra is tender and moist. Stir very gently, being careful not to crush the okra. Transfer the mixture to a serving dish. Mix in the chopped cilantro and serve hot.

Makes 4 to 6 servings.

Kerau ko Tarkaari
BUTTERED PEAS WITH GARLIC AND SPICES

In this simple recipe, tender fresh peas are quickly simmered in clarified butter with a hint of fresh herbs and spices. This cooking method brings out the bright green color of the peas and maintains their sweet flavor. Overcooking robs the peas of their sweetness. This recipe works best with freshly shelled peas, but if they are not available, substitute frozen peas, which are also delicious.

3 tablespoons clarified butter (*gheu*)	¼ teaspoon ground turmeric
¼ teaspoon cumin seeds	A small pinch ground asafetida
2 fresh hot or mild green chilies, split lengthwise	4 cups shelled green peas
8 medium cloves garlic, peeled	½ teaspoon salt
1 tablespoon peeled and finely julienned fresh ginger	1 teaspoon Nepali Garam Masala (page 398)

Heat the clarified butter in a saucepan over medium-high heat. When hot, but not smoking, add the cumin seeds and fry until lightly browned and fragrant, about 5 seconds. Add the green chilies, garlic, ginger, turmeric, and asafetida and fry for 1 minute. Stir in the peas and salt and cook for 5 minutes. Reduce the heat to medium, cover the pan, and cook until the peas are tender and all the juices have evaporated, 8 to 10 minutes. Add the garam masala and stir for 2 minutes. Transfer the peas to a serving dish and serve warm.

Makes 4 to 6 servings.

Kerau ko Munta Tarkaari
PEA VINE SHOOTS

Kerau ko munta *is the Nepali name for pea shoots, which are the tender uppermost green leaves and tendrils of the young pea plant. These delicate shoots are as sweet as fresh peas. The shoots are typically harvested from pea vines before the pods form. The tender shoots are pinched in the uppermost section (about 3 to 4 inches) from the growing point of the plants. These light and flavorful shoots can be eaten raw or lightly stir-fried. They have traditionally been a popular spring delicacy in Asia, and are just beginning to emerge in other parts of the world because of their great taste and nutritional value. Pea shoots are very perishable, and should be used immediately, before they lose their flavor. Look for them at your local farmer's market or in Asian food stores in spring, early summer, and fall.*

I large bunch fresh young pea shoots (about 1½ pounds)
I tablespoon vegetable oil
I medium clove garlic, finely chopped
I teaspoon peeled and finely chopped fresh ginger
¼ teaspoon salt
⅛ teaspoon cayenne pepper

Pick off and discard any tough, large stems and bruised leaves from the pea shoots. Cut the large leaves into 1-inch pieces, but leave the small leaves attached to the stems. Rinse under cold water, drain, and set aside.

Heat the oil in a wide skillet over medium-high heat. When the oil is hot, add the garlic and ginger, and fry until slightly crisp, for less than 1 minute. Add the pea shoots, salt, and cayenne pepper, and cook, stirring frequently, until just tender enough, 5 to 7 minutes. Serve immediately.

Makes 4 to 6 servings.

Chhana-Kerau Tarkaari
PEAS AND CHHANA OR CHEESE

This classic dish originated in northern India, but the Nepalese have adapt-ed it to suit their palate. The traditional version calls for fresh homemade chhana, but you may substitute store-bought paneer cheese. Fresh basket cheese or farmer's cheese are equally delicious substitutes, if ready-made paneer is not available.

2 tablespoons vegetable oil
½ recipe Homemade Chhana (Paneer) Cheese (page 396) or 8 ounces store-bought paneer cheese, cut into ½-inch cubes
3 tablespoons clarified butter (*gheu*)
1 (1-inch) stick cinnamon, halved lengthwise
½ teaspoon cumin seeds
2 bay leaves
½ teaspoon ground turmeric
A small pinch ground asafetida
2 medium onions, finely chopped (about 2 cups)

4 medium cloves garlic, minced
1 tablespoon minced fresh ginger
2 medium tomatoes, finely chopped (about 2 cups)
1 tablespoon ground coriander
1½ teaspoons ground cumin
1 teaspoon salt
1 teaspoon cayenne pepper, or to taste
1 cup plain yogurt mixed with ½ cup of cold water
4 cups frozen peas, thawed and thoroughly drained
½ cup finely chopped cilantro

Heat the oil in a nonstick skillet over medium-low heat. Sauté the cheese cubes in a single layer, turning gently and frequently, until golden brown on all sides, 2 to 3 minutes. With a slotted spoon, remove them, draining as much oil as possible, and transfer them to a paper towel-lined plate to drain. Repeat the process with the remaining cheese. Set aside.

Heat the butter in a heavy saucepan over medium-high heat. When hot, but not smoking, add the cinnamon, cumin, and bay leaves and fry until lightly browned and fragrant, about 5 seconds. Add the turmeric and asafetida, fol-lowed by the onions, garlic, and ginger. Cook, stirring occasionally, until light brown, 5 to 7 minutes.

Reduce the heat to medium, add the tomatoes, coriander, cumin, salt, and cayenne pepper, and mix well. Cover the pan, and cook until the tomatoes are soft and the liquid evaporates, about 5 minutes. Pour in the yogurt mixture and bring the sauce to a boil. Add the peas and browned cheese, and cook, stirring frequently, until the peas are tender and the cheese cubes absorb the sauce, about 10 minutes. The finished product should have a thick sauce, but if you prefer it thinner, add ½ cup of water and bring it to a boil. Mix in the cilantro, transfer it to a serving dish, and serve.

Note: If you are using fresh basket cheese or farmer's cheese, bring the cheese to room temperature before using. Place the cubed cheese on a paper towel to remove any excess moisture before browning. Group the pieces into batches and fry a few at a time. This type of cheese is a little salty, so adjust the seasoning accordingly.

Makes 6 to 8 servings.

Parvar-Alu ko Tarkaari
SAUTÉED PARVAR AND POTATO

Pointed gourd (parvar or parwar) is a tropical vegetable with origins in the Indian subcontinent. The pale green fruit is oblong, tapered at both ends, and marked with a few irregular stripes. Prized for its nutritional value and digestibility, it can be used to make soup, which soothes stomach disorders. It is also delicious simply stir-fried or stewed in a spicy sauce, boiled, or curried and stuffed. Parvar is considered a luxury and is expensive. Fresh parvar is occasionally available in Indian grocery stores, soaked in water to maintain freshness. If fresh parvar is not available, it can also be found frozen and canned in Indian markets. Canned parvar, however, does not have much flavor.

1½ pounds fresh *parvar*	½ teaspoon ground turmeric
¼ cup vegetable oil	2 bay leaves
2 dried red chilies, halved and seeded	A small pinch ground asafetida
	1 tablespoon minced fresh ginger
½ teaspoon fenugreek seeds	3 medium cloves garlic, minced
½ teaspoon ajowan seeds	1 teaspoon ground cumin
3 medium red potatoes, peeled and sliced ¼ inch thick	1½ teaspoons ground coriander
	½ teaspoon salt

With a sharp knife, lightly scrape off the outer coating of each *parvar*. Cut off the pointed top and discard. Halve lengthwise and scoop out the mature seeds, leaving the young seeds intact. Rinse, drain, and set aside.

Heat the oil in a large skillet over medium-high heat until hot, but not smoking. Add the dried chilies, fenugreek, and ajowan and fry until dark brown and fully fragrant, about 5 seconds. Add the potatoes, turmeric, bay leaves, and asafetida. Cook, stirring frequently, until the potatoes are halfway cooked and beginning to brown. Add the *parvar* and cook for 5 minutes. Stir in the ginger, garlic, cumin, coriander, and salt. Reduce the heat to medium-low, cover, and continue cooking until the vegetables are tender. If the liquid evaporates before the vegetables are tender, sprinkle in some water, cover, and cook until tender. Transfer the *parvar* to a platter and serve warm.

Makes 4 to 6 servings.

Bhareko Parvar
STUFFED PARVAR

This is a festive dish cooked for special occasions. Each parvar *is hollowed out, stuffed with ground meat, and cooked until tender. I recommend this recipe only if you have fresh* parvar. *This dish takes time, but the result is extremely rewarding.*

1 pound fresh *parvar*	1 teaspoon Nepali Garam Masala
6 tablespoons vegetable oil	(page 398)
1 medium onion, finely chopped	½ teaspoon ground turmeric
(about 1 cup)	½ teaspoon cayenne pepper
2 large cloves garlic, minced	½ teaspoon salt
1½ teaspoons minced fresh ginger	⅛ teaspoon freshly ground
1 pound ground chicken (or	black pepper
turkey, or half of each)	¼ cup finely chopped cilantro
	2 fresh mild green chilies,
	chopped

With a sharp knife, lightly scrape off the outer coating of the *parvar*. Make a long slit in one side and carefully remove all the seeds to make pockets for stuffing. Sprinkle with salt and set aside.

Heat 2 tablespoons of the oil in a skillet over medium-high heat. Add the onion, garlic, and ginger and cook until lightly browned, 5 to 7 minutes. Add the chicken and cook, stirring to break up the lumps until it is lightly browned, about 10 minutes. Mix in the garam masala, turmeric, cayenne pepper, salt, and black pepper. Reduce the heat to medium-low, cover, and simmer until the meat is cooked through, 10 to 12 minutes. Add the cilantro and green chilies.

Fill each *parvar* with 1 tablespoon of the chicken mixture. Do not overstuff the pockets or the stuffing may come out during the cooking. Secure each squash with kitchen twine.

Heat the remaining ¼ cup of vegetable oil in a wide nonstick skillet over medium-low heat. When the oil is hot, arrange the stuffed *parvar* in the skillet in a single layer. Cook, gently turning, until the parvar are cooked through and light brown on all sides, about 10 minutes. Transfer to a serving dish, remove the twine, and serve hot.

Makes 4 to 6 servings.

Taareko Alu
SPICY SAUTÉED POTATOES

In this recipe, the potato skins are left on because they add an earthy flavor. For best results, use a wide, deep skillet to give the potatoes enough room to brown. Serve as a side dish or a snack with pressed rice flakes (cheura) or warm roti bread.

2 fresh hot green chilies, minced
4 medium cloves garlic, minced
1 tablespoon minced fresh ginger
1 teaspoon ground cumin
1 teaspoon ground coriander
⅛ teaspoon freshly ground black pepper
½ cup mustard oil
1 dried red chili, halved and seeded

1 teaspoon Himalayan herb (*jimbu*)
¼ teaspoon fenugreek seeds
8 medium red potatoes (about 2½ pounds), sliced ½ inch thick
½ teaspoon ground turmeric
A small pinch ground asafetida
1 teaspoon salt

In a small bowl, mix together the green chilies, garlic, ginger, cumin, coriander, and black pepper. Stir in 2 tablespoons of water to make a paste and set aside.

Heat the mustard oil in a cast-iron or nonstick skillet over medium-high heat until the oil faintly smokes. Add the dried chili, *jimbu*, and fenugreek and fry until dark brown and fully fragrant, about 5 seconds. Add the potatoes, turmeric, and asafetida and cook, stirring constantly, until lightly browned and firm, about 7 minutes. Stir in the spice paste and salt. Reduce the heat to medium, cover the pan, and continue cooking, stirring gently, until the potatoes are tender and golden, 7 to 8 minutes. Transfer the potatoes to a serving dish and serve.

Makes 4 to 6 servings.

Useneko Alu
STEAMED NEW POTATOES

Useneko alu *simply means "boiled or steamed potatoes." This recipe is cooked with freshly harvested new potatoes, which have a moister flesh than mature potatoes. The potatoes are steamed in their skins and are served with a freshly ground medley of pungent spices. It is difficult to imagine a Nepali snack without* useneko alu.

2½ pounds new potatoes
1 tablespoon salt
2 medium cloves garlic, peeled
1 (¼-inch) piece fresh ginger, peeled and halved
1 bay leaf

DIPPING SAUCE
4 fresh mild or hot green chilies, or to taste
2 cloves garlic
1½ teaspoons salt
⅛ teaspoon Szechwan pepper (*timmur*)

In a medium-size saucepan, combine the potatoes, salt, garlic, ginger, bay leaf, and enough water to cover, and bring to a boil over high heat. Reduce the heat to low, cover the pan, and continue cooking until the potatoes are tender, about 15 minutes.

While the potatoes are boiling, make the dipping sauce. Place the green chilies, garlic, salt, and timmur in a mortar and pound them with a pestle to create a smooth paste. Place the spice paste in a small bowl and set aside.

Pierce the potatoes with a knife or fork to see if they're done. Do not overcook. Once they are cooked, drain the potatoes in a colander and discard the spices. You may make this dish with peeled or unpeeled potatoes. Transfer the potatoes to a serving dish and serve with the dipping sauce.

Spiced Potato Salad: Toss the potatoes with melted butter, chopped cilantro, chopped green onions, or lemon juice and serve. You may also steam the potatoes instead of boiling. Place the whole unpeeled potatoes in a steamer basket over boiling water and cook, covered, until tender.

Makes 4 to 6 servings.

Alu-Pyaj-Golbheda Tarkaari
POTATO, ONION, AND TOMATO MEDLEY

The following recipe is a succulent combination of potatoes, onions, and toma-toes with several fresh herbs and spices. The vegetables are cooked in their own juices, so they burst with fresh flavor and vibrant color. This dish is served as an everyday side dish with rice, roti bread, or with pressed rice flakes (cheura) for a mid-afternoon snack.

2 tablespoons vegetable oil
4 small onions, cut into wedges
3 to 4 medium red-skin potatoes
  (I pound), peeled and
  quartered
4 medium cloves garlic, chopped
I tablespoon minced fresh ginger
I ½ teaspoons ground coriander
I teaspoon ground cumin
I teaspoon salt

½ teaspoon ground turmeric
¼ teaspoon freshly ground
  black pepper
4 medium tomatoes, cut into
  wedges
2 fresh hot green chilies, chopped
½ cup finely chopped cilantro
3 to 4 green onions (white and
  green parts), finely chopped

Heat the oil in a large, heavy saucepan over medium-high heat. When the oil is hot, but not smoking, add the onion wedges and cook until they just begin to soften, about 5 minutes. Stir in the potatoes, garlic, ginger, coriander, cumin, salt, turmeric, and black pepper. Bring the mixture to a boil. Reduce the heat to medium-low, cover the pan, and continue cooking, stirring from time to time, until the potatoes are half cooked, about 15 minutes.

Uncover and add the tomatoes and green chilies, and cook, stirring gently, until the potatoes are tender, about 10 minutes. The onions should hold their shape and not be mushy. Transfer the mixture to a serving dish. Sprinkle with the cilantro and green onions and serve hot.

Makes 4 to 6 servings.

Pharsi ko Munta
PUMPKIN SHOOTS

Pumpkin shoots (pharsi ko munta) are the young, uppermost tender shoots, tendrils, leaves, and delicate stems from pumpkin plants. They are considered a delicacy. The shoots are harvested from the growing end of the vine (the top 3 to 4 inches) by pinching off the tender ends. The plant will put out a new shoot or growth after the vine has been harvested. Pumpkin shoots have a distinct light flavor that can be described as a cross between squash and spinach. They should be cooked within a day of picking or they will lose their freshness and flavor. Like any leafy green, the volume of this vegetable reduces by half after cooking. Look for these shoots at your local farmer's market or at Indian markets. However, the best way to get them is to grow your own.

1 large bunch pumpkin shoots (8 cups after trimming)	1 large clove garlic, minced
¼ cup clarified butter (gheu)	1½ teaspoons minced fresh ginger
1 dried red chili, halved and seeded	½ teaspoon ground cumin
¼ teaspoon fenugreek seeds	½ teaspoon ground turmeric
	¼ teaspoon salt

Pick through and discard any tough, large stems and matured leaves from the vine shoots. Use only the young shoots with crisp stems and fresh leaves. Snap or bend each stem, remove the fuzzy outer covering and fiber from all sides, and discard. When the fuzzy covering is removed the stems should be shiny. Break the stems into 1½-inch pieces. Separate and tear the leaves into small pieces. Some cooks prefer to remove the tendrils from the pumpkin vine shoots, but I like to include them. Wash, drain, and set the greens aside.

Heat the clarified butter in a heavy saucepan over medium-high heat. When hot, add the dried chili and fenugreek seeds and fry until dark brown and fully fragrant, about 5 seconds. Reduce the heat to medium-low and add the garlic, ginger, cumin, turmeric, salt, and pumpkin shoots. Cover the pan and cook, stirring occasionally, until the shoots are tender and have reduced to half of their original volume, 12 to 15 minutes. Transfer the shoots to a serving dish and serve.

Makes 4 to 6 servings.

Dum-Alu
FRIED POTATOES WITH YOGURT AND SPICES

This is an old family recipe that I have been using for years. It transforms plain potatoes into a dish bursting with flavor. Select smooth-skinned, firm, new potatoes and avoid discolored, bruised, or green-spotted ones. Make sure you use uniformly sized potatoes so they will cook evenly. This recipe can be prepared one day in advance and will taste even better for it because the seasonings will have developed fully.

2 pounds new potatoes
2 cups vegetable oil
2 tablespoons clarified butter
　(*gheu*)
1 (1-inch) stick cinnamon, halved
2 green cardamom pods,
　crushed
2 whole cloves
2 bay leaves
½ teaspoon ground turmeric
A small pinch ground asafetida
2 medium onions, finely chopped
　(about 2 cups)
4 medium cloves garlic, minced
1 tablespoon minced fresh ginger

2 medium tomatoes, chopped
　(about 2 cups)
1½ teaspoons ground coriander
1 teaspoon salt
1 teaspoon ground cumin
1 teaspoon Nepali Garam Masala
　(page 398)
⅛ teaspoon freshly ground
　black pepper
1 cup plain yogurt, stirred
2 to 3 green onions (white and
　pale green parts), finely
　chopped
½ cup finely chopped cilantro
2 hot or mild green chilies,
　chopped

In a medium-size saucepan, place the potatoes and enough water to cover, and bring them to a boil over high heat. Reduce the heat to low and cook until the potatoes are half-cooked, 10 to 12 minutes. Drain and when cool enough to handle, peel the potatoes. Prick each potato all over with a toothpick or fork. This helps the seasoning and sauce to set in. Set aside.

Heat the oil in a deep nonstick skillet over medium-high heat, until hot but not smoking. Add the potatoes, one at a time, in a single layer. You will probably have to do this in two batches. Fry, turning frequently, until they are reddish-brown and a crust begins to form. Remove them with a slotted spoon, draining as much oil as possible, and place on paper towels to drain. Repeat the process with the remaining potatoes. Set aside.

Heat the clarified butter in a large saucepan over medium-high heat. When hot, but not smoking, add the cinnamon, cardamom pods, cloves, and bay leaves and fry until they begin to puff up, darken, and give off a pleasant aroma, about 5 seconds. Add the turmeric and asafetida, followed by the onions, garlic, and ginger, and cook until the onions are soft, about 5 minutes. Stir in the tomatoes, coriander, salt, cumin, garam masala, and black pepper. Cook until the tomatoes soften, all the liquid evaporates, and the oil starts to come away from the sides of the pan. Add the yogurt, 1 tablespoon at a time, mixing to prevent the yogurt from curdling, until it is well-incorporated, 3 to 4 minutes.

Add the browned potatoes and stir gently. Reduce the heat to medium-low, cover the pan, and cook for 5 minutes. Add 1 cup of water and bring the mixture to a boil. Reduce the heat to medium-low, cover the pan, and cook until the sauce has slightly thickened and been absorbed into the potatoes. Remove the pan from heat and let it rest for 10 minutes before serving. Transfer the mixture to a serving dish, mix in the green onions, cilantro, and green chilies, and serve.

Makes 4 to 6 servings.

Paakeko Pharsi ko Tarkaari
YELLOW PUMPKIN CURRY

*The winter vegetable pumpkin (paakeko pharsi) is very common in Nepal.
Pumpkin curry is consumed during the winter months when most fresh veg-
etables are scarce. Peeling this vegetable is somewhat tricky because of its hard
shell. First, cut the pumpkin in half and discard the stem and stringy inside.
You may save the seeds and dry them for future use or toast them for a snack.
This versatile vegetable can be cooked by itself or mixed with lamb or goat.*

¼ cup sesame seeds
3 tablespoons mustard oil
⅛ teaspoon fenugreek seeds
6 cups chopped (1-inch pieces)
  yellow pumpkin
4 hot green chilies, split
  lengthwise
1½ tablespoons minced fresh
  ginger

3 medium cloves garlic, minced
1 teaspoon salt
½ teaspoon ground turmeric
A generous pinch ground asafetida
1½ teaspoons ground coriander
1 teaspoon ground cumin
2 tablespoons fresh lemon or
  lime juice

Heat a small cast-iron skillet over medium heat and toast the sesame seeds, stirring constantly to prevent the seeds from flying all over, until they give off a
pleasant aroma and darken, 2 to 3 minutes. Remove the seeds from the skillet,
pour them into a dry container to halt the toasting, and let them cool. Transfer
the seeds to a spice grinder and grind to a fine powder. Set aside.

Heat the mustard oil in a large saucepan over medium-high heat until faintly
smoking. Add the fenugreek seeds and fry until dark brown and fully fragrant,
about 5 seconds. Add the pumpkin, green chilies, ginger, garlic, salt, turmeric,
and asafetida and mix well. Cook covered, stirring from time to time, until the
pumpkin is soft and tender and can easily be pierced with a fork, about 20
minutes. Add the coriander and cumin and cook until all the liquid has evaporated, 5 to 7 minutes. Remove the pan from the heat and mash the pumpkin
with the back of a spoon. Stir in the toasted sesame seeds and lemon juice. Mix
well and let it stand for 5 minutes before serving. Transfer the pumpkin to a
serving dish and serve warm.

Makes 6 to 8 servings.

Alu Moola ko Tarkaari
WHITE RADISH WITH POTATOES AND TOMATOES

In this recipe, the ever-popular Nepali radish (moola) is cooked with pota-toes, tomatoes, and several fresh herbs and spices. This radish resembles daikon or Japanese radishes, but is more juicy, flavorful, and pungent. Nepalese eat these radishes raw as snacks and cook them in a wide range of dishes. Any variety of white radish will work. They are available in most supermarkets or at Asian or Indian markets.

2 tablespoons vegetable oil
½ teaspoon cumin seeds
1 medium onion, chopped
  (about 1 cup)
2 large cloves garlic, minced
1½ teaspoon minced fresh ginger
¼ teaspoon ground turmeric
3 medium red potatoes (1 pound),
  peeled and cut into
  1-inch cubes
1 teaspoon salt

1 medium white radish or daikon,
  peeled and cut into
  1-inch pieces
2 medium tomatoes, chopped
  (2 cups)
2 fresh hot green chilies,
  chopped
1 teaspoon ground cumin
1 teaspoon ground coriander
¼ cup finely chopped cilantro

Heat the oil in a heavy saucepan over medium-high heat. When the oil is hot, but not smoking, add the cumin seeds and fry until lightly browned and fragrant, about 5 seconds.

Add the onion, garlic, ginger, and turmeric and cook until they are soft. Stir in the potatoes and salt, cover, and cook, stirring frequently, until the potatoes are half cooked, about 10 minutes. Add the radish, tomatoes, green chilies, cumin, and coriander and stir for 2 minutes. Add 1 cup of water and bring the mixture to a boil. Reduce the heat to medium-low, cover, and simmer until the potatoes are cooked through, the radish is crisp-tender, and the sauce has thickened slightly, about 7 minutes. Do not overcook. Transfer the mixture to a serving dish, mix in the cilantro, and serve.

Makes 4 to 6 servings.

Paalungo ko Saag Tarkaari
SPINACH IN MUSTARD OIL

Spinach (paalungo ko saag) has long been one of the most beloved vegetables in Nepal and is served with most every Nepali meal. I like to cook the greens as simply as possible since overcooking robs them of their natural earthy taste and texture. This dish tastes best if served immediately.

2 tablespoons mustard oil
1 to 2 whole red dried chilies, halved and seeded
¼ teaspoon ajowan seeds
4 medium cloves garlic, finely chopped

1 or 2 large bunches (about 2 pounds) fresh spinach, stemmed, washed, and coarsely chopped
1½ teaspoons minced fresh ginger
¼ teaspoon salt

Heat the mustard oil in a saucepan over medium-high heat until the oil faintly smokes. Add the dried chilies and ajowan seeds and fry until dark brown and fully fragrant, 5 seconds. Add the garlic and stir for 30 seconds. Stir in the spinach, ginger, and salt.

Cover and cook, stirring frequently, until the spinach is tender and reduced to about one quarter of its original volume, 7 to 10 minutes. Transfer the spinach to a serving dish and serve. Do not cover the cooked spinach, as it will lose its green color.

Makes 4 servings.

Nauni Paalungo Tarkaari
SPINACH WITH GARLIC BUTTER

Here is another flavorful way of cooking spinach. To prepare this dish, wilt the spinach, squeeze the extra water out, and sauté it in garlic-flavored butter. This recipe works well with any variety of spinach, but I prefer the flat-leaf variety, which is the most tender and cooks quickly.

1 or 2 large bunches (about 2 pounds) fresh flat-leaf spinach, stemmed, washed, and coarsely chopped	2 fresh hot green chilies, split lengthwise
	4 medium cloves garlic, minced
	1½ teaspoons minced fresh ginger
2 tablespoons unsalted butter	¼ teaspoon salt

Place the spinach, with just the water that clings to the leaves, in a medium-size saucepan over medium heat. Cover and cook until wilted and soft, about 5 minutes. As it cooks, the spinach will release a lot of water. Drain the excess water in a colander. With the back of a spoon, gently squeeze the spinach to remove any remaining water. Set aside.

Melt the butter in a saucepan over medium heat. Add the green chilies, garlic, and ginger and cook for 30 seconds. Add the drained spinach and salt, adjust the heat to medium-high, and cook, stirring until all the moisture has evaporated, 5 to 7 minutes. Transfer the spinach to a serving dish and serve.

Makes 4 to 6 servings.

Chamsoor-Paalungo Tarkaari
SPINACH WITH GARDEN CRESS

Chamsoor-Paalungo, *spinach cooked with peppery garden cress is a favorite combination in Nepal. Garden cress* (chamsoor) *has long tender stems, pointed narrow leaves, and a spicy flavor. Cress can be cooked by itself, like any green, but tastes best when combined with other greens. If chamsoor is not available, substitute watercress, which is available in the produce section of regular grocery stores or at Asian markets.*

3 tablespoons mustard oil	2 small bunches (1 pound) garden
1 dried red chili, halved and	cress or watercress, trimmed
seeded	and washed
⅛ teaspoon fenugreek seeds	1½ teaspoons minced fresh ginger
2 to 3 bunches (about	2 large cloves garlic, minced
1½ pounds) fresh spinach,	¼ teaspoon salt
stemmed, washed, and	
coarsely chopped	

Heat the mustard oil in a skillet over medium-high heat until the oil faintly smokes. Add the dried chili and fenugreek seeds and fry until dark brown and fully fragrant, about 5 seconds. Add the spinach, cress, ginger, garlic, and salt. Cook until the greens are tender and most of the liquid has evaporated. Transfer the greens to a serving dish and serve warm.

Makes 4 to 6 servings.

Gheeraula ko Tarkaari
SMOOTH LUFFA GOURD WITH POTATOES

The smooth luffa (gheeraula) is also known as silk gourd, sponge gourd, or toriya and is an extremely popular vegetable in Nepal. It resembles a long cucumber with a smooth green skin marked by fine longitudinal lines. The young gourd is sweet with a delicate and distinctive taste. It is available at Asian and Indian grocery stores and some specialty produce markets. For this recipe, choose only young and tender luffa gourds, avoiding mature ones, which will be bitter with a fibrous texture.

4 to 6 small young smooth luffa
    gourds (8 cups sliced)
2 tablespoons vegetable oil
⅛ teaspoon fenugreek seeds
½ teaspoon ground turmeric
A generous pinch ground asafetida
2 medium red potatoes, peeled
    and cut into ½-inch pieces

1 teaspoon salt
2 fresh mild green chilies, chopped
1½ teaspoons minced fresh ginger
1 teaspoon ground cumin
1 teaspoon cayenne pepper
2 tablespoons clarified butter
    (*gheu*)

Slice off the top and bottom ends of each luffa gourd and lightly scrape off the fuzz with a knife. Peeling is not necessary. Wash thoroughly. Halve lengthwise and scoop out and discard any tough spongy pulp and seeds. Slice the gourd into ½-inch pieces.

Heat the oil in a heavy saucepan over medium-high heat. When hot, but not smoking, add the fenugreek seeds and fry until dark brown and highly fragrant, about 5 seconds. Sprinkle in the turmeric and asafetida, followed by the luffa, potatoes, and salt, and mix well. Reduce the heat to medium-low, cover the pan, and cook, stirring occasionally, until the vegetables are half cooked, about 10 minutes. Add the chilies, ginger, cumin, and cayenne pepper and mix well. The vegetables may release a lot of liquid. Continue cooking, uncovered, until the vegetables are tender and most of the liquid has evaporated, 12 to 15 minutes. Remove the pan from the heat and set it aside, covered.

Just before serving, heat the clarified butter in a small skillet until hot, pour it over the cooked vegetables, and mix well. Transfer the mixture to a serving dish and serve.

Makes 4 to 6 servings.

Karkalo ra Gaaba ko Tarkaari
STEAMED TARO LEAVES

Karkalo *is the Nepali name for taro leaves. Nepalese use all three parts of the taro plant: the leaves* (karkalo), *the young stalks* (gaaba), *and the root* (pidhaalu). *In this recipe, the tender stalks and young leaves are cooked together, producing a delicate flavor and silky texture, similar to spinach. Taro is never eaten raw because it irritates the throat. Once cooked, however, it is fine to eat and lemon juice helps further. The secret to this dish is to use fresh taro leaves and stems. Fresh taro is available at Indian markets under the name* arbi patta. *It is also sold prepackaged in plastic bags.*

1 large bunch (10 to 15) fresh, young taro leaves, stalks, and young shoots	⅛ teaspoon fenugreek seeds
	⅛ teaspoon ajowan seeds
	½ teaspoon salt
2 tablespoons mustard oil	2 tablespoons fresh lemon or
1 dried red chili, halved and seeded	lime juice, or as needed

Note: When cleaning the taro plant, the sap secreted by the stem can cause skin irritation and the temporary discoloration of your fingers so wear rubber gloves or wash your hands frequently.

Separate the taro leaves and stalks with a knife and rinse thoroughly. Place each leaf on a work surface, roll it into a tight cylinder, and tie the ends together to form a loose knot. Bend each stem and peel off the outer covering by pulling the fiber from all sides until you have smooth and silky stems. Cut them into ⅛-inch pieces and rinse them thoroughly. Set aside.

Heat the mustard oil in a small skillet over medium-high heat. When the oil is hot, but not smoking, add the dried chili, fenugreek, and ajowan and fry until dark brown and fragrant, about 5 seconds. Add ½ cup of water and bring it to a rolling boil. Add the taro and salt and reduce the heat to medium-low. Cover the pan, and cook until the taro softens, the excess water evaporates, and the taro is reduced to a silky, smooth paste, 10 to 12 minutes. While cooking, stir frequently to make sure the taro does not burn. Remove the pan from the heat, add the lemon juice, and mix thoroughly. Taste and add the lemon juice and salt as needed. Transfer the mixture to a serving dish and serve hot.

Taro Leaves with Ginger and Garlic: Prepare the taro leaves as directed at left. Heat 2 tablespoons vegetable oil over medium-high heat and sauté ⅛ teaspoon fenugreek seeds until dark, 5 seconds. Stir in 4 mild green chilies (slit lengthwise), 1 chopped onion, 1 chopped red or green bell pepper, 8 chopped cloves garlic, and 1 teaspoon minced fresh ginger. Cook for 5 minutes. Reduce the heat and add the taro leaves, 2 chopped tomatoes, 1 teaspoon ground cumin, 1 teaspoon ground coriander, and ½ teaspoon salt. Cook until the taro softens and the liquid evaporates, 10 to 12 minutes. Remove from the heat and stir in 2 tablespoons lemon juice.

Makes 4 to 6 servings.

Pate Gheeraula ra Mula ko Tarkaari
ANGLED LUFFA GOURD WITH RADISH

Angled luffa (pate gheeraula) is also known as ridged luffa, angled gourd, or Chinese okra. It is a long and narrow gourd, with a sharply ribbed skin. Use only young or immature luffa gourds because once mature, they develop a spongelike fibrous texture and become bitter. They are available at Asian and Indian grocery stores.

I whole dry red chili, halved	I medium white radish or daikon,
¼ cup hot water	peeled and thinly sliced
3 to 4 medium angled luffa	I teaspoon salt
gourds	I ½ teaspoons minced fresh ginger
2 tablespoons vegetable oil	2 teaspoons ground coriander
I teaspoon brown mustard seeds	I large clove garlic, minced
½ teaspoon ground turmeric	I teaspoon ground cumin
A large pinch ground asafetida	

Soak the red chili in the hot water until softened. Drain and coarsely grind with a mortar and pestle.

Slice off the top end and 3 inches of the bottom end of each angled luffa and discard. With a paring knife, remove all the ridges, leaving only smooth white flesh. Wash thoroughly and halve each gourd lengthwise. Scoop out all the mature seeds and fibers, cut them into ¼-inch-thick slices, and set aside.

Heat the oil in a heavy-bottomed pan over medium-high heat. When hot, but not smoking, add the mustard seeds and fry until the seeds pop, darken, and become fully fragrant, about 5 seconds. Sprinkle in the turmeric and asafetida, followed by the luffa gourd, radish, and salt and cook, stirring, for 5 minutes. Add the chili paste, ginger, coriander, garlic, and cumin and stir for 1 minute. Reduce the heat to medium-low, cover the pan, and cook, stirring from time to time, until the vegetables are tender and the liquid has slightly thickened, 15 to 20 minutes. Transfer the mixture to a serving dish and serve.

Makes 4 to 6 servings.

Hariyo Pharsi ko Tarkaari
SPICY ZUCCHINI WITH MUSTARD SEEDS

This spicy recipe works well with any variety of summer squash, but I prefer zucchini. The intense flavor comes from mustard seeds, green chilies, and fresh herbs and spices. You may reduce the amount of green chilies if you prefer a milder version.

4 to 6 medium zucchini (about 2 pounds)
2 tablespoons vegetable oil
½ teaspoon brown mustard seeds
½ teaspoon ground turmeric

A generous pinch ground asafetida
4 to 5 fresh hot green chilies, split lengthwise
1 teaspoon salt
1½ tablespoons minced fresh ginger

Halve the zucchini lengthwise and scrape out the mature seeds, but leave the tender seeds intact. Cut the halves into thin slices.

Heat the oil in a saucepan over medium-high heat. When the oil is hot, but not smoking, add the mustard seeds and fry until they pop, darken, and are fully fragrant, about 5 seconds. Cover the pan until the popping subsides. Stir in the turmeric and asafetida first, followed by the green chilies, salt, and zucchini, and stir well. Reduce the heat to medium, cover the pan, and cook, stirring from time to time, for 12 minutes. Add the ginger, mix well, and cook until the zucchini is tender and all the moisture has evaporated, about 10 minutes. Transfer the zucchini to a serving dish and serve warm.

Makes 4 to 6 servings.

Mismaas Jogi Tarkaari
MIXED VEGETABLE CURRY

*This vegetable curry is made from an assortment of vegetables, gently simmered in a mixture of fresh herbs and spices. I recommend using only fresh vegetables. The most common vegetables are potatoes, peas, onions, cauliflowers, beans, mushrooms, and tomatoes, but you can use any vegetable of your choice. Do not overcook the vegetables or overcrowd them in a small pan, as they will turn into mush. The colorful vegetables can be served with steaming rice or any variety of bread, along with meat curry, pickles, or chutney. They are also served as a mid-afternoon snack with pressed rice flakes (*cheura*).*

¼ cup mustard oil or
    vegetable oil
½ teaspoon fenugreek seeds
½ teaspoon ground turmeric
4 to 5 whole Szechwan peppercorns (*timmur*)
A small pinch ground asafetida
2 medium potatoes, peeled and
    cut into 1-inch pieces
    (about 2 cups)
2 medium onions, quartered
1 small eggplant, cut into 1-inch
    piece (about 1 cup)
1 cup green beans, trimmed and
    cut into 1-inch pieces
1 cup shelled fresh or frozen
    peas, thawed and thoroughly
    drained
1 small carrot, peeled and cut
    into ½-inch slices
3 medium tomatoes, quartered

1½ cups sliced fresh mushrooms
1 small red or green bell pepper,
    cored and cut into 1-inch
    pieces
2 fresh mild or hot green chilies,
    split lengthwise
2 medium cloves garlic, finely
    chopped
1 tablespoon minced fresh ginger
2 teaspoons ground coriander
1½ teaspoons ground cumin
1 teaspoon cayenne pepper
1 teaspoon salt
1 teaspoon Nepali Garam Masala
    (page 398)
½ cup finely chopped cilantro
3 to 4 green onions (white and
    pale green parts), cut into
    1-inch pieces

Heat the oil in a wide, heavy saucepan over medium-high heat until faintly smoking. Add the fenugreek seeds and fry until dark brown and highly fragrant, about 5 seconds. Add the turmeric, *timmur*, and asafetida, followed by the potatoes, and cook, stirring frequently, for 2 minutes. Stir in the onions, eggplant, green beans, peas, and carrot. Reduce the heat to medium, cover the pan, and continue cooking, stirring occasionally, until the vegetables are half cooked, 10 to 12 minutes.

Add the tomatoes, mushrooms, bell pepper, garlic, ginger, coriander, cumin, cayenne pepper, and salt and stir for 2 to 3 minutes. Reduce the heat to medium-low, cover the pan and cook, stirring occasionally, until the vegetables are tender and the liquid has slightly thickened, about 15 minutes.

Stir in the garam masala. The vegetables should cook in their own juices, but if the mixture is dry, add a little water. Mix in the cilantro and green onions, transfer the vegetables to a serving dish, and serve.

Maasu

MEAT

In Nepal, meat is a high-status food and does not feature frequently in the regular diet of most people. Poorer people consume meat only on special occasions and festivities, while the urban middle class consumes meat more frequently. The most common and preferred meat is a freshly slaughtered goat and the Nepali word for goat is the same as the generic word for meat (*khasi* or *boka*). All parts of the animal are eaten, including the liver, intestines, brain, kidney, tongue, tripe, and blood. Meat from castrated goats is called *khasi ko maasu*, young goat meat is called *boka ko maasu*, and both can be purchased in the United States at Indian or Middle Eastern grocery stores and some farms. Most butchers will cut meat according to your specifications, upon request.

Other common meats eaten in Nepal include lamb (*bheda*) or pork (*bangoor* or *banel*). The majority of Nepalese do not eat beef for religious reasons, being Hindu. In many areas of Nepal, certain ethnic groups eat water buffalo (*raango ko maasu*) as their primary source of meat. Water buffalo is extremely lean and tender. It is also versatile and lends itself to spicy cooking. Water buffalo was once a less expensive alternative to goat, but as a greater portion of the population is beginning to recognize its health benefits, it is becoming increasingly expensive. Game, such as boar (*banel*) and venison (*mirga*), is popular in some regions and usually signifies a family celebration. Venison is usually obtained by hunting. Due to a lack of refrigeration, on hunting trips it is sun-dried so that it doesn't spoil. In the high altitude areas of Nepal near the Tibetan boarder, yak meat (*chamari gai*) is consumed fresh and dried. It is similar in flavor to water buffalo, but much leaner and juicier, with a strong, gamy odor.

Religious laws dictate that meat is prohibited on certain days and in combination with certain foods. For example, meat is not to be consumed during Ekaadasi (Auspicious Day), the eleventh day after the full moon, and the eleventh day after the new moon. During this time, meat is not sold in the local markets. During the most important religious festival of Vijaya Dashami, however, a large number of animals are sacrificed and offered to the deities. After religious rites are performed, the animal is cooked and distributed among friends, relatives, and neighbors. At this time, great feasts are prepared in many homes and a large quantity of blessed meat (*prashaad ko maasu*) is consumed. For many families, this is one of the few occasions during the year that they are able to eat meat.

In Nepal, butchered animals are cooked and eaten right after slaughtering, rather than stored. The meat is usually prepared well done. Most frequently, it is cooked in a pressure cooker. Most meat (goat, lamb, water buffalo, and pork), can be used interchangeably in these recipes unless otherwise indicated.

Dahi Haaleko Boka-Khasi ko Maasu
YOGURT-MARINATED GOAT CURRY

This classic Nepali goat curry is marinated in tenderizing yogurt. This dish is best when cooked with leg of goat, but is also delicious with tender cuts of lamb, pork, or water buffalo. Serve it with rice and green vegetables.

2½ to 3 pounds bone-in young goat (preferably from the leg), cut into 1½-inch pieces
¼ cup vegetable oil
1 teaspoon ground turmeric
1 teaspoon salt
2 medium onions, each cut into 6 wedges
2 medium tomatoes, each cut into 6 wedges
1 cup plain yogurt, stirred
6 medium cloves garlic, minced
2 to 3 fresh mild or hot green chilies, split lengthwise
1½ tablespoons minced fresh ginger

1 tablespoon ground coriander
2 teaspoons cayenne pepper, or to taste
4 to 6 green cardamom pods, crushed
1½ teaspoons ground cumin
¼ teaspoon freshly ground black pepper
⅛ teaspoon ground nutmeg
1 (1-inch) stick cinnamon, halved
2 to 3 bay leaves
1 black cardamom pod, crushed
4 whole cloves
1 cup hot water
½ cup finely chopped cilantro

Rinse the goat (mutton) well under cold water and place it in a bowl with the oil, turmeric, and salt, rubbing to coat the meat. Add the onions, tomatoes, yogurt, garlic, green chilies, ginger, coriander, cayenne pepper, green cardamom, cumin, black pepper, nutmeg, cinnamon, bay leaves, black cardamom, and cloves, rubbing again to coat the meat. Cover and marinate for at least 30 minutes at room temperature or refrigerate overnight, but return to room temperature before cooking.

Place the meat in a large saucepan. Cook, uncovered, over medium-high heat, stirring from time to time, until the meat loses its pink color and comes to a boil, 7 to 8 minutes. Stir in the hot water, and return to a full boil. Reduce the heat to medium-low, cover, and simmer, stirring occasionally, until the meat is tender and cooked through, and the sauce has thickened, about 1 hour. Transfer to a serving dish, sprinkle cilantro, and serve hot.

Makes 4 to 6 servings.

Khasi-Boka ko Maasu
GOAT CURRY

This is a basic recipe for cooking goat, but it works equally well with lamb, pork, water buffalo, venison, or even poultry. Traditionally, bone-in goat is used, which contributes more flavor, but boneless meat can also be used. In this recipe, goat is marinated for several hours before cooking and cooked in its own juices. Serve with rice, bread, and vegetables.

2½ to 3 pounds bone-in young goat (preferably from the leg), trimmed and cut into 1½-inch pieces
1 (1-inch) stick cinnamon
2 teaspoons coriander seeds
1½ teaspoons cumin seeds
4 to 6 green cardamom pods, crushed
¼ teaspoon black peppercorns
⅛ teaspoon fennel seeds
2 to 3 bay leaves
1 black cardamom pod, crushed

4 whole cloves
2 to 3 dried red chilies, halved, seeded, and soaked in ¼ cup hot water until soft
¼ cup vegetable oil
4 to 6 medium cloves garlic, minced
1½ tablespoons minced fresh ginger
1 teaspoon ground turmeric
1 teaspoon salt
⅛ teaspoon ground nutmeg
½ cup finely chopped cilantro

Wash the meat thoroughly with cold water, drain, and place it in a medium-size bowl. Set aside while you prepare the spices.

Heat a small cast-iron skillet over medium-low heat and toast the cinnamon, coriander, cumin, green cardamom, peppercorns, fennel, bay leaves, black cardamom pods, and cloves, stirring constantly until they give off a pleasant aroma and are heated through, 2 to 3 minutes. Pour into a dry container to halt the toasting. Cool and remove the seeds from the cardamom and discard the pods. Place the spices in a spice grinder or a mortar and pestle and grind to a fine powder.

Drain the chilies and coarsely grind them into a paste with a mortar and pestle or spice grinder.

In a small bowl, combine the oil, garlic, ginger, salt, nutmeg, chili paste, and toasted spices. Rub the spice mixture over the meat. Cover and allow the meat to marinate for 30 minutes at room temperature or refrigerate it overnight, but bring it back to room temperature before cooking.

Place the marinated meat in a large heavy-bottomed saucepan. Cook, uncovered, over medium-high heat, stirring from time to time, until the meat loses its pink color and comes to a boil, 7 to 8 minutes. Lower the heat, cover, and simmer, stirring often to prevent scorching, until the meat is tender and cooked through, and the juices are absorbed into the meat, about 1 hour. The cooking time depends on the quality and age of the goat. If the meat has not reached the desired tenderness, add ½ cup hot water and continue cooking until it is tender and most of the juices have evaporated. Transfer the meat to a serving dish, sprinkle the cilantro on top, and serve hot.

Makes 4 to 6 servings.

Maasu ko Tarkaari
AJOWAN-FENUGREEK GOAT

This goat dish is cooked with the two most common Nepali spices, fenugreek and ajowan seeds. The spices are added in two successive stages: first, whole spices are fried in hot oil so that the meat browns in the spice-infused oil, then the other ground spices are added and cooked to make a savory sauce. This recipe can also be made with lamb or pork.

3 tablespoons mustard oil
3 dried red chilies, halved and seeded
¼ teaspoon fenugreek seeds
2½ to 3 pounds bone-in young goat (preferably from the leg), cut into 1½-inch pieces
½ teaspoon ajowan seeds
½ teaspoon ground turmeric
A small pinch ground asafetida
4 to 5 medium cloves garlic, minced

1 tablespoon minced fresh ginger
1½ teaspoons ground coriander
1 teaspoon salt
1 teaspoon ground cumin
⅛ teaspoon freshly ground black pepper
2 cups hot water
½ cup finely chopped cilantro
4 to 5 green onions (white and green parts), finely chopped
1 teaspoon Fragrant Garam Masala (page 397)

Heat the mustard oil in a heavy saucepan over medium-high heat. When the oil is faintly smoking, add the dried chilies and fenugreek and fry until dark brown and highly fragrant, about 5 seconds. Add the goat, ajowan seeds, turmeric, and asafetida and cook, stirring constantly, until the meat browns on all sides, about 10 minutes. Mix in the garlic, ginger, coriander, salt, cumin, and black pepper and stir for 1 minute. Adjust the heat to high, add 2 cups of hot water, and bring to a rolling boil, uncovered. Reduce the heat to medium-low, cover, and simmer gently until the meat is tender and cooked through, 35 to 45 minutes. Add the cilantro, green onions, and garam masala and cook for 2 to 3 minutes more. The finished dish should have plenty of sauce. Transfer the mixture to a serving dish and serve hot.

Makes 4 to 6 servings.

Suruwa Maasu
STEWED GOAT WITH SPICES

This dish is also called jhol, ras, *or* umaaleko maasu, *and simply means "soupy boiled meat." The term* suruwa *refers to meat that is gently simmered with fresh herbs and spices to produce a thin soup. This slow-cooking method tenderizes the meat and brings out the flavor of the spices at the same time. The dish is even better the next day when the flavors have more fully developed.*

3 tablespoons clarified butter (*gheu*) or vegetable oil
½ teaspoon ajowan seeds
2½ to 3 pounds bone-in young goat (leg or shoulder), cut into 1½-inch pieces
1 teaspoon ground turmeric
A large pinch ground asafetida
1 medium onion, thinly sliced
6 medium cloves garlic, slivered
1 tablespoon peeled and finely julienned fresh ginger
1 large shallot, minced
2 to 3 fresh mild green chilies, split lengthwise

1 (1-inch) stick cinnamon, halved
1½ teaspoons ground coriander
1 teaspoon ground cumin
1 teaspoon salt
1 teaspoon cayenne pepper or to taste
¼ teaspoon freshly ground black pepper
⅛ teaspoon ground nutmeg
1 black cardamom pod, crushed
2 medium tomatoes, finely chopped or crushed (about 2 cups)
4 to 5 green onions (white and green parts), finely chopped
1 cup finely chopped cilantro

Heat the clarified butter in a heavy saucepan over medium-high heat. When hot, add the ajowan seeds and fry until lightly browned and fragrant, about 5 seconds. Add the goat, turmeric, and asafetida and cook, stirring as needed, until the meat is well browned, 7 to 8 minutes. Add the onion, garlic, ginger, and shallot and continue to cook, stirring constantly, until the onion softens, about 5 minutes. Mix in the green chilies, cinnamon, coriander, cumin, salt, cayenne pepper, black pepper, and nutmeg and stir for 1 minute. Add the tomatoes, green onions, cilantro, and 4 cups of water and bring to a boil. Reduce the heat to medium-low, cover, and simmer, stirring from time to time, until the meat is falling off the bones and the liquid has slightly reduced and thickened, 50 to 55 minutes. Transfer to a serving dish and sprinkle with the remaining cilantro. Serve piping hot.

Makes 4 to 6 servings.

Dashain ko Boka Maasu
DASHAIN GOAT CURRY

This dish gets its name from the most auspicious and joyful Nepali religious festival, Vijaya Dashami, celebrated in September and October, lasting for more than 10 days. During this festival, a large number of goats, ducks, chickens, and water buffaloes are sacrificed and offered to the gods. The meat is consumed as blessed meat (prashaad ko maasu) *along with other celebratory dishes. Goat meat is the preferred meat for this holiday.*

2½ to 3 pounds bone-in young goat (preferably from the leg), cut into 1½-inch pieces
1½ cups plain yogurt, stirred
7 medium cloves garlic, 6 peeled and 1 minced
6 tablespoons vegetable oil
1 tablespoon peeled and finely julienned fresh ginger plus 1 tablespoon minced
2 teaspoons Nepali Garam Masala (page 398)
1 teaspoon salt
½ teaspoon ground turmeric
1 (1-inch) stick cinnamon, halved
2 to 3 bay leaves

4 to 6 green cardamom pods, crushed
4 whole cloves
2 medium onions, thinly sliced (about 2 cups)
2 medium tomatoes, chopped (about 2 cups)
2 to 3 fresh mild green chilies, split lengthwise
2 teaspoons cayenne pepper, or to taste
1½ teaspoon ground coriander
1 teaspoon ground cumin
¼ teaspoon freshly ground black pepper
⅛ teaspoon ground nutmeg
½ cup finely chopped cilantro

Rinse the goat well under cold water, drain, and place it in a heavy-bottomed saucepan. Add ½ cup of the yogurt, the whole cloves of garlic, 2 tablespoons of the oil, the julienned ginger, garam masala, salt, turmeric, cinnamon, bay leaves, cardamom, and cloves. Mix well, rubbing each piece to make sure the meat is well coated. Cook, uncovered, over medium-high heat, stirring from time to time, until the meat loses its pink color and comes to a boil, 7 to 8 minutes. Reduce the heat to medium-low, cover, and simmer, stirring occasionally, until the meat is tender and cooked through, 45 to 50 minutes.

While the meat is cooking, heat the remaining ¼ cup of oil in a separate skillet over medium-high heat. When it is hot but not smoking, add the onions and cook, stirring from time to time, until well-browned, 5 to 7 minutes. Add the tomatoes, green chilies, minced ginger, and minced garlic and cook until the tomatoes are soft, all the juices evaporate, and the oil starts to come away from the sides of the pan, about 5 minutes. Add the cayenne pepper, coriander, cumin, black pepper, nutmeg, and salt to taste and stir well. Stir in the remaining 1 cup of yogurt, 1 tablespoon at a time, mixing well before adding more, and cook until it is completely incorporated into the sauce, about 5 minutes. Pour the sauce into the meat and stir well. Cover and let it rest for 10 minutes, undisturbed, to let the flavors set. Transfer the mixture to a serving dish, mix in the cilantro, and serve.

Makes 4 to 6 servings.

Kesari Maasu
CURRIED GOAT WITH SAFFRON

This saffron-flavored dish is an old family recipe from my mother. Like most Nepali cooks, she never measures or tastes the food while cooking. Instead, she uses her own judgment and adjusts the seasoning simply by smelling the food, and it always turns out to be delicious.

½ cup clarified butter (*gheu*) or vegetable oil
1 (1-inch) stick cinnamon, halved
8 green cardamom pods, crushed
1 black cardamom pod, crushed
6 whole cloves
2 to 3 small bay leaves
3 medium onions, finely chopped (about 3 cups)
2½ to 3 pounds bone-in young goat (preferably from the leg), trimmed and cut into 1½-inch pieces
6 to 8 medium cloves garlic, minced
1½ tablespoons minced fresh ginger

2 to 3 fresh hot green chilies, each split lengthwise
2 teaspoons cayenne pepper or to taste
2 teaspoons ground cumin
1½ teaspoons ground coriander
1 teaspoon salt
1 teaspoon ground turmeric
¼ teaspoon saffron threads
2 tablespoons boiling water
3 medium tomatoes, chopped (about 3 cups)
2 teaspoons Nepali Garam Masala (page 398)
⅛ teaspoon ground nutmeg
½ cup finely chopped cilantro

Heat the clarified butter in a large heavy saucepan over medium-high heat. When hot, add the cinnamon, green and black cardamom pods, cloves, and bay leaves and fry until the spices begin to puff up, darken, and give off a pleasant aroma, about 5 seconds. Add the onions and cook, stirring constantly, until lightly browned, 5 to 7 minutes. Adjust the heat to high, add the goat, and cook, stirring occasionally, until lightly browned, about 10 minutes. Add the garlic and ginger and cook for 2 minutes. Mix in the green chilies, cayenne pepper, cumin, coriander, salt, and turmeric and continue cooking, stirring, for 1 minute. Add ½ cup of water and bring it to a boil. Reduce the heat to medium-low, cover, and cook, stirring from time to time, until the meat is halfway cooked, about 25 minutes.

Crush the saffron in a mortar and pestle and then soak in the boiling water for 10 minutes.

Add the tomatoes, garam masala, and nutmeg to the meat and cook until the tomatoes are soft, about 5 minutes. Add the saffron-infused water and stir well. Starting with 1 cup of water, add ¼ cup at a time, and let it evaporate before adding more. Continue until the meat is tender and the sauce has thickened slightly, 15 to 20 minutes Transfer the meat to a serving dish, add the cilantro, and serve hot.

Makes 4 to 6 servings.

Khasi-Moola-Chhaype
GOAT WITH RADISH AND GREEN ONIONS

In Nepal this dish is prepared with seasonal vegetables. Radishes and green onions complement the goat, making this dish very delicious.

2 fresh mild or hot green chilies, minced
4 to 6 medium cloves garlic, minced
1 tablespoon minced fresh ginger
1½ teaspoons ground cumin
1½ teaspoons ground coriander
1 teaspoon cayenne pepper
½ teaspoon ground turmeric
¼ teaspoon freshly ground black pepper
3 tablespoons vegetable oil
¼ teaspoon fenugreek seeds
1 medium onion, finely chopped (about 1 cup)
A small pinch ground asafetida

2 pounds bone-in young goat meat (leg or shoulder), cut into 1-inch pieces
1 teaspoon salt
½ cup hot water
2 medium white radishes (daikon), peeled and cut into 1-inch pieces (about 2 pounds)
2 medium tomatoes, chopped (about 2 cups)
8 to 10 green onions (white and green parts), cut into 1-inch pieces
½ cup finely chopped cilantro

In a small bowl, combine the green chilies, garlic, ginger, cumin, coriander, cayenne pepper, turmeric, and black pepper. Add 2 to 3 tablespoons of water to make a spice paste and set aside.

Heat the oil in a large heavy saucepan over medium-high heat until hot, but not smoking. Add the fenugreek seeds and fry until dark brown and highly fragrant, about 5 seconds. Add the onion and asafetida and fry until the onion is light brown, 5 to 7 minutes. Add the goat and brown on all sides, about 10 minutes. Add the salt and spice paste and cook, stirring constantly, for 1 minute. Add the hot water and bring to a boil. Reduce the heat to medium-low, cover, and cook, stirring from time to time, until the meat is almost cooked through, about 25 minutes. Add the radishes, tomatoes, and green onions, and mix well. Cover and cook, stirring as needed, until the meat is tender, the radishes are crisp-tender, and all the liquid has evaporated, about 20 minutes. Transfer the mixture to a serving dish, sprinkle with cilantro, and serve.

Goat with Zucchini: You may substitute 2 pounds sliced zucchini for the radishes.

Makes 4 to 6 servings.

Maasu ko Bari
LAMB MEATBALLS

These meatballs (bari) are sometimes shaped into patties and deep-fried.
They can be served as a mid-afternoon snack, appetizer, or as a supplement
to a Nepali meal with any variety of chutney or garnish.

2 pounds lean ground lamb
1 cup dry bread crumbs
1 medium onion, finely chopped
  (about 1 cup)
½ cup finely chopped cilantro
2 to 3 green onions (white and
  pale green parts), finely
  chopped
3 to 4 fresh mild green chilies,
  finely chopped
2 eggs, lightly beaten

4 medium cloves garlic, minced
1 large shallot, minced
2 teaspoons minced fresh ginger
1 teaspoon ground turmeric
1 teaspoon ground coriander
1 teaspoon cayenne pepper
1 teaspoon salt
½ teaspoon ground cumin
¼ teaspoon freshly ground
  black pepper
2 cups vegetable oil

In a large bowl, combine all the ingredients except the oil. Mix well with your
hands until thoroughly mixed. Cover the bowl and let it rest for 7 to 10 minutes, at room temperature, to allow the flavors to develop.

With moistened fingers, form 1½-inch balls. Place them on a tray in a single layer.

Heat the oil in a wide nonstick skillet over medium-high heat until it reaches
350° to 375°F. Test for readiness by placing a small piece of the mixture into
the hot oil. If it bubbles and slowly rises to the surface, it is ready. Gently place
the meatballs into the hot oil. Do not overcrowd. Fry the meatballs gently,
turning carefully so they do not break or stick to the pan. Cook until firm,
cooked through, and golden brown on all sides, 10 to 15 minutes. Remove
with a slotted spoon and drain on paper towels. Repeat with the remaining
balls. Serve warm or at room temperature.

Makes 4 to 6 servings.

Chicken Meatballs: Use 2½ pounds ground chicken in place of the lamb.
Combine all the ingredients as directed above, reducing the garlic to 2 cloves,
the turmeric to ½ teaspoon, and the cayenne pepper to ½ teaspoon. Omit the
coriander and increase the black pepper to ½ teaspoon. Form and cook as
directed above.

Badaami Maasu
LAMB WITH CASHEWS, ALMONDS, AND YOGURT SAUCE

This dish is easy to make and the delicious combination of nuts and yogurt enhances the flavor of the meat. This recipe calls for bone-in lamb, but you can substitute young goat meat or pork. Serve with rice, lentils, or poori bread.

¼ cup plus 2 tablespoons vegetable oil
3 medium onions, coarsely chopped (about 3 cups)
4 fresh hot green chilies, split lengthwise
1½ tablespoons peeled and coarsely chopped fresh ginger
5 medium cloves garlic, coarsely chopped
¼ cup raw cashews, coarsely chopped
10 raw almonds, coarsely chopped
1 tablespoon ground coriander
1½ teaspoons ground cumin
1 teaspoon ground turmeric
1 teaspoon cayenne pepper

1 teaspoon Fragrant Garam Masala (page 397)
1 teaspoon salt
⅛ teaspoon freshly ground black pepper
⅛ teaspoon ground nutmeg
3 medium tomatoes, finely chopped (about 3 cups)
2½ to 3 pounds bone-in lamb (preferably from the leg), trimmed and cut into 1½-inch pieces
1 cup plain yogurt, stirred
¼ cup finely chopped cilantro
2 to 3 green onions (white and pale green parts), finely chopped

Heat ¼ cup of the oil in a heavy saucepan over medium-high heat. When it is hot, but not smoking, add the onions, green chilies, ginger, and garlic and cook, stirring frequently, until the vegetables are soft, about 5 minutes. With a slotted spoon, remove the vegetables, draining as much oil as possible, and transfer the mixture to a food processor or blender. Add the cashews and almonds and grind to a smooth paste. Mix in the coriander, cumin, turmeric, cayenne pepper, garam masala, salt, black pepper, and nutmeg.

Return the mixture to the saucepan with the remaining 2 tablespoons of oil and cook over medium-high heat, stirring constantly, until the mixture is lightly browned, about 5 minutes. Add the tomatoes and continue to cook, stirring, until the tomatoes are soft and all the juices evaporate, about 5 minutes. Add the lamb and cook, uncovered, stirring from time to time, for 10 minutes. Add 1 cup of water and bring to a boil. Reduce the heat to medium-low, cover, and cook, stirring as needed, until the lamb is tender and the sauce has reduced and thickened, about 50 minutes. Add the yogurt, 1 tablespoon as a time, mixing well before adding more, and cook until it is incorporated into the sauce, about 7 minutes. At this stage, the oil will begin to come away from the sides of the pan and may float on the top of the gravy. Mix in the cilantro and green onions, transfer the mixture to a serving dish, and serve hot.

Makes 4 to 6 servings.

Masaledar Maasu
LAMB WITH AROMATIC GRAVY

Masaledar *means a "delicate mixture of herbs and spices," and* maasu *is "meat" in Nepali, so this recipe blends spices and meat in aromatic gravy. The dish can be prepared one day in advance and can be reheated on the stovetop by gently simmering. It is served piping hot with rice, lentils, sautéed vegetables, and warm Nepali breads. Traditionally this dish is made with goat on the bone, but this recipe uses boneless lamb.*

2½ to 3 pounds boneless lamb (or goat), trimmed and cut into 1-inch pieces
2 medium onions, roughly chopped (about 2 cups)
2 to 3 large shallots, chopped
6 medium cloves garlic, peeled
3 fresh mild green chilies, stemmed
1½ tablespoons peeled and roughly chopped fresh ginger
3 dried red chilies, halved and seeded, or to taste
1 tablespoon coriander seeds
1 (1-inch) stick cinnamon, halved
2 teaspoons cumin seeds
¼ teaspoon whole black peppercorns
⅛ teaspoon fenugreek seeds

⅛ teaspoon fennel seeds
4 to 6 green cardamom pods, seeds removed
6 whole cloves
½ cup vegetable oil
2 medium bay leaves
A small pinch ground asafetida
8 blanched whole almonds, ground
1 teaspoon ground turmeric
1 teaspoon salt
¼ teaspoon ground nutmeg
2 medium tomatoes, finely chopped (about 2 cups)
1 cup plain yogurt, stirred
½ cup finely chopped cilantro
5 to 6 green onions (white and pale green parts), finely chopped

Wash the lamb thoroughly with cold water, drain, and set it aside.

Place the onions, shallots, garlic, green chilies, and ginger in a food processor or blender. Add just enough water to facilitate blending and process to a smooth paste.

Heat a small cast-iron skillet over medium-high heat and toast the dried chilies, coriander, cinnamon, cumin, peppercorns, fenugreek, fennel, cardamom, and cloves, stirring constantly, until they give off a pleasant aroma, 2 to 3 minutes. Remove them from the skillet and pour them into a dry container to halt the toasting. Cool, and grind the spices in a spice grinder to a fine powder. A mortar and pestle can also be used.

Heat the oil in a heavy saucepan over medium-high heat. When the oil is hot, but not smoking, add the bay leaves, asafetida, and immediately add the onion mixture. Stir until golden, 5 to 7 minutes. Add the ground spice mixture, almonds, turmeric, salt, and nutmeg and mix well. Add the tomatoes and continue cooking until they are soft and all the juices evaporate, about 5 minutes. Add the yogurt, 1 tablespoon at a time, stirring constantly. Continue cooking until the liquid has evaporated in the spice mixture, about 2 minutes. Add the lamb and cook, uncovered, stirring from time to time, for 10 minutes. Add 1 cup of water and bring to a boil. Reduce the heat to medium-low, cover the pan, and continue cooking, stirring as needed, until the meat is tender, about 50 minutes. If the meat is not tender and the gravy has started to stick to the pan, add ½ cup more water and continue cooking, covered. The dish will be ready when the oil begins to separate from the side of the pan and the gravy is rich, thick, and brown. Remove from the heat. Mix in the cilantro and scallions, transfer the lamb to a serving dish, and serve hot.

Makes 4 to 6 servings.

Sekuwa Maasu
GRILLED LAMB KEBABS

Here is a recipe for boneless lamb marinated in yogurt and spices. The yogurt helps to tenderize the lamb and makes the spices stick to the meat during grilling. This is a wonderfully flavorful meat dish that is quick and easy to prepare. Leftovers can be shredded and made into chowela, a Nepali salad (page 204). It can be served as an appetizer, mid-afternoon snack, or as a supplement to any lunch or dinner menu.

MARINADE
1 teaspoon salt
1 tablespoon fresh lemon or lime juice
½ teaspoon ground turmeric
1 teaspoon Nepali Garam Masala (page 398)
1 tablespoon peeled and minced fresh ginger
3 medium cloves garlic, minced
2 fresh hot green chilies, minced
½ cup plain yogurt, stirred

8 to 10 skewers (if wooden, soak for 30 minutes before use)

2½ to 3 pounds boneless lamb (preferably from the leg), trimmed and cut into 1½-inch pieces
2 tablespoons melted butter or vegetable oil
1 medium red onion, sliced ⅛ inch thick and separated into rings
⅛ teaspoon salt
1 teaspoon fresh lemon or lime juice
1 small cucumber, peeled, halved, seeded, and sliced ¼ inch thick
2 medium tomatoes, each cut into 6 wedges each
10 fresh green chilies

Combine all the marinade ingredients in a medium-size bowl, add the lamb, and mix well, making sure that each piece is coated. Place the lamb and marinade in a heavy, sealable plastic bag, and refrigerate for at least 8 hours. Shake and turn the bag from time to time.

Preheat a charcoal or gas grill to medium-high heat. Remove the lamb from the marinade, and thread onto the skewers. Discard the marinade. For juicy meat, place the pieces close to one another on the skewers. Grill, turning frequently and basting with the melted butter, until the lamb is browned on all sides and cooked through, about 25 minutes. Remove the skewers from the grill and allow the meat to cool a little before removing it from the skewers.

While the lamb is cooking, combine the onions with the salt and lemon juice.

Transfer the meat to a platter. Surround it with the onions, cucumbers, tomatoes, and chilies, and serve immediately.

Makes 4 to 6 servings.

Chowela Maasu
LAMB CHOWELA

Chowela *comes from the Newar community of Nepal. The meat is grilled or roasted, cut into bite-size pieces, and combined with fresh herbs and spices. The intense flavor of this dish is achieved through the addition of tempered spices, or spices fried in oil. This is an extremely versatile dish, and can be served hot, chilled, or at room temperature as a snack, appetizer, or part of a Nepali meal.*

I recipe Grilled Skewered Lamb (page 202), cut into bite-size pieces
I medium red onion, finely chopped (about I cup)
¼ cup finely chopped cilantro
4 to 5 green onions (white and pale green parts), finely chopped
4 fresh mild or hot green chilies, finely chopped
3 tablespoons fresh lemon or lime juice
I tablespoon minced fresh ginger
I teaspoon salt

I teaspoon ground cumin
I teaspoon cayenne pepper
½ teaspoon ground turmeric
¼ teaspoon Szechwan pepper (*timmur*), finely ground with a mortar and pestle
⅛ teaspoon freshly ground black pepper
2 tablespoons mustard oil
¼ teaspoon fenugreek seeds
2 dried red chilies, halved and seeded
3 to 4 medium cloves garlic, slivered

In a medium-size bowl, combine the lamb, onion, cilantro, green onions, green chilies, lemon juice, ginger, salt, cumin, cayenne pepper, turmeric, *timmur*, and black pepper.

Heat the oil in a small skillet over medium-high heat. When the oil is hot, but not smoking, add the fenugreek seeds and dried chilies and fry until the fenugreek turns dark brown and the chilies become reddish-brown and fragrant, about 5 seconds. Add the garlic and fry until it is crisp, but not brown, about 7 seconds. Immediately pour the entire contents of the pan into the meat and toss well. Cover the bowl and allow the seasonings to develop for at least 10 minutes. Transfer the mixture to a serving dish and serve.

Makes 4 to 6 servings.

Piro Bangoor ko Maasu
SPICY PORK

In this recipe, boneless pork is cooked with a spicy blend of herbs and spices. If overcooked, pork has a tendency to dry out and become tough and tasteless, so cook it just until it is tender. The dish can be served with rice, and a selection of chutneys and relishes.

4 to 5 shallots or 1 onion,
  roughly chopped
  (about 1 cup)
4 dried red chilies,
  halved and seeded
6 medium cloves garlic, peeled
1 tablespoon peeled and roughly
  chopped fresh ginger
1½ teaspoons ground coriander
1 teaspoon ground turmeric
1 teaspoon ground cumin

¼ teaspoon freshly ground
  black pepper
¼ cup vegetable oil
1 (1-inch) stick cinnamon
2 small bay leaves
2 green cardamom pods, crushed
4 whole cloves
2½ pounds boneless, lean pork
  (preferably from the loin
  or leg) cut into 1 or
  1½-inch cubes
1 teaspoon salt

Place the shallots, dried chilies, garlic, ginger, coriander, tumeric, cumin, and black pepper in a food processor or blender and process to a smooth paste. Add 2 to 3 tablespoons of water, if needed, to facilitate blending.

Heat the oil in a heavy saucepan over medium-high heat. When it is hot, but not smoking, add the cinnamon, bay leaves, cardamom pods, and cloves and fry until they begin to puff up, darken, and give off a pleasant aroma, about 5 seconds. Add the pork and cook, uncovered, stirring from time to time, until lightly browned about 15 minutes. Add the spice paste and salt, mix well, and continue cooking until all the moisture has evaporated, about 5 minutes. Add ½ cup of water and bring to a boil. Adjust the heat to medium-low, cover the pan, and cook, stirring as needed, until the meat is tender, about 15 minutes. Transfer the pork to a serving dish and serve hot.

Makes 4 to 6 servings.

Raango ko Maasu
WATER BUFFALO WITH GINGER AND GARLIC

Water buffalo meat is commonly eaten in Nepal. It is extremely lean, flavorful, and tender and resembles beef, but is somewhat darker in color. Water buffalo is versatile, and lends itself to spicy cooking. This recipe comes from Tata Didi, a family friend, who uses a generous amount of ginger, garlic, shallots, and spices to make a delicious curry. If buffalo meat is not available, substitute bone-in or boneless, lamb, pork, or goat.

12 medium cloves garlic, 8 minced and 4 sliced
1½ tablespoons minced fresh ginger plus 1 tablespoon julienned
1 teaspoon salt
1 teaspoon ground turmeric
2½ to 3 pounds bone-in water buffalo, cut into 1-inch pieces
¼ cup vegetable oil
2 dried red chilies, halved and seeded

¼ teaspoon fenugreek seeds
4 to 5 large shallots, finely chopped
1 (1-inch) stick cinnamon, halved
2 bay leaves
1 tablespoon ground coriander
1½ teaspoons ground cumin
1 teaspoon cayenne pepper
⅛ teaspoon ground nutmeg
1½ teaspoons Nepali Garam Masala (page 398)

In a bowl, mix together the minced garlic, minced ginger, salt, and turmeric with 1 tablespoon of water to make a paste. Rub over the meat to coat each piece and set aside.

Heat the oil in a heavy saucepan over medium-high heat. When the oil is hot, but not smoking, add the dried chilies and fenugreek and fry until dark brown and highly fragrant, about 5 seconds. Add the shallots, julienned ginger, sliced garlic, cinnamon, and bay leaves and cook, stirring frequently, until golden brown, about 5 minutes. Mix in the coriander, cumin, cayenne pepper, and nutmeg and stir well. Add the spice-rubbed meat and brown well on all sides, stirring constantly, 8 to 10 minutes. Add 1 cup of water and bring to a boil. Reduce the heat to medium-low, cover, and cook, stirring from time to time, until the meat is tender about 50 minutes. Add the garam masala and mix well. Transfer the meat to a serving dish and serve hot.

Makes 4 to 6 servings.

Bafaayeko Bangoor
SPICED BOILED PORK

This dish sounds very easy to make—and it is. The pork is boiled with whole spices and served with dipping spices. Nepalese people prefer to eat their pork meat with the skin and fat on, but you can discard them before serving if you like.

3 pounds boneless pork
    with skin and fat
    (preferably from the leg),
    cut into 3 to 4 large pieces
6 medium cloves garlic, peeled
¼-inch piece fresh ginger,
    peeled and halved
1 (1-inch) stick cinnamon
½ teaspoon salt
¼ teaspoon whole black
    peppercorns
2 black cardamom pods, crushed

⅛ teaspoon Szechwan pepper
    (*timmur*)
3 small bay leaves
6 whole cloves

DIPPING SPICES
3 dried red chilies, halved and
    seeded
¼ cup hot water
2 teaspoons salt
6 whole Szechwan peppercorns
    (*timmur*), finely ground
    with a mortar and pestle

Combine the pork, garlic, ginger, cinnamon, salt, black peppercorns, cardamom, *timmur*, bay leaves, and cloves with enough water to cover in a deep saucepan. Bring the mixture to a boil over high heat, and then reduce the heat to medium-low. Cover the pan, and simmer, stirring from time to time, until the meat is tender, about 55 minutes. If the water evaporates during the cooking process, and the meat is drying out, but has not cooked through, add ¼ cup more water, and continue cooking until the meat is cooked through.

Meanwhile, soak the dried chilies in ¼ cup of hot water until they are softened, about 10 minutes. Drain and grind them to a paste with a mortar and pestle.

Remove the pork from the heat and discard the spices. When cool enough to handle, cut the pork into 1-inch pieces, with the skin and fat on, and transfer it to a platter. In a small bowl, mix the ground chilies, salt, and timmur, and serve it with the pork.

Makes 4 to 6 servings.

Bangoor ko Chowela
PORK CHOWELA

The technique used to prepare this dish is similar to that used to prepare Lamb Chowela (page 204), only the meat is boiled instead of grilled. It is served as a snack or an appetizer or can be served as part of a Nepali lunch or dinner. This dish is equally delicious served cold or at room temperature.

I recipe Spiced Boiled Pork (page 207), skin and fat removed and discarded, cut into ½-inch pieces
½ cup finely chopped cilantro
4 to 5 green onions (white and pale green parts), finely chopped
Salt to taste
3 fresh mild green chilies, chopped
3 tablespoons fresh lemon or lime juice

I tablespoon minced fresh ginger
½ teaspoon ground turmeric
I teaspoon ground cumin
I teaspoon cayenne pepper
⅛ teaspoon freshly ground black pepper
2 tablespoons mustard oil
¼ teaspoon fenugreek seeds
I or 2 dried red chilies, halved and seeded
I medium onion, sliced lengthwise (about I cup)
3 to 4 medium cloves garlic, sliced

In a medium-size bowl, combine the pork, cilantro, green onions, salt, green chilies, lemon juice, ginger, ¼ teaspoon of the turmeric, cumin, cayenne pepper, and black pepper.

Heat the mustard oil in a skillet over medium-high heat until it faintly smokes. Add the fenugreek and dried chilies and fry until the fenugreek seeds turn dark brown and the dried chilies become reddish-brown and fragrant, about 5 seconds. Add the remaining ¼ teaspoon of turmeric, then the onion and garlic and fry until soft, about 5 minutes. Immediately pour the entire contents of the pan into the meat and mix well. Cover the bowl and allow the flavors to develop for 10 minutes or more. Transfer the meat to a serving dish and serve.

Makes 4 to 6 servings.

Bhutuwa Maasu
PAN-FRIED SPICED MEAT

Bhutuwa, *one of the most popular ways of cooking tender cuts of boneless lamb, goat, pork, or water buffalo, is a Nepali technique of browning meat over high heat so that all the liquid evaporates and the oil comes away from the sides of the pan. This technique yields a highly concentrated flavor.*

2½ to 3 pounds boneless lamb, trimmed and cut into ½-inch pieces
½ cup plain yogurt, stirred
4 medium cloves garlic, minced
1 tablespoon minced fresh ginger
1½ teaspoons ground coriander
1 teaspoon salt
1 teaspoon cayenne pepper
1 teaspoon ground cumin
½ teaspoon ground turmeric

⅛ teaspoon freshly ground black pepper
¼ cup mustard oil
1 dried red chili, halved and seeded
¼ teaspoon fenugreek seeds
¼ teaspoon Himalayan herb (*jimbu*)
A small pinch ground asafetida
2 tablespoons vegetable oil
1 large onion, thinly sliced

In a medium-size bowl, combine the meat with the yogurt, garlic, ginger, coriander, salt, cayenne pepper, cumin, turmeric, and black pepper. Let the mixture rest for 5 to 10 minutes at room-temperature so that the meat absorbs the flavors of the spices.

Heat the mustard oil in a large heavy saucepan over medium-high heat. When it is faintly smoking, add the dried chili, fenugreek seeds, and *jimbu* and fry until dark brown and highly fragrant, about 5 seconds. Add the asafetida and spice-coated meat and cook, stirring constantly, until the meat is brown on all sides, about 10 minutes. Reduce the heat to medium-low, cover, and continue cooking, stirring from time to time, until the meat is cooked through, 20 to 25 minutes. Uncover the pan, increase the heat to medium-high, and continue cooking until all the moisture evaporates and the oil comes away from the sides of the pan. Transfer the lamb to a serving dish.

Heat the vegetable oil in the same pan, add the onion and cook over medium-high heat, stirring constantly, until the onions are golden, 5 to 7 minutes. Add them to the meat and serve hot.

Makes 4 to 6 servings.

Mirga ko Sukuti
VENISON JERKY

The term sukuti *refers to any meat that has been preserved by drying or smoking.* Sukuti *is very popular in Nepal and is usually made from deer, water buffalo, yak, or fish. Venison is an especially prized delicacy because of its rarity, since it is obtained only through hunting. Due to the lack of refrigeration in hunting areas, the entire animal is dried before it spoils. The meat is cut into long thin strips, suspended on a rope and slowly dried in the air and sunlight or over a slow fire. This process may take several days depending on the sunlight, temperature, and humidity.*

At home I use a food dehydrator to dry the meat, but you can also dry it in direct sunlight or in the oven. Sun-drying gives the meat a chewier texture. However, the meat should be dried until all the moisture is completely removed or it will begin to spoil immediately.

10 to 12 pounds boneless venison, trimmed and cut into ½-inch-thick strips	1 teaspoon ground turmeric
1 tablespoon granulated garlic	1 teaspoon ground ginger
2 teaspoons salt	1 teaspoon cayenne pepper
	¼ teaspoon freshly ground black pepper

In a medium-size bowl, combine the venison, garlic, salt, turmeric, ginger, cayenne pepper, and black pepper, rubbing to make sure the meat is well coated with spices. Set aside for at least 2 hours at room temperature.

Food-dehydrator method: Arrange the venison evenly in a single layer on two to three dehydrator trays, without overlapping, to allow good circulation. Place the trays in the food dehydrator. Follow the manufacturer's instructions for the drying temperature. Do not over-dry. The finished jerky should be completely dry, but not brittle. To test for dryness, remove a piece of meat, allow it to cool, and check to see that it bends easily, and does not break.

Oven-drying method: Preheat the oven to the lowest temperature (140° to 160°F). Place the venison directly on the oven racks (or place it on racks set on baking sheets). Do not overlap the strips, to allow them good circulation. Place a tray underneath to trap any dripping from the meat. Turn the meat occasionally. Continue until the meat is dry and all the moisture is removed. This process may take 8 to 10 hours depending on the cut of meat. To test for dryness, remove a piece of meat and taste. It should be chewable. Remove it from the oven and place it on a tray in a well-ventilated sunny area to further remove any moisture for 1 to 2 days before storing.

Store the jerky in an airtight container in the refrigerator for up to 6 months.

Makes 3½ to 4 pounds.

Sukuti Saandheko
DRIED MEAT MARINATED WITH SPICES

This dish is perfect to serve as a snack or as an appetizer garnished with tomato wedges. It also makes a spicy accompaniment to plain boiled rice. I use homemade venison jerky, but you can substitute any variety of purchased jerky. Measure the spices carefully because they have a distinct, strong flavor and may overpower the dish.

A large quantity of spiced dried meat can be prepared ahead of time and stored in an airtight container in the refrigerator, but the fresh ingredients, such as green onions, cilantro, fresh chilies, and lemon should be added right before serving. Raw shelled green peas or peanuts can be mixed with the sukuti *to give an extra crunchy texture.*

2 tablespoons vegetable oil
2 pounds Venison Jerky
(page 210)
½ cup finely chopped cilantro
4 to 5 green onions (white and pale green parts), finely chopped
3 tablespoons fresh lemon or lime juice
2 fresh hot or mild green chilies, minced

3 large cloves garlic, minced
1½ teaspoons minced fresh ginger
1 teaspoon cayenne pepper or to taste
½ teaspoon ground cumin
¼ teaspoon ground turmeric
⅛ teaspoon Szechwan pepper (*timmur*), finely ground with a mortar and pestle

Heat the oil in a medium-size nonstick skillet over medium heat until hot. Add the jerky and sauté, stirring constantly, until lightly browned and crispy, 5 minutes. Using a slotted spoon, remove the jerky, draining as much oil as possible, and place it in a bowl. When cool enough to handle, shred the meat into small pieces with your hands or by pounding it in a mortar. Stir in the cilantro, green onions, lemon juice, green chilies, garlic, ginger, cayenne pepper, cumin, turmeric, and *timmur*. Cover and set aside for 30 minutes for the seasonings to set. Transfer to a serving dish and serve at room temperature.

Makes 4 to 6 servings.

Mirga ko Maasu ko Bhutuwa
SAUTÉED VENISON

This recipe is prepared from tender cuts of venison marinated with fresh herbs and spices and sautéed in fenugreek-scented mustard oil.

2 pounds boneless venison,
 cut into ½-inch cubes
2 fresh hot green chilies, minced
4 large cloves garlic, minced
1 tablespoon minced fresh ginger
1½ teaspoons ground coriander
1 teaspoon salt
1 teaspoon ground cumin

1 teaspoon cayenne pepper, or
 to taste
½ teaspoon ground turmeric
⅛ teaspoon ground nutmeg
⅛ teaspoon Szechwan pepper
 (*timmur*), finely ground
 with a mortar and pestle
3 tablespoons mustard oil
⅛ teaspoon fenugreek seeds

In a medium-size bowl, combine the venison with the green chilies, garlic, ginger, coriander, salt, cumin, cayenne pepper, turmeric, nutmeg, and *timmur*, rubbing to make sure each piece is well coated. Cover the bowl and let it rest for at least 30 minutes to allow flavors to set.

Heat the mustard oil in a medium skillet over medium-high heat. When the oil is faintly smoking, add the fenugreek seeds and fry until dark brown and highly fragrant, about 5 seconds. Reduce the heat to medium, add the marinated venison, and cook, stirring frequently, for 5 minutes. Cover the skillet, continue cooking, stirring as needed, until the meat is tender, and all the moisture has evaporated, about 15 minutes. Transfer the meat to a serving dish. Serve hot.

Makes 4 to 6 servings.

Kalejo Taareko
SAUTÉED LIVER WITH SPICES

The Nepalese people have always enjoyed organ meats, especially liver because of its mild flavor and tender texture. Liver is typically cooked during the religious festival of Dashai, which involves slaughtering animals for offerings—making liver freshly available. It is cooked in a variety of ways, but quick pan-frying is the most popular method. In this recipe, the liver is cooked in its own juices with just a hint of spices. It can be served as an appetizer, a snack, or as part of a main meal.

1½ pounds lamb or goat liver
3 medium cloves garlic, minced
1 teaspoon minced fresh ginger
½ teaspoon salt
½ teaspoon ground turmeric
½ teaspoon ground cumin

½ teaspoon ground coriander
¼ teaspoon cayenne pepper
2 whole Szechwan pepper
  (*timmur*), finely ground
  with a mortar and pestle
3 tablespoons vegetable oil

Clean the liver by removing any connecting tissues, veins, and, the outer membrane without tearing the liver itself. Cut it into ½-inch pieces. Rinse the liver thoroughly under cold water, drain, and place in a bowl.

In a separate small bowl, combine the garlic, ginger, salt, turmeric, cumin, coriander, cayenne pepper, and *timmur* and mix well. Add 1 teaspoon of water to make a paste. Combine the paste with the liver, making sure all the pieces are coated. Set aside.

Heat the oil in a medium nonstick skillet over medium-low heat. When it is hot, add the liver and cook, turning frequently, until it starts to shrink and curl up at the edges, about 5 minutes. Cover the skillet and continue cooking, stirring from time to time, until all the moisture has evaporated, and the liver is tender, 10 to 12 minutes. Do not overcook, as it will become chewy and tough. Transfer the liver to a serving dish and serve hot.

Makes 4 servings.

Raajkhaani Taareko
SAUTÉED RAAJKHAANI

Raajkhaani *are goat testicles.* Raaj *means "king" and* khaani *is "food," so it is described as a food of the kings. They are considered a luxury and reputed to have a delicate texture and flavor, compared to other organ meats. It is believed in Nepal that consumption of* raajkhaani *has an aphrodisiac effect. This effect applies only to men and it is presumed that it will have an adverse effect on women.* Raajkhaani *are highly perishable, so they should be cooked as soon as they are available.*

2 pairs goat testicles	**A small pinch freshly ground**
2 tablespoons butter	**black pepper**
I small clove garlic, minced	**⅛ teaspoon ground cayenne**
Salt	**pepper**

With a sharp knife, remove the skin that surrounds each testicle. Halve each one lengthwise and cut them into ½-inch pieces. Rinse and drain.

Melt the butter in a small nonstick skillet over medium-low heat. Add the testicles, garlic, salt, black pepper, and cayenne pepper and cook, stirring constantly, until the meat begins to brown, about 5 minutes. Do not overcook. Transfer the mixture to a serving dish and serve immediately.

Makes 4 servings.

Bhute ko Bhitryaas
FRIED TRIPE

Tripe is called bhitryaas *in Nepali, and is one of the most widely enjoyed organ meats. It can be cooked in various ways, but before cooking, it should be thoroughly cleaned with several changes of water. This is an extremely versatile dish and can be served hot or at room temperature. Serve it as a pre-dinner appetizer or with pressed rice flakes* (cheura) *as a snack food.*

1½ pounds goat or lamb tripe, cleaned, trimmed of any fatty deposits, and cut into several pieces
1 tablespoon salt
1 teaspoon ground turmeric
1 (1-inch) stick cinnamon
2 bay leaves
6 whole cloves
⅛ teaspoon whole black peppercorns

⅛ teaspoon whole Szechwan peppercorns (*timmur*)
¼ cup vegetable oil
1 dried red chili, halved and seeded
1 tablespoon peeled and finely julienned fresh ginger
4 medium cloves garlic, thinly sliced
½ teaspoon ground cumin
½ teaspoon ground coriander

Combine the tripe with the salt, turmeric, cinnamon, bay leaves, cloves, black pepper, and *timmur* with enough water to cover it in a deep saucepan. Bring the mixture to a boil over high heat, and then reduce the heat to medium-low. Cover the pan and simmer, stirring from time to time, until the tripe is fully cooked, about 50 minutes. Drain the tripe, and discard the water and spices. Cut the tripe into ½-inch pieces. Set aside.

Heat the oil in a medium nonstick skillet over medium-high heat. When the oil is hot, but not smoking, add the dried chilies and fry until reddish-brown and fragrant, about 5 seconds. Add the ginger and garlic and sauté until they are crisp, but not brown, about 1 minute. Add the boiled tripe and sauté, stirring constantly, until lightly browned, about 5 minutes. Reduce the heat to medium-low, add the cumin, coriander, and salt to taste, and stir well. Continue frying, stirring frequently, until lightly crisp and browned, another 5 minutes. Transfer the tripe to a platter and serve.

Makes 4 servings.

Bhuttan
STIR-FRIED GOAT KIDNEY

Goat kidney has a mild flavor and holds its shape after cooking. It is often cooked with other organ meats such as liver, heart, and tongue. Like any organ meat, the kidney is very perishable, so it should be purchased fresh and cooked immediately.

6 goat or lamb kidneys	½ teaspoon ground cumin
3 medium cloves garlic, minced	½ teaspoon ground coriander
1 teaspoon minced fresh ginger	½ teaspoon cayenne pepper
Salt to taste	2 tablespoons vegetable oil
½ teaspoon ground turmeric	

Trim white membrane and fat from the kidneys. Rinse in several change of water and cut into ½-inch pieces.

In a medium-size bowl, combine the kidneys with the garlic, ginger, salt to taste, turmeric, cumin, coriander, and cayenne pepper, and mix well.

Heat the oil in a medium-size heavy nonstick skillet over medium-high heat. Add the kidneys and cook, stirring frequently, until the liquid has evaporated, 5 to 7 minutes. Do not overcook. Transfer the mixture to a platter and serve immediately.

Makes 4 to 6 servings.

Tauko ko Tarkaari
SAUTÉED GOAT BRAINS

The brain is one of the most delicate and perishable of all organ meats. In this recipe, the lamb or goat head is first boiled whole, and then the steamed brain is removed gently and pan-sautéed. It is served as a delicacy on very special occasions.

I whole fresh goat or lamb
   head, rinsed
3 small cloves garlic, peeled
I (¼-inch) piece fresh ginger,
   peeled and halved
I (½-inch) stick cinnamon
I green cardamom pod, crushed

I black cardamom pod, crushed
¼ teaspoon coriander seeds
⅛ teaspoon salt
3 bay leaves
6 whole cloves
4 tablespoons butter

In a deep saucepan, combine the goat head, garlic, ginger, cinnamon, green and black cardamom pods, coriander, salt, bay leaves, and cloves. Add enough water to cover by 3 to 4 inches. Bring the mixture to a rolling boil over high heat. Remove any foam and matter that rises to the surface. Reduce the heat to medium-low, cover, and simmer gently until the meat around the head starts to come off and is fully cooked, about I hour. This can be done in a pressure cooker to speed up the process.

Remove the head, place it on a cutting board, and cool. With a sharp knife, carefully cut open the head and remove the brain. Discard the whole spices and bones, but save the stock for a future use. Chop the brain into small pieces and set aside.

Melt the butter in a heavy nonstick skillet over medium-low heat. Add the brains and salt to taste and cook, stirring as needed, until they are firm and lightly browned, 5 to 7 minutes. Adjust the salt. Transfer the brains to a serving dish and serve immediately.

Makes 4 appetizer servings.

Ragati Taareko
SAUTÉED RAGATI

Ragati is one of the most traditional Nepali meat dishes, cooked from goat, lamb, or water buffalo blood. It is served during the religious festival of Dashai, when a large number of animals are sacrificed to the gods. Almost every part of the blessed animals are eaten, and nothing is wasted. The fresh blood is collected during the animal sacrifice in a clean container. The coagulated blood develops a jelly-like texture, and is cut into small pieces, spiced, and sautéed. It is served as an appetizer or snack food or just simply as blessed food. Fresh or frozen blood can be obtained from butchers or in many ethnic markets.

2½ cups fresh goat or lamb
   blood
I large shallot, minced
I teaspoon minced fresh ginger
2 medium cloves garlic, minced
½ teaspoon ground turmeric

½ teaspoon cayenne pepper
4 whole Szechwan peppercorns
   (*timmur*), finely ground with
   a mortar and pestle
Salt to taste
2 tablespoons vegetable oil

Cut the coagulated blood into ½-inch pieces and place them in a bowl. In another small bowl, mix together the shallot, ginger, garlic, turmeric, cayenne pepper, *timmur*, and salt to taste. Add 1 tablespoon of water to form a paste.

Heat the oil in a heavy skillet over medium-high heat. When the oil is hot, add the spice paste and cook, stirring constantly, until it is light brown, about 1 minute. Add the blood and cook, stirring from time to time, until it is well-browned and the oil begins to come away from the sides of the skillet, 15 to 20 minutes. Remove from the heat and serve immediately.

Makes 4 to 6 servings.

Bhutuwa Jibro
TONGUE WITH ONIONS

Fresh tongue is called jibro *in Nepali and, like any organ meat, it can be cooked in many ways, but sautéing with fresh herbs and spices is the most common method. Tongue meat is tough and requires long, slow simmering to make it tender.*

1½ to 2 pounds fresh lamb or
    goat tongues
1 teaspoon salt
4 whole Szechwan peppercorns
    (*timmur*)
8 whole black peppercorns
4 whole cloves
¼ cup vegetable oil

2 medium onions, julienned
1 tablespoon peeled and finely
    julienned fresh ginger
4 large cloves garlic, thinly sliced
½ teaspoon ground turmeric
½ teaspoon ground cumin
½ teaspoon ground coriander
½ teaspoon cayenne pepper

In a deep saucepan, combine the tongues with the salt, *timmur*, black pepper, cloves, and enough water to cover and bring the mixture to a rolling boil over high heat. Remove any foam and scum that rises to the surface. Reduce the heat to medium-low, cover, and simmer, stirring from time to time, until the tongues are tender, about 45 minutes. Drain and discard the water and spices. Place the tongues on a cutting board and when cool enough to handle, peel away the skin with a sharp knife. Discard the skin and cut the meat into ½-inch pieces. Set aside.

Heat the oil in a medium-size nonstick or cast iron skillet over medium-high heat. When the oil is hot, add the tongue and cook, stirring frequently, until it is lightly browned, about 5 minutes. Add the onions, ginger, garlic, turmeric, cumin, coriander, and cayenne pepper and mix well. Continue cooking, stirring when needed, until the onions are soft, about 5 minutes. Add salt if needed. Transfer the mixture to a platter and serve.

Makes 4 to 6 servings.

Bhuttan ko Tarkaari
SAUTÉED ORGAN MEATS

In a country where meat is scarce, the Nepalese have mastered the art of cooking every part of the animal into a delicious dish and the following recipe is a good example. I usually make this recipe when I purchase a whole goat from my local farm and ask the butcher to make a separate package of kidneys, heart, and liver.

3 tablespoons vegetable oil
1 ½ pounds goat or lamb livers, kidneys, and hearts, washed, trimmed of any fat and membranes, and cut into ½-inch pieces
2 fresh hot green chilies, each split lengthwise
2 medium cloves garlic, minced
1 teaspoon minced fresh ginger
½ teaspoon ground turmeric
½ teaspoon ground cumin

½ teaspoon ground coriander
½ teaspoon cayenne pepper
¼ teaspoon salt
4 whole Szechwan pepper (*timmur*), finely ground with a mortar and pestle
2 to 3 green onions (white and pale green parts), finely chopped
¼ cup finely chopped cilantro
½ teaspoon Nepali Garam Masala (page 398)

Heat the oil in a medium nonstick or cast-iron skillet over medium-high heat. When the oil is hot, add the meats and cook, stirring frequently, for 5 minutes. Add the green chilies, garlic, ginger, turmeric, cumin, coriander, cayenne pepper, salt, and *timmur* and mix well. Adjust the heat to medium, cover, and cook, stirring as needed, until the organ meat is tender and browned, the liquid has evaporated, and the oil has begun to separate from the side of the skillet, about 20 minutes. Add the green onions, cilantro, and garam masala and mix well. Transfer the mixture to a serving dish and serve hot.

Makes 4 to 6 servings.

Chara ko Maasu ra Phool

POULTRY AND EGGS

Until recently, chicken (*kukhura*) was rare and high priced in Nepal, but it is now more readily available and cooked more frequently. Traditionally chicken is cooked on the bone because it is more flavorful and succulent than boneless chicken. The skin is removed before cooking so that the spices can better penetrate the chicken. These recipes range from simple, lightly spiced curries to highly spiced dishes, and dishes cooked with vegetables. I prefer to purchase whole chickens rather than precut pieces because this results in more flavorful dishes, but you may use precut pieces for convenience. Farm-raised turkey (*ban kukhura*), duck (*haas*), quail (*battain*), and pheasant (*kaaliz or kaaleej*) are available in the fresh or frozen sections of larger supermarkets, Asian markets, and some farms or farmer's markets.

Eggs are widely enjoyed in Nepal, although some orthodox Brahmins do not eat them. They are not limited to breakfast fare, but are served as snacks, appetizers, or as part of a full meal. Farm-fresh hen eggs are most common, but some people prefer duck eggs, which are more flavorful and higher in fat. Duck eggs have a significant role in Nepal for religious, social, and culinary reasons. In Newar communities, they are used as a sacred (*sagun*) food to promote good luck and prosperity. Eggs are also offered to the gods during religious rituals.

Kukhura ko Pakku
CHICKEN CURRY

This is a simple recipe for chicken curry. To make this curry, purchase a whole young chicken and cut it into serving-size pieces. Alternatively, you can purchase pre-cut chicken pieces, which will be much easier to handle. For best results, marinate these pieces in the morning to prepare an evening meal. The chicken cooks in its own juices without additional water.

2 to 3 dried red chilies, halved
¼ cup hot water
1 (3- to 3½-pound) chicken, skinned and cut into 8 to 10 pieces
1 medium onion, finely chopped (about 1 cup)
¼ cup vegetable oil
1½ tablespoons minced fresh ginger
4 medium cloves garlic, minced
2 teaspoons ground coriander

1½ teaspoons ground cumin
1 teaspoon ground turmeric
1 teaspoon salt
⅛ teaspoon freshly ground black pepper
⅛ teaspoon ground nutmeg
1 (1-inch) stick cinnamon, halved
4 green cardamom pods, crushed
1 black cardamom pod, crushed
6 whole cloves
2 medium bay leaves
½ cup finely chopped cilantro

Soak the chilies in the hot water until softened. Drain and coarsely grind with a mortar and pestle.

Rinse the chicken well under cold water and drain. Prick the chicken all over with a fork or a sharp knife and place it in a large bowl. In a separate small bowl, combine the onion, chili paste, oil, ginger, garlic, coriander, cumin, turmeric, salt, black pepper, and nutmeg. Rub the spice mixture into the chicken with your hands, making sure it is well-coated. Add the cinnamon, green and black cardamom pods, cloves, and bay leaves. Cover and marinate for at least 2 hours in the refrigerator.

Place the chicken with the marinade in a large heavy-bottomed saucepan. Cook, uncovered, over medium-high heat, stirring from time to time, for 10 minutes. Reduce the heat to low, cover, and simmer, stirring often to prevent scorching, until the chicken is tender and cooked through, about 40 minutes. Transfer the chicken to a serving dish, sprinkle with cilantro, and serve hot.

Makes 4 to 6 servings.

Pyaj Haaleko Kukhura ko Maasu
CHICKEN CURRY WITH ONIONS

Here is another easy-to-prepare chicken dish that does not require marinating, but has a delicious spicy flavor. Serve it with the traditional Nepali accompaniments of rice, lentils, and vegetables or with warm bread.

¼ cup vegetable oil
1 (1-inch) stick cinnamon
 2 green cardamom pods,
  crushed
4 whole cloves
2 small bay leaves
2 medium onions, finely chopped
  (about 2 cups)
1 (3- to 3½-pound) chicken,
  skinned and cut into
  8 to 10 small pieces
1 teaspoon salt
1½ teaspoons ground cumin
1½ teaspoons ground coriander

½ teaspoon ground turmeric
2 medium tomatoes, finely
  chopped or pureed
  (about 2 cups)
2 fresh hot green chilies, split
  lengthwise
1 tablespoon minced fresh ginger
3 cloves garlic, minced
1 teaspoon Nepali Garam Masala
  (page 398)
4 to 5 green onions (white and
  pale green parts), finely
  chopped
½ cup finely chopped cilantro

Heat the oil in a large heavy saucepan over medium-high heat. When the oil is hot, but not smoking, add the cinnamon, cardamom pods, cloves, and bay leaves and fry until they begin to puff up, darken, and give off a pleasant aroma, about 5 seconds. Add the onions and cook until lightly browned, 5 to 7 minutes. Adjust the heat to high, add the chicken, and cook, stirring occasionally, until lightly browned. Add the salt, cumin, coriander, and turmeric and stir for another minute. Then add the tomatoes and cook until they are slightly soft, about 2 minutes. Add 1 cup of water and bring the mixture to a boil, uncovered. Reduce the heat to medium-low, cover, and continue cooking for 10 minutes, stirring from time to time to make sure the sauce does not burn or stick to the bottom of the pan. Uncover, add the green chilies, ginger, garlic, and garam masala and continue cooking until the chicken is tender and well coated with the smooth sauce, about 25 minutes. Transfer the chicken to a serving dish, sprinkle the onions and cilantro on top, and serve hot.

Makes 4 to 6 servings.

Kukhura Taareko
STIR-FRIED CHICKEN THIGHS

*This Nepali stir-fry is my favorite way of cooking chicken thighs. Fry the chicken over high heat and add onions when it is almost done to avoid mushiness. It makes a good light lunch served with any Nepali bread or a great snack with pressed rice flakes (*cheura*).*

2½ to 3 pounds skinless, boneless chicken thighs, cut into 1½-inch pieces
½ cup plain yogurt, stirred
1 tablespoon minced fresh ginger
2 medium cloves garlic, minced
1½ teaspoons Nepali Garam Masala (page 398)
1 teaspoon salt
1 teaspoon ground turmeric
½ teaspoon cayenne pepper

¼ cup vegetable oil
2 medium onions, sliced
2 to 3 fresh mild green chilies, jullienned
¼ cup finely chopped cilantro
4 to 6 green onions (white and pale green parts), finely chopped
1 tomato, cut into wedges

In a medium bowl, combine the chicken, yogurt, ginger, garlic, garam masala, salt, turmeric, and cayenne pepper. Set aside at room temperature for 10 minutes.

Heat the oil in a heavy-bottomed large skillet over medium-high heat. When the oil is hot, add the chicken and its marinade and cook until the liquid evaporates and the chicken becomes tender and light brown, 12 to 15 minutes. Add the onions and cook, stirring continuously, until they are soft, about 5 minutes. Mix in the green chilies, cilantro, green onions, and tomato and fry for 2 minutes longer. Transfer the mixture to a serving dish and serve hot.

Makes 4 to 6 servings.

Masaledar Kukhura
CHICKEN WITH AROMATIC SAUCE

This is a slightly more elaborate dish than the preceding recipes as it is cooked in a spicy, seasoned yogurt sauce. This recipe can be prepared one day in advance and reheated on the stovetop by gently simmering until it is heated throughout. This dish can be served with buttered rice, warm bread, vegetables, and pickles.

1 (3- to 3½-pound) chicken, skinned and cut into 8 to 10 pieces
1 teaspoon salt
½ teaspoon ground turmeric
¼ cup vegetable oil plus 2 tablespoons
4 large onions, 3 coarsely chopped (about 3 cups) and 1 halved lengthwise and thinly sliced
4 fresh hot green chilies, split lengthwise
1½ tablespoons peeled and coarsely chopped fresh ginger

4 medium cloves garlic, coarsely chopped
1 tablespoon ground coriander
1½ teaspoons ground cumin
⅛ teaspoon freshly ground black pepper
⅛ teaspoon ground nutmeg
3 medium tomatoes, finely chopped (about 3 cups)
1 cup plain yogurt, stirred
1½ teaspoons Fragrant Garam Masala (page 397)
½ cup finely chopped cilantro
2 to 3 green onions (white and pale green parts), cut into ¼-inch pieces

Rinse the chicken pieces well under cold water and drain. Prick with a fork or a sharp knife and place in a large bowl. With your hands, rub the chicken with the salt and turmeric, and set aside in the refrigerator.

Heat ¼ cup of the oil in a heavy saucepan over medium-high heat. When hot, but not smoking, add the chopped onion, green chilies, ginger, and garlic and cook until onions are soft but not browned, stirring frequently, about 5 minutes. With a slotted spoon transfer the onion mixture to a blender or a food processor, reserving the oil in the pan. Blend the mixture to a smooth paste.

Sauté the sliced onion in the oil remaining in the pan over medium-high heat until crisp and golden brown. With a slotted spoon transfer the onion to a plate lined with paper towels to drain and set aside.

Return the onion paste to the pan. If there is little oil left, add the remaining 2 tablespoons. Stir in the coriander, cumin, black pepper, and nutmeg and cook over medium-high heat until lightly browned, about 2 minutes. Add the tomatoes and continue cooking, stirring, until the tomatoes are soft and the juices evaporate, about 5 minutes. Add the yogurt, 1 tablespoon at a time, mixing after each addition, and cook until it is well incorporated. Add the chicken and 1 cup of water, stir well, and cook, uncovered, for 10 minutes. Reduce the heat to medium-low, cover the pan, and cook until the chicken is tender and the sauce has thickened, about 25 minutes. Stir in the garam masala.

Transfer the chicken to a serving dish, add the fried onions, cilantro, and green onions, and serve piping hot.

Makes 4 to 6 servings.

Kauli-Kukhura
CHICKEN WITH CAULIFLOWER

In this dish, chicken and cauliflower are cooked together, lending each other fla-
vor, and resulting in a delectably flavored and textured dish. Add the cauli-
flower florets at the end of the cooking process, ensuring that they retain their
shape, but have enough time to absorb the spices and flavor of the chicken.

This recipe uses bone-in chicken, which is more flavorful, but you can sub-
stitute skinless, boneless chicken and serve it as a one-dish meal with cheura
(pressed rice flakes) for a mid-afternoon snack or as part of a main meal
with steamed rice.

1 (2½- to 3-pound) chicken, skin removed and cut into 12 to 14 pieces	2 large cloves garlic, finely chopped
¼ cup vegetable oil	1 tablespoon Nepali Garam Masala (page 398)
⅛ teaspoon fenugreek seeds	2 teaspoons cayenne pepper, or to taste
1 bay leaf	
1 medium onion, finely chopped (about 1 cup)	½ teaspoon ground turmeric
2 fresh mild green chilies, chopped	1 teaspoon salt
	½ head cauliflower, cut into 1½-inch florets (about 4 cups)
1 tablespoon minced fresh ginger	¼ cup finely chopped cilantro

Wash the chicken thoroughly with cold water and drain completely. Prick with a fork or a sharp knife and set aside.

Heat the oil in a large heavy saucepan over medium-high heat. When hot, but not smoking, add the fenugreek seeds and fry until dark brown and highly fragrant, about 5 seconds. Add the bay leaf, then immediately add the onion, green chilies, ginger, and garlic and cook until they are lightly browned, stirring frequently, 5 to 7 minutes. Stir in the chicken, garam masala, cayenne pepper, and turmeric and cook, uncovered, stirring from time to time, until the chicken is lightly browned, about 10 minutes. Add the salt and stir well. Reduce the heat to medium-low, cover the pan, and cook until the chicken is almost tender, about 15 minutes. Add the cauliflower and mix well until the florets are evenly coated with spices. Cover the pan and continue cooking, gently stirring as needed, until the chicken is tender and cooked through, the cauliflower is crisp-tender, and the spice mixture is boiled down and absorbed, about 20 minutes. Transfer the mixture to a serving dish, sprinkle with the cilantro, and serve.

Note: It is important to note that cauliflower goes from being undercooked to overcooked very quickly. Since cauliflower has a tendency to become mushy, stir gently.

Makes 4 to 6 servings.

Tandoori Kukhura
TANDOORI CHICKEN

Tandoori chicken is originally from northern India, but it is also very popular in Nepal. Traditionally, the marinated chicken is cooked in a tandoor, a cylindrical clay oven sunk in the earth that is heated to a very high temperature with a charcoal fire. The chicken cooks very quickly in the intense heat, which seals in the juices and flavor. Although the authentic flavor of a tandoor cannot be duplicated in a regular oven or on an outdoor grill, this is my simplified version.

1 (3- to 3½-pound) chicken, skinned and cut into 8 to 10 pieces	1½ cups plain yogurt, stirred
	¼ cup tomato paste
	2 tablespoons vegetable oil
¼ cup fresh lemon or lime juice	1 tablespoon paprika
1½ teaspoons salt, or to taste	1 teaspoon Fragrant Garam
1 teaspoon ground turmeric	Masala (page 397)
1 medium onion, chopped (about 1 cup)	¼ cup butter, melted
	1 medium red onion, thinly sliced
3 fresh mild green chili peppers, stemmed	1 medium cucumber, thinly sliced
¼ cup finely chopped cilantro	2 medium tomatoes, cut into wedges
4 large cloves garlic, peeled	1 lemon, cut into wedges
1 tablespoon peeled and roughly chopped fresh ginger	3 or 4 whole fresh green chili peppers
2 dried red chilies, coarsely broken and seeded	2 to 3 cilantro springs
2 teaspoons coriander seeds	
1 teaspoon cumin seeds	

Rinse the chicken well under cold water and drain. Prick the pieces all over with a fork or sharp knife, making diagonal slits in the fleshy parts to allow the marinade to penetrate. Place the chicken in a bowl and add the lemon juice, salt, and turmeric. Rub over the chicken, and set aside to marinate in the refrigerator.

Combine the onion, green chilies, cilantro, garlic, ginger, dried chilies, coriander, and cumin in a blender or food processor and process until the mixture forms a smooth paste. Add 1 or 2 tablespoons of water to facilitate blending, if necessary. Transfer the mixture to a bowl and stir in the yogurt, tomato paste, oil, paprika, and garam masala. Pour the mixture over the chicken and mix well, making sure that each piece is coated. Place the chicken and marinade in a sealable heavy plastic bag, secure it, and refrigerate for at least 8 hours. Shake and turn the chicken occasionally during the marinating process. When you are ready to proceed, bring the chicken back to room temperature.

Preheat a charcoal or gas grill or broiler to medium-high heat. Place the chicken pieces coated with the marinade on a wire rack and grill or broil them, turning frequently and basting with the melted butter, until well browned on all sides and cooked through, about 30 minutes. Transfer the chicken to a platter, garnish it with the red onion, cucumber, tomatoes, lemon, chili peppers, and cilantro, and serve hot.

Makes 4 to 6 servings.

Kukhura ko Sekuwa
CHICKEN SEKUWA

Sekuwa is the term used to describe any meat dish that is cooked directly under or over a heat source, such as a broiler or grill. In this easy-to-prepare dish, boneless, skinless chicken is tenderized by yogurt and aromatic spices and then cooked by the sekuwa *method. The secret is to not overcook the meat, especially the breast, which tends to dry out very quickly. Chicken* sekuwa *is served as an appetizer with a spicy chutney or it can supplement any lunch or dinner menu.*

2½ to 3 pounds skinless, boneless chicken breasts, cut into 1½-inch pieces

1 tablespoon plus 2½ teaspoons fresh lemon or lime juice

1⅛ teaspoons salt

2 medium red onions, 1 chopped (about 1 cup), and 1 sliced ⅛-inch thick and separated into rings

12 fresh mild green chilies

1 tablespoon peeled and roughly chopped fresh ginger

3 large cloves garlic, peeled

1 cup plain yogurt, stirred

2 tablespoons vegetable oil

1 teaspoon ground paprika

1 teaspoon Nepali Garam Masala (page 398)

½ teaspoon ground cumin

½ teaspoon ground turmeric

2 medium tomatoes, cut into 6 wedges

1 lemon or lime, cut into wedges

2 to 3 sprigs of cilantro

8 to 10 grilling skewers (if wooden, soak for 30 minutes before use)

Place the chicken in a large bowl with 1½ tablespoons of the lemon juice and 1 teaspoon of the salt. Mix thoroughly and set aside for 10 minutes. Put the chopped onion, 2 of the green chilies, the ginger, and garlic in a blender or a food processor and process until they are minced. Transfer the mixture to a small bowl and stir in the yogurt, oil, paprika, garam masala, cumin, and turmeric. Combine the mixture with the chicken, making sure that each piece is well coated. Cover the bowl and marinate it for at least 2 hours in the refrigerator.

Meanwhile, marinate the onion rings in the remaining 1 teaspoon of lemon juice and ⅛ teaspoon of salt.

Preheat a charcoal or gas grill to medium-high heat. Thread the marinated chicken onto the skewers, place them over the rack, and grill, turning frequently, until they are lightly browned on all sides and cooked through, 20 to 25 minutes. Remove them from the grill and allow the chicken to cool a little before removing it from the skewers. Arrange the chicken on a serving dish and surround it with the marinated onion, lemon, and tomato wedges, remaining 10 green chilies, and the cilantro sprigs, and serve.

Makes 4 to 6 servings.

Pine ko Kukhura ra Kerau
GROUND CHICKEN WITH GREEN PEAS

This is a delicious chicken dish that cooks up in minutes and is perfect for a light lunch or a filling snack. This dish is cooked with frozen peas, but you can substitute fresh peas if available, which will make it even tastier, but be sure to increase the cooking time. Serve hot with any griddle-cooked bread, or with pressed rice flakes (cheura).

3 tablespoons clarified butter (*gheu*)
2 medium onions, finely chopped (about 2 cups)
1 (1-inch) stick cinnamon, halved
1 small bay leaf
1 tablespoon minced fresh ginger
2 large cloves garlic, minced
2 pounds ground chicken (or turkey or half of each)

1½ teaspoons Nepali Garam Masala (page 398)
1 teaspoon cayenne pepper
½ teaspoon salt
½ teaspoon ground turmeric
¼ teaspoon freshly ground black pepper
2 cups frozen peas, thawed and thoroughly drained

Heat the clarified butter in a heavy saucepan over medium-high heat, add the onions, cinnamon, and bay leaf, and fry until the onions are lightly browned, 5 to 7 minutes. Stir in the ginger and garlic and cook for 1 minute. Add the ground chicken and cook, stirring continuously and breaking up the lumps, until it is nearly cooked through and lightly browned, about 10 minutes. Stir in the garam masala, cayenne pepper, salt, turmeric, and black pepper and mix well. Add ½ cup of water and bring it to a boil. Reduce the heat to medium-low, cover, and simmer until the meat is cooked through and the liquid has evaporated, about 10 minutes. Add the peas, and cook, stirring occasionally, for 5 minutes. Transfer the mixture to a serving dish and serve hot.

Makes 4 to 6 servings.

Kukhura ko Cutlet
CHICKEN CUTLETS

These spiced chicken cutlets topped with fresh vegetables can be served as a light lunch with buttered rice and vegetables or as a mid-afternoon snack. This dish is best served immediately after cooking, as reheating may dry out the chicken.

6 boneless, skinless chicken breast halves, trimmed (about 2½ pounds)
2 large cloves garlic, minced
1 teaspoon Nepali Garam Masala (page 398)
1 teaspoon vegetable oil
1 teaspoon minced fresh ginger
½ teaspoon freshly ground black pepper

½ teaspoon cayenne pepper
½ teaspoon salt
½ cup plus 2 tablespoons unsalted butter
2 large shallots, minced
1 large onion, julienned
1 small red or green bell pepper, cored and sliced lengthwise
8 ounces fresh mushrooms (any variety), sliced

Place the breasts between 2 pieces of heavy plastic wrap on a cutting board. Pound each chicken breast gently, using a meat mallet or the flat side of a knife until flat and about ¼ inch thick. In a small bowl, combine the garlic, garam masala, oil, ginger, black pepper, cayenne pepper, and salt to make a smooth paste. Rub the paste onto the chicken and coat well.

In a large cast-iron or nonstick skillet, melt ¼ cup of the butter over medium-high heat. Arrange three cutlets in the pan without overlapping and cook, turning as needed, until they are light brown on both sides and the juices run clear when pierced with a knife, about 10 minutes. With a slotted spoon, transfer the chicken to a platter, leaving the excess butter in the skillet. Melt ¼ cup more butter and repeat the process for the remaining 3 chicken breasts.

If there is little butter left in the skillet, melt the remaining 2 tablespoons and cook the shallots, stirring constantly until soft, about 3 minutes. Add the onion, bell peppers, and mushrooms and cook until they are softened and lightly browned, about 5 minutes. Spoon the vegetables over the chicken cutlets and serve immediately.

Makes 4 to 6 servings.

Bhutuwa Chara ko Bhitri
SAUTÉED CHICKEN GIZZARDS

These bite-size gizzards are surprisingly delicious. Chicken hearts and livers, or a combination, may also be used. Ready-to-cook poultry gizzards are available in the meat section of regular grocery stores or specialty butchers. Gizzards can be very tough and need to be boiled until tender before using.

1½ to 2 pounds chicken gizzards	1 large shallot, minced
1 teaspoon salt	2 large cloves garlic, minced
1 (1-inch) stick cinnamon	1 teaspoon minced fresh ginger
2 bay leaves	½ teaspoon ground cumin
4 whole cloves	½ teaspoon ground coriander
⅛ teaspoon Szechwan pepper	¼ teaspoon ground turmeric
(*timmur*)	⅛ teaspoon freshly ground
3 tablespoons vegetable oil	black pepper
2 to 3 fresh mild green chilies,	
minced	

Remove the fat and outer membranes of the gizzards and rinse well. Make a few parallel slashes in each piece (this helps the spices to penetrate), and then cut it in thirds. In a medium-size saucepan, combine the gizzards with ½ teaspoon of the salt, the cinnamon, bay leaves, cloves, *timmur*, and water to cover. Bring to a boil over high heat. Reduce the heat to medium-low, cover, and simmer, stirring from time to time, until the gizzards are tender, about 25 minutes. Drain the gizzards, discard the whole spices, and chop the gizzards into bite-size pieces.

Heat the oil in a medium nonstick skillet over medium-high heat. When hot, but not smoking, add the green chilies, shallot, garlic, and ginger and sauté until soft, stirring constantly. Add the remaining ½ teaspoon of salt, cumin, coriander, turmeric, and black pepper and stir well. Reduce the heat to medium, add the gizzards, and cook, stirring constantly, until they are well browned and the moisture has evaporated, 5 to 7 minutes. Transfer the gizzards to a platter and serve hot.

Makes 4 to 6 servings.

Thulo Kukhura ko Kabaab
SPICY TURKEY KEBABS

This is my favorite recipe for skinless and boneless turkey (or chicken) thighs—
they are lightly marinated, threaded on skewers, and grilled. Turkey meat dries
out very quickly and needs to be basted frequently to keep it moist and succulent.

3 medium red onions, I roughly
chopped (about I cup),
2 thinly sliced and separated
into rings
2 to 3 mild fresh green chilies,
coarsely chopped
4 cloves garlic, chopped
I tablespoon peeled and roughly
chopped fresh ginger
¾ cup plain yogurt, stirred
5 tablespoons fresh lemon or
lime juice
I tablespoon vegetable oil
I tablespoon paprika
2 teaspoons ground coriander
I teaspoon ground cumin

I teaspoon cayenne pepper
I teaspoon Nepali Garam Masala
(page 398)
½ teaspoon ground turmeric
I teaspoon salt
3 to 3½ pounds skinless,
boneless turkey thighs,
trimmed and cut into
1½-inch cubes
¼ cup butter, melted
I medium cucumber, peeled and
thinly sliced

8 to 10 grilling skewers
(if wooden, soak for
30 minutes before use)

Put the chopped onion, green chilies, garlic, and ginger in a blender or a food
processor and process until minced. Transfer the mixture to a small bowl and
mix in the yogurt, 2 tablespoons of the lemon juice, the oil, paprika, coriander, cumin, cayenne pepper, garam masala, turmeric, and ½ teaspoon of the
salt. Combine the mixture with the turkey, making sure that each piece is well
coated. Cover and marinate for at least 2 hours in the refrigerator.

Preheat a charcoal or gas grill to medium-high heat. Thread the turkey onto the
skewers. Place the skewered meat over the grill, and turn frequently, basting with
the butter, until cooked through and browned on all sides, 15 to 20 minutes.

While the turkey is cooking, make the garnish. In a small bowl, combine the
sliced onions, cucumber, remaining lemon juice, and remaining salt and set
aside for 10 minutes. Squeeze out the excess liquid with your hands and drain.

Transfer the turkey kebabs to a serving dish, sprinkle with the garnish, and serve.

Makes 4 to 6 servings.

Thulo Kukhura ko Pakwaan
TURKEY PAKWAAN

*The following recipe was inspired by the Tuladhar family. Although it is tra-
ditionally made with goat meat (khasi), they substitute more widely available turkey drumsticks, which we call "American khasi." When cooked with
a distinct blend of herbs and spices, we find the taste and texture of the succulent dark meat to be similar to goat meat curry. The drumsticks should be
cut into one-inch pieces with the bones. In most supermarkets and butcher
shops, drumsticks are often sold separately, fresh or frozen. Butchers will
gladly cut them into bone-in pieces upon request.*

4 to 4½ pounds turkey
  drumsticks (4 to 6)
1½ tablespoons minced fresh
  ginger
4 large cloves garlic, minced
1½ teaspoons ground cumin
1½ teaspoons ground coriander
1½ teaspoons Nepali Garam
  Masala (page 398)
1 teaspoon cayenne pepper
½ teaspoon ground fennel seeds
¼ teaspoon freshly ground
  black pepper
¼ cup vegetable oil
2 dried red chilies, halved and
  seeded
¼ teaspoon fenugreek seeds
¼ teaspoon cumin seeds

3 medium onions, finely chopped
  (about 3 cups)
4 to 6 green cardamom pods,
  crushed
1 (1-inch) stick cinnamon,
  halved
2 bay leaves
½ teaspoon ground turmeric
4 whole cloves
A small pinch ground asafetida
½ teaspoon salt
3 medium tomatoes, chopped
  (about 3 cups)
½ cup finely chopped cilantro
4 to 5 green onions (white and
  pale green parts), cut into
  ¼-inch pieces
4 fresh mild green chilies,
  cut into ¼-inch strips

Cut the turkey drumsticks, with the bones, into 1-inch pieces. Discard the bony
end and skin and remove the sharp bones that stick out. Wash the turkey thoroughly with cold water and drain. Set aside.

In a small bowl, mix together the ginger, garlic, cumin, coriander, garam masala, cayenne pepper, fennel, and black pepper. Add 1 tablespoon of water to make a paste and set aside.

Heat the oil in a large heavy saucepan over medium-high heat until hot, but not smoking. Add the dried chilies, fenugreek, and cumin and fry until dark brown and highly fragrant, about 5 seconds. Add the onions, cardamom pods, cinnamon, bay leaves, turmeric, cloves, and asafetida and fry, stirring constantly, until the onions turn light brown, 5 to 7 minutes. Stir in the spice paste and cook, stirring constantly, until it is lightly browned, about 1 minute. Add the turkey and cook until lightly browned, about 7 minutes. Add the salt and tomatoes and cook until the tomatoes are soft. Reduce the heat to medium-low, cover, and simmer, stirring from time to time, until the turkey is tender and cooked through and the sauce has thickened enough to coat the meat, about 25 minutes.

Transfer the turkey to a serving dish, top with the cilantro, green onions, and green chilies, and serve hot.

Makes 4 to 6 servings.

Haas ko Maasu Taareko
PAN-FRIED DUCK

Duck (haas) is festival meat in Nepal, and it is served on special occasions. Although the bird has a great deal of fat under the skin, the dark meat is quite lean and flavorful. This simple dish is cooked with minimal spices so as not to overpower the delicate flavor of the duck. Farm-raised ducks are available year-round in supermarkets and Asian food markets.

I (4- to 5-pound) duck
6 to 8 cloves garlic,
   peeled and halved
I (1½-inch) piece fresh ginger,
   peeled and quartered
I (1-inch) stick cinnamon, halved
I teaspoon salt
I teaspoon coriander seeds
½ teaspoon whole black
   peppercorns

⅛ teaspoon Szechwan pepper
   (*timmur*)
4 bay leaves
6 whole cloves
2 tablespoons vegetable oil
I teaspoon Nepali Garam Masala
   (page 398)
½ teaspoon ground turmeric
½ teaspoon cayenne pepper

Rinse the duck under cold water. Remove and discard the neck and giblets and pull out the excess fat from inside the body and neck cavity. Cut the duck into 6 to 8 pieces.

In a large saucepan, combine the duck, garlic, ginger, cinnamon, salt, coriander, black pepper, *timmur*, bay leaves, cloves, and water to cover and bring it to a rolling boil over high heat. Reduce the heat to medium-low, cover, and simmer until the duck is tender, the meat is falling away from the bone, and most of the water has evaporated, about 45 minutes. If there is any water left in the pan, raise the heat to high and cook until all the water has evaporated. Transfer the duck to a bowl and discard the spices.

Heat the oil in a heavy, wide cast-iron skillet over medium-high heat. When the oil is hot, add the meat, garam masala, turmeric, and cayenne pepper and fry until the pieces are browned and lightly crisp, 10 to 12 minutes. Adjust the salt if needed. Transfer the duck to a serving dish and serve.

Makes 4 to 6 servings.

Sano Chara ko Maasu
STEWED CORNISH HEN WITH GINGER AND GARLIC

This flavorful dish is an excellent addition to a celebratory meal. Cornish hens are usually sold in pairs in the frozen meat section and should be thawed before cooking.

2 (1½- to 2-pound) Cornish hens, thawed and skinned, each cut into 6 to 8 serving pieces
1 cup plain yogurt, stirred
1 tablespoon minced fresh ginger plus 1½ tablespoons julienned
12 medium cloves garlic, 3 minced and 9 halved lengthwise
1½ teaspoons ground coriander
1 teaspoon ground cumin
1 teaspoon cayenne pepper
1 teaspoon salt
½ teaspoon ground turmeric
½ teaspoon freshly ground black pepper

1 (1-inch) stick cinnamon
4 green cardamom pods, crushed
2 bay leaves
4 whole cloves
¼ cup vegetable oil, plus 1 tablespoon
2 large onions, sliced
3 to 4 mild green chili peppers, julienned
2 medium tomatoes, chopped (about 2 cups)
1 teaspoon Nepali Garam Masala (page 398)
¼ cup finely chopped cilantro

Rinse the hens, drain, and place in a bowl. Add the yogurt, minced ginger, minced garlic, coriander, cumin, cayenne pepper, salt, turmeric, and black pepper. Mix in the spices, rubbing with your hands. Stir in the cinnamon, cardamom pods, bay leaves, and cloves. Cover and marinate in the refrigerator for at least 2 hours.

Heat ¼ cup of the oil in a heavy saucepan over medium-high heat until hot, but not smoking. Add the onions and cook, stirring constantly, until they are lightly browned, 5 to 7 minutes. Add the julienned ginger, halved garlic cloves, and green chilies and stir for about 1 minute. With a slotted spoon, draining as much oil as possible, transfer the onion mixture to a separate bowl and reserve.

To the remaining oil, add 1 tablespoon more oil, the hens, tomatoes, and garam masala and cook uncovered, stirring from time to time until it boils, about 10 minutes. Lower the heat to medium-low, cover, and simmer, stirring as needed, until the meat is tender and cooked through, 20 to 25 minutes. Stir in the reserved onion mixture, cover, and cook 5 minutes more to blend the flavors. Transfer to a serving dish, sprinkle with the cilantro, and serve hot.

Makes 4 to 6 servings.

Saano Kukhura ko Roast
SPICED ROAST CORNISH HEN

Unlike most Nepali chicken dishes, in this dish the small hens are cooked whole instead of cut up. The hens are roasted with a delicious, aromatic sauce and are best served with plain boiled rice, vegetables, and pickles.

2 (1½- to 2-pound) Cornish hens
3 tablespoons vegetable oil
1 (1-inch) stick cinnamon, halved
4 green cardamom pods, crushed
2 bay leaves
6 whole cloves
2 large onions, finely chopped
　(about 3 cups)
2 medium tomatoes, chopped
　(about 2 cups)
4 medium cloves garlic, minced

1 tablespoon minced fresh ginger
1½ teaspoons ground coriander
1 teaspoon salt
1 teaspoon ground cumin
1 teaspoon cayenne pepper
½ teaspoon freshly ground
　black pepper
½ teaspoon ground turmeric
1 teaspoon Nepali Garam Masala
　(page 398)

Preheat the oven to 350°F. Remove and discard the neck and giblets from the cavities of the hens. Rinse them under cold water, place them in a bowl, and keep them refrigerated while preparing the sauce.

Heat the oil in a medium skillet over medium-high heat. When hot, but not smoking, add the cinnamon, cardamom pods, bay leaves, and cloves and fry until they begin to puff up, darken, and give off a pleasant aroma, about 5 seconds. Add the onions and cook until softened, about 5 minutes. Add the tomatoes, garlic, ginger, coriander, salt, cumin, cayenne pepper, black pepper, and turmeric and cook until the tomatoes are soft and all the juices evaporate, about 5 minutes. Stir in the garam masala and remove the pan from the heat.

Place the hens breast-side up in a roasting pan. Spoon the prepared sauce over and inside the hens. Place the pan in the center of the oven. Roast uncovered, basting frequently with the pan sauce, until the hens are tender, well-browned, and the juices run clear when pierced with the tip of a knife, 25 to 30 minutes. Transfer the hens to a serving dish and serve hot with the sauce.

Makes 4 to 6 servings.

Battain-Dahi-Masala
QUAIL WITH YOGURT AND SPICES

Quail is called battain chara *or* shikaar ko chara *in Nepal. This method of preparing quail is especially loved by my family. This recipe has two steps: first, roast the quail in the oven until tender, and second, add a spiced aromatic sauce for extra flavor. I usually serve this dish with buttered rice, warm bread, or any sautéed vegetables.*

8 whole (4- to 5-ounce) quail
4 tablespoons butter,
    at room temperature
2 teaspoons fresh lemon or
    lime juice
1 teaspoon granulated garlic
½ teaspoon salt
¼ teaspoon freshly ground
    black pepper
2 medium onions, finely chopped
    (about 2 cups)

2 bay leaves
1 tablespoon minced fresh ginger
3 medium cloves garlic, minced
2 medium tomatoes, finely
    chopped (about 2 cups)
1 teaspoon Nepali Garam Masala
    (page 398)
Salt to taste
1 cup plain yogurt, stirred

Preheat the oven to 400°F. Rinse the quail under cold water and pat them dry inside and out. Remove and discard the skins. Cut the birds in half, and prick them all over with the tip of a sharp knife. In a small bowl, combine 2 tablespoons of the butter, lemon juice, garlic, salt, and black pepper to make a paste. Gently rub the spice paste onto the quail, coating them inside and out. Arrange the birds in a roasting pan breast-side up in a single layer. Roast until well browned on both sides, about 25 minutes, turning once. Check for doneness by pricking the meat with a knife. When the juice runs clear, it is ready. Transfer the quail to a platter, cover, and keep warm until ready to serve.

While the quail are cooking, make the sauce. Melt the remaining 2 tablespoons butter in a heavy-bottomed wide saucepan over medium-high heat. Add the onions and bay leaves, and cook, stirring constantly, until the onions are soft, about 5 minutes. Add the ginger and garlic and mix well. Add the tomatoes, garam masala, and salt to taste and cook until the liquid has evaporated, about 5 minutes. Add the yogurt, 1 tablespoon at a time, stirring constantly until it is well incorporated. Cook until the sauce has thickened slightly. Spoon the sauce over the quail, cover, and let the flavors develop, about 15 minutes. Serve immediately.

Makes 4 to 6 servings.

Battain Chara ko Tarkaari
SAUTÉED SPICED QUAIL

A delicacy because of its rarity and wonderful flavor, quail is one of the most tender of all game birds and adapts well to many seasonings and cooking methods. In this recipe, the bird is gently cooked until all the moisture evaporates and the delicious blend of spices coats the quail. Ready-to-cook, farm-raised quail are available year-round, in the fresh or frozen section of some supermarkets, Asian food markets, and specialty butchers. I recommend eating the quail by hand because of its small sharp bones.

8 whole (4- to 5-ounce) quail
1 teaspoon Nepali Garam Masala (page 398)
½ teaspoon ground cumin
½ teaspoon ground coriander
¼ teaspoon freshly ground black pepper
¼ teaspoon cayenne pepper
¼ cup clarified butter (*gheu*)
1 dried red chili, halved and seeded
1 (1-inch) stick cinnamon, halved
2 green cardamom pods, crushed
1 black cardamom pods, crushed

2 bay leaves
¼ teaspoon ajowan seeds
4 whole cloves
1 large onion, finely chopped (about 1½ cups)
2 fresh mild green chilies, chopped
4 large cloves garlic, chopped
1 tablespoon peeled and finely chopped fresh ginger
½ teaspoon ground turmeric
A small pinch ground asafetida
1 teaspoon salt
¼ cup finely chopped cilantro

Rinse the birds under cold water. Remove and discard the skin, necks, hearts, and gizzards. Cut each bird into six pieces and set aside.

In a small bowl, combine the garam masala, cumin, coriander, black pepper, and cayenne pepper. Add ½ cup of water to make a paste and set aside.

Heat the clarified butter in a heavy saucepan over medium-high heat. When it is hot, add the dried chili, cinnamon, green and black cardamom pods, bay leaves, ajowan, and cloves and fry until they begin to puff up, darken, and give off a pleasant aroma, about 5 seconds.

Add the onion, green chilies, garlic, ginger, turmeric, and asafetida and cook until the mixture is lightly browned, about 5 minutes. Mix in the spice paste and cook, stirring for 1 minute. Add the quail and salt and cook until the meat loses its pink color, 5 to 7 minutes. Adjust the heat to medium-low, cover the pan, and continue cooking, stirring from time to time, until the quail is tender, and all the moisture has evaporated, 20 to 25 minutes. Transfer the quail to a serving dish, sprinkle with the cilantro, and serve hot.

Makes 4 to 6 servings.

Kaaleej ko Tarkaari
PHEASANT CURRY

Pheasant is one of the most popular game birds in Nepal, called kaaleej kukhura *or* jangalee kukhura *(chicken of the jungle). Pheasant has traditionally been a mark of skill at any sportsman's table, but farm-raised pheasant are available fresh or frozen at many supermarkets, specialty butchers, or Asian food markets. The bird is similar to chicken, except that it has a gamey flavor, darker color, and firmer texture. The meat also takes much longer to cook than chicken. Yogurt and oil in the marinade help to tenderize the lean meat and keep it moist.*

1 (2- to 3-pound) young pheasant, skinned and cut into 6 to 8 pieces (heart, gizzard, and neck removed)
1 cup yogurt, stirred
6 medium cloves garlic, minced
1½ tablespoons minced fresh ginger
3 tablespoons vegetable oil
1 teaspoon cayenne pepper
1 teaspoon salt
½ teaspoon ground turmeric
2 medium onions, finely chopped (about 2 cups)
2 tomatoes, chopped (about 2 cups)
2 teaspoons ground coriander
1 teaspoon Nepali Garam Masala (page 398)
1 teaspoon ground cumin

In a bowl, combine the pheasant, yogurt, garlic, ginger, 1 tablespoon of the oil, cayenne pepper, salt, and turmeric, rubbing the mixture into the meat. Cover the bowl and set it aside for 45 minutes at room temperature.

Heat the remaining 2 tablespoons of oil in a heavy saucepan over medium-high heat until hot, but not smoking. Add the onions and cook until light brown, 5 to 7 minutes. Add the pheasant and cook until it is lightly browned, about 7 minutes. Add the tomatoes, coriander, garam masala, and cumin and continue cooking until the tomatoes are soft, 5 minutes. Add ¾ cup of water and bring it to a boil, uncovered. Adjust the heat to medium-low, cover the pan, and cook, stirring from time to time, until the pheasant is tender, about 30 minutes. If the pheasant is not yet tender, add ½ cup more water and continue cooking until it is cooked through. Transfer the pheasant to a serving dish and serve hot.

Makes 4 to 6 servings.

Kaaleej ko Ras
PHEASANT STEW

In this recipe, the pheasant is first browned over high heat, which locks in the flavor. It is seasoned with spices, including ajowan seeds, which have a strong distinctive taste and are known to aid in digestion. This dish is best if marinated overnight. It is served with rice, vegetables, and chutney.

3 tablespoons vegetable oil
½ teaspoon ajowan seeds
1 (2- to 3-pound) young pheasant, skinned and cut into 6 to 8 pieces (heart, gizzard, and neck removed)
2 fresh hot green chilies, split lengthwise
4 medium cloves garlic, minced
1 large shallot, minced (about 1 tablespoon)
1 tablespoon minced fresh ginger

2 teaspoons Nepali Garam Masala (page 398)
1 teaspoon salt
½ teaspoon ground turmeric
¼ teaspoon freshly ground black pepper
2 medium tomatoes, finely chopped (about 2 cups)
4 to 5 green onions (white and green parts), finely chopped
1 cup finely chopped cilantro

Heat the oil in a heavy saucepan over medium-high heat. When the oil is hot, but not smoking, add the ajowan seeds and fry until lightly browned and fragrant, about 5 seconds. Add the pheasant and cook, turning the pieces frequently until well-browned on all sides, 5 to 7 minutes. Add the green chilies, garlic, shallot, ginger, garam masala, salt, turmeric, and black pepper and continue cooking, stirring constantly, until the spices are lightly browned, 1 to 2 minutes. Add 3 cups of water, bring it to a rolling boil, and mix in the tomatoes, green onions, and cilantro. Reduce the heat to low, cover the pan, and simmer gently until the pheasant is tender, the meat starts to fall off bones, and the liquid has reduced and thickened slightly, about 30 minutes. Transfer the pheasant to a serving dish and serve piping hot.

Makes 4 to 6 servings.

Phool ko Saada Amlet
NEPALI OMELET

A classic Nepali omelet consists simply of eggs, salt, and pepper, cooked in fragrant mustard oil, which imparts a particularly delicious flavor. Mustard oil is somewhat pungent and strong when raw, so it is heated well before using. Round cast-iron skillets called taapke, *are generally used for cooking omelets to produce an attractive final dish. Omelets can be served at any time as a snack and are an easy food to make when the unexpected guest drops by. A combination of pressed rice flakes (*cheura*) with omelets is a popular snack.*

6 eggs
¼ cup finely chopped cilantro
2 fresh mild green chilies,
    finely chopped
¼ teaspoon salt

¼ teaspoon freshly ground
    black pepper
1½ tablespoons mustard or
    vegetable oil

In a medium-size bowl, whisk together the eggs, cilantro, green chilies, salt, and black pepper until thoroughly mixed, but not foamy.

Heat the oil in a large nonstick or cast-iron skillet over medium-high heat. When the oil is hot, add the egg mixture, shaking the pan back and forth to spread the mixture evenly, and occasionally lifting the edges with a metal spatula to allow the uncooked egg to run underneath, 3 to 4 minutes. When the eggs are almost set, carefully flip the omelet and cook the other side, until it is well set, about 1 minute. Fold the omelet in half, transfer it to a platter, cut it into wedges, and serve immediately.

Vegetable Omelet: Add 1 finely chopped small red onion, 1 finely chopped small tomato, ¼ cup finely chopped cilantro, 3 or 4 finely chopped green onions, 1½ cups thinly sliced mushrooms, and 2 finely chopped fresh mild or hot green chilies. Cook the omelet as directed above, replacing the oil with 2 tablespoons of butter.

Makes 4 to 6 servings.

Phool ko Roti
EGG ROTI

This versatile dish can be made with almost anything, including chopped left-over meat, vegetables, paneer cheese, or tofu. The ingredients are first cooked in a skillet, then well-beaten eggs are poured in and cooked until it resembles thin flat bread. Egg roti is served with any spicy condiments as a snack or a light lunch.

6 eggs
¼ teaspoon salt
¼ teaspoon freshly ground
   black pepper
2 tablespoons vegetable oil
1 cup finely chopped cooked
   chicken or turkey
1 small onion, finely chopped
   (about ½ cup)

½ small red or green bell
   pepper, cored and finely
   chopped (about ½ cup)
½ cup fresh or frozen peas,
   thawed and drained
½ cup fresh or frozen corn
   kernels, thawed and drained
3 to 4 green onions (white and
   pale green parts), finely
   chopped
1 cup thinly sliced mushroom

In a medium-size bowl, whisk together the eggs, salt, and black pepper until thoroughly mixed, but not foamy. Set aside.

Heat the oil in a large nonstick or cast-iron skillet over medium-high heat. When the oil is hot, add the chicken, onions, bell pepper, peas, corn, green onions, and mushrooms and cook until they are soft, 5 to 7 minutes. Slowly pour the egg mixture into the skillet, covering the vegetables evenly. Lower the heat to medium, cover the skillet, and continue cooking, undisturbed, until the egg is well set, about 4 minutes. Carefully flip it, and cook the other side until it is lightly browned, about 1 minute. Transfer the roti to a platter, cut it into wedges, and serve.

Makes 4 to 6 servings.

Phool ko Bhujuri
SPICY SCRAMBLED EGGS

Bhujuri, *the Nepali version of scrambled eggs, is made with herbs, spices, chopped vegetables, or cooked meat. For this recipe, any vegetables can be used.*

3 tablespoons vegetable oil
1 medium onion, finely chopped
  (about 1 cup)
2 fresh mild green chilies,
  finely chopped
2 to 3 green onions (white and
  pale green parts), finely
  chopped
1 teaspoon minced fresh ginger
1 medium clove garlic, finely
  chopped

1 medium tomato, chopped
  (about 1 cup)
¼ cup finely chopped cilantro
1½ cups thinly sliced mushrooms
¼ teaspoon salt
¼ teaspoon ground cumin
¼ teaspoon cayenne pepper, or
  to taste
⅛ teaspoon freshly ground
  black pepper
6 eggs, lightly beaten

Heat the oil in a large nonstick or cast-iron skillet over medium-high heat. When the oil is hot, add the onion, green chilies, green onions, ginger, and garlic and cook, stirring constantly, until the onions are soft, 5 to 7 minutes. Add the tomato, cilantro, mushrooms, salt, cumin, cayenne pepper, and black pepper and continue cooking until all the liquid has evaporated and the mixture is dry, about 7 minutes.

Pour in the beaten eggs and cook until the eggs are almost set. Then scramble them until they firm up and are lightly browned. Transfer the *bhujuri* to a platter and serve immediately.

Makes 4 to 6 servings.

Taareko Phool
SAUTÉED HARD-BOILED EGGS

Hard-boiled eggs topped with fried spices is another easy-to-prepare appetizer or snack. It is served at room temperature, usually accompanied by chutney or pickles.

8 to 10 eggs
¼ cup vegetable oil
4 fresh mild or hot green chilies, julienned
2 tablespoons peeled and finely julienned fresh ginger

6 large cloves garlic, thinly sliced lengthwise
½ teaspoon ground turmeric
½ teaspoon salt
½ teaspoon cayenne pepper
⅛ teaspoon freshly ground black pepper

Using a pin, make a tiny hole in the rounder end of each egg. This helps prevent the shell from cracking while boiling. Place the eggs in a large pot in a single layer, and cover with cold water. Bring them to a boil over high heat. Reduce the heat to medium-low, cover the pan, and cook until the eggs are hard-boiled, about 10 minutes. Drain the water and run the eggs under cold water. Crack them gently and remove the shells.

Heat the oil in a wide cast-iron or nonstick skillet over medium heat. When the oil is hot, add the green chilies, ginger, garlic, and turmeric and fry, stirring constantly, until light brown and crisp, about 2 minutes. With a slotted spoon, transfer the spices to a bowl, draining as much oil as possible. Place the shelled eggs in the remaining hot oil, about 4 to 5 at a time in a single layer, and sauté, turning them gently, until they are lightly browned on all sides. With a slotted spoon, remove them, draining as much oil as possible, and transfer them to a platter. Repeat with the remaining eggs. When they are cool enough to handle, cut each egg lengthwise in half and sprinkle it with the salt, cayenne pepper, and black pepper. Top them with the fried spices and serve.

Makes 4 to 6 servings.

Saandheko Phool
SPICY STUFFED EGGS

Saandheko phool is similar to deviled eggs, but much spicier. It is a delicious party dish with a simple spicy seasoning that gives the boiled eggs a unique flavor and texture. This dish is best served by itself at room temperature as an appetizer or as a part of a meal.

8 to 10 eggs	2 tablespoons vegetable oil
¼ cup sesame seeds	¼ teaspoon fenugreek seeds
1 dried red chili, halved and seeded	⅛ teaspoon Himalayan herb (*jimbu*), sorted
1 teaspoon cumin seeds	2 fresh mild green chilies, julienned
4 whole Szechwan peppers (*timmur*)	½ teaspoon ground turmeric
3 tablespoons plain yogurt	3 to 4 green onions (white and pale green parts), finely chopped
1 teaspoon fresh lemon or lime juice	
¼ teaspoon salt	¼ cup finely chopped cilantro

Using a pin, make a tiny hole in the rounder end of each egg. This helps prevent the shell from cracking while boiling. Place the eggs in a large pot in a single layer, and cover with cold water. Bring them to a boil over high heat. Reduce the heat to medium-low, cover the pan, and cook until the eggs are hard-boiled, about 10 minutes. Drain the water and run the eggs under cold water. Crack them gently and remove the shells. Halve each egg lengthwise and place them on a platter.

Heat a small cast-iron skillet over medium heat and toast the sesame seeds, dried chili, cumin, and timmur, stirring constantly with a wooden spoon to prevent the seeds from flying all over, until they give off a pleasant aroma and the sesame seeds are a few shades darker, about 5 minutes. Pour the spices into a dry container to halt the toasting. Let them cool, transfer them to a spice grinder, and grind to a fine powder. A mortar and pestle can also be used. Place the ground spices in a small bowl and combine with the yogurt, lemon juice, and salt to make a paste.

Heat the oil in a small skillet over medium-high heat. When the oil is hot, but not smoking, add the fenugreek seeds and *jimbu* and fry until dark brown and highly fragrant, about 5 seconds. Add the green chilies, turmeric, and the prepared spice paste and mix well. Transfer everything to a small bowl and cool. Very carefully, dip each egg half into the paste to coat it well. Place the eggs on a tray, sprinkle them with the green onions and cilantro, cover, and refrigerate until ready to serve.

Makes 4 to 6 servings.

Phool ko Tarkaari
EGG CURRY

Simple but elegant, this egg curry has a distinctive flavor, and can be served with lunch or dinner.

6 eggs
¼ cup plus 1 tablespoon vegetable oil
1 medium onion, roughly chopped (about 1 cup)
2 fresh mild or hot green chilies
4 medium cloves garlic, peeled
1 tablespoon peeled and roughly chopped fresh ginger
1 medium tomato, finely chopped (about 1 cup)

2 teaspoons Nepali Garam Masala (page 398)
1 teaspoon salt
½ teaspoon ground turmeric
½ teaspoon cayenne pepper
½ cup plain yogurt, stirred
3 to 4 green onions (white and pale green parts), finely chopped
¼ cup finely chopped cilantro

Using a pin, make a tiny hole in the rounder end of each egg. This helps prevent the shell from cracking while boiling. Place the eggs in a large pot in a single layer, and cover with cold water. Bring them to a boil over high heat. Reduce the heat to medium-low, cover the pan, and cook until the eggs are hard-boiled, about 10 minutes. Drain the water and run the eggs under cold water. Crack them gently and remove the shells.

Heat ¼ cup of the oil in a heavy saucepan over medium-high heat and fry the whole eggs, turning them gently, until they are lightly browned on all sides. With a slotted spoon, remove them, draining as much oil as possible, and transfer them to a platter. When they are cool enough to handle, halve each egg lengthwise, and set it aside.

Combine the onion, green chilies, garlic, and ginger in a blender or food processor and process to make a smooth paste. Add enough water just to facilitate blending. Transfer the blended mixture into the saucepan with the remaining oil. Add the remaining 1 tablespoon of oil and cook over medium-high heat until the mixture is lightly browned, about 5 minutes. Add the tomato, garam masala, salt, turmeric, and cayenne pepper and cook, stirring from time to time, until the tomatoes are soft and all the juices evaporate, 5 to 7 minutes. Mix in the yogurt, 1 tablespoon at a time, stirring constantly. Continue cooking until the yogurt has been absorbed into the sauce, about 2 minutes. Add

1½ cups of water and bring the mixture to a boil. Reduce the heat to medium-low, cover the pan, and continue cooking until the sauce has thickened slightly, 7 to 10 minutes. Carefully place the egg halves in the sauce, one at a time, cover the pan, and cook, stirring gently a few times, for 7 minutes. Try to avoid too much stirring, as the egg yolks may separate from the whites. Transfer the curry to a serving dish, sprinkle with the cilantro and green onions, and serve.

Makes 4 to 6 servings.

Haas ko Phool Taareko
FRIED DUCK EGGS

Duck eggs are slightly larger than large chicken eggs, but more flavorful and higher in fat. This recipe uses only a minimum of spices, to avoid masking the natural taste of the egg. Duck eggs are available in some supermarkets, Asian stores, farmer's markets, and some gourmet food stores. Always select the freshest eggs for better taste. Substitute chicken eggs if duck eggs are not available.

3 tablespoons vegetable oil
3 dried red chilies, halved and seeded
6 duck eggs

Salt to taste
A pinch freshly ground black pepper

Heat the oil in a large nonstick or cast-iron skillet over medium-high heat. When the oil is hot, but not smoking, add the chilies and fry until fully fragrant and reddish brown, about 5 seconds. With a slotted spoon, transfer the chilies to a small bowl and set aside. Crack the eggs into the skillet and season with salt and pepper. Depending on the size of your skillet, you may have to cook the eggs in batches. Reduce the heat to medium-low, cover the skillet, and cook until the whites are completely set. Uncover, gently flip the eggs with a metal spatula, and cook the second side. Do not overcook, as the whites may become rubbery. Transfer the eggs to a plate, garnish them with the fried chilies, and serve immediately.

Makes 4 to 6 servings.

Maacha ra Jhinge Maacha

FISH AND SHRIMP

Fish plays a significant role in Nepali society for religious, social, and culinary reasons. Fish symbolize good luck, prosperity, and happiness. In the Newar community, dried fish is offered to friends and family as *sagun* (blessed) food to bring good luck, success, and good fortune. It is also considered sacred and is offered to various deities during festivals.

Because Nepal is a landlocked country, most fish comes from Himalayan rivers. They are caught by local fishermen, using the old-fashioned fishing techniques with bamboo poles, rods, and fishing traps. The most common fish available are carp, trout, and catfish. In many remote areas of Nepal where there is no transportation or processing facilities, smoking or sun-drying is used to preserve fish. Small dried fish known as *sidra maacha* are very popular and used extensively in Nepali cooking. Until recently, most other fish were imported from India, but the government has successively encouraged commercial fish farming.

No matter what kind of fish one uses, the most important point to remember is that the fish should be absolutely fresh before cooking, keeping in mind that spoilage starts as soon as it is caught if the fish is not kept cold. Nepali techniques for cooking fish are very simple. It is usually marinated and deep-fried or curried. Fish is usually cooked as steaks, and fillets are not a usual custom. Most of the recipes in this chapter use fish steaks, but you can substitute fish fillets if you prefer.

Sarsyun Maacha
MUSTARD OIL FISH

Mustard oil, a very important cooking oil in Nepal, has a nutty taste and aroma. It is always heated to the smoking point before adding any ingredients because the raw oil has a very bitter, sharp flavor. Heating it to a high temperature reduces its pungency.

3 fresh mild or hot green chilies, minced
1 teaspoon minced fresh ginger
1 large clove garlic, minced
1 teaspoon salt
1/2 teaspoon ground turmeric
1/8 teaspoon freshly ground black pepper
1 teaspoon ground brown mustard seeds
1/2 teaspoon ground yellow mustard seeds
2 tablespoons fresh lemon or lime juice
10 to 12 (1-inch-thick) fish steaks (trout, bass, carp), well-rinsed and patted dry
1/2 cup chickpea flour (*besan*)
1 1/2 cups mustard oil

In a medium-size bowl, combine the green chilies, ginger, garlic, salt, turmeric, black pepper, and both mustard seeds. Add the lemon juice, mix into a paste, and set aside for 5 minutes. Place the fish steaks in the bowl and rub well to coat thoroughly with the spice paste. Cover and marinate for 20 minutes in the refrigerator.

Dredge the fish in the chickpea flour, shaking off any excess, and place it on a tray. Heat the oil in a large cast-iron skillet over medium-high heat. When the oil is faintly smoking, carefully place the fish in a single layer in the pan, about four pieces at a time. Do not crowd the pan. Fry, turning 2 to 3 times, until brown on both sides, 5 to 6 minutes. With a slotted spoon, remove the fish, draining as much oil as possible, and transfer to a paper towel-lined platter to drain. Repeat with the remaining fish, adding more oil if needed, and making sure the oil is heated well before adding the fish. Transfer the fried fish to a platter and serve hot.

Makes 4 to 6 servings.

Taareko Maacha
DEEP-FRIED SPICED FISH

This is a quick and easy to prepare deep-fried fish recipe. The fish steaks are first rubbed with turmeric, salt, and lemon to remove any fishy smell before mixing in other spices. For a spicier version, increase the amount of chili (see Spicy Variation). Nepalese like to cook fish with the bones and skin, because this way it keeps its shape and retains flavor, but you can substitute fish fillets. Serve this as a snack accompanied by a spicy chutney or as part of a dinner menu.

10 to 12 (1-inch-thick) fish steaks (trout, bass, carp), well-rinsed and drained
2 tablespoons plus 1 teaspoon fresh lemon or lime juice
1 1/4 teaspoons salt
1/2 teaspoon ground turmeric
2 teaspoons ground yellow mustard seeds
1 clove garlic, minced
1 teaspoon cayenne pepper
1 medium red onion, sliced 1/8-inch-thick and separated into rings
2 cups vegetable oil
1 lemon or lime, cut into wedges
2 medium tomatoes, cut into 6 wedges

Place the fish steaks in a bowl with 2 tablespoons of the lemon juice, 1 teaspoon of the salt, and the turmeric and mix well. Rub each piece gently by hand, making sure the steaks are well coated. Let them stand for 10 minutes to absorb the salt. Add the mustard seeds, garlic, and cayenne pepper and mix well. Cover the bowl and marinate the fish for 20 minutes in the refrigerator.

In the meantime, in a bowl, combine the onion rings with the remaining 1 teaspoon lemon juice and 1/4 teaspoon salt. Set aside to marinate.

Heat the oil in a large cast-iron skillet over medium-high heat until it reaches 350° to 375°F. Test the readiness of the oil by placing a small piece of fish into the hot oil. If it bubbles and rises to the surface immediately, it is ready. Gently drop the fish steaks into the oil, one at a time, in a single layer. Do not crowd the pan. Deep-fry, turning them frequently, until they are firm and golden brown on all sides, 5 to 7 minutes. With a slotted spoon, remove the fish, draining as much oil as possible, and transfer them to a paper towel-lined platter to drain. Repeat the process with the remaining fish.

Transfer the fried fish to a serving dish, surround with the marinated onions, and lemon and tomatoes wedges, and serve.

Spicy Variation: Soak 2 halved and seeded dried red chilies in ¼ cup hot water until softened. Drain the chilies and grind to a paste in a mortar and pestle. Add the chilies to the spice paste above, along with an additional clove of minced garlic, 1 teaspoon minced fresh ginger, ½ teaspoon ground cumin, ½ teaspoon ground coriander, and ⅛ teaspoon black pepper, omitting the cayenne. Prepare the fish as directed above.

Makes 4 to 6 servings.

Maacha ko Tarkaari
FISH CURRY

This simple, mildly spiced fish curry can be prepared a day in advance, as the fish will soak up the gravy, making it even more delicious the next day. Reheat it on the stovetop by gently simmering, but add the lemon, cilantro, and green chili just before serving.

2 dried red chilies, halved and seeded
¼ cup hot water
10 to 12 (1-inch-thick) fish steaks (trout, bass, carp), well rinsed and patted dry
1 teaspoon salt
½ teaspoon ground turmeric
2 medium onions, chopped (about 2 cups)
1 tablespoon peeled and chopped fresh ginger
4 small cloves garlic, peeled
3 tablespoons vegetable oil
1 (1-inch) stick cinnamon, halved

2 bay leaves
3 medium tomatoes, finely chopped (about 3 cups)
1½ teaspoons ground brown mustard seeds
1 teaspoon ground cumin
1 teaspoon ground coriander
⅛ teaspoon freshly ground black pepper
2 tablespoons fresh lemon or lime juice
½ cup finely chopped cilantro
4 fresh hot or mild green chilies, cut into long slivers

Soak the dried chilies in the hot water until softened. Gently rub the fish with the salt and turmeric to coat completely and set aside. Place the onions, chilies with the soaking water, ginger, and garlic in a food processor or blender and process to make a smooth paste.

Heat the oil in a heavy saucepan over medium-high heat until hot, but not smoking. Add the cinnamon and bay leaves and fry until fully fragrant, about 5 seconds. Add the onion paste and cook, stirring frequently, until lightly browned, about 5 minutes. Add the tomatoes, mustard seeds, cumin, coriander, and black pepper and continue cooking, stirring as needed, until the tomatoes are soft and the juices evaporate. Add 1 cup of warm water and bring the mixture to a boil. Reduce the heat to medium-low, cover, and cook, stirring as needed, until the sauce has thickened slightly, about 15 minutes. Add the fish, one piece at a time, and cook covered, stirring gently from time to time, until cooked through, 6 to 8 minutes. Mix in the lemon juice, transfer to a serving dish, and garnish with the cilantro and green chilies. Serve hot.

Makes 4 to 6 servings.

Dahi-Maacha
FISH IN YOGURT SAUCE

Here the fish is sautéed and then simmered in a spiced yogurt sauce resulting in a very flavorful dish.

10 to 12 (1-inch-thick) fish steaks or fillets (any kind), rinsed and patted dry
1 tablespoon fresh lemon or lime juice
2 teaspoons yellow mustard seeds, ground
1 teaspoon salt
½ teaspoon ground turmeric
1½ cups plus 3 tablespoons vegetable oil
1 (1-inch) stick cinnamon, halved
4 green cardamom pods, crushed

3 small bay leaves
4 whole cloves
2 medium onions, finely chopped (about 2 cups)
4 fresh hot or mild green chilies, chopped
1 tablespoon peeled and finely chopped fresh ginger
3 medium cloves garlic, finely chopped
3 medium tomatoes, chopped (about 3 cups)
Salt to taste
1 cup plain yogurt, stirred

In a bowl combine the fish with the lemon juice, mustard, salt, and turmeric; mix well to coat. Heat 1½ cups of the oil in a large cast-iron skillet over medium-high heat until it reaches 350° to 375°F. Test the oil by placing a small piece of fish into the oil—if it bubbles and rises to the surface immediately, it is ready. Fry the fish in the oil, one at a time, in a single layer. Turn as needed, until light brown, about 4 minutes. Remove them with a slotted spoon and transfer to a paper towel-lined platter to drain. Repeat with the remaining fish.

To make the sauce, heat the remaining 3 tablespoons of oil in a wide saucepan over medium-high heat until hot, but not smoking. Add the cinnamon, cardamom pods, bay leaves, and cloves and fry until they begin to puff up, darken, and give off a pleasant aroma, about 5 seconds. Add the onions and cook until lightly browned, 5 to 7 minutes. Add the green chilies, ginger, and garlic and stir for 1 minute. Add the tomatoes and salt and cook until the tomatoes are soft and the juices evaporate. Mix in the yogurt, 1 tablespoon at a time and cook until blended, 2 to 3 minutes. Add 1 cup of hot water and bring to a boil. Reduce the heat to low, add the fish, and stir gently. Cover and cook for 5 minutes to blend the flavors. Remove the pan from the heat and set aside, covered for at least 10 minutes before serving.

Makes 4 to 6 servings.

Maacha ko Ras
FISH CURRY WITH GROUND MUSTARD SEEDS

In Nepal, fish is often cooked with ground mustard seeds, and the two ingredients seem to be a natural combination. Brown mustard seed is called raayo *and is more flavorful and pungent than the yellow mustard seed, which is known as* sarsyun. *This curry can be cooked with either variety.*

2 dried red chilies, halved and seeded	I tablespoon minced fresh ginger
¼ cup hot water	Salt to taste
2 medium tomatoes, finely chopped (about 2 cups)	I tablespoon vegetable oil
5 medium cloves garlic, minced	¼ teaspoon fenugreek seeds
I ½ tablespoons yellow mustard seeds, ground	2½ cups hot water
	I recipe Deep Fried Spiced Fish (page 262), without garnishes
I large shallot, minced	½ cup finely chopped cilantro

Soak the chilies in the hot water until softened. Drain and coarsely grind with a mortar and pestle. In a small bowl, combine the chili paste, tomatoes, garlic, mustard seeds, shallot, ginger, and salt to taste, and set aside.

Heat the oil in a medium-size saucepan over medium-high heat until hot, but not smoking. Add the fenugreek seeds and fry until dark brown and highly fragrant, about 5 seconds. Add the spice paste and cook, stirring frequently, until browned and all the liquid evaporates, about 5 minutes. Stir in 2½ cups of hot water, bring the mixture to a boil, and continue boiling until the liquid has reduced and the sauce has thickened slightly, about 7 minutes.

Add the deep-fried fish, reduce the heat to medium-low, cover the pan, and cook until the flavors blend, 8 to 10 minutes. Transfer to a serving dish, sprinkle with the cilantro, and serve hot.

Makes 4 to 6 servings.

Maacha ko Tauko ko Jhol
FISH HEAD CURRY

This richly seasoned soupy curry is appreciated in Nepal as a wholesome and nutritious meal. Any variety of fish heads can be used, as long as they are fresh. They are available from fishermen or fishmongers, upon request.

2 tablespoons vegetable oil
1 (1-inch) stick cinnamon, halved
2 small bay leaves
4 whole cloves
4 fish heads with bones, gills and viscera removed, cleaned, and split in half
1 medium onion, finely chopped (about 1 cup)
4 large cloves garlic, minced
1 tablespoon minced fresh ginger
½ teaspoon ground turmeric

2 medium tomatoes, finely chopped (about 2 cups)
1 teaspoon ground cumin
1 teaspoon ground coriander
1 teaspoon brown mustard seeds, ground
1 teaspoon cayenne pepper
1 teaspoon salt
⅛ teaspoon freshly ground black pepper
3 cups hot water
½ cup finely chopped cilantro
4 fresh hot or mild green chilies, julienned

Heat the oil in a large saucepan over medium-high heat until hot, but not smoking. Add the cinnamon, bay leaves, and cloves and fry until fully fragrant, about 5 seconds. Add the fish heads and cook, stirring frequently, until lightly browned, about 7 minutes. Add the onion, garlic, ginger, and turmeric and cook, stirring as needed, until the onion is soft, but not browned. Mix in the tomatoes, cumin, coriander, mustard seeds, cayenne pepper, salt, and black pepper. Cook until the tomatoes are soft, about 5 minutes. Add the hot water and bring the mixture to a boil. Reduce the heat to medium, cover the pan, and continue cooking until the sauce has reduced by half, about 15 minutes. Transfer everything to a serving dish, sprinkle with the cilantro and green chilies, and serve hot.

Makes 4 to 6 servings.

Kaagati-Nauni Maacha
LEMON-BUTTERED FISH

The following recipe is one of the easiest and fastest ways to cook fish. All you do is mix the spices with the fish fillets and then pan-fry everything. You can serve the fish with vegetables and the leftover fish can be used to make a quick lunch the next day.

I teaspoon granulated garlic
½ teaspoon ground yellow
    mustard seeds
½ teaspoon cayenne pepper
½ teaspoon salt
⅛ teaspoon freshly ground
    black pepper
2 tablespoons fresh lemon or
    lime juice

2 pounds white fish fillets,
    cut into 2½-inch pieces,
    rinsed, and patted dry
8 to 10 tablespoons unsalted
    butter
I lemon, cut into wedges
I or two sprigs cilantro

In a medium-size bowl, combine the granulated garlic, mustard seeds, cayenne pepper, salt, and black pepper. Add the lemon juice and mix it into a paste. Place the fish fillets in the bowl and mix them with the spice paste, rubbing well to coat thoroughly. Set them aside for 10 minutes in the refrigerator.

Melt 8 tablespoons of the butter in a medium-size nonstick or cast-iron skillet over medium heat, add some of the fish (without crowding), and cook, turning carefully, until golden brown on each side, 6 to 7 minutes. Put the fillets on a plate. Repeat the process with the remaining fillets, adding more butter if needed. Transfer the fish to a platter, garnish with the lemon wedges and cilantro, and serve.

Makes 4 to 6 servings.

Maacha ko Sukuti Saandheko
SPICE-MARINATED DRIED FISH

Dried fish is very popular in Nepal and is used extensively. I usually make my own dried fish in a food dehydrator, but it is also available at Asian markets and specialty food stores. You can find small and medium-size whole dried fish, as well as powdered fish. When selecting the fish, make sure it is freshly dried or smoked, as it tends to spoil quickly. Store-bought varieties may contain salt, so adjust the salt in this recipe accordingly. You can serve this dish as a spicy appetizer or as a side dish.

¼ **cup vegetable oil**
2½ **to 3 pounds dried fish (any variety), skinned, boned, and separated into bite-size pieces**
4 **fresh hot or mild green chilies, julienned**
4 **large cloves garlic, thinly sliced**
I **tablespoon peeled and finely julienned fresh ginger**
Salt to taste

½ **cup finely chopped cilantro**
4 **to 5 green onions (white and pale green parts), finely chopped**
2 **tablespoons fresh lemon or lime juice**
I **teaspoon cayenne pepper**
⅛ **teaspoon Szechwan pepper (*timmur*), finely ground with a mortar and pestle**

Heat the oil in a skillet over medium-low heat. When the oil is hot, fry the fish, stirring constantly, until lightly crispy, 1 to 2 minutes. Do not over cook. Using a slotted spoon, remove the fish, draining as much oil as possible, and place it in a bowl. Add the green chilies, garlic, and ginger to the pan with the remaining oil and fry until crispy, about 1 minute. Mix them with the fish, along with the cilantro, green onions, lemon juice, cayenne pepper, and *timmur*. Taste and adjust the seasonings. Cover the bowl and set it aside for 30 minutes to allow the flavors to develop. Transfer the mixture to a serving dish and serve at room temperature.

Makes 4 to 6 servings.

Maacha ko Bari
SPICY FISH CAKES

There are many ways to make fish cakes. This recipe uses whole fish according to Nepali tradition. The fish cakes can be served as a light snack or appetizer with chutney, or can supplement any Nepali meal.

1 or 2 whole lake trout
    (or other fish of your choice;
    3½ to 4 pounds), cleaned
    and cut into 2 to 3 large
    pieces
1 cup finely chopped cilantro
2 medium red onions,
    1 finely chopped (about 1 cup),
    and 1 sliced ⅛ inch thick
    and separated into rings
4 to 5 green onions (white and
    pale green parts), finely
    chopped
3 to 4 mild fresh green chilies,
    chopped

2 tablespoons plus 1 teaspoon
    fresh lemon or lime juice
2 teaspoons minced fresh ginger
2 medium cloves garlic, minced
1 teaspoon ground cumin
1 teaspoon cayenne pepper
¾ teaspoon salt
⅛ teaspoon freshly ground
    black pepper
2 eggs, lightly beaten
¼ cup dry bread crumbs
2 cups vegetable oil, plus more
    if needed
1 medium tomato, cut into
    6 wedges
1 lemon, cut into wedges

Bring a pot of water large enough to hold the fish to a rolling boil over medium-high heat. Add the fish and cook, uncovered, until the meat is falling off the bones, 15 to 20 minutes. Drain, and when cool enough to handle, carefully separate the meat from the bones, discarding the skin and bones. Place the fish in a large bowl and mix it with the cilantro, chopped onion, green onions, green chilies, 2 tablespoons of the lemon juice, ginger, garlic, cumin, cayenne pepper, ½ teaspoon of the salt, and the black pepper. Using a lightly oiled hand, shape the mixture into twelve 1-inch-thick patties. Dip a patty into the beaten egg, let the excess drip off, roll it in the bread crumbs and shake off the excess, and put it on a platter. Repeat the procedure until all the patties are made. Set aside.

In a small bowl, combine the onion rings with the remaining 1 teaspoon lemon juice and ¼ teaspoon salt. Set aside to marinate while you cook the fish cakes.

Heat the oil in a large nonstick or cast-iron skillet over medium-high heat. When the oil is hot, add the fish cakes and cook, turning carefully once or twice, until lightly browned and crispy on each side, 5 to 6 minutes. With a slotted spoon, remove them, draining as much oil as possible, and transfer them to a paper towel-lined platter to drain. Repeat the process with the remaining fish cakes, adding more oil if needed. Transfer the cakes to a serving dish, surround them with the marinated onions and tomato and lemon wedges, and serve.

Makes 4 to 6 servings.

Jhinge Maacha ko Tarkaari
SHRIMP WITH ONIONS AND TOMATOES

This is an easy-to-make, delicious shrimp dish using a blend of spices. Do not overcook the shrimp because it tends to become dry and overly chewy.

¼ cup butter
1 medium onion, finely chopped (about 1 cup)
4 fresh mild green chilies, chopped
3 medium cloves garlic, minced
1½ teaspoons minced fresh ginger
2 medium ripe tomatoes, chopped (about 2 cups)
½ teaspoon ground turmeric

½ teaspoon ground cumin
⅛ teaspoon freshly ground black pepper
Salt to taste
1½ to 2 pounds large shrimp, shelled, deveined, washed, and patted dry
1 tablespoon fresh lemon or lime juice

Melt the butter in a wide nonstick or cast-iron skillet over medium-high heat. Add the onion, green chilies, garlic, and ginger and cook, stirring frequently, until they are soft, 4 to 5 minutes. Mix in the tomatoes, turmeric, cumin, black pepper, and salt to taste. Continue cooking, stirring from time to time, until the tomatoes are soft and the liquid evaporates, 5 to 7 minutes. Add the shrimp and cook, stirring continuously, until it turns pink, 6 to 8 minutes. Add the lemon juice and stir well. Transfer everything to a serving dish, and serve.

Makes 4 to 6 servings.

Momos

DUMPLINGS

Momo, also known as *momo-cha*, is one of the most popular dishes in Nepal. The *momo* is a bite-size dumpling, filled with meat or vegetables. *Momos* are usually steamed, though they are sometimes fried. The origin of *momo* is uncertain. Because this dish is popular among the Newar community of Kathmandu valley, one prevalent belief is that Newari traders brought them from Tibet. They modified the dish with local ingredients, such as water buffalo meat, and gave the dish a Nepali name. Others believe the dish was introduced to Nepali cuisine by Tibetans who settled in the mountains of Nepal.

Family and friends often gather to spend a joyful, leisurely time preparing *momos*. The dough is rolled very thin, the filling is placed in the center, and then the *momo* is shaped and sealed. Though *momo* shaping is an art, requiring patience, even young children can learn to enjoy the job. They can also help pound the herbs and spices in a mortar and pestle.

Elderly relatives, friends, and the most respected family members are honored with a serving of the first batch of freshly steamed *momos*. Children are generally served a less spicy version. Instead of eating them all at once, guests are served *momos* in small quantities, which keeps them coming for second and third helpings. The hostess always take pleasure serving others before eating her own *momos*.

Freshly steamed momos taste best served piping hot straight from the steamer. If they are served as a meal, six to eight are a good serving. A meat-filled *momo* has to be eaten whole, as the flavorful juice in its steamed pocket will dribble out if it is broken. Though a well-seasoned juicy *momo* does not really need any condiments, it is traditionally accompanied by freshly made

Hot and Fiery Tomato Chutney (page 307). It can also be served with Cilantro Chutney (page 299), Mint Chutney (page 300), Radish Achaar (page 294), or any other chutney of your choice.

Fresh *momo* dough is made by mixing flour with water and kneading until the dough becomes smooth. Making dough is a matter of personal preference, as some cooks prefer white all-purpose flour to whole wheat flour because it makes a smooth and elastic dough, although others like to mix two parts white flour with one part whole wheat. Either way, the dough is kneaded until it is slightly sticky and then left to rest at room temperature for at least a half hour, covered with a damp kitchen cloth, and then rolled out very thin and cut into three-inch circles. Making your own dough wrappers is time-consuming, but the result is rewarding. If you have the time you may find homemade wrappers a bit less fussy to work with, and your *momos* will be tastier than those made with purchased wrappers. Experienced Nepali cooks pride themselves on rolling the thinnest possible wrappers.

In the United States, my family sometimes makes *momos* with commercial dumpling wrappers, known as wonton wrappers or gyoza, found in the Asian sections of larger supermarkets or Asian markets. Commercial wrappers, which come in round or square shapes are convenient if you are in a hurry. If you decide to buy wrappers, make sure they are the paper-thin kind, which become translucent when cooked. These wrappers tend to get soggy quickly, and should be steamed right after filling. If you use frozen wrappers, it is important to thaw them thoroughly and handle them very gently, as they become brittle and tear easily.

Meat Filling

Any type of ground meat, combined with fresh herbs and spices, can be used as *momo* filling. The meat is always cooked inside the wrapper. Sometimes two different kinds of meat and vegetables are cooked together. The best *momo* is always juicy, so sometimes a little oil is added if the meat is very lean to keep the filling moist.

Vegetable Filling

All sorts of vegetables can be combined for filling. They must be chopped very finely and are flavored with fresh herbs and spices and cooked lightly before using for filling. Potato and cabbage are the most popular combination. The filling mixture should not be watery.

Rolling Out the Dough

After the dough has rested, knead it on a floured work surface just until smooth and elastic. Shape the dough into a 12-inch-long rope. Cut it into fifty to fifty-five pieces and form them into balls. Flatten each ball on the floured surface.

With a rolling pin, roll each one into a 3-inch circle. When rolling the dough, leave the center a little thicker than the edges. This will make the wrapper easier to shape and seal around its filling, and will provide extra support to hold the juice that accumulates when steaming. Arrange the disks in a single layer on a lightly floured tray and cover them with a damp towel to prevent them from drying out.

Rolling many wrappers individually can take a lot of time, but there is a faster method. Divide the prepared and rested dough into four or five pieces. With your hands, flatten each piece on a lightly floured surface, and roll it out ⅛ inch thick. With a 3-inch round cookie cutter (or the rim of a drinking glass), cut out as many rounds as you can fit from the sheet. Arrange them as above to keep them from drying out. Repeat the procedure with the rest of the dough. Gather up the dough scraps, roll them out, and continue cutting disks until all the dough is used. When rolling dough this way, use as little flour as possible, or the wrappers cut from the re-rolled scraps will be tough.

Filling the *Momos*

Holding the wrapper in 1 hand, place about 1 tablespoon of filling in the center and use the other hand to gather the edges and seal the stuffing inside by squeezing the edges tightly, making small pleats to securely seal in the filling. Pleats make the *momo* pretty, like a bite-size bag closed tight with a drawstring. Take care not to stuff it too full, or it will leak. Keep the filled *momos* and the unfilled wrappers covered with a damp cloth while working, as the wrappers can dry out and become brittle if exposed to air for too long. Brushing with cold water around the edges of the wrapper helps seal the edges.

Steaming the *Momos*

Grease a steamer tray with oil or cooking spray. You can also line the steamer tray with cabbage or lettuce leaves if you leave ½-inch margin so that steam can circulate. Arrange the *momos* on one or two trays, with the pleated sides up, close together, but not touching. Set aside.

Fill the base of the steamer with 3 to 4 inches of water and bring it to a full boil over medium-high heat. Place the *momo* tray or trays in the steamer. Cover tightly to prevent the steam from escaping. Steam until the dumplings are translucent and juicy, about 10 minutes. If you are using two stacked steamer trays, switch the top with the bottom halfway through the cooking so the momos cook evenly. Do not overcook, or they will dry out, leaving the filling tasteless. Remove them from the steamer and serve immediately. Repeat the procedure with the remaining dumplings. Always keep a kettle of boiling water handy to add to the steamer, as the boiling water evaporates quickly. Steam burns are very painful, so take care to protect your hands and wrists.

Sautéed *Momos*

Pan-fried *momos* are browned and then steamed. They are golden brown and slightly crunchy outside, while still juicy inside. Heat 2 tablespoons of oil in a cast-iron or nonstick skillet over medium heat. Place the *momos* in the skillet pleated side up in one layer without touching each other. Fry until the bottoms are lightly browned, about 5 minutes. Add ¼ cup of cold water and cover the pan. Continue cooking until the liquid has been absorbed and the wrappers are slightly crispy. Transfer them to a platter and serve hot with dipping sauce. Repeat the procedure with the remaining dumplings.

The Next Best Thing to Fresh *Momos*

Leftover *momos* can be refrigerated or frozen. If you want to freeze them, let them cool first, then arrange them in a single layer, without touching, in a freezer bag and seal them airtight. Thaw the frozen *momos* and then sauté as directed above.

Momo ko Pitho
FRESH MOMO WRAPPERS

This is a basic recipe for making momo *wrappers from scratch. Though I use all-purpose flour, some people prefer to mix two-thirds of all-purpose flour with one-third whole wheat. Making your own wrappers takes time, but they are tastier than store-bought ones.*

**3½ cups all-purpose white flour
plus extra for kneading**

½ teaspoon salt (optional)

In a medium-size bowl, combine the flour and salt. Make a well in the center and add ¾ to 1 cup of room temperature water, a little at a time, mixing with your fingers until the flour comes together in a crumbly mass. Transfer the dough to a floured surface and knead until it becomes smooth and elastic, about 5 to 6 minutes. If the dough is too stiff and dry, knead in a little more water to make it elastic and pliable. If the dough is too wet and sticks to your hands, knead in a little more flour until it just barely sticks to itself when folded. (It is easier to start too wet and adjust by adding flour than to add water to dough that is too dry.) Transfer the dough to a bowl, cover it with a damp kitchen towel, and let it rest for 30 minutes or more at room temperature.

Makes 50 to 55 (3-inch) wrappers.

Tarkaari ko Momo
MIXED VEGETABLE FILLING

This is a basic vegetarian stuffing for momos. *The ideal vegetable* momo *is delicate, with a balance of textures and the natural taste of fresh vegetables. The filling can be made of almost any vegetable, finely chopped and lightly cooked with fresh spices. Vegetable* momos *are a very popular appetizer, afternoon snack, or entree served with chutney or a dipping sauce.*

2 tablespoons vegetable oil	½ head fresh green cabbage,
I medium onion, finely chopped	trimmed and shredded
(about I cup)	(about 2 cups)
3 medium cloves garlic, finely	I small bunch fresh spinach,
chopped	stemmed and coarsely
I tablespoon minced fresh ginger	chopped (about 2 cups)
I½ teaspoons ground coriander	I medium carrot, peeled and
I teaspoon ground cumin	shredded (about I cup)
I teaspoon cayenne pepper	I cup (½-inch) cauliflower florets
½ teaspoon ground turmeric	I medium potato, boiled, peeled,
⅛ teaspoon freshly ground	and finely chopped (about
black pepper	I cup)
	I teaspoon salt

Heat the oil in a wide saucepan over medium-high heat. When the oil is hot, but not smoking, add the onion and garlic and cook until they begin to soften, 3 to 4 minutes. Add the ginger, coriander, cumin, cayenne pepper, turmeric, and black pepper and stir for 30 seconds. Add the cabbage, spinach, carrot, cauliflower, potato, and salt and continue cooking, stirring until the liquid evaporates and the mixture is nearly dry. This step is important so that the filling will not soak through its wrapper. Cool the stuffing to a temperature comfortable for handling. See pages 274-276 for directions to complete the *momos.* See page 277 for Fresh Momo Wrappers.

Makes 4 to 6 servings.

Chyau ra Tofu ko Momo
MUSHROOM AND TOFU MOMO FILLING

My daughter Rachana learned the basics of momo *cooking while working in Nepal after her college graduation. She experimented with a variety of vegetable fillings and came up with this recipe.*

2 tablespoons vegetable oil
1 medium red onion, finely chopped (about 1 cup)
4 cups chopped fresh mushrooms (any variety; about 1½ pounds)
2 cups firm tofu
2 medium red potatoes, boiled, peeled, and finely chopped (about 2 cups)

1 small red or green bell pepper, cored and finely chopped (1 cup)
2 fresh hot green chilies, finely chopped
2 medium cloves garlic, minced
1½ teaspoons minced fresh ginger
¼ cup finely chopped cilantro
1 teaspoon salt
¼ teaspoon ground cumin
¼ teaspoon ground coriander

Heat the oil in a wide saucepan over medium-high heat. When the oil is hot, but not smoking, add the onion and cook until it softens, 3 to 4 minutes. Add the mushrooms, tofu, potatoes, bell pepper, green chilies, garlic, and ginger and cook, stirring frequently, until the water from the vegetables has evaporated and the mixture is nearly dry. Add the cilantro, salt, cumin, and coriander and mix well. Transfer the mixture to a bowl and let it cool. See pages 274-276 for directions to complete the *momos*. See page 277 for Fresh Momo Wrappers.

Makes 4 to 6 servings.

Alu ko Momo
SPICY POTATO FILLING

Here is a very simple vegetarian momo *filling made from potatoes that are boiled in their skins, peeled, and mashed before they are seasoned with onion, ginger, garlic, and other spices.*

2 pounds boiling potatoes
¼ cup vegetable oil
2 medium onions, finely chopped
   (about 2 cups)
1 tablespoon minced fresh ginger
3 medium cloves garlic, minced
1½ teaspoons ground coriander
1½ teaspoons Nepali Garam
   Masala (page 398)

1 teaspoon ground cumin
1 teaspoon cayenne pepper
1 teaspoon salt
½ teaspoon ground turmeric
½ cup finely chopped cilantro
4 to 5 green onions (white and
   green parts), finely chopped
2 fresh hot green chilies, finely
   chopped

In a medium-size saucepan, combine the potatoes and enough water to cover, and bring to a boil over high heat. Reduce the heat to medium-low, cover the pan, and continue cooking until the potatoes are tender, 20 to 25 minutes. Drain, and when cool enough to handle, peel and mash the potatoes and set them aside.

Heat the oil in a wide saucepan over medium-high heat. When the oil is hot, but not smoking, add the onions and cook until they begin to soften, about 5 minutes. Add the ginger, garlic, coriander, garam masala, cumin, cayenne pepper, salt, and turmeric and stir for 30 seconds. Add the mashed potatoes and mix well. Remove the pan from the heat and stir in the cilantro, green onions, and green chilies. Cool the stuffing to a temperature comfortable for handling. See pages 274-276 for directions to complete the *momos.* See page 277 for Fresh Momo Wrappers.

Makes 4 to 6 servings.

Maasu ko Momo
LAMB FILLING

Any variety of ground meat, including goat, pork, or water buffalo, can be used for this recipe. Nepalese prefer meat that has a lot of fat, because it produces juicy momos. Traditionally, the spices are ground with water to a smooth paste in a mortar and pestle to bring out more flavors before adding them to the ground meat, though if you are in a hurry, pre-ground spices are almost as good. The seasoning can be altered to suit one's taste, keeping in mind that too many spices will mask the natural flavor of the meat. Momos are best served immediately after steaming, with any variety of freshly made tomato chutney.

2½ pounds ground lamb (preferably leg meat)
1 cup finely chopped cilantro
1 medium onion, finely chopped (about 1 cup)
4 to 5 green onions (white and green parts), finely chopped
3 fresh mild or hot green chilies, chopped

2 tablespoons vegetable oil (use only if the meat is very lean)
4 medium cloves garlic, minced
1 tablespoon minced fresh ginger
1½ teaspoons Nepali Garam Masala (page 398)
1 teaspoon salt
1 teaspoon cayenne pepper
½ teaspoon ground turmeric

In a large bowl, combine all the ingredients and ½ cup of water. Cover the bowl and let it rest for 10 minutes, at room temperature, for the flavors to blend. See pages 274-276 for directions to complete the *momos*. See page 277 for Fresh Momo Wrappers.

Makes 4 to 6 servings.

Bangoor ra Tarkari ko Momo
PORK AND VEGETABLE FILLING

In Nepal, momos *are traditionally filled with only ground meat, but over the past several years, fillings have become more elaborate. These days,* momos *are prepared with virtually any combination of meat, vegetables, tofu, and cheese, and given fancy names such as* meetho momo *(delicious momo),* swaadistha momo *(gourmet momo), and* raseelo momo *(juicy momo). The combination of vegetables and meat probably reflects the trend in Nepal towards health-conscious eating. This recipe was inspired by the Sthapit family, but I have modified it to suit my family's taste.*

I pound ground pork	I teaspoon salt
2 cups chopped fresh mushrooms	I teaspoon ground cumin
(any variety)	I teaspoon ground coriander
I medium onion, finely chopped	I teaspoon cayenne pepper
(about I cup)	½ teaspoon ground turmeric
½ cup finely chopped cilantro	⅛ teaspoon freshly ground
4 to 5 green onions (white and	black pepper
green parts), finely chopped	½ head green cabbage, shredded
2 fresh hot green chilies, finely	(about 2 cups)
chopped	¼ head cauliflower, cut into ½-
4 medium cloves garlic, minced	inch florets (about ½-inch)
I tablespoon minced fresh ginger	I cup shelled fresh peas

In a large bowl, combine the ground pork, mushrooms, onion, cilantro, green onions, green chilies, garlic, ginger, salt, cumin, coriander, cayenne pepper, turmeric, and black pepper. Mix well, working with your hands, until all the ingredients are thoroughly mixed. Cover the bowl and let it rest for 10 minutes, at room temperature, for the herbs and spices to absorb into the meat. Bring a pot of water to a rolling boil over medium-high heat. Add the cabbage, cauliflower, and peas and cook just until they are tender, 3 to 4 minutes. Drain and run them under cold water to halt the cooking. Add them to the pork mixture and mix thoroughly. See pages 274-276 for directions to complete the *momos.* See page 277 for Fresh Momo Wrappers.

Makes 4 to 6 servings.

Kukhura ko Momo
CHICKEN FILLING

Chicken momos have become popular among health conscious people because of their low fat content. You may also use ground turkey, but do not use ground turkey breast, as it tends to dry out. Serve chicken momos as a hot appetizer or as an entree with a tomato-based dipping sauce.

2½ pounds ground chicken	2 medium cloves garlic, minced
1 medium onion, finely chopped	1 teaspoon salt
(about 1 cup)	1 teaspoon ground coriander
¼ cup finely chopped cilantro	½ teaspoon ground turmeric
2 tablespoons vegetable oil	½ teaspoon ground cumin
1 tablespoons minced fresh ginger	½ teaspoon cayenne pepper

In a large bowl, combine all the ingredientes and ¼ cup of water. Mix well, working with your hands. Cover the bowl and let it rest for 10 minutes, at room temperature, for the flavors to blend. See pages 274-276 for directions to complete the *momos*. See page 277 for Fresh Momo Wrappers.

Makes 4 to 6 servings.

Achaar

SALADS, CHUTNEYS, and PICKLES

Nepalese use the term *"achaar"* for a variety of dishes, including salads, chutneys, and pickles. They are an important component of any Nepali meal because they perk up and add tang to traditional dishes. *Achaars* can be prepared from fruits and vegetables, dried legumes, and even some meat and seafood. The most common pickling spices are mustard seeds, fenugreek seeds, sesame seeds, turmeric powder, cayenne pepper, Sezchuan pepper, and Himalayan herb (*jimbu*). In Nepal, *achaars* are made seasonally when fruits and vegetables are in abundance. Properly prepared pickles keep indefinitely and can be used year-round. The most popular achaars are Spicy Potato Achaar with Sesame Seeds (page 290), Cucumber Achaar (page 293), Bitter Melon Achaar (page 296), and Radish Achaar (page 294).

Chutney is often made fresh for each meal, though it can be stored in the refrigerator and used within a few days. The most popular chutneys are made from tomatoes, cilantro, mint, and tamarind. Nepalese are very fond of tomato chutney, and you will see many recipes in this chapter. The most common are Hot and Fiery Tomato Chutney (page 307), Roasted Cherry Tomato Chutney (page 304), and Dried Fish-Tomato Chutney (page 309). Chutneys range from mild to fiery hot and are eaten in small amounts with rice, daal, and vegetables.

A mild-flavored pickle is a nice accompaniment to any heavy or spicy food. Preserved and fermented pickles are bottled and can be stored at room temperature. The most common ones that I have included here are made of cucumber, white radish, lemon, and labsi fruit.

Mismaas Salad
CUCUMBER, ONION, AND TOMATO SALAD

This light, refreshing salad is usually served as an accompaniment to a main dish, but you may also serve it with any variety of snacks. The vegetables can be chopped ahead of time, but the salt, pepper, and lemon juice should be added just before serving to maintain the salad's crunchy texture.

2 medium cucumbers, peeled, halved, seeded, and finely chopped (about 2 cups)
1 large ripe tomato, chopped (about 1½ cups)
1 white radish, chopped (about 1½ cups)

1 medium red onion, finely chopped (about 1 cup)
3 tablespoons fresh lemon or lime juice
¼ teaspoon salt
⅛ teaspoon freshly ground black pepper

In a medium-size bowl, combine the cucumbers, tomato, radish, and onion. Just before serving, toss with the lemon juice, salt, and black pepper. Transfer the salad to a serving dish and serve right away.

Mung Bean Variation: Sort and wash ½ cup whole green mung beans as described on pages 69-70. Soak the beans in water for at least 4 hours, drain and add to the salad with ½ cup finely chopped green pepper, 3 to 4 chopped green onions (white and pale green parts), ¼ cup finely chopped cilantro, and 1 finely chopped fresh green chili. Increase the salt to ½ teaspoon.

Makes 4 to 6 servings.

Kaankro ra Dahi ko Salad
CUCUMBER AND YOGURT SALAD

This cool and refreshing salad goes well with any spicy Nepali dish. For this recipe, I like to use whole milk yogurt, which has a very creamy texture.

2 medium cucumbers, peeled, seeded, and finely chopped (about 2 cups)
1 ¼ teaspoons salt
1 teaspoon cumin seeds
3 cups plain yogurt, stirred

1 fresh mild or hot green chili pepper, finely chopped
⅛ teaspoon freshly ground black pepper
¼ teaspoon cayenne pepper

Place the cucumbers in a bowl and toss with 1 teaspoon of the salt. Set aside until the juices are released, 15 to 20 minutes, stirring a few times. Place the cucumber in a colander and press to squeeze out as much liquid as possible.

Heat a small cast-iron skillet over medium heat and toast the cumin seeds, stirring constantly until they give off a pleasant aroma and are a few shades darker, about 1 minute. Remove the seeds from the skillet and coarsely grind them with a mortar and pestle.

In a bowl, combine the cucumbers, yogurt, green chili, ½ teaspoon of the toasted cumin seeds, remaining ¼ teaspoon salt, and black pepper. Transfer everything to a serving dish and sprinkle with the remaining cumin and cayenne pepper. Cover and refrigerate until ready to serve.

Makes 4 to 6 servings.

Dahi, Pyaj ra Golbheda ko Salad
YOGURT, ONION, AND TOMATO SALAD

Served chilled or at room temperature, this refreshing salad counteracts the effect of a spicy Nepali meal.

I teaspoon cumin seeds
3 cups plain yogurt, stirred
2 medium tomatoes, chopped
 (about 2 cups)
I medium red onion, finely
 chopped (about I cup)
3 to 4 green onions (white and
 pale green parts), finely
 chopped

¼ cup finely chopped cilantro
I fresh mild or hot green chili,
 finely chopped
¼ teaspoon salt
⅛ teaspoon freshly ground
 black pepper
½ teaspoon ground paprika

Heat a small cast-iron skillet over medium heat and toast the cumin seeds, stirring constantly until they give off a pleasant aroma and darken, about I minute. Transfer the seeds to a mortar and pestle and coarsely grind them.

In a bowl, combine the ground cumin seeds, yogurt, tomatoes, red onion, green onions, cilantro, green chili, salt, and black pepper. Transfer to a serving dish and sprinkle with the paprika. Cover and refrigerate until ready to serve.

Makes 4 to 6 servings.

Alu ko Achaar
SPICY POTATO SALAD WITH SESAME SEEDS

Potato achaar *is a popular, addictive, and refreshing potato salad. Only rarely have I come across a traditional Nepali meal that does not include potato* achaar. *For this recipe, use any variety of waxy potato that keeps its shape when boiled. Baking potatoes are not recommended because they produce a dry, starchy* achaar.

8 to 10 small potatoes
(about 3 pounds)
6 fresh (hot or mild) green chilies,
each halved lengthwise
½ cup finely chopped cilantro
¼ cup fresh lemon or lime juice
1 teaspoon cayenne pepper
1 teaspoon salt
½ cup sesame seeds
2 dried red chilies, halved and
seeded
¼ teaspoon Szechwan pepper
(*timmur*)

3 tablespoons mustard oil or
vegetable oil
½ teaspoon fenugreek seeds
¼ teaspoon Himalayan herb
(*jimbu*)
1 medium red or green bell
pepper, cored and diced
(about 1½ cups)
2 tablespoons fresh ginger,
peeled and finely julienned
½ teaspoon ground turmeric
A generous pinch ground asafetida

Place the potatoes and water to cover in a medium-size saucepan, and bring to a boil over high heat. Reduce the heat to medium-low, cover the pan, and continue cooking until the potatoes are tender, 20 to 25 minutes. Drain, and when cool enough to handle, peel and cut the potatoes into 1-inch cubes. Do not pour cold water over them to cool the potatoes, as this will water down their flavor. Place the potatoes in a large bowl and combine them with the green chilies, cilantro, lemon juice, cayenne pepper, and salt. Set aside.

Heat a small cast-iron skillet over medium heat and toast the sesame seeds, dried chilies and *timmur*, stirring constantly to prevent the seeds from flying all over, until they give off a pleasant aroma and the sesame seeds darken, about 3 minutes. Remove the spices from the skillet and pour them into a dry container to halt the toasting and let them cool. Transfer the cool spices to a spice grinder and grind to a fine powder. Stir the spices and ½ cup of water into the potato mixture.

Heat the mustard oil in a small skillet over medium high-heat until faintly smoking. Add the fenugreek and *jimbu*, and fry until dark brown and fragrant, about 5 seconds. Add the bell pepper, ginger, turmeric, and asafetida and fry for 1 minute. Pour the entire contents over the potatoes and mix thoroughly. Taste and adjust the seasonings and lemon juice. Cover the bowl and let the potato achaar stand for 30 minutes at room temperature to absorb the seasonings, stirring occasionally. Transfer the achaar to a serving dish and serve.

Variation: Add 2 cups of chopped cucumbers and ½ cup soaked and dried whole green peas to give a new twist to this dish.

Makes 4 to 6 servings.

Saano Kerau ko Achaar
FIELD PEA ACHAAR

This recipe is made with small Nepali field peas, known as saano kerau. Field peas are similar to common garden peas, except the pods are much narrower and longer, and the peas are green-gray in color and slightly larger than peppercorns. Substitute regular dried peas (green or yellow) if field peas are not available.

2 cups dried small field peas (*sukeko hariyo saano kerau*)	I teaspoon salt
3 to 4 green onions (white and pale green parts), cut into ¼-inch pieces	⅛ teaspoon Szechwan pepper (*timmur*), finely ground with a mortar and pestle
¼ cup finely chopped cilantro	1½ tablespoons mustard oil
3 fresh hot green chilies, julienned	½ teaspoon fenugreek seeds
2 small cloves garlic, finely chopped	I dried red chili, halved and seeded
I tablespoon fresh lemon or lime juice	⅛ teaspoon Himalayan herb (*jimbu*)
I tablespoon minced fresh ginger	½ teaspoon ground turmeric

Sort and wash the field peas as described on pages 69-70. Place the peas in a large bowl, cover them with cold water, and soak for at least 12 hours at room temperature until doubled in size. Drain and rinse the peas thoroughly and transfer them to a bowl. Stir in the green onions, cilantro, green chilies, garlic, lemon juice, ginger, salt, and *timmur*. Set aside.

Heat the mustard oil in a small skillet over medium-high heat. When the oil is faintly smoking, add the fenugreek, dried chili, and *jimbu* and fry until dark brown and fragrant, about 5 seconds. Remove the skillet from the heat, sprinkle with the turmeric, and immediately pour the mustard oil mixture over the peas, and mix thoroughly. Cover the bowl and let stand for 30 minutes at room temperature to absorb the seasonings, stirring occasionally. Transfer it to a serving dish and serve.

Makes 4 to 6 servings.

Koreko Kaankro ko Achaar
CUCUMBER ACHAAR

The refreshing aroma of freshly shredded cucumber brings back warm memories of my childhood in Nepal. Cucumber achaar was prepared fresh daily because it was my father's favorite. This is my family's old recipe and you may adjust the spiciness to your liking.

6 to 8 medium cucumbers, peeled, seeded, and shredded (about 8 cups)
1 tablespoon salt
½ cup sesame seeds
1 cup plain yogurt, stirred
¼ cup finely chopped cilantro
3 tablespoons fresh lemon or lime juice
2 fresh mild green chilies, cut into slivers

1 teaspoon cayenne pepper
⅛ teaspoon Szechwan pepper (*timmur*), finely ground with a mortar and pestle
2 tablespoons mustard oil
½ teaspoon fenugreek seeds
½ teaspoon Himalayan herb (*jimbu*)
½ teaspoon ground turmeric

In a colander, combine the shredded cucumbers and salt. Let them rest in the sink until the juices are released, 15 to 20 minutes. Stir occasionally. Press and squeeze out as much water as possible.

Heat a small cast-iron skillet over medium heat and toast the sesame seeds, stirring constantly to prevent the seeds from flying all over, until they give off a pleasant aroma and darken, about 2 minutes. Remove the seeds to a bowl to halt the toasting, and let them cool. Transfer the seeds to a spice grinder and grind to a fine powder.

Place the cucumbers in a bowl, and add the ground sesame seeds, yogurt, cilantro, lemon juice, green chilies, cayenne pepper, and timmur and mix well.

Heat the mustard oil in a small skillet over medium-high heat. When the oil is faintly smoking, add the fenugreek seeds and jimbu, and fry until they turn dark brown and fragrant, about 5 seconds. Remove the pan from heat and add the turmeric. Pour the entire contents into the cucumber mixture. Mix well, cover, and set aside for 10 minutes to allow the seasonings to develop.

Makes 4 to 6 servings.

Koreko Seto Mula Achaar
RADISH ACHAAR

This spicy radish achaar is a tangy accompaniment to a heavily spiced Nepali meal. Be sure to store this achaar in an airtight container.

1½ pounds white radishes, peeled and julienned or grated (about 4 cups)
1 teaspoon salt
3 tablespoons fresh lemon or lime juice
1 teaspoon cayenne pepper
¼ teaspoon Szechwan pepper (*timmur*), finely ground with a mortar and pestle

2 tablespoons mustard oil
1 dried red chili, halved and seeded
½ teaspoon fenugreek seeds
⅛ teaspoon Himalayan herb (*jimbu*)
½ teaspoon ground turmeric

In a colander, combine the radishes and salt, and let them stand for 10 minutes in the sink. Press to squeeze the excess liquid from the radishes. Transfer the radishes to a bowl and stir in the lemon juice, cayenne pepper, and *timmur*.

Heat the mustard oil in a small skillet over medium high-heat. When the oil is faintly smoking, add the chili, fenugreek, and *jimbu* and fry until dark brown and fragrant, about 5 seconds. Remove the skillet from the heat, sprinkle it with the turmeric, immediately pour the entire contents over the radishes and mix well.

Taste and adjust the salt. Cover the bowl and allow the seasonings to develop, for at least 10 minutes. If not serving the *achaar* right away, cover and refrigerate until serving time. Serve cold or at room temperature.

Makes 4 to 6 servings.

Pyaj ko Achaar
ONION ACHAAR

This fresh onion pickle is tangy and the toasted sesame seeds add a delicious touch. You can use any variety of onions, but I prefer red onions because they are milder and sweeter than yellow or white onions.

¼ cup sesame seeds
2 dried red chilies, seeded and crumbled
⅛ teaspoon Szechwan pepper (*timmur*)
3 tablespoons vegetable oil
¼ teaspoon fenugreek seeds

3 to 4 large red onions, halved and thinly sliced (about 4 cups)
3 fresh mild green chilies, julienned
½ teaspoon ground turmeric
3 tablespoons fresh lemon or lime juice
1½ teaspoons salt

Heat a small cast-iron skillet over medium heat and toast the sesame seeds, chilies, and *timmur*, stirring constantly to prevent the seeds from flying all over, until they give off a pleasant aroma and darken, about 2 minutes. Remove the spices from the skillet, pour them into a dry container to halt the toasting, and let them cool. Transfer the cooled spices to a spice grinder, grind to a fine powder, and set aside.

Heat the oil in a large skillet over medium high-heat. When the oil is hot, but not smoking, add the fenugreek seeds, and fry until dark brown and fragrant, about 5 seconds. Add the onions, green chilies, and turmeric. Cook, stirring constantly, until the raw taste of the onions is gone but they are still crunchy, about 4 minutes. With a slotted spoon, remove the onions, draining any excess oil, and transfer them to a bowl to cool. Combine the cooled onions with the toasted spices, lemon juice, and salt. Let the achaar stand for 10 minutes, transfer it to a serving dish, and serve at room temperature.

Makes 4 to 6 servings.

Variation: For a crunchy achaar, add ½ cup soaked and drained dried whole peas or whole mung beans.

Tito Karela ko Achaar
BITTER MELON ACHAAR

Bitter melon (tito karela), also known as bitter gourd is an acquired taste, but is a very popular vegetable in Nepal. The bitter flavor is due to the presence of quinine, which is reduced by soaking in salt and blanching it before cooking. The pickle is prepared in such a way that the bitterness is almost non-existent—this achaar *perks up any meal.*

4 to 6 medium bitter melons (7 cups sliced)
1 tablespoon plus ½ teaspoon salt
3 tablespoons sesame seeds
1 dried red chili, halved and seeded
2 tablespoons fresh lemon or lime juice
2 teaspoons cayenne pepper

⅛ teaspoon Szechwan pepper (*timmur*), finely ground with a mortar and pestle
2 tablespoons mustard oil
6 to 8 strands Himalayan herb (*jimbu*)
⅛ teaspoon fenugreek seeds
½ teaspoon ground turmeric

Wash the melons thoroughly, but do not peel them. Slice off 1 inch from the top and bottom. Use the cut pieces to rub against the cut surface of the vegetable in a circular motion. A white, foamy substance will be released. Discard the pieces and wash the melons. This process will extract some of the bitterness. Halve the melons lengthwise, scoop out the seeds and spongy pulp with a spoon and discard. Cut each half into ½-inch pieces. In a colander, combine the bitter melon and 1 tablespoon of the salt, and set aside in the sink for 30 minutes. With your fingers, squeeze the juice from the melons, rinse with fresh water, and drain.

Heat a small cast-iron skillet over medium heat and toast the sesame seeds and chilies, stirring constantly to prevent the seeds from flying all over, until they give off a pleasant aroma and the seeds darken, about 2 minutes. Remove the spices from the skillet, pour them into a dry container to halt the toasting, and let them cool. Transfer the cooled spices to a spice grinder, grind them to a fine powder, and set aside.

Bring a medium pot of water to a rolling boil over medium-high heat. Add the bitter melon and boil until tender, but crunchy, 3 to 4 minutes. Drain and run under cold water to halt the cooking. Place them in a bowl and toss with the sesame seed mixture, lemon juice, remaining 1 teaspoon of salt, cayenne pepper, and *timmur*.

Heat the mustard oil in a small skillet over medium-high heat. When the oil is faintly smoking, add the *jimbu* and fenugreek and fry until dark brown and fragrant, about 5 seconds. Remove the skillet from the heat, sprinkle in the turmeric, immediately pour the oil mixture over the bitter melon, and mix thoroughly. Cover the bowl and let the *achaar* stand for 30 minutes at room temperature to absorb the seasonings, stirring occasionally. Transfer to a platter and serve.

Makes 4 to 6 servings.

Paalungo ko Achaar
SPINACH ACHAAR

This delicious and easy achaar *is a simplified adaptation of my mother-in-law's recipe. The spinach is steamed, drained, and mixed with spices.*

2 tablespoons sesame seeds
1 dried red chili, seeded and
    broken into several pieces
1 to 2 large bunches spinach
    (about 2 pounds), stemmed
    and well washed

1 teaspoon fresh lemon or lime
    juice
½ teaspoon cayenne pepper
¼ teaspoon salt
1 tablespoon mustard oil
¼ teaspoon fenugreek seeds
½ teaspoon ground turmeric

Heat a small cast-iron skillet over medium heat and toast the sesame seeds and chili, stirring constantly to prevent the seeds from flying all over, until they give off a pleasant aroma and darken, about 2 minutes. Remove them from the skillet and pour into a dry container to halt the toasting. When cool, transfer them to a spice grinder or a mortar and pestle, and grind into a fine powder.

Place the washed spinach, with only the water clinging to the leaves, in a medium skillet over medium heat. Cover and cook until wilted and soft, about 5 minutes. Remove from the heat and drain off the water in a colander. With the back of a spoon, gently press on the spinach to remove any excess water. Transfer to a medium-size bowl and add the sesame seed powder, lemon juice, cayenne pepper, and salt. Set aside.

Heat the mustard oil in a small skillet over medium-high heat. When the oil is faintly smoking, add the fenugreek and fry until dark brown and fragrant, about 5 seconds. Remove the skillet from the heat, sprinkle with the turmeric, immediately pour the entire contents over the spinach, and mix well. Cover the bowl and allow the seasonings to develop, for about 10 minutes. Transfer the achaar to a platter and serve.

Makes 4 to 6 servings.

Hariyo Dhaniya ko Chutney
CILANTRO CHUTNEY

This dark green chutney has a tangy aroma and spicy refreshing taste. Serve with momos (steamed dumplings, pages 273-283) or fried snacks.

5 cups roughly chopped cilantro
2 medium tomatoes, chopped
  (about 2 cups)
6 fresh hot green chilies,
  roughly chopped
2 tablespoons fresh lemon or
  lime juice

2 medium cloves garlic, peeled
1 teaspoon peeled and roughly
  chopped fresh ginger
½ teaspoon salt
⅛ teaspoon Szechwan pepper
  (*timmur*), finely ground
  with a mortar and pestle

Place the cilantro, tomatoes, green chilies, lemon juice, garlic, ginger, salt, and *timmur* in a food processor or blender and process to make a smooth paste. Transfer the chutney to a bowl and serve. The chutney keeps in the refrigerator for up to 1 week in an airtight container.

Makes 4 to 6 servings.

Baabari ko Chutney
MINT CHUTNEY

Mint (baabari) complements any spicy dish and provides a cooling effect. This chutney can be made with any variety of mint, but select only young and tender sprigs with fresh leaves. Avoid wilted, matured, and dry leaves. Serve it with any fried or steamed appetizers or with a traditional Nepali meal.

4 cups young fresh mint leaves, roughly chopped

1 medium red onion, roughly chopped (about 1 cup)

4 fresh (hot or mild) green chilies, roughly chopped

½ cup plain yogurt

3 tablespoons fresh lemon or lime juice

3 medium cloves garlic, peeled

1 tablespoon peeled and roughly chopped fresh ginger

½ teaspoon salt

Place all the ingredients in a food processor or blender and process until smooth. Transfer to a bowl and serve.

The chutney keeps refrigerated for up to 1 week in an airtight container. It will change color to a pale green, but its flavor does not change.

Makes 4 to 6 servings.

Dhania Baabari ko Chutney
CILANTRO-MINT CHUTNEY

This fragrant chutney has the tangy refreshing flavors of both cilantro and mint. It is served as a dipping sauce with fried appetizers and traditional Nepali meals.

2½ cups firmly packed, coarsely chopped cilantro
2½ cups firmly packed, coarsely chopped young fresh mint
2 medium tomatoes, coarsely chopped (about 2 cups)
4 to 5 green onions (white and light green parts), coarsely chopped
4 fresh hot green chilies, roughly chopped
2 tablespoons fresh lemon or lime juice
2 small shallots, coarsely chopped
2 medium cloves garlic, peeled
½ teaspoon salt

Place all the ingredients in a food processor or blender and process to a smooth paste. Add water, if needed, to facilitate blending, but do not make it runny. Transfer the chutney to a bowl and serve.

The chutney keeps for up to 1 week refrigerated in an airtight container.

Makes 4 to 6 servings.

Tyaamatar ko Chutney
TAMARILLO CHUTNEY

Tyaamatar *is the Nepali word for "tamarillo" or "tree tomato," an attractive egg-shaped fruit with meaty pulp and seeds. It has a tough, bitter skin and is very tart, but flavorful when ripe. Despite its appearance, it is not a true tomato. In Nepal, tamarillos are used primarily in chutneys such as this one. It is made fresh in small quantities and is a delicious accompaniment to any meal. Tamarillos are available at Asian markets, specialty produce stores, and well-stocked supermarkets.*

5 medium ripe tamarillos (preferably red), stemmed	⅛ teaspoon Szechwan pepper (*timmur*), finely ground with a mortar and pestle
8 medium cloves garlic, 4 unpeeled and 4 thinly slivered	1½ tablespoons mustard oil
4 fresh hot green chilies, chopped	⅛ teaspoon fenugreek seeds
½ teaspoon salt	⅛ teaspoon Himalayan herb (*jimbu*)
	1¼ cup finely chopped cilantro

Preheat a charcoal or gas grill to medium-high heat. Roast the tamarillos over the grill, turning frequently, until the skins are blistered, blackened, and very soft. They are ready when the skins peel off easily and they release a pleasant aroma, 10 to 15 minutes. Roast the unpeeled garlic cloves in the same way, turning occasionally, until blackened and soft. Remove from the heat and cool to room temperature. Peel and discard the blackened skins from the tamarillos and garlic.

Place the tamarillo pulp, roasted garlic, green chilies, salt, and *timmur* in a mortar. Use the pestle to grind the mixture to a coarse sauce. You may have to do this in batches. Transfer the sauce to a bowl.

Heat the mustard oil in a small skillet over medium-high heat until faintly smoking. Add the fenugreek and *jimbu* and fry until dark brown and fragrant, about 5 seconds. Add the slivered garlic and fry until golden, about 30 seconds. Remove the skillet from the heat, pour the contents into the tamarillo mixture, and stir well. Cover the bowl and set it aside for at least 10 minutes to allow the flavors to blend. Transfer the chutney to a serving dish and serve.

Makes 4 to 6 servings.

Imili ko Chutney
TAMARIND CHUTNEY

Tamarind (imili) is the reddish-brown fruit of the tamarind tree. The pulp of the fruit has a pleasant flavor with a distinct sweet-and-sour taste. The fibrous pulp is diluted in water and the strained juice is used to make chutney. Dried tamarind pulp is available at Indian and Asian markets or specialty food stores.

2 cups compressed tamarind pulp
4 cups boiling water
2 tablespoons vegetable oil
1 teaspoon cumin seeds
1½ cups dark brown sugar

1 tablespoon cayenne pepper,
  or to taste
2 teaspoons salt
1 teaspoon ground ginger

Break the compressed pulp into small pieces in a bowl. Add the boiling water and soak until the pulp softens, about 1 hour. The tamarind will swell and its volume will increase. Mash the mixture and pour it through a fine-mesh strainer set over a bowl, pressing with the back of a spoon to collect the puree and juice in the bowl. Discard the fiber and seeds. Set the puree aside.

Heat the oil in a medium-size saucepan over medium-high heat. When the oil is hot, but not smoking, add the cumin seeds and fry until lightly browned and fragrant, about 5 seconds. Add the tamarind puree, brown sugar, cayenne pepper, salt, and ginger and bring to a boil. Reduce the heat to medium-low and cook, stirring occasionally, until the sauce reduces by half and the color becomes a rich brown, 15 to 20 minutes. Remove the pan from the heat and let it cool. The chutney will thicken as it cools. Taste for tartness and adjust the seasonings and sugar. Serve the chutney immediately or transfer it to a clean jar. The chutney keeps refrigerated for up to 6 months.

Makes 4 to 6 servings.

Saano Golbheda ko Chutney
ROASTED CHERRY TOMATO CHUTNEY

Roasted tomato chutney is a Nepali classic, prepared fresh daily. Traditionally, the tomatoes are roasted in a small clay pot (makkal) over a charcoal fire, resulting in a smoky flavor. The roasted tomatoes are then crushed in an oval-shaped stone mortar and pestle (khal), and their tangy taste is enhanced by the addition of Nepali timmur.

2 pounds ripe cherry tomatoes, stemmed	½ teaspoon salt
6 to 8 medium cloves garlic, unpeeled	⅛ teaspoon Szechwan pepper (*timmur*), finely ground with a mortar and pestle
4 fresh hot green chilies	¼ cup finely chopped cilantro

Preheat a charcoal or gas grill to medium-high heat. Loosely wrap the tomatoes in heavy-duty foil and roast them over the grill, turning often with tongs. The tomatoes are ready when the skins are blistered, blackened, and separate easily from the pulp. Remove them from the heat and transfer to a bowl. Roast the unpeeled garlic in the same way, turning occasionally, until blackened on all sides and soft. Remove them and set aside. Roast the green chilies until slightly blistered and then set aside. When cool enough to handle, peel and remove the blackened skins from the tomatoes and garlic, but not from the chilies.

Place the roasted garlic, green chilies, salt, and *timmur* in a mortar. Use the pestle to grind the mixture to a smooth paste. Add the roasted tomatoes and grind until smooth. You may have to do this in batches. This process can also be done in a food processor or a blender. Transfer the chutney to a bowl and mix in the cilantro. Taste, adjust the seasonings, and serve immediately or cover and refrigerate until ready to serve.

Makes 4 to 6 servings.

Na Pakaayeko Golbheda ko Chutney
NO-COOK TOMATO CHUTNEY

This recipe is my daughter Sapana's favorite way of preparing a quick chutney. The amount of chili may be adjusted to suit your taste.

6 medium tomatoes, roughly chopped (about 6 cups)
8 to 10 fresh hot green chilies, roughly chopped
½ cup finely chopped cilantro
2 medium cloves garlic, peeled
2 teaspoons peeled and roughly chopped fresh ginger

½ teaspoon salt
⅛ teaspoon Szechwan pepper (*timmur*), finely ground with a mortar and pestle
1 teaspoon mustard oil
1 tablespoon fresh lemon or lime juice

Place the tomatoes, green chilies, cilantro, garlic, ginger, salt, and *timmur* in a food processor or blender and process until smooth. Transfer to a bowl, and mix it with the mustard oil and lemon juice. Taste, adjust the seasonings, and serve immediately or cover and refrigerate until ready to serve. The chutney keeps refrigerated for 2 to 3 days.

Makes 4 to 6 servings.

Taaba ma Poleko Golbheda
ROASTED TOMATO CHUTNEY

A taaba *is a heavy iron skillet or griddle used extensively in Nepal, mainly to make flatbreads* (roti) *or to toast spices. When tomatoes, garlic, and dried chilies are roasted on a* taaba, *they release a wonderful smoky aroma. If you do not have a* taaba, *you may use any cast-iron skillet or griddle.*

8 to 10 medium plum tomatoes, halved	¼-inch piece fresh ginger, peeled and halved
4 medium cloves garlic, sliced	½ teaspoon salt
3 dried red chilies, stemmed	¼ cup finely chopped cilantro

Heat the griddle over medium-high heat and place the tomatoes in it, cut-sides down. Roast, turning frequently, until they are blistered and blackened and bubbles begin to form, 7 to 10 minutes. Push the tomatoes to one side of the skillet, and add the garlic, dried chilies, and ginger and roast until blackened and charred. Remove the pan from the heat and let it cool. There is no need to peel the blackened tomato skins because they add a deep, rusty, rich color to the chutney.

Transfer the tomato mixture to a food processor or blender with the salt and cilantro, and blend to a smooth puree. Transfer the chutney to a serving dish and serve at room temperature. If you are not serving it immediately, cover the bowl and refrigerate it until ready to serve. The chutney keeps refrigerated for 2 to 3 days.

Makes 4 to 6 servings.

Piro Golbheda ko Chutney
HOT AND FIERY TOMATO CHUTNEY

This fiery tomato chutney will spice up any dish, including fried or steamed snacks or appetizers. Make sure to select succulent and fully ripe tomatoes for the best flavor.

6 medium tomatoes
6 medium cloves garlic, peeled
8 fresh hot green chilies
¼ cup finely chopped cilantro
2 teaspoons minced fresh ginger
1 teaspoon salt
¼ teaspoon Szechwan pepper
   (*timmur*), finely ground with
   a mortar and pestle

2 tablespoons mustard oil
3 dried red chilies, halved and
   seeded
½ teaspoon fenugreek seeds
⅛ teaspoon Himalayan herb
   (*jimbu*)

Preheat the oven to 400°F. In a roasting pan, arrange the tomatoes in a single layer and roast until they are soft, blistered, blackened, and most of the liquid has caramelized, about 30 minutes. Add the garlic and green chilies and roast for another 5 minutes. Transfer the roasted vegetables to a food processor or blender and process into a smooth puree. Transfer the mixture to a bowl, mix it with the cilantro, ginger, salt, and *timmur*, and set aside.

Heat the oil in a small skillet over medium-high heat. When the oil is hot, but not smoking, add the dried chilies, fenugreek, and *jimbu* and fry until dark brown and fragrant, about 5 seconds. Remove the skillet from the heat, immediately pour the mustard oil mixture over the tomato puree, and mix thoroughly. Cover the bowl and let the tomato chutney stand for 10 minutes at room temperature to allow the flavors to blend. Transfer the chutney to a bowl and serve. The chutney can be made up to 2 days in advance and kept covered and chilled.

Makes 4 to 6 servings.

Kurelo Haaleko Golbheda ko Achaar
TOMATO CHUTNEY WITH ASPARAGUS

This is a great recipe for two flavorful vegetables—tomatoes and asparagus. In this recipe, steamed asparagus is coated with a zesty tomato sauce seasoned with fenugreek seeds for added flavor. This refreshing chutney goes well with fish, chicken, or any mild meal.

I pound fresh asparagus, sliced diagonally into 1½-inch pieces
4 medium tomatoes, chopped (about 4 cups)
I small red onion, chopped (about ½ cup)
½ cup finely chopped cilantro
4 hot green chilies, chopped
2 medium cloves garlic, peeled
2 teaspoons roughly chopped fresh ginger

I teaspoon salt
⅛ teaspoon Szechwan pepper (*timmur*), finely ground with a mortar and pestle
I tablespoon fresh lemon or lime juice
2 teaspoons mustard oil
⅛ teaspoon fenugreek seeds
½ teaspoon ground turmeric
3 to 4 green onions (green and white parts), finely chopped

Bring a medium-size pot of salted water to a rolling boil over medium-high heat. Add the asparagus and boil until tender, but still crisp, 4 to 5 minutes. Transfer the asparagus to a colander and run cold water over it to halt the cooking. Drain and set aside.

Combine the tomatoes, onion, cilantro, green chilies, garlic, ginger, salt, and *timmur* in a food processor or blender and briefly process to a coarse paste. Transfer the mixture to a bowl and stir in the steamed asparagus and lemon juice.

Heat the oil in a small skillet over medium-high heat. When the oil is hot, but not smoking, add the fenugreek seeds and fry until dark brown and fragrant, about 5 seconds. Remove the skillet from the heat, sprinkle in the turmeric and green onions, and mix. Pour the entire contents into the asparagus mixture and stir well. Set aside for at least 30 minutes to allow the flavors to blend. Transfer the chutney to a serving dish and serve.

Makes 4 to 6 servings.

Golbheda ra Sidra Maacha
DRIED FISH-TOMATO CHUTNEY

Sidra maacha *are tiny dried fish used in pickles and chutneys. Because they have a strong flavor, they are used sparingly. This pungent chutney goes well with fried snacks and adds a spicy tang to any meal. Dried fish are available at Asian food markets or specialty food stores.*

2 tablespoons mustard oil
½ teaspoon fenugreek seeds
6 large tomatoes, chopped
  (about 6 cups)
4 fresh hot green chilies,
  halved lengthwise
1 teaspoon salt
½ teaspoon ground turmeric
¼ teaspoon Szechwan pepper
  (*timmur*), finely ground
  with a mortar and pestle

½ cup finely chopped cilantro
1 cup dried fish
2 tablespoons vegetable oil
3 dried red chilies, stemmed
8 medium cloves garlic,
  thinly sliced
1½ tablespoons peeled and
  julienned fresh ginger

Heat the mustard oil in a medium-size saucepan over medium-high heat until faintly smoking. Add the fenugreek seeds and fry until dark brown and fragrant, about 5 seconds. Add the tomatoes, green chilies, salt, and turmeric and cook, covered, until the tomatoes soften, about 10 minutes. Adjust the heat to medium and cook, stirring from time to time, until the liquid has evaporated and the mixture has thickened, about 20 minutes. Remove from the heat, mix in the *timmur* and cilantro and set aside.

Pinch off and discard the head and tail of each dried fish, along with any visible bones. Break each fish into two to three pieces. Heat the vegetable oil in a small skillet over medium-high heat until hot, but not smoking. Add the dried chilies and fry until dark brown and fragrant, about 5 seconds. Add the garlic and ginger, and fry, stirring until golden and crisp, about 2 minutes. With a slotted spoon, remove the chilies, garlic, and ginger, draining as much oil as possible, and add them to the tomato mixture. Adjust the heat to medium-low, and add the dried fish to the pan. Cook, stirring constantly, until crisp, about 1 minute. Transfer the fish to the tomato chutney, and let it stand for 10 to 15 minutes for the flavors to develop. Transfer the chutney to a serving dish.

Makes 4 to 6 servings.

Gundruk
FERMENTED DRIED GREENS

Gundruk, or fermented, dried greens, are a traditional staple in Nepali cuisine. It is common in the hilly and mountainous regions of Nepal, where vegetables are difficult to grow due to infertile soil and harsh climates.

Gundruk has a slightly sour taste and its flavor varies according to the type of greens used. It can be served plain or with a combination of vegetables, such as soybeans, potatoes, onions, and tomatoes. It can also be paired with lentils in a delicious soup. One of the most popular ways of serving gundruk is gundruk ko jhol (page 101), a vegetable soup served with dhindo (millet or cornmeal porridge; page 126).

Gundruk is prepared during harvesting time, typically in October and November, when these greens are abundant. The leaves are packed into earthenware pots with narrow necks with a wooden ladle. The pots are then placed in the sun to ferment for several days. The fermented greens are removed and spread on a bamboo or straw mat and dried completely before storing for future use.

Gundruk is also pickled by soaking and gently crushing the leaves and mixing them with pickling spices. It can also be mixed with shredded meat to serve as an appetizer.

Gundruk is rarely found in Kathmandu restaurants, but it is popular in many homes. It is certainly an acquired taste. It can be purchased from Nepali stores, but making gundruk is not as complicated as it might seem. In fact, it is quite easy, requiring only a large quantity of greens, a wide-mouth, heavy, clean jar, a spoon, and plenty of sunshine.

1 large bunch mustard greens	Nylon netting or cheesecloth
or any leafy vegetable	Kitchen twine
(radish greens, collard greens,	
cauliflower leaves, or cabbage)	
or a combination	

To prepare the greens, cut off and discard the thick and tough stem ends and any yellow leaves. Wash the leaves thoroughly and drain. Tear the large leaves into two to three pieces, but keep the small leaves whole. Spread them on a large tray lined with cloth or paper towel. Cover the tray with nylon netting or cheesecloth and secure with kitchen twine. Place the tray in the full sun outdoors or air-dry in a well-ventilated area, turning frequently until the moisture is completely removed and the greens are wilted, 2 to 3 hours.

Using a wooden spoon or your hand, pack the wilted greens into a large clean jar, by placing a small amount of the dried greens at a time in the jar, pushing firmly between layers. Make the leaves as compact as possible, and press down firmly until the pot is filled and has no air bubbles or moisture. Cover with a clean cloth and then a plate or a heavy board. Place the jar outside in the direct sun, or if sun is not present, place it in a warm area (above 70°F). Bring the jar indoors in the evening. The next day, uncover the jar, further compress the greens, cover tightly, and allow it to ferment. Fermentation is usually completed in 6 to 7 days, depending upon the temperature. The first signs of fermentation are yellow-brown bubbles and a sour odor. Remove the greens and drain off any excess water, spread them out on a clean cloth, and let them dry completely in the full sun for 3 to 4 days. Make sure there is no moisture present before storing them.

Makes 1 cup.

Note: Gundruk can be made from many leafy green vegetables, including mustard greens (*raayo ko saag or tori ko saag*), radish leaves (*mula ko paat*), cauliflower leaves (*phool govi ko paat*), cabbage leaves (*banda govi ko paat*), kohlrabi leaves (*gyanth govi ko paat*), and turnip leaves (*shalgam ko paat*).

Amala ko Achaar
GOOSEBERRY PICKLE

This recipe uses Indian gooseberries (called amala *in Nepali and* amalaki *in Sanskrit) rather than regular gooseberries. They are green, round, tart berries divided into segments with a single seed in the center. They are very nutritious and are often used in Ayurvedic medicine. Gooseberries are also used to prepare spiced dried fruit chews (page 385 or 388). This pickle complements any Nepali meal.*

4 cups fresh ripe green Indian gooseberries, stemmed	A small pinch ground asafetida
2 tablespoons mustard oil	1 teaspoon ground turmeric
1 dried red chili, halved and seeded	1 teaspoon salt
1 teaspoon fenugreek seeds	¼ teaspoon Szechwan pepper (*timmur*), finely ground with a mortar and pestle
1 teaspoon brown mustard seeds	1 tablespoon vegetable oil

In a medium-size saucepan, place the gooseberries with water to cover, and bring to a boil over medium-high heat. Reduce the heat to low, cover, and continue cooking until the seeds are easily removable, 25 to 30 minutes. Do not overcook. Remove the pan from the heat, drain the gooseberries, and when cool enough to handle, remove and discard the seeds.

Heat the mustard oil in a small skillet over medium-high heat. When the oil is faintly smoking, add the dried chili, fenugreek, and mustard and fry until the fenugreek turns dark brown, the mustard seeds pop, and the chili becomes reddish-brown and fully fragrant, about 5 seconds. Reduce the heat to medium and sprinkle in the asafetida, turmeric, gooseberry pulp, salt, and *timmur* and mix well. Cook, stirring from time to time, until the oil starts to separate from the mixture, 10 to 12 minutes. Remove it from the heat and cool completely.

Transfer the pickle to a clean 16-ounce jar and pour the vegetable oil on top to prevent spoilage. Cover tightly with a lid, and place the jar either in the sun or in a warm area for 7 to 10 days. The pickle will improve as it ages.

Makes 2 cups.

Hariyo Golbheda ko Guleo Achaar
SWEET AND SPICY GREEN TOMATO PICKLE

In Nepal, green tomatoes are usually picked during late summer or early fall before they ripen, and then are preserved to make pickles. This recipe provides a great way to use those tomatoes that just will not ripen. This sweet and spicy pickle has a wonderfully unique taste and will add a refreshing taste to any meal.

¼ cup mustard oil
1 teaspoon fenugreek seeds
8 medium firm green tomatoes, chopped
2 cups packed brown sugar
1 tablespoon cayenne pepper, or to taste
1 teaspoon salt

1 teaspoon ground mustard
1 teaspoon ground ginger
1 teaspoon granulated garlic
1 teaspoon ground cloves
1 teaspoon ground cinnamon
½ teaspoon freshly grated nutmeg
2 bay leaves
¾ cup golden raisins

Heat the oil in a heavy saucepan over medium-high heat. When the oil is hot, but not smoking, add the fenugreek seeds and fry until dark brown and fully fragrant, about 5 seconds. Add the green tomatoes, sugar, cayenne pepper, salt, mustard, ginger, garlic, cloves, cinnamon, nutmeg, and bay leaves and mix well. Bring the mixture to a boil, stirring constantly. Then, reduce the heat to medium-low, cover the pan, and continue cooking, stirring occasionally, until the tomatoes have broken down to a sauce-like consistency, about 45 minutes. In the last 5 minutes of cooking, stir in the raisins. Remove the pickle from the heat and allow it to cool before transferring it to a clean 1-quart jar. Refrigerate until ready to serve. This pickle can be stored in the refrigerator for up to 6 months.

Makes 4 cups.

Kudke Khursaani ko Achaar
GREEN CHILI PICKLE

This is an old-fashioned way to preserve small fresh green chilies. They are sun-dried and skillfully mixed with spices. The pickles keep for more than a year and will become more pungent as they age. This pickle is very hot, so serve only a small quantity and always use a dry, clean spoon to remove the pickles from the jar. In Nepal, bird's eye chilies or bird peppers (jire khursaani) are used, but any type of green chili will work.

3 cups fresh green chilies, stemmed
¼ cup brown mustard seeds
¼ cup cumin seeds
¼ cup coriander seeds
1 tablespoon radish seeds (*mula ko beu*)
1 tablespoon fennel seeds
1½ teaspoons Szechwan pepper (*timmur*)
1 teaspoon fenugreek seeds
1 cup plus 2 tablespoons mustard oil

8 to 10 medium cloves garlic, thinly sliced
3 tablespoons peeled and finely julienned fresh ginger
1½ cups fresh lemon or lime juice
2 teaspoons salt
1½ teaspoons ground turmeric

Cheesecloth
Kitchen twine

If the chilies are long, cut them into 1-inch pieces. Spread them on a large tray lined with a cloth or paper towel. Cover with nylon netting or cheesecloth and secure with kitchen twine. Place the tray outdoors in the full sun or air-dry the chilies in a well-ventilated area, turning them frequently until the moisture is completely removed and they are slightly wilted. This can take from 2 to 12 hours, depending on the weather conditions.

Heat a small cast-iron skillet over medium heat and toast the brown mustard seeds, cumin, coriander, radish seeds, fennel, *timmur*, and fenugreek, until the mixture darkens and gives off a pleasant aroma, 2 to 3 minutes. Remove the spices from the skillet, pour them into a dry container to halt the toasting, and let them cool. Transfer the spices to a spice grinder and process to a fine powder. Set aside.

Heat 1 cup of the mustard oil in a heavy saucepan over medium-high heat. When the oil is faintly smoking, add the garlic, ginger, and sun-dried chilies and fry until crisp, 3 to 4 minutes. Mix in the toasted spice mixture, lemon juice, salt, and turmeric and cook for 5 minutes, stirring as needed. Adjust the heat to medium and cook, uncovered, stirring from time to time, until the mixture has thickened and pulls away from the sides of the pan, about 30 minutes. The finished product should be dry, with no liquid.

Remove the pickle from the heat and let it cool completely before putting it in a clean jar. Leave a ½ inch of space at the top, and pour in the remaining 2 tablespoons of mustard oil. Cover tightly with a lid, place the jar in the sun or a warm area for 8 to 10 days. The pickle is ready to eat and can be stored at room temperature for more than 1 year and tastes better as it ages.

Makes 4 cups.

Lapsi ko Achaar
LAPSI PICKLE

Lapsi or labsi is a small plum-sized fruit native to Nepal. It is greenish-yellow when ripe, with a single, large seed, and extremely sour. The fleshy yellow pulp is used to make pickles, candy, and fruit leather. The tough outer skin is also dried and ground to make a souring agent for some pickles. This is among the most popular of all Nepali fruit pickles. Select only ripe, fresh, and smooth-skinned lapsi fruit and wash them carefully. Discard any bruised and discolored fruit. Lapsi fruit is not available in the United States and the closest possible substitute is Rhubarb Pickle (page 326).

30 to 40 lapsi
1½ cups packed brown sugar
3 bay leaves
8 to 10 green cardamom pods, seeds removed and coarsely crushed with a mortar and pestle
¼ cup vegetable oil
4 dried red chilies, halved and seeded
1 teaspoon fenugreek seeds
⅛ teaspoon Himalayan herb (*jimbu*)
1 teaspoon ground turmeric

A generous pinch ground asafetida
1 cup golden raisins
½ cup raw cashews, coarsely chopped
1 (2-inch) stick cinnamon, halved
2 tablespoons dried coconut chips, coarsely chopped
1½ teaspoons fennel seeds
8 whole cloves
1 tablespoon cayenne pepper
1½ teaspoons salt or as needed
¼ teaspoon Szechwan pepper (*timmur*), finely ground with a mortar and pestle

In a medium-size saucepan, combine the lapsi with water to cover and bring them to a boil over medium-high heat. Reduce the heat to low, cover the pan, and cook until the lapsi are tender and the skins are loose, 20 to 25 minutes. Do not overcook. The pulp and seeds should be intact, but the skin should peel off easily. Drain, and when cool enough to handle, peel off the skins. Set aside.

In a small saucepan, combine the brown sugar, 1½ cups of water, and the bay leaves. Bring the mixture to a boil over medium-high heat, stirring constantly, until the brown sugar is dissolved, about 1 minute. Reduce the heat to medium-low and simmer until the sugar has slightly thickened into a syrup, about 5 minutes. Mix with the ground cardamom and set aside.

Heat the oil in a heavy saucepan over medium high heat. When the oil is hot, but not smoking, add the dried chilies, fenugreek, and *jimbu* and cook until the spices become dark brown and fully fragrant, about 5 seconds. Sprinkle in the turmeric and asafetida, then add the raisins, cashews, cinnamon, coconut chips, fennel, and cloves and fry for 30 seconds. Add the peeled lapsi, cayenne pepper, salt, and *timmur* and fry, stirring constantly, for 1 minute. Add the brown sugar syrup and mix well. Reduce the heat to medium-low and cook, stirring occasionally, until the syrup has thickened, about 20 minutes. Remove the pickle from the heat and let it cool completely before placing it in a clean 1-quart jar. It will keep for more than 1 year at room temperature.

Makes 4 cups.

Phool Govi ko Achaar
PICKLED CAULIFLOWER

To make this spicy and refreshing pickle, use the freshest cauliflower available. The cauliflower is pickled in several toasted aromatic spices, packed in a jar, and placed in the sun to ferment. This pickle keeps at room temperature for more than 6 months and tastes better as it ages. Serve with any bland meal.

I large head cauliflower, cut into I-inch florets (about 6 cups)
2 dried red chilies, halved, seeded, and crumbled
I ½ tablespoons brown mustard seeds
I teaspoon fenugreek seeds
¼ teaspoon Szechwan pepper (*timmur*)

I ½ teaspoons salt
I teaspoon ground turmeric
¼ cup vegetable oil

Nylon netting or cheesecloth
Kitchen twine

Spread the cauliflower florets in a single layer on a large tray. Cover with the netting and secure with kitchen twine. Place the tray in the sun, and let the florets dry until all the excess moisture is removed, and they are slightly wilted, about 4 to 6 hours. If the sun is not present, dry them in the open air for the entire day.

While the cauliflower is drying, toast the spices. Heat a small cast-iron skillet over medium heat and toast the chilies, mustard seeds, fenugreek, and *timmur*, stirring constantly, until they are heated through and give off a pleasant aroma, about 2 minutes. Remove the spices from the skillet, transfer to a dry container to halt the toasting, and cool. Place the spices in a spice grinder and grind to a fine powder. A mortar and pestle can also be used.

In a bowl, combine the sun-dried cauliflower, toasted spices, salt, turmeric, and 2 tablespoons of the oil, making sure the florets are thoroughly coated with the spices.

Pack the cauliflower florets, one by one, into a clean 1-quart jar, pushing firmly until the jar is almost filled. Try to make it as compact as possible. Leave ½ inch of space at the top of the jar. Pour the remaining 2 tablespoons of oil over the cauliflower.

Cover the jar tightly with a lid, and place it outside in the direct sun for several days (but bring it indoors in the evenings). If the sun is not present, place the jar in a warm area and leave it to ferment. The fermentation should take 4 to 5 days, depending on the amount of sunlight and temperature. The formation of gas bubbles indicates fermentation is taking place. The pickle is ready when it has a slightly sour taste. Store it in a cool, dark place. Always use a clean, dry spoon to remove the pickles from the jar.

Cabbage Pickle: This recipe can be prepared with 1 medium head green cabbage in place of the cauliflower. Remove the outer leaves, and finely shred it to make 8 to 10 cups.

Makes 4 cups.

Bhadaure Kaankro ko Achaar
PICKLED CUCUMBER

*Nepali cucumbers differ slightly from the varieties available in the United States. They are eaten fresh when the cucumbers are young, but are also left on the vine to mature so they can be made into pickles. Mature Nepali cucumbers are large, oblong, and brown-skinned with a crisp flesh, resembling small watermelons. Pickled cucumber is eaten frequently. During the festival of Dashai, when a large amount of meat and rich foods are consumed, the pickled cucumber is served to provide a cooling effect. Traditionally, it is prepared and stored in an old-fashioned clay pot with a wide mouth and a thick interior (*maata ko ghaito*), which helps maintain a cool temperature even during fermentation. The wide mouth facilitates the packing in and pressing of the cucumber pieces.*

I large Nepali cucumber or 4 to
   6 large unwaxed cucumbers
   (10 to 12 cups sliced)
¼ cup brown mustard seeds,
   finely ground
1½ tablespoons salt
I tablespoon cayenne pepper
I teaspoon ground turmeric

½ teaspoon Szechwan pepper
   (*timmur*), finely ground
   with a mortar and pestle
5 tablespoons vegetable oil

Cheesecloth
Kitchen twine

Halve the cucumbers lengthwise, scoop out and discard the mature seeds. Quarter each cucumber lengthwise and cut the quarters into 1-inch pieces. Cover with cheesecloth and secure with kitchen twine. Place the cucumbers in a single layer (skin-side down) on a tray. Use two or three trays if needed. Place the trays in the sun, and let the cucumbers dry until all the excess moisture is removed and they are slightly wilted, 4 to 6 hours. If the sun is not out, dry them in the open air for the entire day (6 to 8 hours).

In a large bowl, combine the mustard seeds, salt, cayenne pepper, turmeric, and *timmur*. Add 3 tablespoons of the oil to create a paste. Add the cucumbers and mix with your hands, making sure they are well coated with the spices. Cover the bowl and set aside for 20 minutes.

Pack the cucumbers, one by one, into a clean 2½-quart wide-mouth jar. Push firmly until the jar is almost filled and there is no space between the cucumbers. Leave ½ inch of space at the top of the jar and pour the remaining 2 tablespoons of oil over the cucumbers. If the jar is not packed properly, air pockets will develop leading to spoilage.

Cover the jar tightly with a lid, and place it outside in the direct sun for several days (but bring it indoors in the evenings). If the sun is not present, place the jar in a warm area and leave it to ferment. The fermentation should take 4 to 5 days, depending on the temperature. The formation of gas bubbles indicates the fermentation is taking place. The pickle is ready when the cucumbers are still crunchy with a slightly sour taste. Store in the refrigerator to avoid excess souring. Always use a dry, clean spoon to remove the pickles from the jar.

Makes 10 cups.

Masala ko Ledo Achaar
SPICY LEMON PICKLE

Here is a simplified adaptation of this classic aromatic Nepali ledo achaar *from my grandmother's kitchen.* Ledo achaar *is a spicy lemon pickle. Preparing this pickle requires skill, and is a time-consuming process, but the result is definitely worthwhile. I can still remember the aroma of spices being pounded in the mortar and pestle. On a sunny day, experienced pickle makers were called to our house to prepare the pickles. They would cut, dry, grind, and cook the vegetables, fruits, nuts, herbs, and spices all day in the sun. At the end of the day, they had made enough pickles for the entire year.*

12 lemons	1½ teaspoons radish seeds
¾ cup sesame seeds	(*mula ko beu*)
½ cup cumin seeds	1 teaspoon ajowan seeds
½ cup coriander seeds	2 teaspoons fenugreek seeds
½ cup brown mustard seeds	1 teaspoon freshly ground
10 dried red chilies, halved,	black pepper
seeded, and broken	4 whole cloves
into several pieces	1 (2-inch) stick cinnamon,
10 green cardamom pods,	broken into several pieces
seeds removed	1 cup mustard oil
2 black cardamom pods,	1 tablespoon Himalayan herb
seeds removed	(*jimbu*)
1 tablespoon fennel seeds	1½ teaspoons ground turmeric
1 tablespoon yellow mustard	¼ teaspoon ground asafetida
seeds	1 cup fresh lemon or lime juice
1½ teaspoons Szechwan pepper	2 teaspoons salt
(*timmur*)	1 tablespoon vegetable oil

Remove and discard the peel, membranes, and seeds from the lemons. Reserve the pulp and any juice that has collected.

Heat a medium-size cast-iron skillet over medium heat. Toast the sesame seeds, cumin, coriander, brown mustard seeds, chilies, green and black cardamom, fennel seeds, yellow mustard seeds, *timmur*, radish seeds, ajowan, 1 teaspoon of the fenugreek, the black pepper, cloves, and cinnamon, stirring constantly, until the spice mixture darkens and gives off a pleasant aroma, 2 to 3 minutes. Remove the spices from the skillet and pour them into a dry container to halt the toasting. When cool, transfer the spices to a spice grinder and grind to a fine powder. You may have to do this in two or three batches. Pour the mixture through a sieve and regrind any spices that do not pass through. Set aside.

Heat the mustard oil in a heavy saucepan over medium-high heat. When the oil is faintly smoking, add the remaining 1 teaspoon fenugreek and *jimbu*, and fry until dark brown and fragrant, about 5 seconds. Remove the pan from the heat, add the turmeric, asafetida, and toasted spice mixture, and mix thoroughly. Return the pan to the heat, add the reserved lemon pulp and cook, stirring, until the mixture boils. Add the lemon juice and salt and cook, uncovered, for 10 minutes. Adjust the heat to medium-low, cover the pan and cook, stirring from time to time, until the liquid has reduced and thickened and become a rich dark brown, about 45 minutes more. The pickles are done when the oil separates from the spice mixture. Remove the pickle from the heat and cool.

Transfer the pickle into a 2-quart jar. Pour the vegetable oil on top, cover tightly with a lid, and place the jar either in the sun or in a warm, sunny area for 1 month. The pickle is then ready to be eaten. It will keep for more than a year in the refrigerator, and will improve as it ages.

Note: For everyday use, place a small amount of the pickle into a smaller jar and use it from there. Do not use a wet spoon to scoop the pickle from the jar, and never put back pickle that has been taken out of the jar.

Makes 6 cups.

Kaagati ra Khursaani ko Achaar
LEMON-CHILI PICKLE

In this quick and easy recipe, lemons are combined with spices and pickled in the sun. The pickling process takes about one month, and this pickle improves in taste with time.

1 tablespoon fennel seeds
1 tablespoon yellow mustard
   seeds
1 teaspoon ajowan seeds
1 teaspoon fenugreek seeds
6 lemons, peeled, seeded, and
   cut into 1-inch pieces

6 fresh hot green chilies, cut
   into ½-inch pieces
1½ tablespoons finely peeled
   and julienned fresh ginger
2 teaspoons salt
A pinch ground asafetida
3 tablespoons mustard oil

Heat a small cast-iron skillet over medium heat and toast the fennel seeds, mustard seeds, ajowan, and fenugreek, stirring constantly until they give off a pleasant aroma and darken, 2 to 3 minutes. Remove the spices from the skillet, pour them into a dry container to halt the toasting, and cool. Transfer the spices to a spice grinder and grind to a fine powder. Set aside.

In a bowl, combine the lemons, green chilies, ginger, salt, asafetida, and toasted spices. Add 2 tablespoons of the mustard oil and mix well. Place the mixture in a clean 1-quart jar, and pour the remaining 1 tablespoon of oil on top of the pickle. Close the lid tightly and place the jar in the sun or in a warm area for 1 month. Shake the jar occasionally. The pickle is ready when the color lightens and the spice mixture thickens.

Makes 4 cups.

Gulio-Piro Kaagati ko Achaar
SWEET LIME PICKLE

This pickle can be prepared from either limes or lemons. It has a sweet, tart, and citrusy taste. This pickle goes well with fried snacks, and adds a spicy twist to any mild Nepali meal.

1 tablespoon brown mustard seeds	10 to 12 small limes (about 1½ pounds)
½ teaspoon fenugreek seeds	1 cup white or brown sugar
2 dried red chilies, halved and seeded	2 tablespoons salt
	1 teaspoon ground turmeric

Heat a small skillet over medium heat and toast the mustard, fenugreek, and dried chilies, stirring constantly, until they give off a pleasant aroma and darken, about 1 minute. Remove the spices from the skillet, pour them into a dry container to halt the toasting, and let them cool. Transfer the spices to a spice grinder and grind to a fine powder.

With a sharp knife, cut off a piece from the top and bottom of each lime and quarter them lengthwise. Remove and discard any seeds. Place the limes in a clean 1-quart jar, and add the toasted spices, sugar, salt, and turmeric. Close the lid tightly and shake vigorously to mix. Place the jar in direct sunlight (bring it indoors in the evenings). If the sun is not present, place the jar in a warm area. Shake the jar once a day so the spices penetrate the limes evenly.

The pickle is ready when the color changes to light brown, the limes soften, and the spice mixture thickens, 6 to 7 weeks. Store in a cool, dark place. The pickle will taste better as it ages.

Makes 4 cups.

Rhubarb ko Achaar
RHUBARB PICKLE

This spicy, sweet, and tart chutney is prepared from rhubarb and spices. Rhubarb is a perennial plant with juicy red stalks resembling celery stalks, and large, coarse leaves. The leaves of this plant are toxic and not edible; only the red stalks are used. Due to its intense sourness, rhubarb is usually cooked with sugar. Many Nepalese living in the United States have described rhubarb chutney as similar in taste and texture to Nepali Lapsi Pickle (page 316) when cooked with the same spices.

3 ½ pounds rhubarb
   (10 to 12 cups sliced)
2 tablespoons vegetable oil
5 whole dried red chilies,
   halved and seeded
1 teaspoon fenugreek seeds
½ teaspoon cumin seeds
½ teaspoon ajowan seeds

1 cup packed brown sugar, or
   to taste
1 ½ teaspoons salt
1 teaspoon fennel seeds
1 teaspoon ground cinnamon
½ teaspoon ground nutmeg
½ teaspoon ground cloves

Trim the rhubarb, discarding the ends and leaves. Rhubarb stalks are best when used young and peeling is not necessary. If the rhubarb is tough, peel off the outermost stringy covering with a vegetable peeler. Slice the rhubarb into ¼-inch pieces and set aside.

Heat the oil in a heavy saucepan over medium-high heat. When the oil is hot, but not smoking, add the dried chilies, fenugreek, cumin, and ajowan and fry until dark brown and fully fragrant, about 5 seconds. Add the rhubarb, sugar, salt, fennel, cinnamon, nutmeg, and cloves and mix well. Bring the mixture to a boil, stirring constantly. Then, reduce the heat to medium-low, cover the pan, and simmer until the rhubarb is tender and the liquid has thickened, about 45 minutes. It should resemble a thick jam. Remove the pickle from the heat and adjust the seasonings and sugar. Serve immediately or cool and transfer to a clean 1-quart jar and refrigerate.

Makes 4 cups.

Khaade ko Mula Achaar
WHITE RADISH PICKLE

Radish pickles are commonly served with Nepali meals. The spicy, sharp, refreshing, pickle boosts the appetite and is thought to aid in digestion. Any variety of long, white radishes (such as daikon) can be used as long as they are fresh, with smooth skins. Avoid radishes that are limp, woody, or withered. Traditionally, pickles are made on sunny days, which results in a faster fermentation. This pickle will keep well for six months if refrigerated.

2 small white radishes, peeled
 and cut into bite-size pieces
 (about 6 cups)
3 tablespoons brown mustard
 seeds, finely ground
1 tablespoon cayenne pepper
2 teaspoons salt
1 teaspoon ground turmeric
¼ teaspoon Szechwan pepper
 (*timmur*), finely ground
 with a mortar and pestle

2 tablespoons vegetable oil
2 tablespoons mustard oil
½ teaspoon fenugreek seeds
⅛ teaspoon Himalayan herb
 (*jimbu*)

Nylon netting or cheesecloth
Kitchen twine

Place the radishes in a single layer on a wide, large tray. Cover with the netting and secure with kitchen twine. Place the tray in the sun, and let them dry until slightly wilted, about 4 to 6 hours. If the sun is not present, dry them in the open air for the entire day. When the moisture from the radishes is completely removed, place them in a large bowl with the mustard seeds, cayenne pepper, salt, turmeric, *timmur*, and vegetable oil. Mix with your hands, making sure the radishes are thoroughly coated with the spices. Cover the bowl and let it stand for 30 minutes before placing the mixture in a jar.

Select a clean, wide-mouth jar and pack the radishes into the jar, one by one, pushing firmly until the jar is almost filled. Make sure there is no space between the radishes, but leave a ½ inch of space at the top of the jar.

Heat the mustard oil in a small skillet over medium-high heat. When the oil is faintly smoking, add the fenugreek seeds and *jimbu* strands and fry until dark brown and fragrant, about 5 seconds. Remove the skillet from the heat and let it cool. Pour the entire contents into the packed radish jar. Cover tightly with a lid, and place it outside in the direct sun for several days (bring it indoors in the evenings). If the sun is not present, place the jar in a warm area and leave it to ferment. The fermentation should take 4 to 5 days, depending on the amount of sunlight and the temperature. The formation of gas bubbles indicates that fermentation is taking place. The pickle is ready when the radishes are still crunchy and have a slightly sour taste. If you prefer a stronger and more sour pickle, increase the fermentation time. Store the pickles in the refrigerator for up to 6 months Always use a dry, clean spoon to remove the pickles from the jar.

Makes 6 cups.

Kaagati ko Achaar
PICKLED LIME

This popular pickle, made from thin-skinned limes, is one of the simplest ways of preserving limes. In Nepal, lime pickle is believed to have medicinal value. Some Nepalese suck a small piece of lime pickle to relieve nausea. The sour-salty pickle is also irresistible to many pregnant women and young girls.

10 to 12 small limes (about 1½ pounds)	¼ cup salt

With a sharp knife, cut off a piece from the top and bottom of each lime and quarter them lengthwise. Remove and discard any seeds. Rub each piece of lime with the salt. Place the limes in a clean 1-quart jar. Close the lid tightly and shake vigorously. Place the jar in direct sunlight (bring it indoors in the evenings). If the sun is not present, place the jar in a warm area. Shake the jar once a day.

The pickle will be ready after the limes soften, the skins become tender, the juice thickens, and the color becomes light brown, 6 to 7 weeks. The pickle keeps at room temperature for more than 1 year and tastes better as it ages.

Makes 4 cups.

Til ko Chhope
ROASTED SESAME SEED PICKLE

This is not a pickle in the traditional Western sense, but a Nepalese dry pickle or chhope. *Made from toasted ground sesame seeds, it is incredibly versatile and perks up any Nepali dish. Toasting sesame seeds brings out a nutty flavor, so I do not recommend using pre-ground seeds. In addition, the seeds turn rancid quickly due to their high oil content, so only make a small amount of this pickle at a time. Traditionally, the souring agent used for this pickle is* chook amilo, *which is made by boiling the juice from a large Nepali variety of lemon* (nibuwa) *until it becomes dark brown. For this recipe, I use regular lemon juice, which works well.*

3 cups sesame seeds	1½ teaspoons salt
8 to 10 dried red chilies, halved and seeded	3 to 4 tablespoons fresh lemon or lime juice
1 teaspoon Szechwan pepper (*timmur*)	

Heat a large cast-iron skillet over medium heat and toast the sesame seeds, stirring constantly to prevent the seeds from flying all over, until they give off a pleasant aroma and darken, 2 to 3 minutes. Remove the seeds from the skillet, pour them into a dry container to halt the toasting, and let them cool. Place the chilies and *timmur* in the same skillet, and toast them until they are smoky and darken slightly, about 1 minute. When roasting the chilies, cover the pan because the fumes can be irritating.

Transfer the roasted sesame seeds, chilies, and *timmur* to a spice grinder and grind to a fine powder. You may have to do this in two batches. Use a spoon to loosen any clumps that form on the bottom of the grinder. Transfer the powder to a mixing bowl and stir in the salt and lemon juice. The mixture should resemble wet sand. Taste and adjust the salt and lemon juice. Serve right away or store in an airtight container in a cool place for up to 3 months.

Makes 3 cups.

Guleo Khaana

SWEETS

Nepali sweets, are served throughout the day: with breakfast, with afternoon tea, and after dinner. These confections are made from a wide variety of ingredients, including milk, fruits, vegetables, nuts, and seeds. They are usually quite sweet and are often flavored with green cardamom, saffron, and certain essences.

Some sweets are prepared for special occasions, such as weddings, religious ceremonies, and family feasts. These are usually bought from professional sweet makers (*haluwai pasale*), not made at home. During the most important religious festivals, such as Vijaya Dashami (a ten-day celebration marking the victory of the goddess Druga over the devil), Laxmi Puja (the celebration of the goddess Laxmi), and Bhai Tika and Tihaar festivals (brother's and sister's day), many delicately flavored and elaborate sweets are prepared. They are consumed as blessed food or shared and exchanged with family and friends to celebrate the joyous occasion.

Mana-Bhog
WHEAT FLOUR PUDDING

In Nepali, mana *translates as "mind" and* bhog *is "pure food," so the mana-bhog is defined "as an offering to the mind." Made from wheat flour, it is similar in texture to a thick pudding. It is also associated with auspicious occasions and considered one of the purest forms of food to be offered to the deities* (naivedya) *during religious festivals. This is a popular dessert that is quick and easy to prepare and best served warm. Traditionally, it is paired with poori (page 110) for a delicious breakfast or snack.*

1 cup sugar
Seeds of 4 to 5 green cardamom
   pods, coarsely ground with a
   mortar and pestle
¾ cup clarified butter (*gheu*) or
   unsalted butter

1½ cups all-purpose flour
½ cup golden raisins
¼ cup halved raw cashews
2 tablespoons finely chopped
   dried coconut chips

In a medium-size saucepan, combine the sugar, ground cardamom, and 2 cups of water and bring to a boil over medium heat. Cook until the sugar dissolves and a thin syrup forms, about 5 minutes. Set aside.

Melt the butter in a heavy saucepan over medium-low heat. Add the flour, and cook, stirring constantly, until it is light golden brown with a pleasant nutty aroma, 15 to 20 minutes. Be careful not to burn the flour.

Stir in the raisins, cashews, and coconut. Slowly add the sugar syrup, stirring constantly. Cook until all the syrup is absorbed and the *mana-bhog* starts to pull away from the sides of the pan. The finished dish should be soft and creamy. Transfer it to a serving dish and serve hot.

Makes 4 to 6 servings.

Sooji ko Haluwa
SEMOLINA PUDDING

Sooji ko haluwa is a delicious semolina pudding. It is a favorite for children, who often eat this delicious treat for breakfast. Serve it immediately, when it is still warm and fluffy.

⅛ teaspoon saffron threads
4 cups whole milk, heated
1 cup clarified butter (*gheu*)
1½ cups fine semolina
¼ cup coarsely chopped raw cashews
¼ cup golden raisins
¼ cup finely chopped dried coconut chips
2 tablespoons finely chopped raw almonds
Seeds of 6 green cardamom pods, finely ground with a mortar and pestle
1 cup sugar

Rub the saffron threads between your fingers to crush them, and place them in a mortar and pestle or small bowl. Add 2 tablespoons of the milk and mix with a pestle or spoon until the saffron is thoroughly dissolved. Set aside.

Heat the butter in a heavy saucepan over medium-low heat. Add the semolina and cook, stirring constantly, until it is light brown with a pleasant, nutty aroma, about 25 minutes. Stir in the cashews, raisins, coconut, almonds, and ground cardamom. Gently pour in the remaining warm milk, sugar, and saffron-infused milk and stir well. Continue cooking until all the milk has been absorbed and the haluwa has become fluffy, 5 to 7 minutes. Transfer to a platter and serve hot.

Makes 4 to 6 servings.

Gaajar ko Haluwa
CARROT PUDDING

Gaajar ko haluwa is a favorite family dessert. The recipe is easy to prepare, but requires constant attention and stirring while cooking. It can be served hot, warm, or at room temperature, topped with chopped nuts. This dessert can be made ahead of time and can be stored in the refrigerator for up to one week. When serving, reheat slowly in a saucepan or in the microwave.

⅛ teaspoon saffron threads
8 cups whole milk
¼ cup clarified butter (*gheu*) or unsalted butter
1½ pounds carrots, peeled and coarsely grated
½ cup blanched raw almonds, finely ground

Seeds of 6 green cardamom pods, finely ground with a mortar and pestle
1 cup sugar
2 tablespoons golden raisins
2 tablespoons chopped raw cashews
2 tablespoons raw pistachios, coarsely ground with a mortar and pestle

Rub the saffron threads between your fingers to crush them, and place them in a mortar and pestle or small bowl. Add 2 tablespoons of the milk and mix with a pestle or spoon until the saffron is thoroughly dissolved. Set aside.

Heat the butter in a heavy saucepan or nonstick pan over medium heat. Add the shredded carrots and any liquid and cook, stirring continuously, until the carrots are soft and the liquid has almost evaporated, about 10 minutes.

Increase the heat to medium-high, add the remaining milk, almonds, and cardamom and mix well. Cook, stirring frequently, until the mixture comes to a full boil. Reduce the heat to medium-low, cover, and cook, stirring from time to time, until the milk has thickened and the mixture has reduced by about half, about 30 minutes. Add the sugar, raisins, cashews, and saffron-infused milk and continue cooking, stirring and scraping the sides of the pan, until the mixture begins to pull away from the sides of the pan to create a thick solid mass, 10 to 15 minutes. Transfer the *haluwa* to a serving dish. Sprinkle with the pistachios and serve.

Makes 4 to 6 servings.

Kheer
RICE PUDDING

Traditionally in Nepal, I prepared kheer *with* govindbhog *rice, a fragrant delicate medium-grain rice similar in flavor to basmati, though it can be made with any variety of white rice.* Kheer *is associated with auspicious occasions and religious ceremonies, but is also enjoyed on a regular basis.*

¾ cup medium-grain white rice
1 tablespoon clarified butter
  (*gheu*)
⅛ teaspoon saffron threads plus
  6 to 8 threads for garnish
8 cups plus 1 tablespoon whole
  milk
Seeds of 4 to 6 green cardamom
  pods, finely ground with a
  mortar and pestle

1 cup sugar, or to taste
2 tablespoons chopped blanched
  raw almonds
2 tablespoons finely chopped
  dried unsweetened coconut
2 tablespoons golden raisins
2 tablespoons coarsely chopped
  raw pistachios

Rinse and soak the rice as directed on page 46. Drain and combine the rice and clarified butter. Mix well and set aside. This process will prevent the grains from sticking together while cooking.

Gently crush the saffron with a mortar and pestle. Dissolve in 1 tablespoon of the milk and set aside.

Bring the milk and ground cardamom to a boil in a heavy-bottomed saucepan over medium-high heat. Stir occasionally to prevent the milk from burning. Reduce the heat to medium and continue cooking, stirring occasionally, until the milk has slightly thickened, about 15 minutes. Then, stir in the rice mixture. Reduce the heat to medium-low and simmer until the rice grains have softened, about 20 minutes. Mix in the sugar, almonds, coconut, and raisins. Continue cooking, stirring, until the mixture has condensed into a thick, smooth pudding. Stir in the saffron-infused milk. Transfer the *kheer* to a serving dish, sprinkle it with the chopped pistachios and saffron threads, and serve immediately.

Note: Refrigeration will thicken the *kheer* and decrease its sweetness.

Makes 4 to 6 servings.

Makai ko Tachauera
FRESH CORN PUDDING

Makai ko tachauera *is a delicious old-fashioned family recipe. This creamy corn pudding was a culinary treat growing up in Nepal. It was usually prepared during the peak growing season when the corn was freshest.*

5 to 6 ears sweet corn
¼ cup clarified butter (*gheu*) or unsalted butter
3½ cups whole milk
Seeds of 4 green cardamom pods, finely ground with a mortar and pestle

¾ cup sugar
2 tablespoons golden raisins
2 tablespoons blanched slivered raw almonds

Remove the husks and silks from the corn. With a sharp knife, slice off the kernels. Scrape down the base of the cob with the side of the knife, and extract as much milky juice as possible into a bowl. Set aside.

Heat the butter in a large skillet over medium-high heat. Add the corn with all its juices and cook, stirring until all the juice evaporates, for 5 minutes. Add the milk and ground cardamom and cook, stirring occasionally, until the milk boils. Reduce the heat, cover, and continue cooking until the corn is tender, the milk thickens, and the mixture reduces to about half its original volume, 7 to 10 minutes. Add the sugar, raisins, and almonds, mix well, and cook for 5 minutes more. Serve warm.

Makes 4 to 6 servings.

Makhana ko Kheer
PUFFED LOTUS SEED PUDDING

Makhana *are puffed dried lotus seeds, which have a pleasant, delicate flavor. This recipe uses the lotus seeds to make a dessert, similar to rice pudding, in which the seeds are boiled with milk, cardamom, and saffron, and garnished with dried fruits. It is served warm or at room temperature.*

⅛ teaspoon saffron threads
6 cups plus 2 tablespoons whole milk
3 tablespoons clarified butter (*gheu*) or unsalted butter
5 cups puffed lotus seeds (*makhana*)
Seeds of 6 green cardamom pods, coarsely ground with a mortar and pestle

¾ cup sugar
2 tablespoons coarsely chopped raw almonds
2 tablespoons golden raisins
1 tablespoon coarsely chopped raw pistachios

Gently crush the saffron with a mortar and pestle. Dissolve it in 2 tablespoons of the milk and set aside.

Heat the butter in a heavy saucepan over medium-low heat. Add the lotus seeds and sauté, stirring constantly, until light brown, 5 to 7 minutes.

Increase the heat to high, add the remaining 6 cups of milk and cardamom, and bring to a boil. Reduce the heat to medium-low, cover, and continue cooking, stirring occasionally, until the lotus seeds soften and the milk thickens slightly, about 25 minutes. Add the sugar, almonds, raisins, and saffron-infused milk and cook until the mixture has condensed into a thick pudding. Transfer the *kheer* to a serving dish, sprinkle it with the chopped pistachios, and serve warm.

Makes 4 to 6 servings.

Kesari Barfi
SAFFRON FUDGE

*Barfi is a traditional fudge made from any combination of flours, lentils, nuts, fruits, vegetables, and thickened milk (*khuwaa*). It can be eaten any time of the day (like candy) as a snack or as an after-dinner dessert.*

⅛ teaspoon saffron threads
½ cup clarified butter (*gheu*) or
    unsalted butter
1 cup sugar
1½ cups whole milk
3 cups non-fat powdered dry milk
¼ cup blanched raw almonds,
    finely ground

¼ cup shredded unsweetened
    coconut
Seeds of 8 to 10 green car-
    damom pods, finely ground
    with a mortar and pestle
½ cup raw pistachios, coarsely
    ground with a mortar
    and pestle

Grease a 9 x 13-inch pan and set aside.

Rub the saffron threads between your fingers to crush them, and place them in a mortar and pestle or small bowl with 1 tablespoon of water. Continue mixing with a pestle or spoon until the saffron is thoroughly dissolved. Set aside.

Heat the butter in a medium-size saucepan over medium-low heat. Gradually add the sugar and mix well, stirring constantly. Increase the heat to medium-high, add the milk, bring it to a boil. Stir in the powdered milk, almonds, coconut, and ground cardamom and cook until the liquid evaporates and the mixture starts to pull away from the sides of the pan forming a thick, solid mass, about 10 minutes. Stir in the saffron-infused water and mix well. At this stage, the mixture will stick to the bottom of the pan, so stir constantly.

Transfer the mixture to the prepared pan and spread it evenly. Sprinkle the *barfi* with the pistachios and gently press into the surface. Set the pan aside for 1 hour until it sets. Then cut into 1-inch diamond-shapes. Carefully remove the pieces from the pan, arrange them on a decorative platter, and serve. If not serving them immediately, refrigerate the *barfi* in an airtight container for up to 2 weeks, but bring it to room temperature before serving.

Makes 25 to 30 pieces.

Badaam ko Barfi
ALMOND FUDGE

Almonds add a soft crunch and delicious sweetness to this barfi. *For the best results, use freshly ground almonds.*

2 cups blanched raw almonds
plus 1 tablespoon coarsely
chopped
2 cups whole milk
1½ cups sugar

½ cup clarified butter (*gheu*) or
unsalted butter
Seeds of 10 green cardamom
pods, finely ground with a
mortar and pestle

Grease a 9 x 13-inch pan and set aside.

Place the blanched almonds and milk in a food processor or blender and process until the almonds are coarsely ground.

Place the almond mixture in a heavy-bottomed saucepan, and cook over medium-low heat, stirring frequently, until all the moisture has evaporated and the mixture has reduced to a thick paste, about 15 minutes. Stir in the sugar. Add the butter, 1 tablespoon at a time, mixing well after each addition. Do not allow the mixture to burn or stick to the bottom of the pan. Continue cooking until the mixture begins to pull away from the sides of the pan to form a thick mass. Stir in the ground cardamom.

Transfer the *barfi* to the prepared pan, and spread evenly. Sprinkle the ground almonds on top and gently press them into the surface. Set the pan aside for 1 hour until it sets. Then cut the *barfi* into 1-inch diamonds. Carefully remove the pieces from the pan, arrange on a decorative platter, and serve. If not serving immediately, refrigerate in an airtight container for up to 2 weeks, but bring to room temperature before serving.

Makes 25 to 30 pieces.

Maalpuwa
MAALPUWA FRITTERS

Maalpuwa or maalpua are sweet, thick, fried Nepali pancakes flavored with fennel seeds. The sweet bread is delicious by itself or can be served with fresh fruit and a hot beverage. These are best eaten hot, but can also be served at room temperature.

1 to 1½ cups milk, or as needed	1½ tablespoons fennel seeds
¾ cup sugar, or to taste (or half white and half brown sugar)	2½ cups all-purpose flour
	3 to 4 cups vegetable oil
1 medium very ripe banana, peeled and mashed	

In a medium-size bowl, combine the milk, sugar, banana, and fennel seeds. Gradually add the flour, beating well to make a smooth batter without lumps. Beat with a fork to make it fluffy. Cover with plastic wrap or a damp towel and set the batter aside for at least 30 minutes at room temperature. If the rested batter is too thick, add 1 to 2 tablespoons of water; if it feels too thin add more flour. The consistency of the batter should be similar to pudding.

Heat the oil in a skillet over medium-high heat until it reaches 350° to 375°F. Test for readiness by placing a small drop of batter into the hot oil. If it bubbles and rises to the surface immediately, it is ready. Pour 2 tablespoons of the batter directly into the hot oil to form an irregular 3-inch circle. The batter will sink at first, but will rise to the surface slowly. Turn over and fry the other side until golden brown. Remove with a slotted spoon and drain on paper towels. Repeat with the remaining batter. Serve immediately or keep warm, covered until ready to serve.

Note: While frying, maintain the oil temperature at 350° to 375° F for even cooking. If the temperature is not hot enough, the *maalpuwa* will absorb a lot of fat. If the oil is too hot, it will brown too quickly but remain uncooked inside.

Makes 12 to 15 fritters.

Besan ko Laddu
SWEET CHICKPEA BALLS

Laddus are traditional sweet balls that can be made from any type of flour such as chickpea, wheat, semolina, or a blend of these. It is a popular confection, eaten any time of the day with various beverages.

I cup clarified butter (*gheu*) or
    unsalted butter
2 cups chickpea flour (*besan*)
1½ cups shredded unsweetened
    coconut
½ cup blanched raw almonds,
    finely chopped

½ cup raw pistachio nuts,
    finely chopped
2 tablespoons walnuts, chopped
Seeds of 8 to 10 green cardamom
    pods, finely ground with a
    mortar and pestle
I cup sugar

Melt the butter in a heavy saucepan over medium-low heat. Gradually add the chickpea flour, stirring constantly, until the flour becomes rich golden brown and has a pleasant nutty aroma. Do not burn the flour, for this may produce a bitter taste. Add the coconut, almonds, pistachio nuts, walnuts, and cardamom and mix well. Remove the pan from the heat and allow the mixture to cool slightly. Stir the sugar into the cooled mixture.

With your hands, form 1-inch balls of the chickpea flour mixture. Carefully place the balls on a tray to harden for 15 to 20 minutes. Transfer the balls to a platter and serve. *Laddu* keeps in a well-sealed container, refrigerated, for 4 to 5 weeks.

Makes 20 to 22 pieces.

Lumbini Laddu
LUMBINI LADDU

Although these sweet balls are named after Lumbini, the birthplace of Gautam Buddha, this recipe does not come from Lumbini. In fact, there is no connection. When my children were young, I often prepared these delicious sweets. They loved the crunchy texture and nutty flavor of these sweet balls, named them Lumbini Laddu, and the name simply stuck.

1¼ cups clarified butter (*gheu*)
3½ cups all-purpose flour
1 cup shelled raw, unsalted sunflower seeds
½ cup unsweetened shredded coconut
¼ cup golden raisins

2 tablespoons coarsely chopped raw almonds
Seeds of 8 to 10 green cardamom pods, finely ground with a mortar and pestle
¾ cup sugar
3 tablespoons coarsely ground raw pistachios

Melt the butter in a heavy saucepan over medium-low heat, add the flour, and cook, stirring constantly, until light golden brown with a pleasant nutty aroma, 15 to 20 minutes. Add the sunflower seeds, coconut, raisins, almonds, and cardamom and mix well. Remove the pan from the heat and let the mixture cool slightly.

Stir in the sugar. When it is cool enough to handle comfortably, Form the mixture into 1-inch balls. Roll the balls in the chopped pistachios, pressing gently so they stick. Carefully place the balls on a tray. Transfer the laddu to a platter and serve. Store refrigerated in a well-sealed container for 4 to 5 weeks.

Makes 25 pieces.

Motichur ko Laddu
CHICKPEA FRITTERS IN SYRUP

Motichur ko laddus *are golden yellow balls made from chickpea flour served in sugar syrup. Chickpea flour batter is dropped into hot oil to form tiny fritters and a flat perforated spatula (*jhanjar*) is then used to extract them. Finally they are soaked in a saffron-cardamom syrup, and rolled into round balls.*

2 cups chickpea flour (*besan*)
¼ teaspoon saffron threads
1 tablespoon boiling water
2½ cups sugar
Seeds of 8 to 10 green cardamom
   pods

3 to 4 cups vegetable oil
2 tablespoons chopped blanched
   raw almonds
2 tablespoons coarsely ground
   raw pistachios
2 tablespoons golden raisins

Place the chickpea flour in a medium-size bowl and gradually add ½ cup of water, a little at a time, beating well to make a smooth and creamy batter. The batter should be pourable. If it is too thick, add more water; if it feels too thin, add more flour and mix well. Set aside.

Gently crush the saffron threads with a mortar and pestle and dissolve in the boiling water. Set aside.

In a wide saucepan, combine the sugar, cardamom seeds, and 4 cups of water. Bring the mixture to a boil over medium-high heat, stirring constantly, until the sugar is dissolved, about 2 minutes. Reduce the heat to medium-low and simmer it until a thick syrup forms, 5 to 7 minutes. Add the saffron-infused water and mix well. Keep warm.

Heat the oil in a deep heavy skillet over medium-high heat until it reaches 350° to 375°F. Test the readiness of the oil by dropping a little batter into the hot oil. If it bubbles and rises to the surface immediately, it is ready. Hold a large perforated spatula (*jhajar*) over the frying pan and pour 2 to 3 tablespoons of batter on the spatula. Tap and shake the spatula until the batter falls through the holes, making round drops. Fry the drops until they are light brown and crisp, 40 to 50 seconds. Remove them with a slotted spoon, draining as much oil as possible, and immediately place them in the warm sugar syrup. Repeat the process until all the batter is used up. Make sure to mix the drops and the syrup until the drops are well-coated. Stir in the almonds, pistachios, and raisins, cover the saucepan, and set aside for 1 to 2 hours so the drops can absorb the syrup.

Working with a small handful of the mixture, roll and squeeze it between your palms to form 1-inch balls. Carefully place the balls on a tray to harden for a few minutes. Repeat the procedure for the remaining mixture. Transfer the *laddu* to a platter and serve at room temperature. Store in the refrigerator in a well-sealed container for up to 1 month.

Makes 20 to 22 pieces.

Gulaab Jaamun
DUMPLINGS IN SAFFRON-CARDAMOM SYRUP

A very popular dessert, gulaab jaamun, *also called* gup-chup, *are round fried dumplings soaked in saffron-cardamom syrup. They resemble small reddish-brown plums and have a soft, spongy texture.* Gulaab jaamun *are made for special occasions, holidays, religious festivals, and wedding ceremonies. Traditionally, they are made from* khuwaa *(page 351), but this is a simplified recipe. They are served warm or at room temperature, and can be served alone or with beverages, fruit, or yogurt to tone down the sweetness and richness.*

⅛ teaspoon saffron threads	I teaspoon baking soda
4 cups sugar	¼ cup unsalted butter, melted
6 green cardamom pods, crushed	¾ cup whole milk, or as needed
Seeds of 4 green cardamon pods, coarsely ground with a mortar and pestle	¼ cup raw pistachios, coarsely chopped
2½ cups nonfat powdered milk	¼ cup raw almonds, coarsely chopped
½ cup all-purpose white flour	3 to 4 cups vegetable oil

Gently crush the saffron with a mortar and pestle. Dissolve it in I tablespoon of water and set aside.

In a wide saucepan, combine the sugar, 6 whole cardamom pods, and 4 cups of water and bring to a boil over medium-high heat, stirring constantly, until the sugar has dissolved, about 2 minutes. Reduce the heat to medium-low and simmer until the mixture has slightly thickened, about 5 minutes. Remove the pan from the heat, stir in the saffron-infused water, and set it aside, covered.

In a medium-size bowl, combine the powdered milk, flour, and baking soda and mix well by hand. Stir in the butter and mix thoroughly. Gradually add the milk, a little at a time, to form a dough that holds together. Knead the dough until it is soft and pliable and can be easily molded into small balls. If the dough is too sticky, add some flour; if it feels too firm, add a little water, and knead it some more. Cover the bowl and set aside at room temperature for 20 to 25 minutes.

To make the filling, combine the pistachios, almonds and ground cardamom seeds in a small bowl and mix well. Set aside.

When the dough is well rested, remove it from the bowl, place it on a flat surface, and knead it again for 1 minute. Divide the dough into 25 equal pieces. Roll each piece into a small ball. Make an indentation in the ball, place a pinch of the filling in the center, close the dough around the filling, and reroll to smooth it. If there are cracks, seal them and reroll into a smooth ball. Cover the balls with a damp kitchen towel and set aside until ready to fry.

Heat the oil in a medium heavy skillet over medium-high heat until it reaches 350° to 375°F. Test the readiness of the oil by placing a small piece of dough into the hot oil. If it bubbles and slowly rises to the surface, it is ready. Drop four to five balls at a time into the hot oil. They will first sink to the bottom and then will rise to the surface slowly. Fry them gently, turning, until they are reddish-brown on all sides, 3 to 5 minutes. Do not cook the *gulaab jaamun* over high heat, or the outside will burn before the inside cooks.

Remove the fried balls from the pan with a slotted spoon and drain the excess oil. Gently submerge the balls in the warm syrup, and let them soak for at least 2 hours, until they are soft and spongy. Serve the *gulaab jaamun* warm or at room temperature. Store them (in the syrup) in the refrigerator for up to 1 week, but bring them back to room temperature or warm them before serving.

Makes 25 balls.

Jilphi
SYRUP-FILLED LOOPS

Jilphi, *also known as* jalebi *or* jeri, *are one of the most common sweets in Nepal. They are deep-fried, pretzel-shaped yellow-orange loops dipped in saffron syrup. Jilphi taste best when freshly made as they are crisp and the filling is succulent and aromatic. When they cool, they lose their crispiness, and the filling crystallizes, but they are still delicious. Traditionally,* jilphi *are paired with a soft Nepali bread called* Swaari *(page 105). Jilphi are very rich, so I usually serve them with fruit, yogurt, or pressed rice flakes* (cheura), *to tone down their sweetness.*

2¾ cups all-purpose flour	4 cups sugar
3½ tablespoons rice flour	6 to 8 green cardamom pods,
2 tablespoons plain yogurt	crushed
⅛ teaspoon saffron threads	2 to 3 cups vegetable oil

In a large bowl, combine both flours. In a separate bowl, mix together the yogurt and 2 cups of water. Gradually add the yogurt mixture to the flour and mix until the batter has a creamy consistency without lumps.

Cover the bowl and let it stand in a warm place, such as pantry or an oven with a pilot light, to ferment for 12 to 16 hours. Once fermented, the mixture will double in volume and bubbles will form on the surface. The batter should have a pleasant faintly sour aroma. With a whisk or fork, mix the batter again for 2 minutes. If necessary, add 1 to 2 tablespoons of water to make a smooth, pourable batter.

Gently crush the saffron with a mortar and pestle. Dissolve it in 2 tablespoons water and set aside.

In a wide saucepan, combine the sugar, 3 cups of water, and the cardamom pods and mix well. Bring the mixture to a boil over medium-high heat, stirring constantly, until the sugar has dissolved, about 2 minutes. Reduce the heat to medium-low and simmer until slightly thickened about 5 minutes. Remove the pan from the heat, stir in the saffron-infused water, and set it aside, covered.

Heat the oil in a heavy wide skillet over medium-high heat until it reaches 350° to 375°F. Test the readiness of the oil by placing a little batter into the hot oil. If it bubbles and rises to the surface immediately, it is ready. Place the batter in a pastry bag or a heavy plastic bag with one corner snipped off. Do not overfill the bag. There should be enough space to twist the top of the bag. Squeeze the batter directly into the hot oil in a circular motion to make a spiral loop about 4 inches in diameter that somewhat resembles a pretzel. Fry four to five *jilphi* at a time, turning them a few times, until crisp and golden brown on both sides.

With a slotted spoon, remove the *jilphi*, draining as much oil as possible, and immediately submerge in the warm syrup until it has filled the coils. With a slotted spoon, immediately remove the *jilphi*, draining the excess syrup, and transfer it to a platter. Repeat the procedure for the remaining batter. If the syrup has thickened, add 1 tablespoon of water and reheat it slowly. Serve the *jilphi* at room temperature.

Makes 20 to 22 pieces.

Doodh ko Rabadi
MILK DESSERT

Rabadi *is a delicate sweet dish that is prepared by slowly boiling milk until it has reduced to a cream-like consistency. You can serve* rabadi *plain or with chopped fruits and nuts. This recipe is time-consuming, but is well worth the effort for its cool, creamy, and delectable taste.*

1 gallon whole milk	⅓ cup sugar
2 green cardamom pods, crushed	2 tablespoons coarsely chopped
Seeds of 4 green cardamom	raw pistachios
pods, finely ground with a	6 to 8 saffron threads, crushed
mortar and pestle	

Bring the milk and 2 crushed cardamom pods to a rolling boil in a heavy saucepan over medium-high heat, stirring constantly. Reduce the heat to medium-low and simmer, stirring from time to time, until the milk has thickened and reduced to half its original volume. As the milk thickens, stir it often to prevent scorching. This process may take 45 minutes to 1 hour.

Remove the pan from the heat, add the sugar, and mix well. Discard the cardamom pods. Transfer the mixture to a serving dish and sprinkle it with the pistachios, ground cardamom seeds, and crushed saffron. Cover and refrigerate the *rabadi* for several hours before serving.

Makes 6 to 8 servings.

Doodh ko Khuwaa
MILK KHUWAA

Khuwaa is milk cooked down to the consistency of soft cream cheese. It is the basis of many Nepali sweets. In areas where there is no access to refrigeration, khuwaa is one of the best ways to preserve milk. In Nepal, a well-trained sweet maker (haluwai) spends hours boiling the milk, stirring constantly to prevent scorching, until the milk solidifies. Because this process is very time-consuming, khuwaa is usually purchased rather than made at home. Farmers make khuwaa over a wood fire, and then bring it to Kathmandu markets to sell.

I gallon whole milk

In a heavy-bottomed saucepan, bring the milk to a rolling boil over medium-high heat. Reduce the heat to medium-low and simmer, stirring from time to time, until the milk thickens and reduces to a semi-solid consistency. This process may take 1½ hours or more. As the milk thickens, stir more often to prevent scorching. Remove it from the heat and let it rest at room temperature until it thickens to the consistency of cream cheese, 10 to 15 minutes. Store in the refrigerater in a sealed container for up to 2 months.

Makes 4 to 5 cups.

Bhuteko Khuwaa
GOLDEN FRIED KHUWAA

My husband associates this dish with his childhood in Nepal. His great-grandmother would sauté the khuwaa, *flavored with cardamom and cashews, and serve it for a delicious snack.*

1 tablespoon clarified butter (*gheu*)	Seeds of 4 green cardamom pods, finely ground with a mortar and pestle
1 recipe Milk Khuwaa (page 351)	
3 tablespoons sugar	
2 tablespoons chopped raw cashew nuts	

Heat the butter in a medium skillet over medium-low heat. Add the *khuwaa*, a little at a time, mixing well after each addition. Sauté it, stirring constantly, until it is golden brown, 5 to 7 minutes. Add the sugar, cashews, and cardamom seeds and continue sautéing until the butter starts to come away from the sides of the pan, about 2 minutes. Transfer the fried *khuwaa* to a serving dish and serve it at room temperature.

Makes 4 to 6 servings.

Kesari Peda
SAFFRON PEDA

Peda, *small, flat, round patties prepared from thickened milk, are another popular Nepali sweet. Traditionally, they are made from* khuwaa *(page 351), but this simplified version uses paneer.*

I gallon whole milk	I ½ cups powdered dry milk
½ cup fresh lemon or lime juice	I ½ cups sugar
¼ cup clarified butter (*gheu*) or unsalted butter	2 tablespoons chopped raw pistachios
I cup heavy cream	6 to 8 saffron threads, lightly crushed
Seeds of 4 green cardamom pods, half finely ground with a mortar and pestle	
	Cheesecloth

Place the milk in a heavy saucepan over medium-high heat and bring it to a rolling boil. When the milk begins to foam and threatens to boil over, quickly pour in the lemon juice and mix well. The milk will immediately curdle. Remove it from the heat. Line a strainer or colander with 3 layers of cheesecloth. Place the colander in the sink and pour the curdled milk into the colander. Squeeze out any excess liquid with your hands, removing as much moisture as possible. Wrap the curds in paper towels, and press to absorb any remaining moisture. Unwrap and knead the cheese on a flat work surface until it has a smooth dough-like consistency.

Heat the butter in a wide skillet over medium-low heat. Add the curds and fry gently, stirring constantly, until all the moisture has evaporated. Stir in the cream and ground cardamom seeds. Then add the powdered milk and sugar and cook, stirring until the mixture thickens and pulls away from the sides of the pan, 10 to 15 minutes. Transfer the mixture to a bowl and cool.

Scoop out I ½ tablespoons of the mixture and form it into a smooth ball. Holding the ball in your palm, flatten it slightly. With your opposite hand, gently push your thumb into the center to create a small well, and then press a pinch of chopped pistachios, cardamom seeds, and saffron into the well. Place the peda on a tray. Repeat the process with the remaining "dough." *Peda* keeps refrigerated in an airtight container for 2 weeks. Bring them back to room temperature before serving.

Makes 35 to 40 pieces.

Rasbari
CHHANA CHEESE BALLS IN CARDAMOM SYRUP

Rasbari *is a popular sweet dish made for special occasions. In Nepali,* ras *is "juice" and* bari *is "balls," so* rasbari *translates to "savory balls in juice." To make* rasbari, *the fresh cheese is shaped into small balls and then simmered in a delicately flavored syrup until they double in size and become light and spongy, with a delicious dairy-rich taste.* Rasbari *are best served at room temperature, right after they are made. Once they have been refrigerated, their texture and flavor begin to change, and they lose their spongy texture.*

I recipe freshly made Homemade Chhana (Paneer) Cheese (page 396)	4 to 5 green cardamom pods, crushed
5 cups sugar	½ teaspoon rose essence (optional)

Place the cheese on a work surface and knead it with the heel of your hand until it becomes a soft and pliable dough, 3 to 5 minutes. Scoop up about 2 tablespoons of the cheese dough and roll it into a smooth ball. Repeat the process with the remaining cheese. Set the balls aside and cover them with a damp kitchen towel.

In a large wide saucepan, combine the sugar, cardamom pods, and 8 cups of water. Bring the mixture to a boil over medium-high heat, stirring from time to time, for 5 minutes. Gently add the cheese balls, one at a time, adding as many as the pan can hold in a single layer. Do not crowd the pan, there needs to be enough room between the balls to allow for swelling. Reduce the heat to medium, cover the pan, and continue cooking until the balls double in size, about 20 minutes. With a slotted spoon, remove the cheese balls and place them in a bowl with ½ cup of syrup and set aside while you make the second batch. If the syrup has thickened, add ¼ cup of water. Repeat the process with the remaining cheese balls.

Transfer all the *rasbari* to a large bowl with the remaining syrup. Add the rose essence, cover, and set aside for at least 2 hours at room temperature. Once the *rasbari* have cooled, they will shrink and firm up slightly. Serve at room temperature or refrigerate them for up to a week in an airtight container.

Makes 20 to 25 balls.

Sikarni

SAFFRON-PISTACHIO SIKARNI

This classic recipe was passed down by my mother years ago, and I have been making it for festive occasions and family get-togethers ever since. Sikarni *is a versatile dish that takes on the flavor of whatever it is mixed with, such as ground almonds, chopped mango, or sliced strawberries. Adjust its sweetness to suit your taste.*

1 recipe Homemade Yogurt (page 394)
⅛ teaspoon saffron threads plus 8 to 10 saffron threads for garnish
2 tablespoons milk
1½ cups sugar

Seeds of 8 to 10 green cardamom pods, finely ground with a mortar and pestle
½ cup raw pistachios, coarsely chopped

Cheesecloth

Line a large colander with 3 layers of cheesecloth. Place the yogurt in the colander, and bring in the corners and tie together to form a bag. Set the colander with the yogurt over a large bowl, and drain the whey. Make sure the bottom of the colander is high enough, so the yogurt does not touch the drained whey. Place the colander and bowl in the refrigerator and check in a few hours to make sure the whey has not reached the colander. You may need to remove the whey once or twice as the yogurt continues to drain. To facilitate the draining, adjust the bag, shifting it about and turning it upside-down in the colander from time to time. Drain until the yogurt reduces to about half its original volume, or until it resembles soft cream cheese. This will take 12 to 16 hours.

Gently crush ⅛ teaspoon of the saffron with a mortar and pestle. Dissolve in the milk and set aside.

Remove the yogurt from the cheesecloth and transfer to a bowl. Add the saffron-infused milk, sugar, and cardamom seeds and beat until it is light and creamy. Stir in ¼ cup of the chopped pistachios. Transfer the mixture to a decorative platter, sprinkle with the remaining chopped pistachios and saffron threads. Serve it immediately or cover and refrigerate until you are ready to serve. *Sikarni* keeps covered in the refrigerator for up to 4 days. If any whey rises to the surface, stir to incorporate it into the yogurt mixture.

Makes 6 to 8 servings.

Doodh-Bari
MILK PATTIES IN PISTACHIO CREAM

Doodh-bari *is an exceptionally flavorful, dairy-rich dessert of cheese pat-ties soaked in thickened milk, delicately flavored with cardamom and saffron and garnished with pistachios. Serve* doodh-bari *plain or with fresh fruits.*

PISTACHIO CREAM
⅛ teaspoon saffron threads, lightly crushed with a mortar and pestle
8 cups plus 2 tablespoons whole milk
¼ cup sugar
¼ cup shelled pistachios, coarsely ground with a mortar and pestle (reserve 1 tablespoon for garnish)
Seeds of 4 green cardamom pods, finely ground with a mortar and pestle

CHEESE PATTIES
½ gallon whole milk
4 cups cultured buttermilk

SYRUP
2 cups sugar

Cheesecloth

To make the pistachio cream, gently crush the saffron with a mortar and pes-tle. Dissolve it in 2 tablespoons of the milk and set aside. Bring the remaining 8 cups of milk to a rolling boil in a heavy saucepan over medium-high heat, stirring constantly. Reduce the heat to medium low and simmer, stirring occa-sionally, until the milk has thickened to a creamy consistency and reduced by half, about 25 minutes. Stir in the saffron-infused milk, sugar, pistachios, and cardamom seeds. Remove the pan from the heat and set aside.

To make the cheese patties, bring the milk to a rolling boil in a large heavy saucepan over high heat, stirring constantly, to prevent a skin from forming on the surface. Be careful not to let the milk burn or stick to the bottom of the pan (for there is nothing more unpleasant than burned milk!). When the milk threatens to bubble over, stir in the buttermilk. The milk will immediately start to separate into soft curds and whey. Stir gently. Remove the pan from the heat and allow the curdled milk to sit undisturbed for 2 minutes.

Line a strainer or colander with 3 layers of cheesecloth or a clean sheer white fabric. Place the colander over a large bowl. Pour the curdled milk into the colander and let the whey drain into the bowl while the fresh cheese remains in the cheesecloth. Pull together the 4 corners of the cheesecloth and tie them to make a bundle. Twist the bundle and squeeze out as much liquid as possible.

Hang the cheesecloth bundle on the kitchen faucet for 45 minutes to 1 hour to allow the whey to drain further. When the whey has stopped dripping, remove the bundle and wrap it with several layers of paper towels or a clean dry kitchen towel. Place the bundle on a flat surface and squeeze and roll it to extract additional moisture. Unwrap, remove the cheese, place it in a bowl, and knead until it is smooth, 2 to 3 minutes. Divide the cheese into twenty-five equal pieces and shape them into 1-inch patties. Set aside.

To make the syrup, in a large saucepan, combine the sugar and 5 cups of water and bring to a boil over medium-high heat. Boil for 5 minutes and then gently add the cheese patties. Reduce the heat to medium, cover, and cook until the patties expand, about 20 minutes. With a slotted spoon, transfer them to a bowl, and set aside. When they are cool enough to handle, gently squeeze each patty to remove excess syrup.

Arrange the patties in single layer on a platter. Pour the cream sauce over the patties, cover, and soak for at least 2 hours at room temperature. Garnish with the reserved pistachios just before serving. Serve them chilled or at room temperature. Refrigerate any leftover patties for up to 1 week in an airtight container.

Makes 25 milk patties.

Juju Dhau
SWEETENED YOGURT

Juju dhau *is a sweetened, custard-like yogurt that comes from Bhaktapur, Nepal, and is an important component of all feasts and celebrations. Although cow's milk is used to make regular yogurt, buffalo milk (*bhaisi*) is traditionally used for this dessert, resulting in a richer taste and texture. To make* juju dhau, *the milk is boiled, sweetened, mixed with culture, and poured into a decorative, red clay pot called* kataaro. *It is then placed in a warm place, on a bed of paddy husks (the papery covering of rice grains), and wrapped in several thick blankets to maintain a warm temperature while the yogurt sets. Because the clay pots are porous, the excess liquid from the yogurt slowly evaporates, leaving a delicious, thick yogurt. It is served in the* kataaro. *This is my version of* juju dhau, *prepared with cow's milk. Serve it chilled with any meal, by itself, or for dessert.*

½ gallon whole milk
1 cup sugar
¼ cup powdered milk
Seeds of 6 green cardamom pods, finely ground with a mortar and pestle

¾ cup plain yogurt with active cultures
¼ cup raw pistachios, coarsely chopped
12 to 15 saffron threads, crushed in a mortar and pestle

Combine the milk, sugar, powdered milk, and cardamom seeds in a heavy saucepan over medium-high heat. Bring it to a rolling boil, stirring constantly to prevent sticking, and remove any skin that forms on the surface. Reduce the heat to medium-low and simmer, stirring from time to time, until the milk has thickened, about 15 minutes. Remove it from the heat and allow the milk to cool to lukewarm. You can speed up the cooling process by setting the pan in a bowl of ice and stirring it continuously until the milk has cooled.

In a small bowl, mix ½ cup of the lukewarm milk mixture with the yogurt. Add the mixture back to the warm milk. To mix thoroughly, pour the milk into another bowl, transfer it back to the pan, and repeat this two to three times. Transfer the mixture to a clay pot or other container, and cover.

Wrap the container with a thick kitchen towel. Place it in a warm spot, such as a pantry or on top of the refrigerator, to allow the culture to grow. It is important that the yogurt is kept warm and undisturbed until it sets, at least 6 hours. To test if the yogurt has set, slowly tilt the container. If it pulls away from the side of the container, it is ready.

Sprinkle the yogurt with the pistachios and saffron. Refrigerate it in the same container for at least 6 hours before using. It will thicken further as it chills. The finished dish should be thick and creamy.

Makes 8 cups.

Phalphul ko Mithai
FRUIT SALAD IN CARDAMOM SYRUP

This colorful fruit salad is made with the freshest seasonal fruits. The syrup helps to preserve the texture and shape of the fruits. It is best served the day it is made, but may be refrigerated for up to two days. Spoon the fruit salad into attractive bowls and serve by itself or with other Nepali sweets.

4 ripe mangoes, peeled and
cut into ½-inch pieces
(about 4 cups)
I apple, peeled, cored, and cut
into ½-inch pieces
(about I cup)
I pint strawberries, sliced
(about 2 cups)
½ pineapple, peeled, cored, and
chopped (about 2 cups)
I small papaya, peeled, seeded,
and cut into ½-inch pieces
(about 3 cups)

½ medium cantaloupe or
honeydew, peeled, seeded,
and chopped (about 2 cups)
¾ cup sugar
I tablespoon fresh lemon or
lime juice
Seeds of 8 green cardamom
pods, crushed with a mortar
and pestle

Combine all of the fruits in a bowl and set aside.

In a small saucepan, combine the sugar, lemon juice, cardamom seeds, and I cup of water and mix well. Bring to a boil over medium-low heat, stirring constantly, until slightly thickened, about 5 minutes. There should only be enough syrup to coat the fruit. Remove the pan from the heat and allow the syrup to cool to lukewarm. Pour the syrup over the mixed fruits. Cover and chill for at least 1 hour before serving.

Makes 4 to 6 servings.

Dahi Phalphul ko Salad
FRUIT SALAD WITH YOGURT

This light fruit salad is a refreshing way to end a spicy meal. This salad is simple to prepare, and you can use any combination of seasonal fruits.

10 cups whole milk yogurt
⅛ teaspoon saffron threads
2 tablespoons milk
6 cups chopped assorted fruits (mangoes, pineapple, seedless grapes, strawberries, pears, peaches, bananas)
1 cup sugar

Seeds of 4 to 6 green cardamom pods, finely ground with a mortar and pestle
¼ cup raw pistachios, coarsely ground

Cheesecloth

Line a colander with three layers of cheesecloth. Place the colander over a large bowl. Place the yogurt in the colander and let the whey drain for 2 hours.

Gently crush the saffron with a mortar and pestle. Dissolve in the milk and set aside.

Remove the yogurt and place it in a medium-size bowl. Stir in the fruit, sugar, ground cardamom seeds, and saffron-infused milk. Transfer the salad to a serving dish and garnish it with the pistachios. Chill for at least 1 hour and then serve.

Makes 4 to 6 servings.

Cheeso-Taato Peeune

BEVERAGES

If you have ever traveled to Nepal or are familiar with Nepali customs, you know that Nepali hospitality is expressed by offering all guests some kind of beverage, whether it is just a glass of water or one of many hot and cold drinks. Among the most beloved beverages is hot tea. Tea drinking is an important part of Nepali culture and it is served throughout the day, most commonly prepared with milk and sugar. Another popular beverage served during the warmer months is fruit *sharbat*. Made from fresh lemons, it is a cool, refreshing yogurt drink. Yogurt is one of the five divine liquids (*pancha-amrit*) offered to deities. The others are milk, clarified butter, sugarcane juice, and honey.

Lassi
YOGURT DRINK

Lassi, a delicious sweet beverage made with yogurt, is a refreshing drink served during hot summer days.

4 cups plain yogurt
½ cup sugar, or to taste
Seeds of 2 green cardamom
    pods, finely ground with a
    mortar and pestle

⅛ teaspoon saffron threads,
    lightly crushed with a
    mortar and pestle
1 cup ice cubes or crushed ice

Combine the yogurt, sugar, cardamom seeds, saffron, and 2 cups of cold water in a blender and process at high speed until well blended. With the blender running, add the ice cubes one at a time through the feeder hole. Continue to process until the ice is finely ground. Pour the *lassi* into tall glasses and serve chilled.

Fruit Lassi: To make mango lassis, omit the saffron and add 2 peeled and chopped ripe mangoes or 2 cups canned mango pulp and 1 teaspoon rosewater (optional) with the ice and process as directed above. Garnish each glass with a sprinkling of coarsely chopped raw pistachios. Other fruits, such as strawberries, bananas, peaches, pears, or grapes can be used as well, but reduce the water to ½ cup. You may also use honey or maple syrup instead of sugar.

Almond-Pistachio Lassi: Add ¼ cup blanched raw almonds, ¼ cup raw pistachios, and ½ cup honey diluted with 1 tablespoon warm water with the ice and process as directed above.

Makes 4 servings.

Aamp ra Doodh ko Sharbat
MANGO MILK SHAKE

Fresh mangoes are the principal ingredient in this beverage. Make this delicious, easy-to-make, refreshing drink on hot summer days, when mangoes are in season.

3 medium ripe mangoes, peeled
  and roughly chopped
3 cups whole milk
½ cup sugar, or to taste

Seeds of 2 green cardamom
  pods, finely ground with a
  mortar and pestle

Combine all the ingredients in a blender and process at high speed until well blended and smooth. Transfer the milkshake to a pitcher, and chill for at least 1 hour before serving.

Makes 4 servings.

Kaagati ko Sharbat
NEPALI LEMONADE

This refreshing lemonade is often served to welcome guests on hot days. Serve the lemonade chilled, garnished with lime slices.

1 cup fresh lemon or lime juice	6 to 8 fresh mint leaves, crushed
1 cup sugar, or to taste	Ice cubes or crushed ice
1 lemon or lime, sliced	

In a large pitcher, combine the lemon juice, sugar, and 6 cups of cold water and mix thoroughly to dissolve the sugar. Add the lemon slices and mint, and chill. When you are ready to serve, pour the lemonade into glasses of crushed ice.

Mint-Ginger Lemonade: In a saucepan, combine 1 (¼-inch) piece ginger, 1½ cups sugar, and 7 cups of water and bring them to a quick rolling boil over high heat. Reduce the heat to low, cover, and simmer gently for 10 minutes. Uncover and allow the mixture to cool to room temperature. Pour the entire contents into a pitcher with 1 cup fresh lemon juice. Gently bruise 6 to 8 mint leaves and add them to the pitcher. Garnish with additional mint leaves.

Makes 4 servings.

Bael ko Phal ko Sharbat
WOOD APPLE DRINK

Wood-apple (bael) is also known as elephant apple, monkey fruit, Indian quince, or holy fruit. It is a sweet, aromatic, hard-shelled fruit found throughout South Asia, and its yellow-orange pulp is used to prepare cooling drinks. This fruit is also known to have healing powers, and is used for digestive disorders. It makes a delicious sharbat. *Do try this recipe if you can get hold of wood-apples!*

I large ripe wood apple	Ice cubes or crushed ice
½ cup sugar, or to taste	
Seeds of 3 green cardamom pods, finely ground with a mortar and pestle	

Break open the shell of the wood-apple, remove its gummy pulp and seeds, discarding the shell and seeds. Combine the pulp, sugar, cardamom seeds, and I cup of cold water in a medium-size bowl. Whisk the mixture until smooth and pour into a pitcher. Chill and serve over crushed ice.

Makes 4 servings.

Mohi
BUTTERMILK DRINK

Mohi *is an old-fashioned drink, prepared from the liquid leftover after churning butter. I remember drinking it at my husband's maternal grandparents' home in Dhading, Nepal, where a meal without yogurt and* mohi *is unthinkable. A tall glass was always served to visitors as a gesture of hospitality. This is my version of* mohi *prepared from ready-made cultured buttermilk.*

¼ teaspoon cumin seeds
2 cups cultured buttermilk
½ cup crushed ice

Salt to taste (some buttermilk
   contains salt)

Heat a small skillet over medium heat and toast cumin seeds, stirring constantly, until they give off a pleasant aroma, about 1 minute. Transfer to mortar and pestle and grind coarsely.

Combine the cumin, buttermilk, ice, salt, and 1 cup of cold water in a blender and process at high speed until well blended. Pour the mixture into tall glasses and serve.

Makes 4 servings.

Badaam-Pista-Kesari Doodh
WARM MILK WITH
ALMONDS, PISTACHIOS, AND SAFFRON

A family favorite, this hot beverage is nourishing and filling. It is usually served hot but is equally good chilled.

4 to 6 saffron threads
6 cups plus 2 tablespoons whole
  or low-fat milk
¼ cup blanched raw almonds
2 tablespoons raw pistachios

2 tablespoons sugar, or to taste
Seeds of 2 green cardamom
  pods, finely ground with a
  mortar and pestle
A small pinch ground cinnamon

Gently crush the saffron with a mortar and pestle. Dissolve in 2 tablespoons of the milk and set aside.

Place the almonds, pistachios, and 2 tablespoons of milk in a blender and grind to a fine paste.

Bring the remaining milk to a rolling boil in a medium-size saucepan over medium-high heat, stirring constantly. Add the nut mixture, sugar, ground cardamom seeds, and saffron-infused milk. Lower the heat and simmer until all the ingredients are mixed well, about 5 minutes. Pour the milk into glasses and garnish each with a sprinkle of ground cinnamon. Cool the milk to a comfortable drinking temperature and serve.

Makes 4 servings.

Aduwa Haaleko Doodh
HOT GINGER MILK

In this recipe, fresh ginger is simmered with milk until it releases its flavor, for a delicious, aromatic and healthy drink. It is usually served hot after dinner or before bedtime.

1 (⅛-inch) piece fresh ginger
6 cups whole or low-fat milk

2 tablespoons sugar, or to taste

In a heavy-bottomed saucepan, bring the milk and ginger to a boil over medium-high heat, stirring constantly. Reduce the heat to medium-low and simmer for 5 minutes. Add sugar and mix well. Remove and discard the ginger and pour the milk into glasses. Cool the milk to a comfortable drinking temperature and serve.

Makes 4 servings.

Taato Kaagati ra Aduwa
HOT LEMON DRINK

This refreshing drink is served any time of the day throughout the year. It is prepared by boiling fresh ginger, lemon juice, and water.

¼ cup fresh lemon or lime juice
1 (½-inch) piece fresh ginger,
** peeled and halved**

2 tablespoons sugar, or to taste

In a saucepan, bring 6 cups of water to a rolling boil over high heat. Add the lemon juice, ginger, and sugar, and reduce the heat to low. Simmer until the ginger releases its flavor, about 5 minutes. Pour the entire contents into a teapot. There is no need to remove the ginger, as it will sink to the bottom and continue flavoring the beverage. Serve hot.

Makes 4 servings.

Doodh Haaleko Chiya
MILK TEA

Milk tea (chiya) is the most widely consumed hot beverage in Nepal, where it is enjoyed throughout the day, starting in the early morning. Many people drink several cups of milky tea instead of breakfast, followed by an early lunch. These days, tea bags have become more popular in Nepal, but loose black tea is still preferred for its richer flavor, color, and usually, lower price. Tea is grown mainly in the eastern parts of Nepal and Nepali tea is now export-ed all over the world. The chiya I grew up with was made with loose black tea leaves, boiled with water, milk, and sugar, sometimes flavored with spices (cardamom, cloves, cinnamon, and fresh ginger).

I tablespoon good quality loose black tea leaves	I cup whole milk Sugar to taste

In a medium-size saucepan, bring 6 cups of water to a rolling boil over medi-um-high heat. Add the tea leaves and continue boiling until the water has become dark reddish-brown, about I minute. Reduce the heat to medium-low. Add the milk and sugar, and simmer until the tea becomes light brown. Make sure the tea is not too watery, or mild. Strain into individual cups and serve immediately.

Cardamom Tea: Add 2 cracked green cardamom pods while boiling the water.

Fresh Ginger Tea: Add I teaspoon minced fresh ginger while boiling the water.

Spiced Tea: Decrease the water to 3 cups and bring it to a boil with I (I-inch) stick cinnamon, 2 (I-inch) slices fresh ginger, 3 crushed green cardamom pods, 3 to 4 whole cloves, and 5 black peppercorns, and increase the milk to 3 cups.

Helpful Suggestions:

As a rule, for each cup of tea, you will need I½ cups of water, because the water evaporates during the continued boiling and simmering.

Always boil the water vigorously before adding the tea leaves and spices. This helps bring out the color and aroma of the tea.

Too many loose tea leaves may make the tea bitter and too strong, so adjust the measurements to suit your taste.

Too much milk makes the tea flavorless.

As it sits around, tea loses its flavor so it should be served immediately after brewing.

Makes 4 servings.

Peeneko Masala ko Chiya
MASALA TEA

Masala tea is a strong, aromatic, refreshing tea prepared with milk, sugar, and a combination of freshly ground spices. Ready-made spice mixtures are easily available at Indian grocery stores, but I recommend making your own because it will be fresher and will taste better.

4 cups whole or low-fat milk	½ to 1 teaspoon Spice Mixture
1 tablespoon good quality loose	for Tea (page 400) or
black tea leaves	Fragrant Masala Tea
	(page 401)
	Sugar to taste

In a medium-size saucepan, combine the milk, tea leaves, spice mixture, and 2 cups of water and bring to a rapid boil over medium-high heat. Reduce the heat to medium-low and simmer, stirring continuously to prevent it from boiling over, until the tea becomes light brown. Add the sugar according to taste. Strain the tea directly into individual cups and serve immediately.

Makes 4 servings.

Pokhara Bazaar ko Chiya
POKHARA BAZAAR TEA

*In 1996, my daughter Rachana and I trekked the Pokhara-Jomsom-Muktinath trail in Nepal. Some of the more memorable events were the stops at roadside tea vendors or teahouses (*chiya pasal*), where a hot pot of steaming tea was always ready. Tea houses are where one meets friends and catches up on the local news, daily events, and gossip. The tea served was delicious, strong, and aromatic.*

Each morning, the tea vendor prepared a big pot of fresh tea and when the first batch was finished, another batch was made. During my trek, the tea vendor showed me how he prepared the delicious tea. He used loose, broken black tea leaves, and boiled them with water, milk, and sugar until it reached just the right color and flavor. He then strained it through a thin cloth and served it steaming hot.

3 cups whole or low-fat milk	1½ teaspoons minced fresh ginger
½ cup sugar or to taste	8 whole black peppercorns
3 tablespoon loose black tea (preferably strong, full-bodied, Nepali tea)	

In a medium-size saucepan, combine the milk, sugar, tea, ginger, peppercorns, and 6 cups of water and bring them to a boil over medium-high heat. Reduce the heat to medium-low, and continue to simmer until the tea becomes light brown. Strain the tea directly into individual cups and serve it immediately.

Makes 4 servings.

Nunelo Chiya
SHERPA TEA

For centuries, people of the high Himalayas have enjoyed tea made with yak butter, salt, and milk. This beverage is believed to restore strength, and provide energy and warmth necessary in the harsh climate and high altitude. The tea is served hot in individual wooden bowls and consumed throughout the day. As a token of hospitality, a cup of butter tea is always served to visitors.

3 tablespoons loose black tea
  leaves
I cup whole milk

½ cup butter
⅛ teaspoon salt

In a saucepan, bring 6 cups of water to a rapid boil over medium-high heat. Add the tea leaves and continue boiling until the water has become dark reddish-brown, about I minute. Strain the tea into a blender. Add the milk, butter, and salt and process until mixed well. Pour the tea into a teapot, and keep warm. When you are ready, pour it into individual cups and serve.

Makes 4 servings.

Sittal Chiya
NEPALI HERBAL TEA

This relaxing, easy-to-make herbal tea is prepared with several whole spices, dried gooseberry, and goddess basil leaves. I usually prepare a large pot of this tea, and drink it throughout the day. Most of the ingredients are readily available in Indian grocery stores.

3 tablespoons dried green
   gooseberries (*amala*)
I (I-inch) stick cinnamon
I (¼-inch) piece fresh ginger,
   peeled and halved
4 green cardamom pods, crushed
2 black cardamom pods, crushed

I teaspoon whole cloves
I teaspoon dried goddess basil
   leaves (*tulasi*)
2 bay leaves
¼ cup sugar, or to taste
2 tablespoons fresh lemon or
   lime juice

In a large saucepan, combine 8 cups of water, the gooseberries, cinnamon, ginger, green and black cardamom pods, cloves, basil, and bay leaves and bring them to a rapid boil over medium-high heat.

Reduce the heat to low and simmer until the flavors of the spices are released, about 25 minutes. If the tea becomes too strong, add some water to adjust the taste. Stir in the sugar and lemon juice. Strain and serve.

Makes 6 servings.

Tulasi ko Chiya
GODDESS BASIL TEA

This refreshing aromatic tea is believed to relieve stress. It may be prepared with either fresh or dried basil, but the best flavor comes from fresh leaves. Tulasi, known as goddess or holy basil, is one of the most important herbs in Nepal. It is believed to have medicinal value, and is used widely to cure many ailments. The plant is also considered sacred and worshiped.

10 to 15 fresh goddess basil leaves (*tulasi*), lightly crushed or 2 tablespoons dried basil

1 (¼-inch) piece fresh ginger, peeled and halved
Sweetener of your choice (sugar, honey)

In a saucepan, combine 4 cups of water, the *tulasi*, and ginger and bring them to a rapid boil over medium-high heat. Reduce the heat to low and simmer until the ginger and basil release their flavors, about 10 minutes. Add the sweetener according to taste. The resulting tea will be light green in color and have a wonderful fragrance. Pour into cups and serve immediately.

Makes 4 servings.

Baasna-Aune-Masala Haru

AFTER-MEAL REFRESHERS

Nepali meals are always finished off with a special selection of fragrant whole spices, dried fruits and nuts, sweet or salted fruit nuggets (*titaura*), betel nuts (*supaari*), and ready-made digestive powders. A mixture of whole cloves, green or black cardamom seeds, and cinnamon sticks, for example are often chewed and sucked to refresh the palate. Some people find betel nuts the most satisfying and they chew them by themselves or with cloves and cardamom throughout the day. A mixture made of fennel seeds, finely shredded betel nuts, and aromatic flavorings is also chewed to cleanse the mouth. Nepalese also enjoy a popular digestive chew prepared from green betel leaves, locally known as *paan*. The leaves are neatly rolled and folded into a triangular pouch that is filled with different combinations of ingredients, such as betel nuts, cardamom seeds, cloves, dried fruits, fennel seeds, and coconut chips, and chewed slowly to refresh the palate. When habitually chewed, betel leaves stain the teeth and turn the mouth a deep red color. Betel leaf chewing is an acquired taste and some people find it too strong.

Many Nepali households own a traditional container, called *paan batta*, an elaborate box with beautiful intricate carvings. The boxes are usually made of silver, but can also be made from anything, from wood to precious metals. The bigger boxes have compartments to hold different ingredients. It is customary at the end of the meal, for the host or the hostess to bring out the *paan batta* filled with fragrant whole spices, betel nuts, or dried fruits and offer it to the guests, whether it is a formal or informal occasion. There is a custom in Nepal of presenting a silver *paan batta* to the bride as a wedding present so that she may serve and impress her guests once she goes to her husband's house.

Baasna Aune Masala Haru
BASIC AFTER-MEAL REFRESHER

The following recipe uses the most common combination of refreshing ingredients, typically served in a Nepali paan batta.

I cup green cardamom pods	½ cup areca or betel nuts,
½ cup black cardamom pods	chopped
I cup whole cloves	½ cup churpi (*yak cheese chew*)
½ cup cinnamon sticks, broken	
into I-inch pieces	

Place each ingredient in a compartment of a *paan batta* or other divided container and serve.

Makes 4 cups.

Masala Haru
DRIED FRUIT AND NUT REFRESHER

A combination of different dried fruits and nuts, chopped into bite-size pieces, is another after-meal refresher in Nepal. Sugar or rock candy are available in Indian markets. This popular snack is a natural energy booster and a cure for sweet cravings.

I cup raw almonds	I cup shelled raw pistachios
I cup raw cashews	I cup dark or golden raisins
I cup walnuts	I cup puffed lotus seeds
I cup pitted dried dates	(*makhana*)
I cup chopped dried coconut	½ cup rock candy (*misri*)

Chop the almonds, cashews, walnuts, and dates into uniform-size pieces. Combine with the coconut, pistachios, raisins, lotus seeds, and sugar candy. Transfer the mixture to a decorative serving dish and serve.

Makes 8 cups.

Saunp, Misri, Naribal
FENNEL SEED REFRESHER

Fennel seeds are used extensively as an after-meal digestive or palate cleanser after a spicy Nepali meal. A small quantity is chewed slowly just like an after-dinner mint. They are served toasted by themselves or with a combination of shredded coconut, tiny candy balls, roasted melon seeds, and tiny pieces of rock candy. Sometimes the fennel seeds are coated with multi-colored candy coatings, which are available at Indian stores.

1½ cups fennel seeds	¼ cup old-fashioned rock candy
½ cup finely chopped dried coconut	(*misri*)

Heat a small cast-iron skillet over medium heat, and toast the fennel seeds, stirring constantly, until they give off a pleasant aroma, 2 to 3 minutes. Pour them into a dry bowl to halt the toasting.

In the same skillet, toast the coconut, stirring and shaking the skillet, until crispy and light brown, about 1 minute. Mix it with the fennel. Let the mixture cool completely, then stir in the rock candy. Store in an airtight container and serve as needed.

Makes 2¼ cups.

Baasna Aune Masala
FRAGRANT AND COLORFUL
MOUTH-FRESHENING BLEND

This refreshing combination of crunchy and colorful seeds, nuts, and spices is generally chewed after a meal. The fragrant and mildly sweet mixture helps with digestion and serves as a mouth freshener after a spicy meal. This recipe is versatile, and you alter the blend according to your personal preferences. All ingredients are available at Indian stores.

I cup fennel seeds
½ cup sesame seeds
½ cup melon seeds
½ cup candy-coated fennel seeds
¼ cup thinly shredded betel nuts

Seeds of 12 green cardamom pods
Seeds of 8 black cardamom pods
2 tablespoons sweetened dried shredded coconut

Heat a small cast-iron skillet over medium heat and toast the fennel seeds, stirring constantly until they give off a pleasant aroma, 2 to 3 minutes. Pour them into a dry bowl to halt the toasting.

In the same skillet, toast the sesame seeds, stirring constantly with a wooden spoon to prevent the seeds from flying all over, until they give off a pleasant aroma and darken, 2 to 3 minutes. Mix them with the fennel seeds. Toast the melon seeds in the same skillet for 1 minute. Add them to the fennel-sesame mixture.

Let the mixture cool completely, and then stir in the candy-coated fennel seeds, betel nuts, green and black cardamom seeds, and coconut. Transfer the mixture to an airtight container and serve as needed.

Makes 3 cups.

Kaagati ko Sankhatro
DRIED LEMON CHEWS

Popular sankhatro *chews are very refreshing, with a tart and fruity flavor. They are slowly chewed any time of the day or after meals. They are also used as a home remedy to aid digestion and to cure stomach disorders and nausea. Sankhatro are traditionally prepared from Nepali lemons* (nibuwa)*, large, oblong fruit with a thick yellow and rough skin. They are extremely sour and are used for making pickles and chutneys. The juice extracted from the* nibuwa *is made into a concentrated dark brown liquid* (chook amilo)*, which is used as a souring agent in many pickles. For this recipe, I use large, regular lemons, which are equally delicious.*

15 lemons	Cheesecloth
¼ cup salt	Kitchen twine

Wash the lemons thoroughly and wipe them with a clean cloth or paper towel. With a sharp knife, cut off a small piece from the top end of each lemon, then make two cuts, cutting halfway through as if you were making 4 wedges, making sure the bottom is still attached. Pick out any visible seeds and discard.

Rub the salt on lemons and into the cuts. Select a clean jar, big enough to fit all the lemons, and place them inside. Close the lid tightly and shake the jar vigorously. Place the jar outside in the direct sun (but bring it indoors in the evenings). If the sun is not present, place the jar in a warm area. Shake the jar once a day until the lemons soften, the skins become tender, and the color lightens. This process may take 3 to 4 weeks.

Remove the lemons from the jar and place them on a flat tray in a single layer. Cover with cheesecloth and secure with kitchen twine. Situate the tray in the full sun and let the lemons dry slowly. Always bring the tray indoors after the sun has set. Alternatively, use a food dehydrator, following the manufacturer's instructions. Dry the lemons until all the moisture evaporates and the pulp has a chewy texture. Cut the lemons into bite-size pieces. Store in airtight containers for up to a year at room temperature.

Makes 4 cups.

Amala ko Titaura
GREEN GOOSEBERRY NUGGETS

Amala *is the Nepali name for the Indian gooseberry, which is a small, round, light yellow colored fruit that has a sour taste. The fruit is one of the richest known natural sources of vitamin C. It is known as a medicinal fruit used for healing and rejuvenation in Ayurvedic medicine. Upon chewing, the fruit is initially quite sour, but when followed by water it produces a very sweet and refreshing aftertaste. In this recipe, the berries are boiled until the seeds separate from the pulp. The fruit is then lightly spiced, formed into nuggets, and dried. Chew these any time of the day or after meals.*

10 cups fresh green gooseberries, washed and stemmed	½ teaspoon ground cumin
	A small pinch ground asafetida
1 tablespoon minced fresh ginger	1 tablespoon vegetable oil
1 teaspoon salt	
1 teaspoon cayenne pepper	Cheesecloth
½ teaspoon ground turmeric	

Place the gooseberries and water to cover in a medium-size saucepan, and bring to a boil over medium-high heat. Reduce the heat to low, cover the pan, and cook until the fruit is tender and the seeds are easily removable, 25 to 30 minutes. Drain and when cool enough to handle, separate the seeds from the pulp, and discard the seeds.

Place the gooseberry pulp in a bowl and mash it well. Stir in the ginger, salt, cayenne pepper, turmeric, cumin, and asafetida. Before making the nuggets, grease one or two wicker trays (*naanglo*) with a little oil. Shape the gooseberry mixture into grape-size nuggets, and place them on the prepared tray close together, but not touching.

Place the tray outside in the full sun, cover with cheesecloth and let the nuggets dry slowly. Always bring the tray indoors after the sun has set. Once the nuggets are slightly firm on top, gently turn them over to allow the bottom sides to dry evenly. The nuggets should be dried in 2 to 3 days, depending upon the amount of sunlight. Alternatively, you can dry the nuggets in a food dehydrator according to the manufacturer's instructions. When the nuggets are fully dried, they will shrink and become light brown. The nuggets can be stored in an airtight container for up to 6 months.

Gooseberry Chips: Instead of mashing the boiled pulp, separate it into segments. Mix the segments with the spices and dry as directed above. You can also make gooseberry chips with raw berries. Thinly slice the berries and discard the seeds. Mix the slices with the spices and set them aside for 1 hour for the flavors to develop. Then dry as directed above. Cutting each berry by hand is a time-consuming process, but this method will give the chips a better color and flavor.

Makes 2½ cups.

Guleo Lapsi ko Titaura
SPICY LAPSI CHEWS

Lapsi ko titaura *is one of the most favorite and delicious fruit chews made from the Nepali native fruit,* lapsi *or* labsi *(Nepalese hog plums). The fruit is greenish-yellow when ripe, and has a large hard seed that is almost the size of the whole fruit itself. The plum-sized fruit has a pleasant flavor, but is extremely sour, even when completely ripe. The pulp is firmly attached to the seed and difficult to separate, so it must be boiled first. The pulp is mixed with sugar and spices, made into nuggets, and sun-dried. Lapsi are not available in the United States. If you get hold of this fruit though, this recipe is a must!*

75 to 80 medium lapsi fruits	A small pinch ground asafetida
2½ to 3 cups sugar, or to taste	1 tablespoon vegetable oil
1 tablespoon cayenne pepper	
2 teaspoons salt	Cheesecloth
Seeds of 10 to 12 green	Kitchen twine
cardamom pods, finely ground	
with a mortar and pestle	

Place the fruit and water to cover in a medium-size saucepan and bring to a boil over medium-high heat. Reduce the heat to medium-low, cover the pan, and cook until the *lapsi* are tender, the skins loosen, and the seeds easily separate from the pulp, 25 to 30 minutes. Drain, and when cool enough to handle, peel off the skins. Separate the pulp and discard the seeds and skins.

In a bowl, combine the pulp, sugar, cayenne pepper, salt, cardamom seeds, and asafetida. Knead the mixture vigorously by hand, making sure the spices are well incorporated. The pulp will be sticky and slippery. Before making the nuggets, grease one or two wicker trays (*nanglo*) with oil. Form grape-size nuggets and drop them onto the prepared tray, placing them close together, but not touching.

Cover the tray with cheesecloth and secure with kitchen twine. Place it in the full sun, but always bring the tray indoors after the sun has set. Once the nuggets are slightly firm on top, gently turn them over to allow the bottom sides to dry evenly. The nuggets should be completely dried in 4 to 5 days, depending upon the temperature, humidity, and amount of sunlight. Take care to completely dry them, or they may mold. Alternatively, you can use a food dehydrator, following the manufacturer's instructions The lapsi chews keep stored in an airtight container for up to 6 months.

Makes 60 to 65 small servings.

Lapsi Rolls Variation: Add the seeds of 3 black cardamom pods ground with a mortar and pestle, and ½ teaspoon ground cinnamon to the above mixture. Spread the mixture on the prepared tray about ½ inch thick. Leave 1 inch around the edges so that the leather can be removed easily. Dry as instructed above. Remove the leather and cut it into pieces and/or roll it in sugar to protect it from air and moisture.

Note: The boiled tough skin of the lapsi fruit can also be dried with or without seasonings. It becomes very brittle so it is not good for chewing, but is used as a souring agent for some pickles.

Saamaanaya Pakaaune Bidhi ra Masalaa ko Mishran

BASIC RECIPES AND SPICE BLENDS

Gheu
NEPALI CLARIFIED BUTTER

Clarified butter is simply butter that has been simmered until it separates. The clear golden liquid that remains is called gheu *in Nepal. It adds a unique flavor to the food that it is cooked with. It also has a higher smoking point than regular butter and therefore may even be used in deep-frying without burning.* Gheu *is used extensively in Nepali cuisine, and is considered the secret ingredient in sweets. It has a pure, clean flavor and keeps at room temperature. I usually make* gheu *at home. It is also available ready-made at Indian food stores or some well-stocked larger supermarkets, only here they call it* ghee.

2 pounds unsalted butter   **2 large bay leaves**

Cut the butter into small chunks and place it in a heavy saucepan with the bay leaves. Heat over low heat, stirring from time to time, until completely melted. Then, raise the temperature to medium and cook, stirring occasionally, until the butter crackles and bubbles, 4 to 5 minutes. Reduce the heat to medium-low and simmer until it separates into three layers—a top layer of white foam, clear liquid in the middle, and a bottom layer of golden brown milky solids—35 to 40 minutes. Do not stir, but check the butter frequently to make sure it is not burning. Carefully skim off any white foam without disturbing the bottom.

Remove the pan from the heat and set aside for 10 minutes to allow the milk solids to further settle to the bottom. When the liquid has slightly cooled and it is easy to handle, pour or spoon the clear golden liquid into a wide-mouth container, leaving as much of the sediment in the pan as you can. You may also strain the liquid through a cheesecloth-lined strainer or a paper towel. Discard the bay leaves and milky solids. Cover the *gheu* and store it either in the refrigerator or at room temperature. Once cooled, the *gheu* will have rich golden color, buttery aroma, and will solidify, but not harden.

Spiced Clarified Butter: Simmer cinnamon sticks, cardamom pods, or a combination of other whole spices and herbs to make spice-infused *gheu*, but remove them before pouring the *gheu* into a storage container.

Makes 2³⁄4 to 3 cups.

Dahi
HOMEMADE YOGURT

Yogurt (dahi) is considered one of the most important dairy products in Nepal. Making it at home is simple and most of the equipment needed is already in your kitchen. Yogurt also plays an important role in religious rituals and other traditions. For example, it is eaten to purify oneself on fasting days and consumed as a sacred food, before departing from home. Many Nepalese believe that yogurt brings good luck, so a fresh container of yogurt is placed in entryways. On auspicious occasions, yogurt is mixed with vermillion powder to prepare a red paste (achheta ko tika) applied to the forehead for family blessings. Yogurt is considered a healing food in Nepal and used to cure indigestion, and hangovers, and to counter the effects of spicy or rich foods.

I gallon whole milk	**I cup plain yogurt with active cultures**

Heat the milk in a heavy saucepan over medium-high heat. Stir constantly to prevent sticking and remove any skin that forms on the surface. Once it has boiled, remove the pan from the heat and let it cool. You can speed up the cooling process by setting the pan in a bowl of ice and stirring continuously until the milk has cooled to lukewarm.

In a small bowl, mix ½ cup of the lukewarm milk with the yogurt. Return the mixture back to the warm milk. To mix thoroughly, pour the milk into another bowl, transfer it back to the pan, and pour it back and forth two to three times. Transfer the mixture to a clean container and cover it with a lid.

Wrap the container in a kitchen towel. Place it in a warm spot, such as a pantry or on top of the refrigerator. Alternatively, preheat the oven to its lowest setting for 10 minutes. Turn it off and place the mixture in the oven. To maintain the temperature, turn the oven on again every few hours. If your oven has a pilot light, there is no need to turn it on as the yogurt will set from just the heat of the pilot light. It is important that the yogurt is kept warm and not disturbed until it is set, at least 6 hours. Do not shake or stir the milk during this process. To test if the yogurt has set, slowly tilt the container. If the yogurt pulls away from the side of the container, then it is ready. Once the yogurt has set, refrigerate it immediately. The longer it is left at room temperature, the more tart it becomes.

Makes 16 cups yogurt.

Helpful Hints: If you prefer to make a smaller quantity of yogurt, use I quart of milk and ¼ cup plain yogurt with active cultures.

You may also place the yogurt in a cardboard box lined with a clean kitchen towel, which will help keep it warm. You can also set the yogurt on a rack on top of a food warmer set to the lowest setting.

If there is a large amount of whey floating on top of the set yogurt, your incubation period might have been too long. If your yogurt is too watery, there may have been insufficient starter culture, the culture may not have been properly mixed with the milk, or the mixture may have been disturbed during the incubation period. If the temperature is too high or too low during incubation, the mixture will be liquidy.

If you use low-fat or skim milk, the yogurt will have a less creamy consistency. You can thicken it, by boiling it until reduced and thickened or add 2 to 3 tablespoons of dry milk powder before heating the mixture.

Chhana
HOMEMADE CHEESE (PANEER)

Homemade cheese, called chhana *in Nepali, is a versatile ingredient that absorbs the flavors of the food it is cooked with. It can be cubed and fried and added to almost any vegetable dish with a sauce, coated with chickpea flour and fried, or used in sweet dishes. If properly refrigerated,* chhana *keeps for four to five days, but it is best used within a day or two of making it.*

I gallon whole milk	**Cheesecloth**
I to I ¼ cups fresh lemon or lime juice, strained	

Pour the milk into a heavy saucepan and bring it to a rolling boil over high heat, stirring constantly. Be careful not to let it burn. When the milk threatens to boil over, quickly stir in the lemon juice. It will immediately separate into soft curds and whey. Stir gently. Remove the pan from the heat and allow the curdled milk to sit undisturbed for 2 minutes.

Line a strainer or colander with three layers of cheesecloth. Place the colander over a large bowl. Pour the curdled milk into the colander and let the whey drain. The whey can be used for the next batch of *chhana* or as a base for soup, vegetable dishes, or to cook rice.

Pull the corners of the cheesecloth together and tie them into a bundle. Twist the bundle and squeeze out as much liquid as possible. Hang the cheesecloth bundle on the kitchen faucet for at least 45 minutes to allow the whey to drain further. When it has stopped dripping, remove the bundle and wrap it in paper towels or a clean dry kitchen towel. Place the bundle on a flat surface and squeeze and roll it to extract any additional moisture. Unwrap it, remove the cheese, place it in a bowl, and knead it until smooth, 2 to 3 minutes. Use as directed in recipes or transfer the cheese to a baking sheet and spread 1 inch thick. Cut it into cubes or other shapes. If not using the *chhana* immediately, refrigerate it in an airtight container for 3 to 4 days.

Note: You can use any of the following ingredients in place of the lemon juice: 2 cups plain yogurt; ¾ cup white vinegar, diluted with a little water; 6 cups cultured buttermilk; or 3 cups *chhana* whey saved from a previous batch.

Makes 4 to 4½ cups.

Baasna Aaune Garam Masala
FRAGRANT GARAM MASALA

This spice blend is more aromatic and milder than basic Nepali Garam Masala (page 398), where cumin and coriander dominate. Just a pinch of this fragrant mixture lends a wonderful aroma to any dish. It is usually added towards the end of the cooking process or sprinkled over cooked dishes as a last-minute garnish.

Seeds of 20 to 22 green
cardamom pods (about 2½
tablespoons)
Seeds of 3 to 4 black cardamom
pods (about 2 teaspoons)
1 tablespoon whole cloves
1 (3-inch) stick cinnamon,
broken into several pieces

3 small bay leaves, crumbled
1 tablespoon whole black
peppercorns
½ whole nutmeg, broken into
several pieces
2 tablespoons coriander seeds
1 tablespoon cumin seeds

Heat a small cast-iron skillet over medium-low heat. When it is hot, add the spices and toast them, stirring constantly and swirling the pan, until they give off a pleasant aroma, 2 to 3 minutes. Pour them into a dry container to halt the toasting. Let them cool, transfer to a spice grinder or mortar and pestle and grind to a fine powder. Sieve, and regrind any bits of the mixture that do not pass through the sieve. Store the mixture in a container with a tight-fitting lid. It can be stored for up to several months without losing much of its flavor, but make sure to keep the container tightly closed after each use.

Makes ¾ cup.

Garam Masala
NEPALI GARAM MASALA

Garam masala is an aromatic combination of several toasted and ground spices. There are many variations of this spice blend and each family has their own version. The most common and basic components of the mixture are cumin, coriander, black pepper, nutmeg, green cardamom, cinnamon, and cloves. Premixed and ground garam masala or curry powders are also readily available at Indian markets and in the spice section of some supermarkets. They bear little resemblance in flavor and taste to freshly ground homemade blends. If not bought from reputable stores, the mixture may be stale and/or include cheap fillers. If you use a ready-made garam masala, use less than the amount mentioned in my recipes because they may overpower the dish.

Making your own garam masala is easy and assures a fresher and more intensely flavored spice mix. The trick to making successful spice blends is to purchase whole spices, gently toast them until they give off a pleasant aroma, cool them, and grind them to a powder. The ground spices should be stored in a cool, dry place in an airtight container. Whole spices have a longer shelf life than ground spices because they have seed coatings and bark to protect the flavors, which are released once they are crushed. Therefore, it is always best to make spice blends in small quantities. Nepali garam masala can also be used as a marinade or a dry rub, and a small amount of garam masala sprinkled on prepared food also gives the dish more flavor.

½ cup cumin seeds
½ cup coriander seeds
1 tablespoon whole black
  peppercorns
3 to 4 small bay leaves
3 (1-inch) sticks cinnamon,
  broken into several pieces

8 green cardamom pods, crushed
2 black cardamom pods, crushed
1 tablespoon whole cloves
1 small whole nutmeg, broken
  into several pieces

Heat a cast-iron skillet over medium-low heat. When it is hot, add all of the spices and toast them, stirring constantly and swirling the pan, until they give off a pleasant aroma and darken, 3 to 4 minutes. The heat will draw out the natural oils of the spices and mellow the flavors. Pour the spices into a dry container to halt the toasting. Let them cool, remove the seeds from the green and black cardamom pods. Discard the pods and return the seeds to the spice mixture. Working in small batches, grind to a fine powder in a spice grinder, blender, or mortar and pestle. Sieve, and regrind any bits of the mixture that do not pass through the sieve. Store the garam masala in a sealed container with a tight-fitting lid. It can be stored for up to several months without losing much of its flavor, but make sure to keep the container tightly closed after each use.

Note: To make a larger batch, you can double the amount of spices and toast the spices in batches, if necessary. The toasting process only takes a few minutes and the spices burn very quickly and become bitter if not watched carefully. Traditionally the whole spices are sun-dried for a few days before grinding. If you like, you can put the spices on a large tray and place them in the full sun for 3 to 4 days. Stir the mixture two to three times each day and always bring the tray indoors after the sun has set.

Makes 1¼ cups.

Chiya ko Masala
SPICE MIXTURE FOR TEA

This combination of spices is used to make a delicious masala tea (see facing page). The secret to making masala tea is to slowly and carefully toast the whole spices over gentle heat. Traditionally, the spices are sun-dried until the subtle flavors are captured, then they are pounded in a mortar and pestle. It is believed that sun-drying brings out a deeper flavor than pan-toasting. Once the whole spices are ground, they start to lose their flavor, so be sure to store them in an airtight container. Make this in small quantities to ensure freshness. You can experiment to find your favorite combination by adjusting the spices to your liking.

4 tablespoons green cardamom
   seeds
Seeds of 5 black cardamom
   pods, (about 2¼ teaspoons)
1 tablespoon whole cloves
1 (2-inch) stick cinnamon,
   broken into several pieces

1 teaspoon fennel seeds
⅛ teaspoon whole black
   peppercorns
¾ teaspoon ground ginger

Heat a small cast-iron skillet over medium-high heat. When it is hot, add the green and black cardamom seeds, cloves, cinnamon, fennel seeds, and peppercorns and toast them, stirring constantly, until they give off a pleasant aroma, about 2 minutes. Pour into a dry container to halt the toasting. Once they are cooled, grind them in a spice grinder or mortar and pestle until finely ground. Add the ginger and mix well. Transfer to an airtight glass jar. To make tea, use ⅛ to ¼ teaspoon per cup of boiling water, or according to personal preference.

Makes ¾ cup.

Chiya ko Baasna Aaune Masala
FRAGRANT MASALA TEA

This masala tea blend gives a simple twist to any tea preparation, and there is no need to toast the spices. Add the spice blend while boiling the water.

Seeds of 1 cup green cardamom
    Pods
1 teaspoon whole cloves

1 (2-inch) stick cinnamon,
    broken into several pieces

Mix all the spices together. Working in small batches, grind the spice mixture to a fine powder in a spice grinder, blender, or mortar and pestle. Sieve, and regrind any bits of the mixture that do not pass through the sieve. Store in a container with a tight-fitting lid. The mixture can be stored up to 1 year without losing much of its flavor, but make sure to keep the container tightly closed after each use. Use ⅛ to ¼ teaspoon per cup of boiling water, or a little more for a pot of tea.

Makes ¼ cup.

Khaana ko Tayaari

PLANNING AND SERVING NEPALI MEALS

A typical Nepali meal consists of a generous serving of boiled rice, accompanied by a choice of several sautéed or curried vegetables, lentils and beans, occasionally a small serving of meat, pickles, and perhaps some cooling yogurt. A single plate of rice is rarely enough to satisfy most Nepalese, so it is almost always followed by a second, and in many cases, a third helping. Most of the recipes in this book yield four to six servings, but they are easily doubled. Consider increasing the amount of rice when you are cooking for Nepalese gatherings. For meals that are more elaborate, you may want to serve appetizers, beverages, and breads, along with a fancy rice dish, and increase the variety of side dishes. To conclude the meal, serve your favorite desserts and after-meal refreshers.

In many of my recipes, whole spices, such as bay leaves, cinnamon sticks, green and black cardamom pods, cloves, and dried red chilies or fresh green chilies are left in the dish before serving. They continue to release their fragrance and flavor, and add visual appeal to the dish. Remind your guests to be careful about these whole spices and push them to the side of the plate to avoid burning their mouths. You may remove them before serving, but Nepalese usually chew on whole spices, except for bay leaves.

Many of the dishes can be made ahead of time and reheated before serving. The following are a variety of menu suggestions for different occasions. If Nepalese cooking is new to you, start with the simple everyday basic menu.

I. SIMPLE EVERYDAY MENUS

MENU 1: (VEGETARIAN)
Plain Steamed Rice (*Bhaat-Bhuja*)
Black Urad Daal (*Jhaaneko Kaalo Maas ko Daal*)
Hot and Fiery Tomato Chutney (*Piro Golbheda ko Chutney*)
Cucumber and Yogurt Salad (*Kaankro ra Dahi ko Salad*)
Cauliflower with Potato and Peas (*Phool-Govi, Alu, Kerau Tarkaari*)
Spinach with Garden Cress (*Chamsoor-Palungo Tarkaari*)

MENU 2: (VEGETARIAN)
Basmati Rice with Butter (*Gheu Haaleko Bhuja*)
Split Pigeon Pea Daal (*Rahar ko Daal*)
Whole Wheat Flatbread (*Phulka-Roti*)
Julienne Radish Achaar (*Koreko Seto Mula Achaar*)
Mixed Vegetable Curry (*Mismaas Jogi Tarkaari*)
Mustard Greens (*Sit le khaeko Rayo ko Saag*)
Spiced Yogurt (*Homemade Dahi*)

MENU 3: (NON-VEGETARIAN)
Plain Steamed Rice (*Bhaat-Bhuja*)
Yellow Mung Beans (*Pahelo Moong ko Daal*)
Cucumber Achaar (*Koreko Kaankro ko Achaar*)
Cucumber, Onion, and Tomato Salad (*Tarkaari ko Mismaas Salad*)
Spicy Sautéed Potatoes (*Taareko Alu*)
Spicy Zucchini with Mustard Seeds (*Hariyo Pharsi ko Tarkaari*)
Goat Curry (*Khasi-Boka ko Maasu*)

MENU 4: (NON-VEGETARIAN)
Plain Steamed Rice (*Bhaat-Bhuja*)
Maharani Daal (*Maharani Daal*)
Flaky Roti Bread (*Patre-roti*)
Dried Fish-Tomato Chutney (*Golbheda ra Sidra Maacha*)
Chicken Curry with Onions (*Pyaj Haaleko Kukhura ko Maasu*)
Green Beans and Potatoes (*Simi ra Alu ko Tarkaari*)
Spinach with Garlic Butter (*Nauni Paalungo Tarkaari*)

MENU 5: (NON-VEGETARIAN)
Basmati Rice with Butter (*Gheu Haaleko Bhuja*)
Kwanti Soup (*Kwanti ko Ras*)
Tomato Chutney with Asparagus (*Kurelo Haaleko Golbheda ko Achaar*)
Deep-Fried Spiced Fish (*Taareko Maacha*)
Spicy Potato Achaar with Sesame Seeds (*Alu ko Achaar*)
Sautéed Okra (*Taareko Ram Toriya*)
Sweetened Yogurt (*Juju Dhau*)

II. MENUS FOR ENTERTAINING

MENU 1:
Sautéed Chicken Gizzards (*Bhutura Chara ko Bhitri*)
Assorted Spiced Nuts (*Taareko Piro Kaaju-Badaam*)
Basmati Rice with Butter (*Gheu Haaleko Bhuja*)
Poori Bread (*Poori*)
Black Urad Daal (*Jhaaneko Kaalo Maas ko Daal*)
Bamboo Shoots, Potatoes and Black-Eyed Beans (*Taama-Alu-Bodi ko Tarkaari*)
Asparagus Salad (*Saandheko Kurelo*)
Spicy Potato Achaar with Sesame Seeds (*Alu ko Achaar*)
Mushroom Curry (*Chyau ko Tarkaari*)
Goat Curry (*Khasi-Boka ko Maasu*)
Fish in Yogurt Sauce (*Dahi-Maacha*)
Saffron-Pistachio Sikarni (*Sikarni*)
Sweet Chickpea Balls (*Besan ko Laddu*)

MENU 2:
Spiced Peanuts, Soybeans, and Shredded Chicken (*Saandheko Bhatmaas-Badaam-Kukhura*)
Dried Meat Marinated with Spices (*Sukuti Saandheko*)
Soybean Salad (*Hariyo Bhatmaas Saandheko*)
Phulauna Croquettes (*Maas ko Phulauna*)
Cilantro-Mint Chutney (*Dhania Baabari ko Chutney*)
Saffron Rice (*Kesari Bhuja*)
Buttered Daal (*Daal Makhani*)
Potato-Stuffed Bread (*Alu-Roti*)
Dried Fish-Tomato Chutney (*Golbheda ra Sidra Maacha*)

Pan-Fried Asparagus (*Kurelo ra Alu Taareko*)
Taro Leaves with Ginger and Garlic (*Karkalo ko Tarkaari*)
Roasted Eggplant with Sesame Seeds (*Bhanta Saandheko*)
Chicken with Aromatic Sauce (*Masaledar Kukhura*)
Lamb Meatballs (*Maasu ko Bari*)
Nepali Rice Pudding (*Kheer*)

MENU 3:
Spicy Stuffed Eggs (*Saandheko Phool*)
Fish Sticks (*Maacha ko Chop*)
No-Cook Tomato Chutney (*Na Pakaayeko Golbheda ko Chutney*)
Savory Snack Mix (*Furindaana*)
Mixed Vegetable Pulau (*Tarkaari ko Pulau*)
Maharani Daal (*Maharani Daal*)
Spinach Poori Bread (*Poori*)
Cucumber Achaar (*Koreko Kaankro ko Achaar*)
Okra-Tomato-Onion Medley (*Raam Toriya ko Ras Tarkaari*)
Spiced Chayote Squash (*Iskush ko Tarkaari*)
Spicy Sautéed Potatoes (*Taareko Alu*)
Stewed Cornish Hen with Ginger-Garlic (*Sano Chara ko Maasu*)
Lamb with Cashew, Almond, and Yogurt Sauce (*Badaami Maasu*)
Roasted Sesame Seed Pickle (*Til Ko Chhope*)
Almond Fudge (*Badaam ko Barfi*)
Dumplings in Saffron-Cardamom Syrup (*Gulaab Jaamun*)
Fruit Salad with Yogurt (*Dahi Phalphul ko Salad*)

III. AFTERNOON SNACKS, LIGHT LUNCHES, AND OFFERINGS FOR UNEXPECTED GUESTS

MENU I:
Create a menu by choosing one of the following:

Pressed Rice Flakes (*Cheura*)
Cauliflower with Potato and Peas (*Phool-Govi, Alu, Kerau Tarkaari*)
Mixed Vegetable Curry (*Mismaas Jogi Tarkaari*)
Spicy Sautéed Potato (*Taareko Alu*)

Curried Dried Peas (*Thulo Kerau ko Tarkaari*)
Brown Chickpeas with Onions (*Kaalo Chana ko Tarkaari*)
Stir-Fried Mixed Sprouted Beans (*Taareko Kwanti*)
Egg Roti (*Phool ko Roti*)
Cauliflower Chicken (*Kauli-Kukhura*)
Fish Curry (*Maacha ko Tarkaari*)

MENU 2:
Pressed Rice Flakes with Green Peas (*Matar-Cheura*)
Any chutney of your choice
Fruit Salad with Yogurt (*Dahi Phalphul ko Salad*)
Syrup-Filled Loops (*Jilphi*)

MENU 3:
Poori Bread (*Poori*)
Potato-Onion-Tomato Medley (*Alu-Pyaj-Golbheda Tarkaari*)
Easy Chickpea Curry (*Chana ko Tarkaari*)
Hot and Fiery Tomato Chutney (*Piro Golbheda Ko Chutney*)
Dumplings in Saffron-Cardamom Syrup (*Gulaab Jaamun*)

MENU 4:
Mung Roti (*Moong ko Roti*), Buckwheat Bread (*Phaapar Ko Roti*), or
    Chataamari Bread (*Chataamari*)
Any vegetable of your choice
Fruit Salad with Yogurt (*Dahi Phalphul ko Salad*)

MENU 5:
Any dumpling (*Momo*)
No-Cook Tomato Chutney (*Na Pakaayeko Golbheda ko Chutney*) or
    Fresh Cilantro Mint Chutney (*Dhania Baabari ko Chutney*)
Sweetened Yogurt (*Juju Dhau*)

MENU 6:

Create a menu by choosing any of the following snacks served with any chutney, pickles, and sweets:

Savory Snack Mix (*Furindaana*)
Snack Crackers (*Nimki*)
Vegetable Stuffed Samosas (*Tarkaari ko Samosa*)
Mixed Vegetable Patties (*Tarkaari ko Chop*)
Potato Chops with Ground Meat (*Maasu Bhareko Alu ko chop*)
Batter-Fried Vegetables (*Pakauda*)

Pakaaune Saamaagri ra Bhaadaa Kuda Haru

NEPALI INGREDIENTS AND KITCHEN EQUIPMENT

INGREDIENTS

The following describes some of the special ingredients used in this book. Most ingredients are available in Indian, East Asian, and Middle Eastern grocery stores or some health food stores and larger supermarkets.

Ajowan Seeds (*Jwaano*)

Also known as ajowan, ajwain, Bishop's weed, omum, or carom seeds, they are used extensively in Nepali cooking. These tiny gray-brown seeds have a striped surface and resemble celery seeds, but have a somewhat sharper and more pungent flavor. If the seeds are chewed plain, they are quite strong, bitter, and stinging, but their aftertaste is quite pleasant. They are usually lightly fried to release their flavor and added at the beginning stages of the cooking process. The seeds are sometimes also crushed in a mortar and pestle and added to batters. Ajowan seeds are one of the most important spices in the much-loved sprouted bean soup (Kwanti, page 99). The seeds are also chewed on their own to help with bloating, to relieve flatulence, and to aid digestion. It is believed that ajowan soup helps lactating mothers increase and maintain milk supplies. The seeds should be stored in an airtight container in a cool, dark place.

Asafetida (*Heeng*)

Also called *hingu* (Sanskrit) or devil's dung, asafetida is used extensively in

Nepali cooking to flavor and preserve food, as well as for its medicinal properties. Asafetida comes from an herbaceous fennel-like perennial plant. When mature, the stems are cut close to the roots releasing a milky substance that solidifies into a brownish, gummy mass. Asafetida is sometimes described as having an unpleasant and overpowering smell, due in part to the presence of sulfur. In Nepali, there is a saying, *"hing ne bhai pani hing ko taalo cha"* ("even if the asafetida is used up, its aroma lingers in the wrapping cloth"). However, when used with discretion, this spice mellows and adds a pleasant aroma to prepared food. The flavor of asafetida is definitely an acquired taste, although some people describe it as similar to shallots or garlic.

Asafetida is commonly used in the preparation of daals, vegetable curries, and pickles. It is used in minute amounts, otherwise it will overpower a dish. It is readily available, labeled as *hing* at Indian grocery stores in powdered or solid forms. Most powdered forms are combined with rice, corn, or wheat flour to prevent lumping, or to reduce its overpowering smell, and sometimes to increase its weight. The powdered form is convenient, but of a less intense flavor. Solid pieces of asafetida are brown in color and come in irregular shapes. Some people prefer to buy the solid form because its flavor is more concentrated. In my recipes, I use the powdered form, but if you decide to purchase solid asafetida, you can grind it as needed. Asafetida should be stored in an airtight container because of its strong smell.

Atta Flour (*Gahu ko Pitho*)
Also known as chapatti or durham whole wheat flour, this fine-textured flour is processed from low-gluten wheat and used in making most unleavened breads. Since this flour is low in gluten, it is easier to knead and roll.

Bay Leaves (*Tejpaat*)
From an aromatic evergreen tree, this herb is also known as Indian cassia, cinnamon leaves, and *tej patta*. The leaves are oblong shaped and usually have three prominent veins. The dried leaves have a warm, sweet, and distinct cinnamon aroma. They are usually lightly sautéed for all kinds of spiced meat and fish curries, savory rice dishes, lentils, and some vegetables and are usually removed from the dish before it is served. Bay leaves are one of the important spice ingredients in the preparation of Nepali Garam Masala (page 398). The leaves are also known to have some medicinal properties and for the treatment of colic and diarrhea. They are available in Indian food markets under the name "Indian Bay Leaves." They should be stored in an airtight container in a cool dark place.

Black-Eyed Peas (*Bodi*)

Also known as cow peas, these kidney-shaped beans are tan or cream colored with small black markings or "eyes," which they maintain even after cooking. The outer skin of the bean is somewhat thick and not easily digestible, so they should be cooked thoroughly. Like any other dried bean, they should be soaked for more than six hours or until soft before cooking. They can be mixed with vegetables and cooked as a curried dish.

Buckwheat Flour (*Phaapar ko Pitho*)

Buckwheat belongs to the sorrel and rhubarb family and has triangular seeds. It is not related to wheat and is not a true grain, and has no gluten. It has a nutty flavor and is a high source of protein. It is available at Indian and health food stores, and at some regular supermarkets. It should be stored in an air-tight container.

Cardamom, Black Pods (*Alainchi*)

Native to the sub-Himalayan region, black cardamom is the dried fruit of a perennial herbaceous plant of the ginger family. Apart from its usage in India, Nepal, and other Asian countries, black cardamom is not common. The pod is oval shaped and dark brown, tough and leathery with deep wrinkles. Each pod contains several moist brown seeds that are sticky, flavorful, and once crushed, emit a pleasant smoky aroma with a hint of camphor. When cooked, the spice enhances and intensifies the taste of food without overpowering a dish. Some people describe black cardamom as an inferior substitute to green cardamom, but it is considered a valuable spice in Nepal. It is one of the ingredients used to make Nepali garam masala spice blends (pages 397 and 398), and is also used in meat curries, rice dishes, and pickles.

Many Nepalese chew black cardamom to freshen the breath and palate. It is also used as a home remedy for digestive disorders and considered beneficial to teeth and gums. It is available in Indian food stores. Look for pods with moist, sweet seeds, and a smoky fragrance. Old pods with splits and cracks will have poor quality seeds with no flavor. The seeds quickly lose their flavor once the pods are opened, so store the pods whole and grind the seeds as needed.

Cardamom, Green (*Sukumel*)

The dried unripened fruit of a perennial bushy plant of the ginger family, green cardamom pods are three-sided, smooth-skinned, and contain reddish-brown seeds. The seeds are sticky and have a highly aromatic flavor with a hint of eucalyptus. Because of its high price, it is used sparingly. When a recipe calls for whole cardamom, the pods are cracked leaving the seeds intact, adding a subtle flavor to a dish. Sometimes the pods are removed before the food is served. For recipes that call for ground cardamom, I prefer to crush the seeds in a mortar and pestle freshly rather than use preground cardamom because the seeds begin to lose their flavor once the pods are opened.

Cardamom is one of the most important ingredients in Nepali sweets, and is also popular in meat and vegetable curries, sweet preserved pickles, and beverages. It is also one of the ingredients used to make the Nepali Fragrant Garam Masala (page 397). Cardamom seeds are also chewed after dinner or any time of the day to freshen the breath. Many people carry a small bag of cardamom pods to chew as needed. Cardamom is also used in Ayurvedic medicine to treat various maladies such as digestive disorders and headaches, and is known to cure nausea and vomiting. Cardamom pods, both green and bleached white, are available whole, seeded, or ground in Indian food stores and most supermarkets. Look for high-quality whole pods, which are plump, and have brownish-black seeds with a strong scent. If the pod is wrinkled and dried up, the seeds will have no flavor.

Chickpeas, Brown (*Kaalo Chana*)
Brown chickpeas are similar to white chickpeas in shape, but are smaller and more wrinkled, with a thick seed coating. They also have a different flavor and texture. They should be soaked in water before cooking. They can be cooked in bean dishes, toasted, fried to make crunchy snacks, or sprouted.

Chickpeas, White (*Sukeko Chana*)
Also known as Bengal gram or garbanzo beans, chickpeas are irregular-shaped beans somewhat larger than peas. They have a thick wrinkled skin and are normally soaked in water before using, which cuts down the cooking time. After soaking, the beans double in size and the wrinkles smooth out. They are cooked in daals, mixed with salads, or sprouted.

Chickpeas, Yellow Split (*Chana ko Daal*)
These are also known as split Bengal gram and come from the brown variety of chickpeas. They resemble yellow split peas or pigeon peas, but are slightly larger and have a bright yellow color. This daal takes a long time to cook and will not disintegrate, but holds its shape. It is usually presoaked before cooking. Yellow split chickpeas are difficult to digest, and are always cooked with a generous amount of ginger and asafetida.

Chickpea Flour (*Besan*)
Also known as Bengal gram flour or chana flour, this flour is pale, yellow colored, and finely milled from brown chickpeas. It has a nutty flavor and is used

often as a batter for fritters, sweet dishes, and as a thickener. Look for this flour in Indian grocery stores or larger well-stocked supermarkets.

Cilantro (*Hariyo Dhania ko Paat*)

Also called fresh coriander or Chinese parsley, cilantro is the fresh leaves and stems of the coriander plant. The seeds and leaves have completely different flavors and aromas and cannot be substituted for one another. Fresh cilantro has a distinct and sharp flavor, whereas the seeds are much milder. A small amount of chopped fresh coriander is sprinkled on nearly every dish as a garnish and to add extra flavor. It is also combined with highly seasoned meat or vegetables to tone down spiciness.

Cilantro is sold year-round in most supermarkets and in Indian, Latin American, and Asian food markets. Make sure it is bright green and avoid wilted leaves. It can be stored in the refrigerator for up to one week in a plastic bag lined with a paper towel. The rooted variety can be kept longer in a glass of water, root-end down, covered with a plastic bag in the refrigerator. Change the water every other day and use as needed.

Cinnamon and Cassia Bark (*Daalchini*)

One of the oldest known and most aromatic spices, cinnamon is the dried inner bark of a tropical evergreen tree. The bark is reddish-brown in color, pungent, sharp tasting, and easily breakable. It is used either whole or ground to flavor sauces, rice, desserts, syrups, and is brewed with milky tea (page 372). Cinnamon is also one of the components of Nepali spice blends, such as garam masala (page 398). It is available whole or ground in any supermarket or Indian food store. Cinnamon sticks keep indefinitely, but ground cinnamon loses its flavor more quickly. Both should be stored in an airtight container. In Nepal, a small stick of cinnamon is sometimes chewed with cardamom and cloves after a heavily spiced meal to freshen the breath and palate.

Clarified Butter (*Gheu*)

Clarified butter is made by heating unsalted butter until all the milk solids separate and can be removed. This butter imparts a wonderful flavor and is extensively used in Nepali cooking. It is easy to make at home (page 393) and is available in Indian grocery stores under the name, *ghee* in jars of various sizes.

Cloves (*Lwang*)

The dried buds of a tropical evergreen tree, cloves are reddish-brown in color with a rounded flower head. They are one of the most important Nepali spices, used both for culinary and medicinal purposes. In Sanskrit, cloves are called *deva kusuma*, meaning "the flower of the gods" or "auspicious bud." Cloves are either used whole or ground to flavor many Nepali dishes such as meat, poultry, vegetable stews, and rice, but rarely in sweet dishes. When gently sautéed, the spice swells and releases a pleasant aroma. Cloves are also used in pickles and are an important component in Nepali Garam Masala mixtures (pages 397-98). Cloves can overpower a dish, particularly when ground, so they should be used sparingly. Buy them whole, not ground, as ground cloves lose their potency quickly.

Aside from its culinary use, cloves are also used to freshen one's mouth. Nepalese chew cloves throughout the day, alone or with green or black cardamom or cinnamon sticks and betel nuts. Chewing cloves is certainly a cultivated taste, and at first, they can be bitingly sharp, hot, and leave a numb sensation in the mouth, but once you get used to it you enjoy the taste. Cloves act as a quick home remedy for relieving toothaches by simply tucking them in the affected corner of the mouth and chewing slowly to release the oil. This also helps to minimize tooth decay and eliminates halitosis. Cloves are used to cure nausea and flatulence and promote digestion, especially after eating fatty and spicy food.

Coriander Seeds (*Dhaniya ko Geda*)

The dried, ripe fruit of a hardy annual plant from the parsley family, coriander seeds are beige or yellowish-brown in color, slightly smaller than peppercorns, with longitudinal ridges, that can be easily split into halves. They have a very pleasant and sweet aroma, with a hint of citrus. It is a valued spice in Nepali cooking and extensively used as a flavoring agent in nearly almost all dishes. Coriander is an important ingredient used in Nepali Garam Masala mixtures (pages 397-98). The combination of cumin and coriander is one of the most common seasonings in Nepali cuisine. In many recipes, both coriander leaves (cilantro) and seeds are used in the same dish to create a wonderful flavor. Coriander seeds are available both whole and ground at Indian grocery stores. I usually purchase whole seeds and grind them in small quantities as needed because ground seeds lose their potency quickly. To bring out their flavor, you can also toast the seeds carefully before grinding and store them in an airtight container.

Cumin Seeds (*Jeera*)

In Sanskrit, cumin seeds are called *sugandhan jeeraka*, meaning "good smelling," indicating that the spice has been in use for a very long time. Cumin seeds are gray green, oblong, ridged, and thicker in the middle with pointed ends, somewhat resembling caraway or fennel seeds in appearance. They have a sharp, pungent, and slightly bitter taste. The seeds are either used whole, ground, or lightly crushed, and are used extensively in Nepali cooking. Cumin seeds are an essential ingredient in Nepali spice blends (pages 397-98). Ground cumin has a distinct, strong, and powerful flavor and should be used carefully in measured quantities; otherwise, it may dominate a dish. Cumin seeds are available either whole or ground at most supermarkets. The flavor of ground cumin seeds loses its potency once it ages, so grind it fresh or purchase it in small quantities.

Cumin Seeds, Black (*Kaalo Jeera*)

The black variety of cumin seeds comes from a small, slender, annual herb. It is similar to regular cumin seeds except for their dark brown color and length. These seeds are warm, pungent, and mildly bitter, with a sweet scent. They are called *shahi jeera* in Hindi, meaning "king cumin" because of their distinct features. This spice is used more widely in Indian-Kashmiri cuisine than Nepali. Because it is relatively rare, black cumin is used only in small amounts.

Fennel Seeds (*Saunp* or *Saunf*)

The strong-smelling fennel plant has bright green stalks, lacy, dark green leaves, and mustard yellow flowers, which turn into seed-heads when ripe. They are collected before they mature and are dried. These slightly curved seeds are oval shaped with ridges, greenish-yellow, and look somewhat like plump cumin seeds. They are an aromatic spice with a mild licorice flavor. All parts of the fennel plant are edible, including the young tender shoots, leaves, and stalks, as well as the seeds. Fennel seeds are offered at the end of the meal as a digestive or to freshen the mouth. The seeds are sometimes toasted to bring out the flavor and mixed with coconut, melon seeds, and sugar crystals before chewing. They are available in most supermarkets and the higher quality seeds will be bright green, which indicates freshness. The seeds can be ground in a spice grinder or with a mortar and pestle as the recipe indicates.

Fenugreek Seeds (*Methi ko Geda*)

An indispensable spice in Nepali cooking, these brownish-yellow rectangular seeds are very hard and highly aromatic. They come from an annual herb of the legume family that grows about two feet high with white flowers that form long, slender pods. When the pods mature, they are dried, and the seeds are removed. The seeds have a very strong, unpleasantly bitter taste in the raw stage, but when cooked, they emit a wonderful aroma. They are used in small quantities, and in many recipes, the whole seeds are first fried in oil to bring out the maximum flavor. The seeds can also be soaked, sprouted, and used in salads or pickles. The young and fresh green leaves (*methi ko saag*) of the fenugreek plant are also used; they have a pleasant bitter flavor that is an acquired taste. Frying fenugreek seeds gives off an unpleasant smell that may linger for days without proper ventilation. Fenugreek seeds, as well as fresh and dried leaves, are available in Indian grocery stores.

Ginger (*Aduwa* or *adua*)

Although fresh ginger is sometimes called gingerroot, it is actually an underground creeping rhizome. The attractive plant has long leaves, and grows up to three feet tall, forming rhizomes that are dug up from the ground as they mature. Fresh ginger has cream to light brown colored skin with a pale yellow flesh, and provides the freshest flavor and spicy biting taste. Fresh, dried whole, and powdered ginger are available at Indian and Asian food stores and many supermarkets. For best results, always choose ginger that is firm and unwrinkled. It can be kept for several weeks in the refrigerator, wrapped in a paper towel to absorb moisture. Peeled and sliced ginger does not keep very well, so it should be peeled as needed. Fresh ginger paste is also available at some Asian and Indian grocery stores and should be refrigerated after opening. Powdered ginger is convenient, but has a different flavor and should not be substituted for fresh ginger. Aside from its culinary use, both fresh and dried ginger are valued for their medicinal properties, particularly to soothe the digestive system, indigestion, loss of appetite, and especially flatulence. They are also used to relieve coughs and sore throats.

Goddess Basil (*Tulasi*)

Considered sacred in the Hindu tradition, this annual herb is traditionally grown in the courtyard or in a pot of many Nepali homes and worshiped in the morning and evening. Goddess Basil has small aromatic leaves, which are either green or purplish. In addition to their religious uses, fresh or dried basil is used to make a soothing herbal tea, and is believed to help treat common colds, headaches, and stomach disorders.

Green Gooseberry (*Amala*)

Also called Indian gooseberry, *emblica*, or *amalaki*, green gooseberries come from trees grown at the foot of the Himalayan mountains. The tree has feathery leaves, and the fruit is light yellow to green, round, firm, and tart. It is picked by hand or by shaking it from the tree. It is then gathered from the ground and transported to markets in a conical wicker basket (*doko*). Nepalese regard whole gooseberries as sacred and offer it to deities during worship. They may be eaten raw, but are usually dried, made into preserves, or pickled with spices. Gooseberry possesses high nutritive value and is known for its medicinal properties. They are believed to help prevent aging and to treat diarrhea and hemorrhages. Gooseberries are available in Indian markets, frozen and dried, but occasionally you may find fresh ones.

Himalayan herb (*Jimbu*)

Also known as Himalayan aromatic leaf garlic, *jimbu* is a dried aromatic herb that is virtually unknown outside the Himalayan region. The herb looks like dry brownish-green grass and has a distinct flavor somewhat similar to garlic and shallots. It is found wild throughout many regions of Nepal. The leaves and tender stems are carefully picked and dried, which weakens the flavor, but this is reversed by browning it in hot oil until fully fragrant. Nepalese have a remarkable fondness for this herb and they use it as a tempering spice to flavor daals, vegetables, salads, and pickles. Generally, a small pinch of *jimbu* is sufficient to flavor a dish and it should be used with discretion. The fried herb lends texture and visual appeal to any dish. As the herb ages, it loses its flavor, so purchase it in small quantities. *Jimbu* is only available in Nepal, but some people substitute the dried roots of the garlic bulb, although this does not produce the same flavor as *jimbu*.

Kidney Beans (*Raajma ko Daal*)

These kidney-shaped beans have a red firm skin with cream-colored flesh, and are cooked similar to other beans. They are first soaked in water to improve the texture and to quicken the cooking time. They are slowly simmered with fresh herbs and spices until tender.

Lentils, Red or Pink (*Musuro ko Daal*)

Also known as *masoor daal*, these round lentils have brown seed coatings and are very popular in Nepal. They are available whole (*singo musuro ko daal*) or split (*musuro ko daal*). When cooked, whole lentils retain their shape, and do not disintegrate into mush. The split, skinless variety is quick cooking with a delicate nutty flavor and turns golden yellow when cooked. The whole lentils with skins can be sprouted or stir-fried and made into crunchy snacks. Generally, neither variety needs soaking before cooking.

Mango Powder (*Amchoor*)

Made from tart, unripe, green mangoes, which are peeled, sliced, dried, and finely ground, mango powder is very tart with a pleasant, mild, citrus flavor. It is used as a spice to add tartness to various dishes. It is more common in vegetable dishes than meat dishes, and is frequently used to flavor snacks. The light brown-colored powder is available in Indian grocery stores in sealed plastic bags.

Mung Beans (*Moong Daal*)

Also known as green grams or *mugi ko daal*, these legumes are extensively used in Nepali cooking. They are known for their lightness and for being easily digestible. These tiny oval-shaped beans come in three forms. Split yellow mung beans without skins (*pahelo moong ko daal*) are the most common daal in Nepal and are considered the most delicious and easiest to digest. They can be soaked, drained, and fried into crunchy snacks. This daal is also frequently prescribed for sick people with digestive disorders. Split green mung beans with skins (*khoste moong ko daal*) are used to prepare basic daal or combined with rice to make a soft rice porridge. Whole green mung beans with skins (*singo moong ko daal*) are cooked by themselves or combined with other legumes. They can be soaked and used in salads, stir-fried, deep-fried, or sprouted, and are used to make the traditional Nepali mixed sprouted bean dish Kwanti (page 97).

Mustard Oil (*Tori ko Tel*)

Mustard oil is an extremely pungent, yellow-colored oil that comes from pressed mustard seeds. In the raw state, the oil has a bitter, sharp flavor, but once it is heated to the smoking point, the pungency mellows and the oil imparts its delicious flavor to food that it is cooked with. Nepalese apply mustard oil to hair to promote healthy growth and use it in massage for relief from aches and pains. Mustard oil is available in Indian and Asian stores, and some well-stocked supermarkets.

Mustard Seeds (*Rayo* or *Sarsyun*)

These small round seeds come from the mustard plant, a common annual field crop. They range from reddish-brown to a dark brown color, but when crushed they are yellow on the inside. They have a pungent, sharp flavor, but when fried in oil, they impart a mellow nutty flavor. Nepalese use ground or coarsely ground mustard seeds to make pickles because of their wonderful preservative properties, which discourage mold and bacteria. They are also used to perk up vegetable dishes. Yellow mustard seeds (*sarsyun*) are used to cook fish and are believed to eliminate fishy odors. The tender leaves of the mustard plant, called mustard greens (*raayo ko saag*), are also used. The seeds are pressed to extract fragrant mustard oil. Mustard is used as a home remedy to cure flatulence and to promote digestion. Mustard seeds are available whole, split, or powdered at Indian grocery stores, Asian markets, and regular grocery stores.

Nepalese Hog Plum (*Labsi*)

Also known as *lapsi* or *lausi*, these are a native fruit of Nepal. The tall subtropical tree can be found growing in many parts of the country. The fruit is greenish-yellow when ripe and roughly resembles a small oval-shaped plum. It is extremely sour, even when fully ripe, and has a high vitamin C content. The fruit has a tough fibrous skin and pale yellow flesh, which is firmly attached to a large brown seed. The pulp is difficult to separate from the seeds, but once cooked it separates easily. A ripe labsi has a pleasantly tart flavor and some people like to eat it fresh, but it is mainly used to make dried fruit nuggets or fruit leather (page 388), both sweet and salted. It is also pickled, cooked with vegetables, or used as a souring agent. The stony seeds (*champati*) are used as a cooking fuel and some children play with the seeds like round marbles. Labsi is not available outside Nepal.

Nutmeg (*Jaiphal*)
Known for its strongly aromatic, warm, fresh, and nutty flavor, nutmeg comes from the fruit of the nutmeg tree. It is an ingredient in Nepali Garam Masala (page 398). Ground nutmeg is frequently used to season strong-flavored meat like game, venison, and organ meats. It is also used with cardamom to prepare milk-based sweet dishes and yogurt desserts. Nutmeg should be used in moderation, a small pinch is generally sufficient to flavor a moderate-sized dish. Purchase whole nutmeg and grind or grate it as needed, because its flavor deteriorates and it loses its potency soon after grinding. Whole nutmegs keep indefinitely if they are stored in an airtight container, away from sunlight. In addition to its culinary uses, it is also used as a home remedy to aid digestion, treat diarrhea, cure nausea, and improve appetite. Nutmeg oil is also used in soap, perfume, and ointments.

Peas, Dried (*Sukeko Thulo Kerau*)
Available in green and yellow varieties, these peas are used whole or split, with or without the skins. When split and skinless, they are consumed as daal, while the whole peas are eaten as a form of vegetable curry. They can also be soaked, sprouted, and made into salads, or mixed with other vegetables. They are sometimes toasted and puffed for snack foods. Dried peas do not require soaking before cooking, but soaking shortens the cooking time.

Field Peas (*Sukeko Hariyo Saano Kerau*)
These tiny peas resemble garden peas, with smaller and narrower pods, each containing tightly packed almost round, smooth peas. Once dried, they become green-gray in color and resemble mung beans, but are much harder. Field peas are usually grown for drying, but are also eaten fresh. The podded bushy plants are sold bundled in the market during the spring. The dried peas require

soaking for more than twelve hours before using them. They are most commonly pickled, used in salads, or cooked with vegetables.

Peppercorns (*Marich*)

One of the most widely used spices in the world, black pepper is also known as *pippali* in Sanskrit, which means "berry." Black pepper has a very pungent, hot, and biting taste. Because of its spicy taste, it should be used in moderation. It is available whole, finely ground, or crushed in supermarkets. Although preground pepper is convenient, the essential oils released by grinding peppercorns fade quickly, so it is best if purchased whole and ground as needed. It should be stored in an airtight container away from sunlight. Peppercorns are recognized as having medicinal qualities such as promoting digestion, reducing bloating and flatulence, and relieving nausea.

Pigeon Peas (*Rahar ko Daal*)

Also known as red gram, yellow lentils, arhar, or toor, pigeon peas are usually sold split without skins. This daal has a slightly nutty taste, is easy to digest, and resembles yellow split chickpeas. In Nepal, *rahar ko daal* is considered the king of daal. They are available dry and oiled. The oily kind looks glossy because it is coated with castor oil to prevent spoilage. Oiled pigeon peas should be rinsed in hot water before cooking. They are cooked by themselves or can be mixed with other legumes.

Poppy Seeds (*Khus Khus*)

These small, dried, pale yellow, black, or beige seeds come from the capsules of the opium poppy. They add a crunchy texture and nutty flavor to any dish, and are especially popular as a topping for breads. They can be purchased at Indian grocery stores and most supermarkets. These seeds contain oil, which turns rancid quickly, so it is best if they are stored in the refrigerator.

Nigella Seeds (*Mungrelo*)

Also known as black cumin, black onion seeds, and *kalonji*, these are small, triangular, black seeds, with a rough surface and white interior. They have a lingering flavor described as peppery, nutty, and bitter. The whole seed is not very strong, but when crushed they have a distinct pungent flavor. Nigella seeds are often confused with onion seeds, but they are quite different and should not be substituted. The seeds are usually fried or toasted to enhance their flavor, and cooked with meat and fish curries, with mild vegetables such as pumpkin, and used extensively in pickles. They are available whole in small packets in Indian grocery stores.

Radish Seeds (*Mula ko Beu*)

The dried edible seeds of the radish plant, radish seeds are reddish-brown in color with a pungent, sharp, and peppery taste, and a hint of radish flavor. When the radish plant reaches its full height, its yellow flowers become seedpods. The seeds are harvested, separated, and collected by threshing. They are used in small quantities because of their overpowering taste and mainly as a pickling spice. The seeds are used in the ground form and they can be easily crushed with a mortar and pestle.

Rice Flakes, Pressed (*Cheura* or *Chewra*)

Also known as *bajee*, pressed rice flakes are prepared from soaked or parboiled rice that has been flattened by large heavy rollers into flat flakes. They are dehydrated and the finished product is a ready-to-eat rice flake. In Nepal, the old-fashioned method of pounding the grains in a heavy wooden mortar with a pole still exists in many villages, although it is slowly being replaced by machines. The dried rice flakes have uneven edges and a rough texture, and resemble rolled oats. They are extremely light, with no particular aroma, a bland taste, and vary in thickness, texture, and color according to the types of rice. *Cheura* is very popular throughout Nepal because it can be consumed without further cooking, it stores well, is easy to carry, and is light and healthy. Plain, toasted, or fried rice flakes are eaten with vegetables or meat, eggs, yogurt, pickles, and as a mid-day snack between meals. It is also served as a breakfast food. *Cheura* is sold in plastic bags in Indian grocery stores under the name *poha*, *chidwa*, or *chura*. Before use, the flakes need to be picked over to remove any foreign matter. Store them in a cool dry place in a covered container to keep out moisture.

Rice Flour (*Chaamal ko Pitho*)

This white flour is made by grinding rice grains into powder. It is available in Indian or East Asian grocery stores and some health food stores, as well as well-stocked supermarkets. Store in a dry, tightly closed container.

Saffron (*Kesar*)

The dried stigmas of the saffron crocus flower are known as saffron. Each flower contains three bright red stigmas that are handpicked, an extremely labor-intensive process, making it one of the world's most expensive spices. The stigmas are dried until they shrink into slender, delicate thread-like, strands with a bright orange-red color and delicate aroma. Saffron is used in small amounts to flavor various Nepali dishes. The threads are usually crushed and infused in warm liquids to extract their full aroma and flavor and to give an even color to the dish. Some cookbooks suggest toasting saffron strands before crushing them to extract more flavor. I do not recommend this method and it is not necessary to bring out the intense aroma. Saffron is also available in the ground form in an airtight container, dated and labeled with the source in Indian, Middle Eastern, and regular supermarkets. Good-quality saffron has a strong pleasant flavor, and is light, glossy, and soft to touch. It should be stored in a cool dry place away from sunlight, for its flavor diminishes and it becomes dry and brittle as it ages. Ground saffron loses its potency more quickly and can be easily adulterated with fillers unless you get it from a reputed spice vendor.

Sesame Seeds (*Til*)
Sesame seeds are flat, small, oval seeds that come from the annual tropical sesame plant. They can be white, black, or various shades of brown. White sesame seeds are shiny, slippery, and easy to crush and remain white even after cooking. They are used mainly in desserts and bread preparations. The black varieties have a strong bitter taste and are not used much in Nepali cooking, but they are considered sacred and are used in various religious ceremonies and rituals. Light brown sesame seeds are much preferred and are usually toasted to bring out their nutty flavor. They are available at most supermarkets and in Indian, South Asian, and Middle Eastern grocery stores. Due to their high oil content, sesame seeds turn rancid quickly. It is best if they are purchased in small amounts and used as needed. They should be kept in an airtight container in a cool and dry place.

Soybeans (*Bhatmaas*)
Also known as *bhatmaas ko kosa* and edamame, soybeans grow on an annual bushy plant that produces green shell beans covered with fuzz. The shelled beans are similar in size and color to green peas and slightly smooth to the touch, with a firm and crisp texture. Soybeans have received universal recognition because of their nutritional value, especially their high protein content. Both fresh and presoaked beans are an excellent source of fiber and are used to make vegetable curries, stews, and soups. They are also sprouted and used in soups. Toasted soybeans make an ideal snack. Fresh green soybeans are occasionally available at Asian and Indian grocery stores, and frozen and dried soybeans are available at many well-stocked supermarkets.

Tamarind (*Imili* or *Imilee*)
Thick reddish-brown pods of a large tropical evergreen tree with ferny leaves native to Asia, tamarinds are three to six inches long, irregularly curved at the ends, and shaped somewhat like a large peapod. As the pod matures, they

develop shiny, black seeds surrounded by pulp and coarse fiber. When dried, the brittle shells crack open and the pulp dehydrates into a sticky, sweet-and-sour paste. Tamarind is used as a souring agent in many Nepali dishes. It is available at Indian or Asian grocery stores in different forms: compressed (with or without seeds) into fibrous blocks, concentrated, powdered, and sometimes whole dried pods. If you are using compressed pulp, you need to soak it in water before using.

Szechwan Pepper (*Timmur*)

Also known as *ban timmur* or Nepali pepper, this is a highly pungent, sharp tasting dried berry from the prickly ash shrub family. It is often mistaken for black pepper, but it has an entirely different flavor and is, in fact, not related to the black pepper family. When the berry matures, it splits into two halves with a shiny black seed. It has a rough, wrinkled, and uneven surface and the aroma lies in the split covering of the pod, not in the seed. Nepalese describe its taste as *per-peraune*, which means "biting taste with an anesthetic feeling on the tongue." It should be used only in moderation; otherwise, it will overpower the dish.

Timmur is the most commonly used spice in Nepali pickles and chutneys. Whole *timmur* is also used to flavor some vegetable and lentil dishes, but it is removed before serving so that the unpleasant bite can be avoided. It is also used to cook Nepali wild mushrooms to remove any toxic elements. While trekking in the Muktinath area, I observed locals using *timmur* extensively to flavor yak meat, to make jerky, *momos* (stuffed dumplings), lentils, and vegetables. *Timmur* is found wild throughout the hilly slopes of Nepal where the temperature is cold. During the rainy season, some use *timmur* to cure leech bites. It is also used as a home remedy to cure stomach ailments and toothaches. The recipes in this book usually suggest grinding the berries in a mortar and pestle to bring out the maximum flavor, but you can also use a spice grinder. Use a sieve to remove the husks. Nepali *timmur* is not available outside Nepal, but you may substitute Szechwan pepper or Chinese pepper, which has a similar, if milder flavor.

Turmeric (*Besar*)

Used in nearly all Nepali dishes to add color and flavor, ground (*besar*) and fresh turmeric (*haledo*) are the most important spices in Nepali cuisine. The plant is native to southeastern Asia (probably India) and is cultivated throughout the warmer areas of the world. The plant belongs to the ginger family and has a rhizome, which looks similar to fresh ginger but has short, round, finger-like stems and an orange color. To produce ground turmeric, fresh turmeric is boiled or steamed, peeled, dried, and ground to a powder. Making your own ground turmeric is a lengthy process, and requires a lot of time and effort, but some people prefer this authentic version. Preground turmeric is yellow-orange in color, lightly aromatic, slightly bitter, and pungent. A small amount (¼ to 1 teaspoon) of turmeric is sufficient to color and flavor a dish. Excessive turmeric can overwhelm the other flavors of the food. Turmeric is added to nearly all dishes, including breads and pickles. It also has antiseptic properties and therefore is rubbed onto slaughtered animals to help preserve the meat. Fish is rubbed with salt and turmeric to eliminate any fishy smell. Because of its color, turmeric is sometimes confused with saffron, but the flavors are in no way similar. Turmeric has a religious significance in many Hindu ceremonies and rituals. Turmeric is available either fresh, dried, or powdered at Indian grocery stores. The color of ground turmeric tends to fade and becomes unpleasant if the spice has aged. One has to be very careful when using turmeric powder, as it tends to stain clothes, cooking utensils, cutting boards, and work surfaces and is difficult to clean.

Urad Beans (*Maas ko Daal*)

Also known as black gram, urad beans resemble whole mung beans, but are smaller and have a dull black seed coat. It takes a long time to soften this daal while cooking, and it is known to be the slowest cooking bean and difficult to digest. When cooked, each bean doubles in size and becomes slippery. Since the beans are heavy and hard to digest, many people cook them with a generous amount of ginger, garlic, and ground asafetida. They are available in three forms: Split white urad beans without skins (*maas ko chhata ko daal*), these creamy-white or ivory-colored skinned split beans resemble yellow split mung beans in texture but have a blander taste. Split black urad beans with skins (*kaalo maas ko daal*), used for a popular Nepali daal preparation called *Jhaaneko kaalo maas ko daal*. They are also combined with rice to make soft rice porridge. They are soaked, ground, and used to make many snacks. The soaked and ground batters are mixed with chopped vegetables and made into sun-dried nuggets (pages 91-92). Whole black urad beans with skins (*singo maas ko daal*) are small, oval, shiny or dusky black beans. They are cooked the same way as any basic daal dish, or soaked and sprouted.

Urad Flour (*Maas ko Pitho*)

This is an off-white colored flour made from dried, split, and skinless urad beans. It is used by itself, or combined with other flours and made into breads or savory fried snacks. Look for urad flour in Indian grocery stores.

KITCHEN EQUIPMENT

The Nepali kitchen is very simple. Most food is cooked on the stovetop and villagers in rural parts of Nepal still use homemade clay stoves (*chulo*) and cook on wood or charcoal fires. Gas, kerosene, and electric stoves, however, have replaced these clay stoves in Kathmandu and many other parts of Nepal. Traditionally, kitchens occupied the top floor of the house and wood was the main source of cooking, so pots and pans were designed to fit wood-burning stoves. Some traditional cooking utensils made of iron, brass, copper, and bronze, with elaborate engraving, are still used in Nepali households, but they have slowly been replaced by modern and more functional utensils. To prepare the dishes in this book, you do not need to purchase special kitchen equipment. However, listed below are some of the more commonly used items that can be useful in making authentic Nepali dishes. Most of these are available in Indian or Asian supermarkets.

Rolling Pins (*Chauka* and *Belna*)

Chauka, small round platforms usually made of wood, stone, or marble are used for rolling out dough. *Belna* are rolling pins usually made of wood. They are wide in the middle and have tapered ends. Their grip and weight is suited for rolling thin, round breads.

Wok-Shaped Pan (*Karahi*)

A wide, round-bottomed pan, with two side handles, resembling the Chinese wok. It can be used for almost any method of cooking, including deep-frying, stir-frying, steaming, or braising. A *karahi* is made of heavy cast-iron and can withstand high cooking temperatures. It also absorbs heat quickly, distributes it evenly, and retains it for maximum efficiency, even at low temperatures. This pan comes in a variety of sizes and materials, such as brass, iron, and stainless steel, and the two handles on the sides make it easy to rotate or move while cooking. This pan is the choice of many cooks, and it is one of the most indispensable cooking utensils in Nepali kitchens.

Pressure Cooker (*Presar Kooker*)

A pressure cooker is a pot in which steam pressure builds up so that food cooks quickly at high temperatures. It is available in stainless steel or heavy-duty aluminum, which are both good conductors of heat. Pressure cookers are popular in modern Nepali kitchens as they cook food in a short time.

Spice Box (*Sanduke* or *Masala Dani*)

This round stainless steel spice box that stores dry spices is found in most

Nepali homes. It contains seven round bowls, along with a small teaspoon measure, which fits inside the box. It has a tight-fitting lid to ensure that the spices are not exposed to air and do not mix together. The bowls are filled with commonly used spices, such as ground cumin, ground coriander, fenugreek seeds, ground chili, garam masala, ground turmeric, and salt. The *sanduke* is generally kept by the side of the stove.

Dumpling Steamer (*Momo pakaune bhada*)

The stacked steamer is mainly used for steaming stuffed dumplings (*momos*). It is made of aluminum or stainless steel and comprised of two to three racks with holes allowing steam to pass through. The bottom pot holds water and has a domed lid, which prevents water from dripping onto the steamed food. The top rack accommodates a large quantity of food. They are generally available in Asian supermarkets.

Griddle (*Taaba* or *Taawa*)

This heavy iron griddle or skillet is used to cook Nepali breads. It is slightly concave and comes in various sizes, but the most common ones are nine inches in diameter. A *taaba* does not usually have a handle, but some varieties do have a circular loop handle, and modern ones have wooden handles. After much use, *taabas* become well seasoned.

Frying Pan (*Tai Taapke*)

This classic Nepali pan is used especially for deep-frying. It is made of heavy cast-iron, has a flat bottom, and a long handle, which does not get hot during cooking. There are many sizes and varieties, some smaller *taapkes* are designed for frying eggs so that they cook without breaking the yolk. A *tai taapke* is great for cooking Nepali *sel* (page 122), as it distributes heat evenly.

Iron Pan (*Falaam ko Taapke*)

This traditional iron pan with a long handle and rounded bottom is mainly used to prepare black urad beans (*maas ko daal*). It is known for its excellent heat distribution during cooking. The pan is heavy, durable, and ideal for cooking vegetables or preparing entire meals.

Round Tray and Bowls (*Thaal-Kachaura*)

Traditionally Nepali meals are served on a *thaal-kachaura*. A number of small bowls, known as *kachaura*, are placed on a tray. Meat, vegetables, and daals are placed in the bowl, while rice and bread are placed directly on the tray. This way the rice does not get mixed up with other dishes and it lets you sample each individual dish separately.

Divided Plates with Compartments (*Khande Thaal*)

This is a metal tray that is divided into compartments. It can be round or square, and the most common ones are made of stainless steel. When using a *khande thaal*, rice is placed in the largest compartment and the vegetables, meats, lentils, pickles, and curry dishes are placed in the surrounding compartments. This allows you to taste each dish individually and to mix the tastes and textures to see what combination and sequence you prefer. *Thaals* are one of the most important and indispensable items in the Nepali kitchen.

Mortar and Pestle (*Khal*)

This multi-purpose grinding tool is used to grind herbs, spices, nuts, and seeds into powders and pastes. A mortar and pestle is one of the most practical kitchen tools. They are made of a variety of materials, such as stone, brass, iron, marble, or hardwood. They are especially effective when grinding small quantities of ingredients.

Round Wicker Tray (*Nanglo*)

Made from sturdy bamboo strips and reeds, this tray is mainly used to separate hulls, stones, and foreign material from grains. It is one of the most important and practical kitchen items used for sorting, sun-drying spices and vegetables, or just storing objects.

Nepali-English

GLOSSARY

aamp	mango
aandra-bhudi	tripe
achaar	pickle or chutney
achheta ko tika	paste made from vermilion powder, rice grains, and yogurt, applied on the center of forehead symbolizing good luck
aduwa	fresh ginger
aipan	an auspicious religious design made with thin rice paste
alainchi	black cardamom pods
alu	potato
amala	green gooseberries
amchoor	powdered dried mangoes
anarsa-roti	sweet rice bread flavored with white poppy seeds
anna	grain or food
anna-prasana	rice-feeding ceremony
annapurna	goddess of grains (goddess of prosperity and abundance)
arsa-roti	molasses rice bread
atta flour	durum wheat flour
ayurveda	ancient Indian art of natural medicine
baabari	mint
baara	deep-fried spongy doughnut-shaped patties prepared from beans

baasi	stale, old, leftover
badaam	almond
badam	peanuts
badian	Indian lentil nuggets
bael	wood apple
bakulla simi	fava beans
banda govi	cabbage
banda ko paat	cabbage leaves
bangoor (banel)	pork
barela	balsam apple
barfi	fudge-like sweet made from flour, thickened milk, nuts, fruits, and vegetables
bari	small, round, Nepali-style meatballs or patties made from seasoned ground meat
basmati (baasmati)	long-grain fragrant white rice
battain	quail
besan	chickpea flour
besar	turmeric
bhaadaa-kuda	kitchen equipment
bhaat	cooked rice
bhaat-ko-maad	starchy water obtained from boiling rice
bhai-tika (tihaar)	brother's/sister's day
bhanta	eggplant
bhatmaas	fresh or dried soybeans
bheda-ko-maasu	lamb meat
bhitryaas	tripe
bhogate	pomelo
bhuja	cooked rice
bhujuri	scrambled
bhutuwa	fried
biraula	mixed sprouted beans
bire-noon	black salt
bodi	black-eyed peas
boka ko maasu	goat meat
bungo	banana blossom
chaaku	unrefined sugar made into dark brown firm chunks
chaamal	uncooked rice
chaamal ko pitho	rice flour
chamari-gai	yak

chamena	appetizer or snacks
chamkera	sprinkle
chamsoor	garden cress
chana ko daal	yellow split chickpeas or split Bengal gram
chapatti flour	durum whole wheat flour
chataamari	rice flour bread
chauka-belna	rolling pins and platform
cheura (chewra)	pressed rice flakes
chhana	paneer cheese
chhata ko daal	split white urad beans without skins
chhaype	green onions
chhope	dry-powdered pickle usually made from sesame seeds
chimta	metal tong
chiplo daal	slippery textured daal
chiya	tea
chiya pasal	teahouse or roadside tea vendors
chook-amilo	souring agent for pickles
chop	oval or round patties made from vegetables, meat, or fish
chowela	Nepali spiced meat salad
chukar (chyakhura)	partridge
chulo	clay stoves
chyau	mushroom
daal	all dried legumes, lentils, beans, and peas
daal maharani	daal dish fit to serve a queen
daal-bhaat	rice and lentils together
daal-bhaat-tarkaari	lentil, rice, and vegetables
daalchini	cinnamon
dahi	plain yogurt
dahi-cheura	mixture of yogurt and pressed rice flakes
dal-badi	sun-dried lentil nuggets made with spicy lentil paste (Indian)
dashain	Nepali religious festival
dhaniya (dhania) ko geda	coriander seeds
dhaniya	cilantro or fresh coriander
dhindo	thick cornmeal or millet porridge
doodh	milk
doodh-bari	dessert cheese patties soaked in thickened milk
dum-alu	potato dish

Ekaadasi	the eleventh day after and before the full moon
falaam ko taapke	iron pot or pan
farsi ko phool	squash blossom
furindaana	popular snack made from a mixture of nuts, seeds, lentils, beans, peas, and rice flakes
gaaba	young stalks of taro plant
gaajar	carrot
garam masala	blend of ground spices
gheeraula	smooth luffa gourd
gheu	clarified butter
golbheda	tomato
gulaab jaamun	a popular dessert dumpling in fragrant syrup
guleo	sweet
gundruk	fermented greens
gyanth govi	kohlrabi
gyanth govi ko paat	kohlrabi leaves
haas	duck
haluwa	sweet dish made with flour, vegetables, and fruits
haluwai ko pasal	sweet shop
hariyo bhatmaas	fresh soybeans
hariyo bhatmaas kosa	soybeans in the pod
hariyo chana	fresh green chickpeas
hariyo dhania ko paat	cilantro
hariyo pharsi	green squash
heeng	asafetida
Imili	tamarind
iskush	chayote squash
jaato	a circular milling or grinding stone on a pivot
jaipatri	mace
jaiphal	nutmeg
Janai purnima	Nepali festival when a special sprouted bean soup is eaten
jaulo	rice porridge with lentils and vegetables
jeera	cumin seeds
jhanne	spice-infused tempering oil

jhol-tarkaari	curried vegetable dish
jilphi (jalebi, jeri)	deep-fried, pretzel-shaped confection in syrup
jimbu	an aromatic Himalayan herb
jinge maacha	shrimp
jire-khursaani	bird's eye chili pepper
juju-dhau	sweetened yogurt
jwaano	ajowan, ajwain, Bishop's weed, omum, or carom seeds
jwaano ko ras	ajowan soup
kaagati	lemon or lime
kaaju	cashew nuts
kaaleej (kaaliz)	pheasant
kaalo	black
kaalo chana	dried, dark brown chickpeas
kaalo jeera	black cumin seeds
kaalo maas ko daal	split black urad beans with skin
kaalo noon	black salt
kaankro	cucumber
kadi	smooth and creamy soup-like dish of yogurt and chickpea flour
kalejo	liver
karahi	wok-shaped round-bottomed pot
karkalo ko paat	taro leaves
kasaudi	traditional rice pot with round bottom and narrow neck
kauli ko paat	cauliflower leaves
kera	banana
kerau	green peas
kerau ko daal	split pea daal
kerau ko munta	pea shoots
kesar	saffron
khal	mortar and pestle
khande thaal	divided plates with compartments
khasi ko maasu	castrated goat meat
kheer	rice pudding
khichari	soft cooked rice and daal dish
khoste moong ko daal	split green mung beans with skins
khudo	molasses
khursaani	chili
khus khus	poppy seeds

khuwaa	thickened milk; base for many sweets
kokyaoone	irritating sensation to the throat when taro is eaten raw
kukhura	chicken
kulfi	Indian ice cream
kurelo	asparagus
kwanti	mixed sprouted beans
kwanti purnima	Nepali religious festival where sprouted bean soup is eaten
laakha-mari	Newari ceremonial sweet bread
laddu	sweet dessert balls
lapsi	Nepalese hog plum
lapsi ko titaura	lapsi fruit candy or nuggets or fruit rolls
lasoon ko poti	garlic
lassi	yogurt drink
lauka	bottle gourd, opo squash
lava	unhusked and puffed rice
Laxmi Puja	celebration of the goddess Laxmi
ledo achaar	ground spice pickle
lwang	cloves
maalpuwa	sweetened batter-fried pancakes flavored with fennel seeds
maas ko daal	urad beans or black gram daal
maas ko phulaura	deep-fried lentil balls
maas ko pitho	urad flour
maasu	meat
maata ko ghaito	earthen pots with wide necks for making pickles
maida ko pitho	all-purpose white flour
makai	corn
makhana	puffed lotus seed
makkal	small portable clay pot with charcoal fire
mamuri	golden brown, crusty, thin rice cake
mana-bhog	fluffy wheat haluwa
marich	peppercorn
marsi chaamal	medium- to short-grain white rice
masala	spices
masala-dani	spice box
maseura	sun-dried nuggets made with lentils and vegetables
masino chaamal	long-grain white rice
matar	green peas

methi ko geda	fenugreek seeds
millet	kodo
mirga ko maasu	deer meat
mismaas	mixed
misri	rock candy
mithai	sweets
mohi	buttermilk
momo	stuffed dumpling
moong	mung beans
moong (mugi) ko daal	split yellow mung beans without skin
moong ko roti	bread prepared from split yellow mung bean batter
moong ko titaura	sun-dried split yellow mung bean nuggets
mula	radish
mula ko beu	radish seeds
mula ko paat	radish leaves
mungrelo	nigella seeds
musuro ko daal	red or pink lentils
naan	Indian leavened bread baked in tandoor ovens
naivedya	sacred offering to deities
naanglo	round wicker tray
naribal	coconut
nauni	homemade butter
neuro	fiddlehead ferns
nibuwa	Nepali lemon
nimki	snack crackers
paakeko pharsi	yellow pumpkin
paalungo ko saag	spinach
paan	betel leaf chew
paan-batta	traditional container filled with fragrant whole spices, betel nuts, dried fruits
paani	water
pahelo moong ko daal	split yellow mung beans without skins
pakaaune	cooking
pakauda	chickpea batter-fried savory fritters
panyu	a large flat or round spoon with long handle
parvar (parwar)	pointed gourd
pate gheeraula	angled luffa gourd

pathi bharne	ceremonial game with rice grains played by mother-in-law and daughter-in-law during marriage ceremony
patre-roti	flaky flatbread with multiple layers
peda	flat, round, sweet thickened milk patty
phaapar ko roti	buckwheat bread
pharsi ko munta	pumpkin vine shoots
phool	eggs
phool-govi	cauliflower
phulaura	deep-fried croquette
phulka-roti	whole wheat flatbread
pidhaalu	taro tubers
piro	spicy
pista	pistachio
pitho	flour
pooja ko saamaan	a small tray filled with offerings to the gods (flower, raw rice, vermilion powder, incense)
poori	deep-fried puffed bread
prashaad	food offered to gods and blessed
prashaad ko maasu	blessed meat
pulau	flavorful rice dish
pyaj	onion
quaanti	mixed sprouted beans
raajkhaani	goat testicles
raajma daal	dried kidney beans
raam-toriya	okra
raango ko maasu	water buffalo meat
raato bodi	dried kidney beans
raayo ko geda (or *sarsyun*)	mustard seeds
raayo ko saag	mustard greens
rabadi	sweets made from thickened milk
ragati	animal blood
rahar ko daal	yellow split pigeon peas or toor daal
ras	soup
rasbari	sweet dish made from fresh chhana cheese in fragrant syrup

roti	bread
rukh-katahar	green jackfruit
saada bhaat	plain rice
saag	green leaves
saal ko paat	saal leaves
saandheko	a method of cooking marinated and spice-tempered food
saano kerau	small field peas
sagun food	food served to bring luck, success, and good fortune
sakhar khanda	sweet potato
samosa	deep-fried triangular turnover
sanduke	spice box
sankhatro	lemon chew
sattu	toasted corn, wheat, millet, and barley flour
saunp	fennel seeds
sel-roti	crisp, sweet rice bread resembling a large, thin, puffed-up doughnut
shalgam ko paat	turnip leaves
sharbat	beverage
sidra maacha	small dried fish
sikarni	yogurt dessert flavored with cardamom and saffron
silauto-baccha	heavy rectangular stone slab and roller grinding stone
simi	green beans
singo maas ko daal	whole black urad beans with skins
singo moong ko daal	whole green mung beans with skins
singo musuro ko daal	brownish-green whole lentils
sishnu	nettle greens
sukeko chana	dried chickpeas
sukeko hariyo thulo kerau	dried whole green peas
sukeko pahelo kerau	dried yellow peas
sukumel	green cardamom pods
sukuti	dried meat (jerky)
supaari	betel nuts
suruwa maasu	soupy boiled meat
swaari	soft deep-fried wheat bread
taaba (or *taawa*)	heavy cast-iron griddle
taama	bamboo shoots

taapke	cast-iron pot with long handle and rounded bottom
taareko	fried
tachauera	corn pudding
tai taapke	frying pan
tane-bodi	long beans
taraju	hand-held scale
tarbuja	watermelon
tarika	method
tarkaari	vegetable
tarkaari bazaar	vegetable market
tarul	Nepali yam
tejpaat	bay leaves
thaal-kachaura	round tray with bowl
tharak marne	completely cooked rice
thulo chana	dried whole yellow chickpeas
thulo kerau	whole dried peas, both green and yellow
til	sesame seed
timmur	Szechwan pepper
titaura	fruit nuggets
tito karela	bitter melon or bitter gourd
tori ko saag	mustard leaves
tori ko tel	mustard oil
tsaampa	roasted flour made from corn, wheat, millet, barley
tulasi	goddess basil
tyaamatar	tamarillo or tree tomato
umaaleko	boiled
usineko chaamal	parboiled rice
yoh-mari	steamed rice flour bread
yomari punhi	post-harvest celebration

INDEX

apples
   Phalphul ko Mithai (Fruit Salad in
      Cardamom Syrup), 360
Arsa Roti (Molasses Rice Flour Bread), 119
asefetida (*heeng*), 411–12
Asian eggplant
   Nepali Bhanta Tarkaari (Sautéed Asian
      Eggplant), 148
   See also eggplant
asparagus
   Kurelo Haaleko Golbheda ko Achaar
      (Tomato Chutney with
      Asparagus), 308
   Kurelo ka Alu Taareko (Sautéed
      Asparagus), 131
   Saandheko Kurelo (Asparagus Salad), 132
asparagus beans. *See* long beans
atta flour (*gabu ko pitho*), 412
   Alu-Roti (Potato-Stuffed Bread),
      112–13
   Makai ko Roti (Corn Bread), 116
   Patre-roti (Flaky Roti Bread), 108–9
   Phulka-Roti (Whole Wheat
      Flatbread), 106–7
   Poori (Poori Bread), 110–11

Baabari ko Chutney (Mint Chutney), 300
Baasi-Bhaat Bhutuwa (Fried Rice), 60
Baasna Aaune Garam Masala (Fragrant
   Garam Masala), 397
Baasna Aune Masala (Fragrant and
   Colorful Mouth Freshening
   Blend), 384
Baasna Aune Masala Haru (Basic After-
   Meal Refresher), 381
Badaami Maasu (Lamb with Cashews,
   Almonds, and Yogurt Sauce),
   198–99
Badaam ko Barfi (Almond Fudge), 340
Badaam-Pista-Kesari Doodh (Warm Milk
   with Almonds, Pistachios, and
   Saffron), 370

Bael ko Phal ko Sharbat (Wood Apple
   Drink), 368
Bafaayeko Bangoor (Spiced Boiled
   Pork), 207
Bakulla Simi Tarkaari (Spiced Fava
   Beans), 138
balsam apple (*barela*)
   Barela ko Tarkaari (Sautéed Balsam
      Apple), 133
bamboo shoots
   Taama-Alu-Bodi ko Tarkaari (Bamboo
      Shoots, Potatoes, and Black-
      Eyed Peas), 134–35
banana blossoms
   Kera ko Bungo Tarkaari (Banana
      Blossom Curry), 136
bananas
   Dahi Phalphul ko Salad (Fruit Salad
      with Yogurt), 361
   Maalpuwa (Maalpuwa Fritters), 341
   Sel-Roti (Banana Rice Bread),
      122–23
Banda Govi Taareko (Stir-Fried Cabbage),
   142
Bangoor ko Chowela (Pork Chowela), 208
Bangoor ra Tarkari ko Momo (Pork and
   Vegetable Filling), 282
Barela ko Tarkaari (Sautéed Balsam
   Apple), 133
Battain Chara ko Tarkaari (Sautéed Spiced
   Quail), 246–47
Battain-Dahi-Masala (Quail with Yogurt
   and Spices), 245
bay leaves (*tejpaat*), 412
Besan ko Laddu (Sweet Chickpea
   Balls), 342
betel nuts
   Baasna Aune Masala (Fragrant and
      Colorful Mouth Freshening
      Blend), 384
   Baasna Aune Masala Haru (Basic
      After-Meal Refresher), 381